ALONZO T. JONES

General Conference Bulletins

The Third Angel's Message

General Conference Bulletins 1893

by

Alonzo T. Jones

This book is a collection of sermons presented by Alonzo T. Jones
at the 1893 General Conference session of Seventh-day Adventists.

"I have been reading the Bulletins of 1893 and 1897. They contain most decided testimony in the affirmative, testimony which if presented to the people will prove a power for the truth. The Spirit of the Lord was upon these ministers as they bore their testimony before thousands of people."

Ellen G. White - Letter 204, 1908

© **2020**

ISBN: 978-0-9945585-6-5

Contents

Sermon 1 7
Sermon 2 18
Sermon 3 45
Sermon 4 57
Sermon 5 69
Sermon 6 83
Sermon 7 97
Sermon 8 109
Sermon 9 120
Sermon 10 136
Sermon 11 150
Sermon 12 158
Sermon 13 175
Sermon 14 187
Sermon 15 197
Sermon 16 207
Sermon 17 217
Sermon 18 229
Sermon 19 243
Sermon 20 251
Sermon 21 262
Sermon 22 278
Sermon 23 290
Sermon 24 306

Sermon 1

January 27, 1893

As we begin our Bible study I think it would be well to spend this hour, at any rate, in considering what we came for, and how we are to come to get any good. I suppose that every one came expecting to hear things we never thought of before; and not only expecting to hear things we never thought of before, but expecting to learn things we never thought of before. It is very easy to hear things we never thought of before, but we do not always learn what we hear. But I suppose we have come expecting to learn things we never thought of before. It is simply saying we have come expecting the Lord to give us new revelations of Himself, of His word, and of His way altogether. I have come for this.

This text is good advice for us all: "Verily I say unto you, Whosoever shall not receive the kingdom of God as a little child, he shall not enter therein." Mark 10:15. Thus we have come to learn of the kingdom of God, to receive things of the kingdom of God, things new and old, old things in a new way, and new things in a new way. Whosoever shall not receive it as a little child, shall not enter therein; cannot have it. Hence, we are all to come here and to sit down at the feet of Christ, looking to Him as our teacher, expecting to receive what He has to tell us, coming as a little child. Because, not only is this text here which speaks thus about those who would receive the kingdom of God, but in Matthew it is put in such a way as to cover all the time after we receive the kingdom of God from the first. "At the same time came the disciples unto Jesus, saying, Who is the greatest in the kingdom of heaven? And Jesus called a little child unto him, and set him in the midst of them, and said, Verily I say unto you, except ye be converted, and become as little children, ye shall not enter into the kingdom of heaven." Matt. 18:1-3.

Now if any one should say that the other text refers to any who are receiving the kingdom of God for the first time and admit the truth that they can receive it only as a little child, confessing that they know nothing of it themselves and cannot bring themselves to a knowledge of it, this verse shows that it goes beyond that, and that the idea goes with it even after we have received the kingdom of God; for in order to be converted we are to be as a little child, receive the kingdom of God as a little child, allowing that we know nothing of ourselves, no wisdom of our own. It is not our own wisdom that can make it plain to us, can open the way by which we can understand it all right as it is. We must leave all our wisdom out in order to gain it and by being converted become as a little child. "Except ye be converted and become as a little child, ye shall not enter the kingdom of God." What kind of children are mentioned? Little children. Little children have not much pride of opinion of their own. Grown up ones are not so ready to learn. Then this is spoken as giving us a model and example as to how we are to come to the word of God to learn.

There is another verse that tells us the same thing and perhaps in a more forcible manner. "And if any man think that he knoweth anything, he knoweth nothing yet as he ought to know it." 1 Cor. 8:2. How many people does that cover? "Any man," all of us that have come here. Any one then who has come here, will it refer to us as personally as that? Every one. Any one of us then who have come here, that thinks he knows anything, how much does that cover? Thinks he knows how much? Thinks he knows what? "Anything." Does that cover all things then? Yes sir. Then the text covers all people and all things that may be known. Then if any one of us thinks he knows anything, what does he know? How much does he know? He knows nothing yet as he ought to.

Well, then, we will all assent that that is true, shall we? Just set that down for yourself. If you came here thinking you knew something, you must decide you do not know that as you ought to know it. Then shall we come to this study in that way? Shall we all come to this study tomorrow, next day, each time we come here, and just settle it in our minds that we do not know anything as we ought to know it? I do not care if it is the oldest minister in our ranks; he must come and say, "I do not know anything yet as I ought to know it; teach thou me." And we will learn. Every one that comes to this house that way will learn something every lesson he hears. And this includes that same oldest minister in the ranks. He will learn more than any of the rest of us, if he sits down like that. But how long a time does that text cover? How long will it remain there? Will we go beyond that time during this institute, think you? No sir. Very good then, we have that settled, for the whole institute, if we thought we knew anything.

There are some things we thought we knew pretty well. If there is one thing we thought we knew, just put it down, we don't know anything. We are always learning the most out of those texts that we already know best. Don't forget that. We are always learning the most out of the texts with which we are already the most familiar. Then don't you see that any one who takes any text or thought, and studies upon it for a long time and thinks he has got all the thought out of it that is in it, he just shuts himself off there? When he says, "Now I know it," he shuts himself off from learning what is really in that text.

Brother Porter here in the lesson of the previous hour spoke to us of God's purpose in making known to us these things. What kind of purpose was that spoken of? An "eternal purpose." And the Scripture is God's expression to us of His thoughts in that eternal purpose. The Scripture is the expression of God's thoughts on that purpose, in carrying out and setting forth and making known that purpose. Well then, what kind of purpose is it? Eternal. How deep then are His thoughts? How far-reaching is that purpose? Eternal. How deep then are the thoughts expressed in the scriptures? Eternal. In how many expressions in the Scriptures and in how many scriptures is the thought of eternal depth? In how many passages? *Every one*. Then it does take all the Scriptures that are written for the Lord to express to us what He wants to tell us, of His eternal purpose? Yes sir. Then how deep is the thought in each passage of Scripture and the words that are used to tell it? Eternal. Then just as soon as any man catches one of these thoughts and thinks, I know it now and have got it, how far short is he? How far short is he from having the thought that is really there, from having the thought that is in that passage? (Voices: As far as his mind is from God's mind). When he says, I have the truth; I have the thought, he has shut up his own mind from the wisdom of the knowledge of God, putting himself and his own mind in the place of God and His thoughts. The man that does that cannot learn any more. Don't you see, that at that instant he shuts himself out forever from learning? And the man who does that, of course can learn nothing beyond himself, and of course will never have the knowledge of God.

The expressions of thought conveyed in the statements of the Scriptures are as eternal depths. Then what limit can we set to ourselves in the study of these? No limit at all. Then does not that present the splendid picture and the grand prospect that the eternal and the whole mind of God is wide open before us for us to study upon? Well then, let us not forget that that is the field of study upon which we are to enter.

We have been in it a good while, and let us be careful that we do not think we know something. Let us be sure that we have not been inveigled into the idea of thinking that we know something as we are to know it. Let us just settle it now by the word of God that we do not know that thing at all. There is knowledge in each line of thought for us to catch. And until all the depths and eternities are past we will never get to the place where we will have the right to think we know that thing and are done with it. Shall we? Well then, I am glad to know that we have such a subject as that to study upon, and such a length of time as that (eternity) in which to study it. Well then let us be *glad* to start with. That text is going to remain with us as long as we are in the world at least, and it won't go then; it will go in this shape of course; the Bible, the word of God as put up in this shape, will go. No doubt these Bibles will be burned up just as any other book of paper and leather. But the word of God will not be burned up. That text in this shape (in print) will last as long as the world does, but after that it will still exist in this shape (the body). Then that text will still remain with us all the time, even eternally. "And if any man think that he knoweth anything, he knoweth nothing yet as he ought to know." No, no man knows it. Are not you glad, brethren, are not you glad?

But we must not linger too long upon any one of these texts, for there are several texts we want to bring up tonight. Taking the thought we had a moment ago, we have come here expecting to learn many things that are new and many new things about what we have learned formerly. We have not come though, to learn anything but the truth. That is what we want. The only thing there is any power in, the only thing there is any good in, the only thing there is any sanctifying force in, is the truth, the truth as it is in Jesus of course, because there is no truth in any other way. Then coming with that purpose, to know only the truth, that is all we are to study, that is all we are to ask about. It is none of your business or mine whether a thing be old or new or who says it in this institute or whether it is for us to study or for any one else, is it? The thing for us to ask is, Is it true? If it be true, then take the Lord's word as He has given it to us, no difference by whom He says it, no difference in what way it comes, no difference if it comes in exactly the opposite way in which way we expected it to come – and the probabilities are that it will, "for your ways are not my ways, saith the Lord." Then when we have a way fixed up, we may expect it to come another way.

The Lord will not allow any one to dictate to Him or to lay out plans for Him. We may take the Lord in that text, "O God, verily thou art a God that hidest thyself." But we can see Him. He will hide Himself; we cannot fix the ways in which He is going to do things always, but the best of it is we will let Him have His own way to do things, and we will be in a position to do it all the time. Then we will be perfectly safe. Then we will never need to have any anxieties, need never have any thing to do with the management of it ourselves. He is all wise; everything goes straight with Him, and we simply keep ourselves ready to see Him do it at any time. And we have nothing to do but to enjoy ourselves in seeing Him do things. I have been greatly blessed in the study of the Bible and in watching the Lord do things. And when it is the darkest, the most mysterious, then it is the best study, because it takes us clear out of ourselves to see Him do it. If we could see just how it was coming out always it would not seem interesting. When it is the darkest, we can watch the more intently and with more interest, to see the Lord straighten it out.

So then we are to learn the truth only – no difference who speaks it. The Lord will speak it, of course, no difference by whom it is spoken or the way it comes. If we knew it before, thank God somebody else knows it now. If we did not know it before, then thank the Lord we now know it. The only thing to ask is, Is it true? You all know those verses in 2 Thess. 2:9, 10: "Even him, whose coming is after the working of Satan with all power and signs and lying wonders, and with all deceivableness of unrighteousness in them that perish; because they received not the love of the truth." Any one who loves the truth and will receive the love of the truth, Satan will never have any chance to work in with all signs and lying wonders and all deceivableness of unrighteousness. No sir. Because Jesus has said it (John 8:32): "Ye shall know the truth, and the truth shall make you free." Then every one who receives the love of the truth, this will make them free. Then the one in whom Satan is to work all signs and lying wonders, is he free? No, he is a fearful slave. As long as we have it settled in our minds that the only thing we shall ever seek or expect is the truth, and love it because it is the truth, and take it because it is the truth, then we need not be uneasy about whether Satan is going to deceive us or not.

Notice the last half of the verse. The effect of the truth is to make us free. The first half is the best promise in the Bible, if we could measure promises. But we cannot do that because one is just as important as another. All are the thoughts of God, and His thoughts are eternal. But this is an excellent promise, "Ye shall know the truth." That, it seems to me, is a most wonderful promise. "Ye shall know the truth." Think you know it? Wonder if you know it? Wonder whether such and such a thing is true? No sir. "Ye shall *know* the truth." That is the promise of Jesus Christ to you and to me, that when we trust in Him and follow Him, we shall know the truth. And as certain as we yield to Him and follow Him, He will take care that we know the truth, and we trust Him for it.

"Then said Jesus to those Jews which believed on Him, If ye continue in my word, then are ye my disciples indeed. And ye shall know the truth, and the truth shall make you free." How are we to know the truth? Continue in His word, be His disciples indeed, and ye shall know the truth. Then His word is the word of truth. "Ye shall know the truth." We want to stick to that promise. It seems to me that if that promise were the only one in the Bible it would be all we would need. "Ye shall know the truth." Because Christ has promised that, this is for you and for me, when we follow Him and when we yield to Him. And because this is so, it seems to me that we ought to be the gladdest people on the earth, for that promise given, "Ye shall know the truth."

There will be plenty of opportunities, assuredly – there have been some already, no doubt, in just the first lessons which have been given – some opportunities already for persons in the classes to say, Well, now, is that so? Probably some opportunity has already been offered for some to say, "Well now, I do not know about that." There will be countless instances doubtless, before the six weeks are past, that the Lord has given us to study His word and ways, numberless times in which we will be called upon to say, Well now is that so? What is the promise? "Ye shall know the truth." Now the Lord does not want us to take things because some one says them. God does not want us to say when anyone says a thing, Well, that is so, because he says it. That is not the thing. We are to know it is true, because God says it. And I say that there is the promise, "Ye shall know." There will be the opportunity for the query to arise, Is that so? How about that. There is the query, but there is the promise with it. Do not forget it. Jesus has said to you every time that query arises, "Ye shall know the truth." Then, when that query arises from some thought in the lesson, what is the answer to you and me? What are we then to consider? What is the place for us to occupy just then? Here is some brother who will be speaking some day, and he will make a statement perhaps, reading a passage or two or three passages, and catch a thought there that is new to me, make an expression here that is new to me, and the query comes, Well now is that so? What is the answer to me? "Ye shall know the truth." Then what am I to do just then with that new thought, with that query? Am I now just to hold that query, that new thought, that which is to me a new thought? Am I not to hold that right before Christ, and ask Him the truth? Or wouldn't I better go to some of the brethren and ask, "What do you think about that?

Brother A. says so and so. What do you think about that? That is new to me, and I kind of half doubt it." "Well, I doubt it too," says the other brother. Well then, of course it cannot be so; that settles it. It is not so. It is none of your business what I think about it.

I remember once in a camp meeting a brother read some scriptures right straight through – it was about all he did do; it was a Bible reading – but the thoughts he brought out in the Bible reading were new to a large number in the audience. About half a dozen came in a flock to me and asked, "Well, now, Brother Jones, what do you think about that?" I said, "It is none of your business what I think about it; what do you think about it yourself?" "Well, we do not know what to think about it," they replied. Then I said, "Find out." Suppose I had said I do not believe it. Then they would have gone off and said, "I do not believe that, because Brother Jones said he did not." Suppose I had said it was so. They would have said, "That is so. Brother Jones says that is so." So I propose to tell you nothing about what I think. It is none of your business. You know for yourselves what is the truth. That is the position I propose to occupy in this institute. I expect to find some things coming out here that are new. I have never found a meeting yet where we have studied the Bible that the Lord did not give us something that was new, beautiful, grand, and glorious. But the place I propose to occupy is right upon that promise, "Ye shall know the truth."

But I find people, and doubtless you have too, who seem to get upon the idea that the only sure way to know the truth is to raise all the objections they can and have them answered. But when I have raised and presented all the objections I know against a point and they are all answered, then am I sure what is truth? Am I sure of it? No, because there are objections I never thought of. Don't you see? On that line can I ever be sure that it is the truth until every objection that is possible is brought against it by every mind in the universe – can I be sure of it until then? When these are all answered would that make me sure it was so? If it would, how can I live long enough to hear all the objections answered? Can we get at the truth in that way? Is there any possibility of getting at the truth by raising objections and having them answered? No sir. What is the use of starting on a road of which you will never reach the end – a wrong road of course? Better not start on it at all.

Another word. Can there be any objections against the truth? Think of that closely. Well, when something is presented, are you and I to say, "I see an objection against that?" Is that the position we are to take? No; we are to ask whether it is the *truth*, and if it is, there is no objection, there can be no objection against it. Our objection is a fraud. Don't you see? The thing we are to ask is, Is it the truth?

And then another way the people have of getting at the truth is to hear both sides of it. You have heard that thing yourself. "That is one side," they say, "but now I want to hear the other side before I decide." What is one side of the truth? Well, here is one side of the truth, and there is the other side of the truth. Then where is the truth?

You get on the either side of the truth and it is error. I have heard one side, and I want to hear another side of it! Then how can I tell what is the truth, anyhow? But suppose I have heard actual truth (and that is the need of it), and I am not satisfied until I hear the other side. What is the other side? Taking this one side to be the truth, what is the other side? Error. Then we can decide best what is truth by hearing a lot of lies, can we? "Well," says one, "I have heard your side of it, and it looks to me as though it were true, but I want to hear the other side!" The truth is the word of God. Then he proposes by waiting to hear the other side, to know whether it is true or not by comparing it with a lot of lies and thus make a lot of lies a test of the truth.

We do not want to hear the other side. All we want is the truth. Here is one side of the truth, and there is the other side of the truth. He hears both sides according to his own plan; then how does he arrive at the truth? In his own way. He has heard this and that.

Where is the truth? He must find it out some way. Does he not compare one side with the other and weigh one against the other and strike the balance and judge where the truth is? Well, when he has done that, can he know he has the truth? Is he sure that is the truth? Is my mind, my judgment, my ability to weigh arguments and decide upon the truth – is that the infallible test of truth? Is a man's judgment, his faculties, the test of truth at all? When we want to test the truth so as to know it is the truth, the test must be an infallible one. Is not that so? It must be one that will never fail. To discern the truth and declare it, it must be one that will never miss under any circumstances amid ten thousand arguments and errors. The one by which we must test the truth must be such a one as will strike the truth among ten million diverse opinions, and strike it without fail in succession – every thought that may be raised among men. Is not that so? Man's mind we know is not the test of truth. It is only his own idea and the truth that he settles upon. "But your thoughts are not my thoughts, neither are your ways my ways, says the Lord."

Now brethren, in the time in which we are, there are two reasons why that thing could not be worked, even if it were correct. One is, that the truth of God is developing so rapidly that we have not time to hunt out all the objections and listen to the arguments on both sides, because we would be everlastingly behind while we were listening to a lot of arguments and objection. But we do not want to stand in that place when probation closes. The time is too short for that, and we would be left out when we get there. But there is the promise, "Ye shall know the truth."

Turn again to John 14:16, 17: "I will pray the Father and he shall give you another Comforter that he may abide with you forever, even the Spirit of truth." Spirit of what? Truth. Oh! Thank the Lord for the promise, "I will pray the Father." What is Christ doing tonight for us, who are here in this institute? Praying the Father. He will send us the Comforter? The Spirit of truth. What is the position to occupy before we come to the class each day? Taking part in that prayer, that we may have the Spirit of truth, isn't it?

So then Jesus is praying, and by the way, as Jesus is doing it are not we in good company when we do it? Let us spend a good deal of time at it then during this institute. Let us spend a good deal of time in His company during this institute. What do you say? [Congregation: "Amen."] I will pray the Father and He *will* give you – He does not say I will pray the Father that He *may* do it, as though it was to be decided after He had prayed, but I will pray the Father and He *shall* give you. Of course His prayer is heard for He makes intercession for us. He presents our prayers according to the will of God. And so then He prayed and we pray that He may give us this Comforter, and He does. When we ask we know we receive, for He says so. If we ask anything according to His will, what then? He hears us. And this is the confidence we have in Him tonight. This is the confidence we have in Him that if we ask anything according to His will He hears us. Then if we have that confidence in the Lord, we can have a good time throughout this institute. Ask anything according to His will and He hears us. Then it is His will that we should have the Holy Spirit. Then we can go to Him every day, and every hour of the day, asking Him for that Spirit of truth and know that we shall receive it, know He hears us, and if we know He hears us, we know we have the petitions we desired of Him.

Now put these things together.

We ask anything according to His will, and He hears us. Every time we ask, He hears. Then when He hears, then what? We know we may have it? Shall have it? *Have* it. Then what are we to do? When we have asked according to His will we know He hears us. And we have what we ask for, then what are we to do? Let us thank Him for it. Then before we come to the institute each morning let us ask the Lord for the Holy Spirit according to His will, then when we have asked, yield wholly to the Lord, and thank Him that it is done, and come expecting Him to teach, and that He will teach the teacher, and through Him teach us.

"That I may abide with you." How long? Forever. Good. the Spirit of truth is able to take the truth and make known the truth at any moment amid ten thousand times ten thousand phases of error. How long? Forever. Isn't that good? Is not that a good promise that He shall give to us the Spirit of truth, and He will stay there forever? "Even the Spirit of truth, whom the world cannot receive, because it seeth him not neither knoweth him; but ye know him; for he dwelleth with you and shall be in you."

"Howbeit when he, the Spirit of truth, is come, he will guide you." What will He do? Guide you. He will do it; that is positive. When He comes, He will do that. Well, brethren, can't we trust Him, then? Let us put the three things together, "Ye shall know the truth;" "I will pray the Father," and He shall guide you." Then can't we trust Him? Can't we surrender everything to Him right off without a single hesitation about anything? "Ye shall know the truth." "The Father shall give you the Spirit of truth, and He will guide you." Then shall we not yield everything to Him and trust Him and expect Him to guide us in every study we have here?

"Howbeit when he, the Spirit of truth, is come, he will guide you into all truth: for he shall not speak of himself; but whatsoever he shall hear, that shall he speak; and he will shew you things to come." Will He? He will show us things to come. Good. Doesn't the Lord want us to see things that are coming before they overtake us? Hasn't He told us that the people who will now see what is coming upon us by what is being transacted before us, will trust no longer to human inventions, but will feel that the Holy Spirit must be recognized and received? How will we see what is coming upon us? By what is being transacted before us. Jesus will show us things to come. He does not want us to be taken by surprise in any of these things. He wants us to know what is coming beforehand, to be fully armed, and not to be surprised and overtaken.

"He shall glorify me: for he shall receive of mine, and shall show it unto you." And what is He? "I am the truth, and the Spirit of truth." He takes what is His and shows it to us. Then when the Spirit of truth takes only that which is the Lord's (and that is all He will ever show to us) He does not stand out independently and do great things of Himself, just as Jesus did not do that, but yielded everything that the Father might move and work in Him. So the Holy Spirit in His place does the same things as Jesus did exactly. He does not show of Himself, but finds what God told to Jesus and tells that to you and me. So He gives us the truth of God as it is in Jesus. He is the God of truth? "All things that the Father hath are mine. Therefore, said I, that he shall take of mine and shall show it unto you." Then we have the scripture, "But as it is written, Eye hath not seen, nor ear heard, neither hath entered into the heart of man, the things which God hath prepared for them that love him." There is the eternal purpose, and the depths of it. That is where we are to stand, asking, taking part in that prayer of Jesus every day, that we may have the spirit of truth here in our studies and all our work, guiding us into truth.

Note the following from *Steps to Christ*, pp. 105, 129, 130.

> "Never should the Bible be studied without prayer. Before opening its pages we should ask for the enlightenment of the Holy Spirit, and it will be given. When Nathaniel came to Jesus, the Saviour exclaimed, 'Behold an Israelite indeed, in whom is no guile.' Nathaniel said, "Whence knowest thou me?" Jesus answered, "Before that Philip called thee, when thou wast under the fig tree, I saw thee." And Jesus will see us also in the secret places of prayer, if we will seek Him for light, that we may know what is truth. Angels from the world of light will be with those who in humility of heart seek for divine guidance.
>
> The Holy Spirit exalts and glorifies the Saviour. It is His office to present Christ, the purity of His righteousness, and the great salvation that we have through Him. Jesus says, "He shall receive of mine, and shall show it unto you." The Spirit of truth is the only effectual teacher of divine truth. How must God esteem the human race, since He gave His Son to die for them and appoints His Spirit to be man's teacher and continual guide.
>
> God intends that even in this life the truths of His word shall be ever unfolding to His people. There is only one way in which this knowledge can be obtained. We call attention to an understanding of God's word only through the illumination of that Spirit by which

> the word was given. "The things of God knoweth no man, but the Spirit of God"; "for the Spirit searcheth all things, yea, the deep things of God." And the Saviour's promises to His followers was, "When he, the Spirit of truth, is come, he will guide you into all truth . . . for he shall receive of mine, and shall show it unto you."
>
> God desires man to exercise his reasoning powers; and the study of the Bible will strengthen and elevate the mind as no other study can. Yet we are to beware of deifying reason, which is subject to the weakness and infirmity of humanity. If we would not have the Scriptures clouded to our understanding, so that the plainest truths shall not be comprehended, we must have the simplicity and faith of a little child, ready to learn and beseeching the aid of the Holy Spirit. A sense of the power and wisdom of God, and of our inability to comprehend His greatness, should inspire us with humility, and we would enter His presence, with holy awe. When we come to the Bible, reason must acknowledge an Authority superior to itself, and heart and intellect must bow to the great I AM.

From this time forth as long as we live, when we read His word just as it is, let us never set up an "if" against it. Is there any "if" about it? Can there be any "if"? There is no "if" in it at all. It is just what it says. Thank God it is so, and let Him tell us what it means, and how it is to.

I read again from *Gospel Workers* p. 126:

> "God desires us to receive the truth upon its own merits – because it is truth. The Bible must not be interpreted to suit the ideas of men, however long they may have held these ideas to be true.

That means that I must not interpret the Bible to suit this man (speaker pointing to himself). It means you, too.

> The spirit in which we come to the investigation of the Scriptures, will determine the character of the assistant at your side (*Ibid.*, p. 127).

There is an important thing. We are coming in here every day for the investigation of the Scriptures. Now the word is, The spirit in which you come will determine the character of the assistant at your side.

> Angels from the world of light will be with those who in humility of heart seek for divine guidance. But if the Bible is opened with irreverence, with a feeling of self-sufficiency, if the heart is filled with prejudice, Satan is beside you, and he will set the plain statements of God's word in a perverted light (*Ibid.*).

Let us not have Satan for an assistant. Then let us be certain we join with Jesus in that prayer before we come – and remain in it while we stay. "We should study the Bible for ourselves. No man should be relied upon to think for us." That does not say we are not to be led by a man, if God is leading the man, or by a woman either, if God is leading the woman. You know too, that a certain man once would have done well to have consented to be led by an ass. But he proposed to be led by the Lord alone. He didn't propose to have anybody lead him, but he got into mischief. Let us not choose who shall lead us, except that God shall lead us.

A man was once talking against the Spirit of prophecy and telling how easy Seventh-day Adventists were deceived how deluded they were, that their teachers got up and told them certain things, and they just swallowed them down whole. I said to myself, that I wished he would try it, try to get things down there in that way. It is a fact that Seventh-day Adventists are hard to lead. I am glad of it in one way. I want every Seventh-day Adventist to be so hard to lead that nobody in the universe can lead him but Jesus Christ. Yes, sir. But oh, brethren, let us get where it will not be nearly so hard for Him to lead us. But I am glad they are so hard to lead that nobody can do it but Him. Let us get into that place as soon as possible, and then let us just be led as easy as a lamb by Him, by the Lamb of God that He is.

> We must not become set in our ideas and think that no one should interfere with our opinions. When a point of doctrine that you do not understand comes to your attention, go to God on your knees, that you may understand what is true, and not be found as were the Jews, fighting against God. . . It is impossible for any mind to comprehend all the richness and greatness of even one promise of God. One catches the glory of one point of view, and another the beauty and grace from another point, and the soul is filled with the heavenly light. If we saw all the glory, the spirit would faint. But we can bear far greater revelations from God's abundant promises than we now enjoy. It makes my heart sad to think how we lose sight of the fullness of blessing designed for us. We content ourselves with momentary flashes of spiritual illumination, when we might walk day after day in the light of His presence. . . He whose office it is to bring all things to the remembrance of God's people and to guide them into all truth, may be with us in the investigation of His holy word (*Ibid.,* pp. 129-131).

Oh, what a promise that is, that we shall know the truth! Then He gives us the Spirit of truth to guide into the truth. And that Spirit is such a perfect guide, such an infallible one that it will silence every other voice than that which comes from Him who is truth and life. Well, then, brethren, let us enter upon the study in this spirit and remain in this spirit, and God will teach us. And as it was said in the days of Job, and in the book, "Who teaches like him?"

Sermon 2

January 30, 1893

I will take a text tonight that will last a week at least. It is a familiar statement to all, I think. It is as follows:

> The people who will now see what is soon to come upon us by what is being transacted before us, will no longer trust in human inventions, and will feel that the Holy Spirit must be recognized, received, presented before the people.

Tonight, to begin with and to lay the foundation for what is to come, we will look at the situation as it exists tonight before us in the United States government. And for this reason I shall relate the experiences of the hearing that took place lately in Washington; beginning with that, and simply state the facts as they are before us tonight, and then afterward we can find out the bearing of the facts that already exist.

When the first movement was made for religious legislation by Congress in the United States, you will remember that we began to circulate a petition, which was, in effect, a remonstrance against anything of the kind, containing these words:

> *To the Honorable, the Senate of the United States:*
>
> We, the undersigned, adult residents of the United States, twenty one years of age or more, hereby respectfully, but earnestly, petition your Honorable Body not to pass any bill in regard to the observance of the Sabbath, or the Lord's day, or any other religious or ecclesiastical institution or rite; nor to favor in any way the adoption of any resolution for the amendment of the National Constitution that would in any way tend, either directly or indirectly, to give preference to the principles of any religion or of any religious body above another, or that will in any way sanction legislation upon the subject of religion; but that the total separation between religion and State, assured by the National Constitution as it now is, may forever remain as our fathers established it.

And the Sunday closing of the World's Fair, when that came up, this was likewise brought before Congress under this protest:

> We the undersigned, citizens of the United States, hereby respectfully, but decidedly, protest against the Congress of the United States committing the United States Government to a union of religion and the State in the passage of any bill or resolution

> to close the World's Columbian Exposition on Sunday, or in any other way committing the Government to a course of religious legislation.

The Breckinridge bill was protested against in the same way; the bill to stop the delivery of ice on Sunday, last year, in Congress, was protested against in the same way so that our protest in this respect has been against Congress touching the subject in any way at all. But it did do it, as we expected always, of course, that it would.

While we were circulating these petitions men would not believe that there was enough of importance in it to sign their names to the petitions, even when they believed that the petition was all right in itself. Men would admit that that was all right. They would say, "I believe all that; but it is not of enough importance to pay any attention to; I would not take the time to sign my name to it, although I am in favor of all that you are saying. No such thing as that will ever be done." And because there were so many of that kind of people who did not believe that it would ever be done, it was done. And when they found out it was done, they began to try to have it undone. They began to wake up to see that they were mistaken and that it had been done, and then seeing their mistake, they began trying to retrieve it by asking that the World's Fair should be open on Sunday. And the reasons they urge for the opening of the Fair are precisely the same reasons that were given for closing it.

This movement for opening originated in Chicago. The Chicago *Herald* started it, and the city council of Chicago took it up and drafted a memorial to Congress, which the city council, with the mayor at its head, as representatives from the city of Chicago, took to Washington and presented the first day of the four days' hearing. Some of the reasons that were given upon which they asked that the Fair should be opened on Sunday, I will read:

> The wish of the Council is,
>
> That the gates of the world's Columbian Exposition be not closed Sunday.
>
> That all machinery be stopped, and that noise be suppressed that day, to the end that quiet may prevail, which is in keeping with the Sabbath.

That recognizes Sunday as the Sabbath, and of course there is a certain quiet that becomes it, and they wanted it open with the machinery stopped "that the quiet may prevail." That is the same reason that the other folks want it shut on Sunday. They want the same thing.

> That suitable accommodations be provided within the Exposition grounds for holding religious services the Sabbath day, to the end that all the denominations may have worship conducted according to their several customs without obstruction or hindrance.

That is the same reason that the other folks wanted it shut – so that they could have religious services in their churches.

> We recognize and rejoice in the fact that our country is and always has been a Christian Nation...

And the leading reason urged by the churches for closing it is that "this is a Christian Nation."

> We are of the opinion that more good will be accomplished by permitting these people and all others who desire it, to visit the inside of the grounds than will follow from keeping them out... We believe that the United States, as a Christian country, should open the gates Sunday as a recognition of the fact that in no branch of human interest or thought has there been more progress during that four hundred years of time than in the Christian Church.

That is exactly the reason that the other folks gave for shutting it: that the United States, as a Christian nation, should shut the Fair on Sunday as a recognition of the advancement made in Christian ideas.

> Would it not be a good thing to throw the sanctify of religious worship about the great temple dedicated to the things of use and beauty?

And the reason given for shutting the Fair was that it would be a good thing to throw the sanctity of religion over the whole Fair.

So you can see the reasons that were given for opening it are precisely the reasons that were given for shutting it.

The Chicago *Tribune*, in mentioning the letter that Cardinal Gibbons wrote on the subject, introduced it in this form, in its issue of December 3, 1892:

> There is a strong and growing sentiment in some religious circles in favor of the repeal of the World's Fair Sunday closing act. One eminent divine after another is coming out in favor of this liberal movement. The possibilities for a series of religious demonstrations at the Park become more and more manifest. With the leading religious and moral teachers of Europe and America to conduct services every Sunday, with sacred music produced by choruses embracing, perhaps, thousands of trained voices, Sunday at the World's Fair will be one of the grandest recognitions of the Sabbath known to modern history.

So the other folks said if the Fair be closed on Sunday and the solemnity of the Sabbath overspreads it and this nation sets the grand example of the recognition of the Sabbath, it will be "one of the grandest exhibitions of the Sabbath known to modern history."

More than this: those who worked for the opening of the Fair pandered to the church interests precisely as the others did in working for the shutting of it. As soon a these things appeared in print I wrote a letter to Brother A. Moon, sending him these marked passages, and I said to him, "You can readily see that the reasons that are given by these people for opening the Fair are precisely the reasons that were given for shutting it.

Now that being so, for us to join with them would be to recognize the legitimacy of the legislation and the reasons for the legislation, whereas every one of these reasons is directly against everything that we have been working for all these years in Congress. So this makes it plain enough that we cannot put a single one of our petitions along with theirs. We cannot take a single step along with them; we can not work with them at all or connect with them in any way in the way they are working or upon the reasons which they give for opening the Fair. We will have to maintain the position that the legislation is not and never was right at all. The only thing we can do therefore is to hold that the thing ought to be undone. The only position which we can take is that the Sunday part of the legislation should be unconditionally repealed.

Brother Moon immediately replied that he had seen these statements and had already taken the position that I spoke of in my letter. You will remember that about the same time I wrote an article which appeared in the *Sentinel* setting forth the same facts and taking the same position; saying that we did not care a turn of the hand whether the Fair was opened or shut on Sunday but we did care more than could be told whether the subject should be dealt with at all by Congress.

Therefore Brother Moon told the Chairman of the Committee and the gentlemen who were managing that side of the question in Washington that neither we nor our petitions could be counted at all in connection with that movement. The Chairman of the Committee asked Brother Moon what our position was. He told the Committee what our position was and how many petitions there were there. Of course all the names that were gathered upon that first petition, nearly four hundred thousand, are just as good today as they were then, whenever any congressman chooses to call them up and present them. They are everlastingly against the whole thing. Therefore the Chairman, when Brother Moon told him what our position was and the reasons for it said to him: "You write out your position as regards this legislation, and I will present it as a bill in the House so as to give you a basis upon which to present your petitions and for your arguments to be heard." Brother Moon, in that room, dictated to Mr. Thompson of Chicago, what we desired, and Chairman Durborow introduced it with his own name on it.

Following is the bill:

> 52nd CONGRESS, 2D SESSION. H. RES. 177
>
> *In the House of Representatives, December 20, 1892. Referred to the Select Committee on the Columbian Exposition and ordered to be printed.*
>
> Mr. Durborow introduced the following joint resolution:
>
> > Joint Resolution to repeal the religious legislation pertaining to the World's Columbian Exposition.

> Whereas the United States Constitution specifically states that "Congress shall make no laws respecting an establishment of religion, or prohibiting the free exercise thereof"; Therefore be it–
>
> *Resolved by the Senate and House of Representatives of the United States of America in Congress assembled*, That the act of Congress approved August fifth, eighteen hundred and ninety-two, appropriating five millions of Columbian half dollars to provide for celebrating the four hundredth anniversary of the discovery of America by Christopher Columbus by holding an international exposition of arts, industries, manufactures, and products of the soil, mine, and sea in the city of Chicago, in the State of Illinois, on the condition that the said exposition shall not be opened to the public on the first day of the week, commonly called Sunday; and also that section four of 'an act to aid in carrying out the act of Congress approved April twenty-fifth, eighteen hundred and ninety, entitled An act to provide for celebrating the four hundredth anniversary of the discovery of America by Christopher Columbus by holding an international exposition of the arts, industries, manufactures, and products of the soil, mine, and sea in the city of Chicago, in the State of Illinois,' be, and the same is hereby, amended so as to leave the matter of Sunday observance entirely within the power of the regularly constituted authorities of the World's Columbian Exposition.

Then that being understood that that was introduced with the understanding and for the express purpose of opening the way for us to present our petitions and to be heard upon the question, we proceeded upon that idea. The arrangement for the hearing was made. Brother Moon tells me that if the hearing could have been had before Christmas he is perfectly satisfied that we would have been heard; but the hearing was not appointed until after the holidays, and Congress took a recess during the holidays and when Congress reconvened it was discovered that the Chairman of that Committee was another man altogether. I was informed that he had a dinner with Elliott F. Shepard in the meantime. Whether that had any effect upon his digestion or some other part of his make-up I do not know. At any rate that or something caused him to repudiate all that he had done and shut out the principle which he had embodied in that resolution and presented in order that we might be heard.

Dr. Lewis, the Seventh-day Baptist, went to Congress to be heard. He told me that he went to Mr. Durborow, the chairman of the committee, and asked to be heard. Mr. Durborow asked him what he represented and what his argument was to be. Mr. Lewis told him that it would be upon the point of the unconstitutionality of the legislation already taken by Congress. Mr. Durborow told him that the Committee had decided not to hear any arguments at all upon the principle but only upon the policy of the legislation; not to consider any question at all as to whether it was constitutional or not, but that Congress had done it, and it was presumed that Congress had the right to do it. And any mention as to the propriety of the legislation would be entirely left out, and it was only considered now as to whether it would be better policy for the country to open the Fair or shut it on the Sunday that had been adopted by Congress.

When that was done Dr. Lewis had nothing at all to say, and made no calculation to say anything. But the third day and among the last minutes of the day, Mr. Durborow called upon him to speak, giving him five minutes. Dr. Lewis told him that he did not have anything to say, that he did not have his documents with them, and that he had no intention to speak under the circumstances. But Mr. Durborow rather insisted that he should, that he had five minutes to occupy if he chose. So he occupied them though in rather a perfunctory way.

Samuel P. Putnam was there for the same purpose, having several thousand of petitions in his pocket. He is president of the Free Thought Federation of America. He went to Mr. Durborow for a portion of time to be appointed him, and he received the same information – that any arguments as to the constitutionality of the question or the principle involved was not to be considered at all, but only the policy of the legislation. That being so, Mr. Putnam made no further request. But he likewise was called upon to speak, but was given only a very few minutes, which he occupied as best he could.

I did not get there long enough beforehand to find all that out. Brother Moon knew it, but I did not have a chance to talk with him. My train was late, and I arrived there in time, by hurrying, to get to the committee room as the argument was opened. So I did not have time to learn anything about the situation at all. After the hearing Mr. Thompson of Chicago came to me and asked me if I would take the balance of the time that day, the last half hour. I had written to Brother Moon that whatever arrangements they should make I would conform to when I got there. I supposed that was the arrangement. I told Mr. Thompson if they thought best I would speak that day, but I would like to wait until after the American Sabbath Union had spoken, but if they would rather, I would take the time. And so when I began I began on the only thing I knew. It was to call in question the legislation, but that was the thing they had decided not to have discussed. I noticed immediately that they were restless. The chairman was very restless. But I did not know what was the matter.

So I will take up the question right there now. It is true that the chairman made a statement in opening the hearing that I understand now, but did not then. He said:

> The meeting today will be held for the purpose of giving a hearing to those favoring the legislation that is before the Committee. I think it would be proper to state to the Committee that the present case is somewhat different from the case as presented a year ago, and that the proposition before the Committee is to *modify existing* law, not *create* law, as was the proposition a year ago. Therefore the discussion before the Committee on this occasion it is expected *will be held very closely* within the lines of *modification* presented in the resolution before the Committee, copies of which are on the desk and which can be furnished to you, which provides for the *modification* of the closing of the gates of the Columbian Exposition on Sunday by permitting them to be opened under restrictions as stated in these resolutions.

That expression, "Not to create law," was the statement that I did not understand then, but do now.

Well, it was fortunate in another sense that I spoke that half hour, because there was no time afterward when I could have had a half hour. The longest time occupied by anybody after that was about twenty-five minutes, and the most of the fifty-seven speakers had only an average of about ten minutes allowed them.

Although the chairman shut out the argument I was making upon the constitution, yet other members of the Committee asked questions until the whole half hour was consumed, and every one of their questions was presented in such a way that I was compelled to strike the constitution and the unconstitutionality of what they had done, in answering the questions. And so the argument they wanted to shut out was presented in spite of the efforts of the chairman. And the very things that he refused to listen to from us were presented by others in a great deal stronger way than we should or could have stated them. My argument before the Committee is as follows:

> *Mr. Durborow:* You have just thirty minutes left, Mr. Jones.
>
> *Mr. Jones:* Mr. Chairman, I expect to speak in favor of this legislation that is now before the Committee for a larger number of reasons than could be given in the half hour which I may have to speak, but I shall endeavor to touch upon such reasons as have not been dwelt upon very particularly hitherto. I shall start with one that has been touched by Mayor Washburne, to some extent, but which may be referred to a little more fully, and then I shall go from that to the consideration of other points.
>
> My first point is that this subject, of whether the gates of the World's Fair shall be closed or opened on Sunday, is a subject with which the national government has nothing at all to do. It is entirely beyond its jurisdiction in any sense whatever. There are three distinct considerations–
>
> *Mr. Robinson:* – What church do you belong to?
>
> *Mr. Jones:* I do not see what that has to do with the question.
>
> *Mr. Durborow:* The gentleman certainly has the right to ask the question.
>
> *Mr. Jones:* Very well; I beg your pardon. I did not know that the gentleman was a member of the Committee. I am perfectly willing to answer the question, though I cannot see what bearing it has upon this discussion. I am a member of the Seventh-day Adventist Church. But I speak here today as a citizen of the United States and upon the principles of the government of the United States. And I may say further that in the way that Congress has touched this question, I may probably speak upon it as a Seventh-day Adventist. As Congress has entered the field of religion already, we have the right to follow it there, if necessity should require.
>
> What I was about to say is that three distinct considerations in the Constitution of the United States forbid Congress to touch this question. The first is well defined by George Bancroft in a letter which he wrote Dr. Philip Schaff, Aug. 30, 1887, which reads as follows:

My Dear Mr. Schaff,

I have yours of the 12th. By the Constitution no power is held by Congress except such as shall have been granted to it. Congress therefore from the beginning was as much without the power to make a law respecting the establishment of religion as it is now after the amendment has been passed. The power had not been granted and therefore did not exist, for Congress has no powers except such as are granted, but a feeling had got abroad that there should have been a Bill of Rights and therefore to satisfy the craving, a series of articles were framed in the nature of a Bill of Rights, not because such a declaration was needed, but because the people wished to see certain principles distinctly put forward as a part of the Constitution. The first amendment, so far as it relates to an establishment of religion, was proposed without passion, accepted in the several States without passion, and so found its place as the opening words of the amendments in the quietest manner possible. . .

George Bancroft

This is shown by the Tenth Amendment to the Constitution which says that "the powers not delegated to the United States by the Constitution, nor prohibited by it to the States, are reserved to the States respectively, or to the people." As no power has been granted to Congress on the subject of religion, *that* is reserved to the States or to the people. That is where we ask that this shall be left, just where the Constitution has left it. It is a question reserved to the States. It is for the State of Illinois alone, so far as any State can have anything to say upon the subject, to say whether that Fair shall be opened or shut on Sunday. If the State of Illinois should not say anything on the subject, it is still left with the people. It is for the people in their own capacity as such, to act as they please in the matter, without any interference or dictation by Congress.

Not only is that so on that point, but if the Constitution had not said a word on the subject of religion, there would have been no power in Congress to touch this question. But the people have spoken; the constitution has spoken and denied the right of the United States government to touch the question and has reserved that right to the States or to the people. Not only did it do that but it went further and actually prohibited the government of the United States from touching the question. This lack of power would have been complete and total without the prohibition, because the powers not delegated are reserved. But they went further and not only reserved this power but expressly prohibited Congress from exercising it. It is trebly unconstitutional for Congress to touch the question. It was so at the beginning of the government, and this is why we insist that this legislation shall be undone, and leave it where the Constitution has left it – to the States or to the people.

Mr. Houk: The language of the Constitution, I believe, is that Congress shall make no law respecting the establishment of religion.

Mr. Jones: I am going to follow this question a little further and notice that amendment. The amendment does not read, as it is often misquoted, "Congress shall make no law respecting *the* establishment of religion;" but "Congress shall make no law respecting *an* establishment of religion, or prohibiting the free exercise thereof." There are two meanings in this clause. When the Constitution was made, all that it said upon this subject was that "no religious test shall ever be required as a qualification to any office or public trust under the United States." Some of the States had established religions at the time; I think all except Virginia. Virginia had released herself in a campaign directly touching this question. The first part of the clause was intended to prohibit Congress from making any law respecting any of these religions which were established already in those States, and the second part of the clause prohibits Congress from touching the subject of religion on its own part, in any way. In the State of Virginia from 1776 – with the exception of the interval when the war was highest – to December 26, 1787, there was a campaign conducted over the same question that is now involved in this legislation.

The English Church was the established church in Virginia, and the Presbyterians, the Quakers, and the Baptists sent a memorial to the General Assembly of Virginia, asking that as the Colonies had declared themselves free and independent of British rule in civil things, so the State of Virginia should declare itself free from British rule in religious things and that they should not be taxed to support a religion which they did not believe, nor even any religion which they did believe. And the English Church was disestablished. Then a movement was made to establish the "Christian religion" and to legislate in favor of the Christian religion" by passing a bill establishing a provision for teachers of that religion. Madison and Jefferson took the opposition to that bill, and by vigorous efforts defeated it, and in its place secured the passage of a bill "establishing religious freedom in Virginia," which is the model of all the state constitutions from that day to this, on the subject of religion and the State.

Now then, that campaign in Virginia against the establishment of the Christian religion there, embodied the same principle that is involved in this legislation of today, and as that was distinctly shut out, so we ask that this shall be also and Congress and the government step back to the place where it was before and where it belongs. Madison went right out of that campaign into the convention which formed the Constitution of the United States and carried with him into that convention the principles which he had advocated in the campaign and put those principles into the United States Constitution, and the intention of all was, and is, that Congress shall have nothing at all to do with the subject of religious observances.

Washington, in 1797, made a treaty with Tripoli, which explicitly declared that "The government of the United States is not in any sense founded upon the Christian religion." And when Congress has legislated upon this question with direct reference to the Christian religion, therein again it has gone contrary to the express intent of those who made the Constitution and established the supreme law, as expressed in their own words. And for this reason we ask that the thing shall be undone and Congress put the government right back where it was before that legislation was established, and leave the question where it belongs.

Mr. Durborow: Your objections are simply constitutional?

Mr. Jones: There are some others, but the foundation of all is the unconstitutionality of it. Those who sent up the petitions here and those who worked for the movement in this Capitol knew that it was unconstitutional when they asked it. A gentleman who spent six months at this Capitol for this legislation, has argued for more than twenty-five years, in print and in speech, that any Sunday legislation by Congress or legislation in behalf of the Christian Sabbath would be unconstitutional. And yet he worked here six months to get Congress to do that without any change in the Constitution. For twenty-five years, he, with the Association to which he belongs, has been working to get an amendment to the Constitution recognizing the Christian religion and making this a "Christian nation" so that there would be a constitutional basis for Sunday legislation. But now in the face of that twenty-five years' history and work and in the face of their own arguments, they have gone right ahead, and got Congress to do it, when they knew it was unconstitutional.

Another reason why we ask the repeal of it is that it was secured upon false representations. The representations which they made to Congress in order to secure this legislation were all false. They represented before Congress that the mass of the people of the United States were in favor of their cause, which has been demonstrated over and over to be false. It was forcibly demonstrated in the city of Chicago not quite a month ago. There the American Sabbath Union held a convention – a national convention. They had four mass-meetings the first night of the time in which the convention was held. One of those mass-meetings I attended. It was reported in the Chicago papers, of which I have copies here. I will read the Chicago report of it so that it will be seen that I have not put any of my feelings into it. The Chicago *Tribune* of December 14, 1892, had this report:

IT WAS VOTED DOWN

> The American Sabbath Union suffered a defeat last night at one of its meetings which so surprised the leaders present, that the incident was a veritable sensation. It was an unexpected blow, and the more grievous because it was administered by one of the most sabbatarian of all Christian denominations.

Mr. Jones: This was not the first instance of the kind, as some present here will remember.

Rev. W. F. Crafts: – That's a good joke.

> The Union opened a national convention here yesterday afternoon and made arrangements for four mass-meetings throughout the city last night to forward the movement. One of these meetings was held at the M. E. Church, South Park Avenue and 33rd St. It was a small mass-meeting, but everything went on smoothly for a time and the 'American Sabbath' had everything its own way. Dr. H. H. George, a leader in the movement, Mr. Locke, and others advocated the closing of the World's Fair on Sunday, and vigorously denounced the efforts of the directors and of the mayor and city council to have Congress repeal the closing act. These speeches were warmly if not unanimously approved by frequent amens and clapping of hands. No one looked for any opposition, and so the following resolutions were drawn up in a confident and emphatic manner:
>
>> *Whereas*, We are informed by the Chicago press that our City Council through the influence of Mayor Washburne has appointed a committee of its members to go to Washington for the purpose of influencing Congress to reverse its action with reference to closing the World's Fair on Sunday; and,
>>
>> *Whereas*, The Chicago directors have opened headquarters in Washington for

the same purpose, notwithstanding the acceptance of two and one half million dollars' appropriation from Congress on the express conditions that the gates should not be opened to the public on Sunday; and,

Whereas, there are seven thousand saloons running open every Sunday, contrary to the State law; therefore, be it–

Resolved, First, That we enter a most earnest protest against such official action on the part of the mayor and city council in using such measures in opposition to the action of Congress and spending the people's money in attempting to reverse the very conditions upon which the appropriation of Congress was received.

Resolved, That we deprecate and condemn the action of the directors, who received the money from Congress upon condition that the Fair should not be opened Sunday (*a bona fide* contract), and are now using all possible effort to influence Congress to set aside said condition.

Resolved, That in our judgment it would be more proper for the mayor and city council to close the saloons on Sunday in accordance with the State law, than to endeavor to influence Congress to open the Exposition Sunday, contrary to law.

There was applause at the end, and then the chairman of the meeting, Rev. H. H. Axrell, put the resolutions to vote. To his and others surprise the "Ayes" and "Noes" seemed equal, with the volume of tone apparently in favor of the latter. The chairman then said, that a rising vote would seem to be in order, and he requested all in favor of the resolutions to stand up. The secretary counted thirty on their feet.

All opposed will arise.

The rest of the audience, with the exception of four who seemed to have no opinion on the matter, stood up, and the secretary looking astonished at the evident majority paid little attention to counting heads, and declared that there were at least thirty-five against the resolution, and what seemed strangest was that many of them were women.

After a moment of wonder the chairman said he would like to have some explanation for the action of the majority.

Mr. Jones: I was there and gave the reason why we were opposed to the resolutions. The next day in their convention this thing was called up and quite fully considered. And so I read the report from the Chicago *Times* of the following day:

Gloom pervaded the meeting of the American Sabbath Union yesterday morning. The unexpected set-back received at the meeting held at the South Park Methodist Church the evening before had dampened the ardor of the delegates, and only a baker's dozen were in their seats when the presiding officer of that session, Dr. H. H. George, of Beaver Falls, Penn., called the meeting to order. The cause of the depression was the outcome of the meeting the night before. Four mass-meetings were held Tuesday night. At the first three, resolutions were adopted in favor of Sunday closing of the World's Fair. At the last the resolution was defeated, the attendance, it is now claimed, being principally of Adventists. That was the reason of the gloom which pervaded the South Park Church yesterday.

The committee appointed to prepare a telegram to Congress reported the following:

> The National Convention of the American Sabbath Union, meeting in this city, respectfully request our Congress, and especially the Committee on the World's Fair, that no action be taken to repeal the Sunday closing law. Mass-meetings were held in four different parts of the city last night to protest against this repeal as an act dishonorable to Congress and the nation.

> Dr. Mandeville was on his feet in an instant.

> That should not read four mass-meetings, for one meeting was opposed to the resolutions, he said. "It should read three mass-meetings."

> Yes, protested the committeeman, but our resolution covers that point. It says the meetings were held to protest – it does not tell what they did.

> But Dr. Mandeville would not be hoodwinked by any double dealing of the sort, and the resolution was made to say that three mass-meetings vigorously protested against the repeal of the Sunday closing law.

And the Secretary of the American Sabbath Union for the State of Illinois wrote a correction to the Chicago Evening Post in which he denounced those who voted against their resolutions as "brass interlopers," and for having "massed their forces to defeat the object of this mass-meeting." That opened the way for me to reply, which I read here as a part of my argument and which explains this point a little more fully before this Committee:

> *Chicago, December 17:* Editor of the Evening Post: I would not needlessly add to the afflictions of the American Sabbath Union, but in justice to the people denounced in Rev. Mr. McLean's letter in the Evening Post of Thursday, as well as to bring that letter within the boundary of facts, Mr. McLean's correction needs to be corrected. That he should not have a clear understanding of the situation at the South Park Church mass-meeting of Tuesday night, is not strange. He was not there. I was there, and, therefore, beg a little space to correct his correction. He states that the Seventh-day Adventists, "evidently supposing it would be a fine stroke of policy, in order to defeat the object of the meeting, massed their forces," from the region of the meeting, "with the result as published." This is a total misapprehension. There was not a particle of policy about it; there was no thought beforehand of defeating the object of the meeting; and our forces were not massed. That there was no massing of forces will readily appear to all from the fact that while there are one hundred and ninety-four Seventh-day Adventists in this quarter of the city, there were only about forty at the mass meeting. And whereas, there are fully three hundred Seventh-day Adventists in the other three divisions of the city – west side, north side, and Englewood – there were none in attendance at the Sunday union mass meetings in those three quarters. If we had done as we are charged with doing, at least three, instead of only one, of their mass-meetings would have been carried against their resolution. Mr. McLean ought to be thankful that we are not so black as he has painted us, and that they escaped as well as they did.

> But why should they denounce us? Was it not–[#]
>
> *The Chairman* (Mr. Durborow): I don't want any more of such stuff as that. I do not see what bearing that has on this question. Please confine yourself to proper lines of argument.
>
> *Mr. Jones:* It shows this: that their representation of forty millions of people – the masses of the country – is not true. When forty people can go to a mass-meeting and outvote them it shows that the masses are not with them.
>
> *Mr. Durborow:* We are here on a matter of changing some legislation. I think we might as well drop that. The congressmen undoubtedly knew what they were doing when they passed that bill.
>
> *Mr. Jones:* I am not casting any reflection upon Congress in this. I am not saying that the Congress knew that these representations were false. But is it not possible for congressmen to be deceived, and seriously to consider representations which were false?
>
> *Mr. Durborow:* I don't think your whole argument is very respectful to the Congress of the United States.

You see he shut me off from showing that these representations were false and said he did not "want any more of that stuff," but he got it. Rev. H. W. Cross, a Presbyterian minister from Ohio went to Washington to make a five minutes' speech. And the third day of the hearing he set forth this m"atter stronger than I could have done. I think I had better give his speech right here. It is as follows:

> SPEECH OF REV. H. W. CROSS BEFORE THE COMMITTEE
>
> *Mr. Durborow:* Rev. H. W. Cross of Ohio will speak for five minutes.
>
> *Rev. H. W. Cross:* Mr. Chairman and gentlemen of the Committee: The real object of my being here to speak a word, is in favor of intellectual honesty on the part of the orthodox churches. I am a minister of an orthodox church. I notice in my territory that these church petitions are exceedingly delusive as to the number of those that sign them or vote for them.
>
> Now for example, in one instance in our State the Presbyterians passed a resolution, saying that we represent so many, aggregating a certain membership; and then the Christian Endeavor Society, composed of many of the same church members alluded to by that Presbyterian church, will pass a like resolution, and say we represent fifty, seventy, or one hundred members. And then it will be brought before the Sunday school. And many of the persons who are counted as voting for the resolutions will have been counted three, four, or five times, and it is almost on the principle of voting early and often – which is so much opposed in secular politics. I am witness to this fact. There was one petition claiming to represent eighty church members that signed the petition to Congress but they were not present at all. It was at a Sunday school, and the vote was taken by the Sunday school superintendent, and there were children that voted for those resolutions that were not old enough to know whether the expression "World's Fair" meant the pretty girls in the next pew or the Columbian Exposition in Chicago.

[#] *On page 44*

> I deem it my duty to inform this Committee of the facts in that case. The real animus of these petitions is religious. But you cannot tell by the wording of the petitions just what they mean; it is the spirit back of them that shows this. The columns of the religious press and the exhortations of class leaders and Sunday school superintendents – it is what they say to the few that were voting, that tell what these petitions mean. I deem our legislators thoroughly competent, intellectually and morally, to decide this question without any imperious dictation from any sect or group of sects, as to whether this opening of the great educational exposition is consistent with the civil Sabbath. I notice a tendency in my own church papers and in other orthodox church papers to gloat over the fact that "we (that is this group of denominations having this common idea) have been strong enough by our own strength, to grasp Congress. We have hurled Congress against the Seventh-day Adventists, against the Seventh-day Baptists, and against the Roman Catholic citizens, and against various other of our citizens." Now it seems to me that is hardly a desirable thing to do in this country.
>
> I cannot speak to you, gentlemen of the Committee, in the manner and to the extent that I had prepared myself, owing to the fact that I have but five or six minutes allowed me, and so I have simply presented these two points: that these petitions are exceedingly delusive as to the number who sign them, inasmuch as one and the same identical people have spoken many times, and in a great variety of instances, at conventions as individual signers, at Sunday-schools, as members of the Society of Christian Endeavor – the same persons have voted again and again. And when you come to figure out the vast aggregate it is exceedingly delusive, and if the interests of the civil Sabbath. . .
>
> *Mr. Durborow:* – Mr. Cross, your time has expired.
>
> *Mr. Cross:* Very well, then; I will leave my sentence unfinished. I bow to the decision.

Another speech which most powerfully set forth this that the Committee refused to hear from me, was that of Mr. Thomas J. Morgan, a laboring man from Chicago. He had his speech written out to be read. But after hearing some of the church representatives, he was so stirred by their misrepresentations, that he, when he came to speak, forgot all about his written speech, the passing of time, and everything else, till the Chairman told him his twenty-five minutes were gone. I will give his speech here also. So I read:

After stating whom he represented and that he had received word "from 375 labor organizations, coming from every town and city in the United States, in which there is sufficient industry carried on to promote or encourage the organization of a body of workmen," and covering up to date "thirty-three States of the Union," he said:

> ### SPEECH OF THOS. J. MORGAN
>
> Now Mr. Chairman, having stated the authority that is vested in me, I wish to say that I appear before this Committee under very great embarrassment. I did not know until two hours before I took the train that I should be able to reach this Committee. I arrived here at eleven o'clock last night, and being in a new place, in unaccustomed conditions,

I lost my sleep. In addition to that I am just from the bench. you see [holding up his hands] I am a workman; there are the callouses and corns that are a necessary incident to manual labor. I come unprepared by education to meet the arguments presented here or to present my case with the force and fluency that gentlemen in the opposition have, having been forced by my condition to labor all my life-time since nine years of age, without a single vacation; absolutely denied the opportunities of education except that which was wrested from my sleeping hours.

I am also embarrassed by the fact that I find myself, for the first time in my life, in the midst of a lot of friends of labor, whose existence I never before was aware of; and I am absolutely astounded as well as embarrassed at the statements they make. They not only claim to speak in the name of labor, such as we have it in the United States; but, lo and behold, they speak with the voice of authority from my fellow-workers in Great Britain, from which country I came. Not only that, but they take the name of a man whom I honor more, possibly, that any other, and hurl authority from that source at this Committee – that man is Karl Marx. They speak in the name of the social Democrats of Germany also; and I, being a Social Democrat, being an Englishman, and associated intimately with the reform movement of that country, and being here in the United States for twenty-three years an active labor reformer – why, you can imagine my embarrassment and astonishment when I find myself in the presence of these advocates and friends of Karl Marx, the Social Democrats of England, and the friends of labor reform here in the United States. [Turning to the Clergymen] I regret exceedingly that I cannot grasp your hands in fraternal friendship. I am sorry that I have to say, Oh, save us from our friends. I am embarrassed in being compelled to say that I am here with authority to absolutely repudiate you and charge you with false representation.

When I heard the statements they made, I thought I will approach this matter with kindness, gentleness, etc.; I thought to myself, I hope I will have the power to deal with this question in the same spirit; but I am afraid I have overstepped the limits already. I have this thing so near at heart that ordinary composure is absolutely destroyed when I find that we are attacked, that our interests are so misrepresented, that our desires and wants are so distorted, by these men who claim to speak with authority.

[To the clergymen] You bring men's names from England who are absolutely unknown. What is the matter with Joseph Arch? What is the matter with Tom Mann? What is the matter with Ben Tillott? Can you speak in their names? No. You bring some unknown names here to add force to your misrepresentation. You have never been the friends of labor and at this time you have no right to speak in that sense.

When you brought your references here my mind ran back at once to England, to Joseph Arch, a layman in the church, whose zeal for the Christian religion was too great to be contained. As a layman he taught, under the hedge-rows, the moral truths that Christ enunciated, and he found in his efforts to lift up his class that the whole array of clergymen of Great Britain were against him, as we find the whole array of the clergy of the United States except the Catholic Church arrayed against us.

[Voices from the clergymen expressing disapproval.]

Possibly that statement I made that the *whole* clergy was arrayed against us is not strictly true. I hope to save myself from any statement that is not absolutely based upon facts. Possibly I would be right if I said that the evangelical churches of the United States, as here represented, are absolutely opposed to us and to our interests. Probably I should except the Catholic Church; possibly I will admit that. I tell you I am embarrassed. Possibly you will give me some consideration at least in that respect. I wanted to undo the work that you have been doing here and I will do it to the best of my ability.

Joseph Arch, to whom I referred who now lives, and from whom you have got no word, who was lifted from the hedge-row into the House of Parliament, was placed there by the people, and he promised to make it possible for them to live in decency and respectability. After he had accomplished that, the clergymen of Great Britain called him to a great meeting in Exeter Hall, at which there were present two hundred clergymen. They asked him to explain the purposes of his organization, and he did so. It was to lift the people out of absolute ignorance, into the comforts and decencies of manhood; it was to kill the saloon, to empty the jail, to give men in the agricultural districts a chance to live, as decent human beings. He had accomplished a great deal in that direction and he not only told the ministers, "We not only did it without your help, but we did it in the face of your absolute effort in antagonism." And he said, "After we have accomplished this work you call us to account! We give you the results of our work. We did that without your help. We will go right along. All that we ask you is that if you can not see your way to help us, get out of the way and leave us alone to do our work." This is my answer to your English production.

You speak here of the Social Democrats of German. What right have you? You have no authority at all. You go to work and take this little bit and that little bit from the work of Karl Marx, the Social Democrats, and the result of their convention and present it here with authority. I am a Social Democrat. I belong to that organization, and have done all I could to proselyte, in my humble way, the minds of the workmen of the United States, to the principles they hold. And I want to tell you clergymen that the principles held by the Social Democrats of Germany are the principles enunciated by Jesus Christ and which you do not understand.

[Voices: "Hear, hear."]

Mr. Chairman, I not only speak with this authority that I have expressed, but I want to call attention to the relative position that we occupy toward this World's Fair matter, in comparison with this body of clergymen organized like a machine [turning to the ministers]. I want to call up one after another to do his portion of the work.

Mr. Durborow: Mr. Morgan, the Committee is at this end of the table.

Mr. Morgan: My general statement as to my unfitness for this kind of work will excuse me, I hope. If the friends of the Church had been kinder to me when I was a child, had they taught me to read and write, I possibly would have been able to follow all the requirements of refined and common etiquette and society. Thanks to them, possibly I shall make some bad breaks, for which I ask to be excused.

I was going to say, Mr. Chairman, that in addition to the authority that I have here set forth, I wish to say that we workmen of Chicago particularly and especially demand the right to be heard with more consideration than our opponents. As soon as the word went forth that it was proposed to have an exposition, a world's exposition, in the United States, the labor organizations everywhere responded with gladness to that proposition, and as soon as it was settled that the World's Fair should be held somewhere in the United States, Chicago workmen put forth their claim to Chicago as the proper geographical point to have a world's exposition located. They backed up their request that Chicago should be the place with petitions from labor organizations throughout the United States, to such an extent that Congressman Hawley was able to stand up in the Congress of the United States and say, "I hold in my hand petitions from organized labor from every State in the Union, except New York, asking that the Fair shall be located in Chicago." That Fair was located there. But even before it was located there, the demand was made by Congress that Chicago should show its ability to conduct that Fair, be subscribing for ten millions of her stock. The workmen put their hands into their pockets and with dimes and fifty cent pieces and dollars subscribed for half a million of her stock.

What did the Church do? Did the Church demand that there should be an exposition of the world's products and man's ingenuity? If they did they did it silently. The workmen responded in this substantial fashion; and since then they have built the Fair and consecrated it with their blood. Hundred and hundreds of workmen have been killed and maimed in the construction of that mighty work. And I think that because of these reasons what we have to say should have additional weight attached to it.

Not only that, but giving all due credit to the master minds who designed and planned that wonderful exposition, giving them all due credit, the products exhibited there come from this kind of hands [Holding up his own labor-hardened hands]. And after we have built the Fair, sacrificed our lives in doing so, after we have contributed by our ingenuity and labor in placing there the exhibits, these men, who had no hand in it, neither in designing, constructing or in anything else connected with it, have come and shut the gate and turned the lock on us workmen! And then they come here with the miserable plea that they are instructed, that they are justified in speaking for labor! It is absolutely astounding, the assumption these men have in making their plea. I cannot comprehend how they could risk their reputation for veracity, for honesty, and for truth – and that is all the stock in trade that the clergy have, and if that is lost they are gone, how they could risk their veracity and honesty in making these statements. One of them comes here this morning and says, "I hold a petition from a labor Union in New York City." What labor union?

Rev. Mr. W. F. Crafts: The engineers of the United States.

Mr. Morgan: – Who?

Mr. Crafts: The Brotherhood of Locomotive Engineers.

Mr. Morgan: No! Look here; that claim, that statement that is made, that they do not duplicate things is basely, maliciously false. They do duplicate things. And they bring in a single petition from one of the local unions in the state of New York and you make people believe you have got another organization.

Mr. Crafts: – O no.

Mr. Morgan: Well, of course my comprehensive faculties are not equal to grasp your way of managing these things. Another statement is made that because the engineers of the United States speak, that settles the question; that they are the most intelligent of all workmen in the United States. I absolutely repudiate that statement.

[Here Mr. Morgan spoke a few words touching some rather personal matters between the organization which he represented and the organization of engineers, which we think it best for us not to seem to take any part in by printing and circulating as widely as this document will be spread – Publishers (original document)].

Then the plea is made that the opening of the Fair will necessitate extra work upon the part of the engineers. Let me call your attention to this fact, that if the Worlds's Fair is closed on Sunday people will be absolutely prohibited from enjoying its privileges on that day. That day will be given to traveling. Men will start on Sunday, reach Chicago Sunday night or Monday, spend the week at the Fair, take the train the latest hour Saturday night or the earliest hour Sunday morning.

Mr. Durborow: Mr. Morgan, you have been speaking just twenty-five minutes and have consumed the time allotted to you. I understand that you desire Mr. Askew to follow you and unless you give way to him, of course you would occupy his time.

Mr. Morgan: O, excuse me, Mr. Chairman. I did not think I had been talking so long. But really I would like to have a little more time. I have a paper here which I would like very much to present.

Mr. Durborow: If you have the consent of the other speakers, of course it will be all right.

Dr. W. H. Thomas: – I will give you my time.

Mr. Durborow: Simply state a synopsis of your paper if you can, and give it as quickly as possible.

Mr. Morgan: I will read it as rapidly as possible, and you can read it at your leisure.

[Reading] In regard to the religious side of this matter, I wish to say that the working men attribute the action of Congress in closing the World's Fair on Sunday to the activity and influence of the Protestant evangelical church, and that in the accomplishment of its purpose the representatives of these churches assume to be the guardians of the economical and moral interests of the working people, and in their name and behalf urge Congress to close the gates of the World's Fair on Sunday.

We are here duly authorized by the only organized and formal movement made by workingmen in relation to the closing of the Fair on Sunday to absolutely deny the right of these churches or their representatives to speak or act for us in this matter, and to prove to you by documentary evidence we present that all such representations made to Congress by these churches were willfully or ignorantly fraudulent.

In this connection we desire to call the attention of congressmen who may have been influenced by the action of these churches, and who are sincerely interested in the religious side of this question, to the fact that the indifference or active antagonism of the working classes toward the Church is at present and has been for years past, a subject of the most serious consideration by the clergy. We respectfully represent that one of the principal causes of this latent and active hostility to the Church is due to the fact that its representatives are so far removed economically and socially from the wage-working classes as to entirely fail to understand their wants, desires and aspirations, and hence as a result, when they do speak in our name, they misrepresent us, as they have in this case. This has occurred so frequently and universally that the respect and reverence for the Church held by the working people in the past, has been destroyed to such an extent that the Church itself has become alarmed. With a few exceptions, and upon rare occasions, a suggestion to have a clergyman open or participate in our conventions or mass-meetings would be met with contemptuous ridicule. Tens of thousands of wage-workers who like myself have passed from infancy to manhood within the folds of the Church, and in being forced from it, have retained a fervid love for the moral principles taught by the Carpenter of Nazareth, realize not only the wickedness embodied in the acts of the clergy in shutting the workers out of the fair, but also understand the effect it will have in further alienating the working classes from and intensifying their hostility toward the Church.

Speaking as we do, with this intimate personal knowledge, we respectfully, but most earnestly, urge congressmen who have been influenced by religious considerations to undo this ill-advised and injurious act of the Church.

Rev. Mr. Martyn, in advocating the closing of the Fair on Sunday, declared that neither literature nor art had any effect whatever upon the moral status of the people. Our reply is that this statement is a libel upon literature and art and a monstrous insult to all scholars and artists, and an absolute denial of the advantages of secular education, whereas we insist that every advance in general knowledge is necessarily an advance in public morals, and that the knowledge of individuals, and hence their moral status, is affected largely by their environment.

Place a working man within the gates of the World's Fair, bring him in contact with the wonders of nature as there shown, and the marvels of man's production gathered from the whole world, and in open-eyed wonder he will be lifted out of his ordinary self, all his lowest and basest instincts and habits will be for the time submerged, and deep into his mind and heart will be pressed, as never before, a comprehension of nature's varied resources and the limitless ingenuity and power of the human mind, which will ever after be a profitable source of reflection, a subject of conversation, instructive alike to himself and his associates, that must necessarily make him a better man, a more skillful, and hence a more valuable, worker and a more useful citizen.

These conclusions are reached not from abstract reasoning, but through practical personal experience, and were I a clergyman or an active member of the Church, having the moral welfare of the people at heart, I would consider it an imperative duty not only to open wide the gates of the fair on Sunday, but to advocate the organization of special means to bring the masses within its intellectual and moral influences on that particular day.

In the consideration of the moral side of the subject I asserted that the influence of a visit to the World's Fair would make the laboring man a more skillful and hence a more valuable worker. To the great army of unknown inventors a day in the World's Fair would be an inspiration of inestimable value, not alone to themselves but to the nation and to the human race. Again I speak from actual experience, being personally benefited by visits to expositions similar in character to the World's Fair, but in size and scope comparatively insignificant.

Those guarding the industrial and commercial interests of Great Britain and France thoroughly understand this view of the case. In Birmingham, England, where I came from, one of the greatest manufacturing towns in the world, such exhibits on a small scale were permanent institutions. Special delegations of workers were regularly sent to the world's expositions of London and Paris, and from personal conversation with one of the French workmen delegated to visit the centennial and exposition at Vienna, I learned that the French people were equally alert to the importance of this particular matter.

I am also advised by one of my associates, actively interested and aiding in this work of opening the gates of the World's Fair on Sunday, that in Germany in the industrial towns along the Rhine the workingmen's societies regularly sent delegations to both London and Paris to report upon the exhibits relating to their particular trades and that such visits were so arranged, for economical reasons, that the delegates reached Vienna or Paris on Saturday night or Sunday morning, visited the exposition during Sunday, and departed for home Sunday night or Monday morning.

Comparatively few of the workers in the United States have had the advantage of those stimuli to thought and invention, nor have the manufacturing and commercial class as yet reached a full realization of its importance. Hence I press this view of the matter, hoping that it may aid in opening the gates of the World's Fair on Sunday to the hundreds of thousands of workers in Chicago and its neighboring towns and to encourage by that privilege the visits of as many wage-workers throughout the nation as may by months of self-denial and sacrifice save sufficient to pay the expenses of a visit to the World's Fair, such visit being necessarily limited to a few days.

Now I return to my own speech, where it was interrupted by the Chairman of the committee.

Mr. Jones: Well, very good. I will take it, then, that Congress knew what they were doing. Here is the record of it in the Senate; that is where this part of the legislation began, because the legislation in the House touched only the closing of the government exhibit and passed the House that way and said nothing about closing the Fair on Sunday. When it came to the Senate, there this part of the legislation originated. I shall read from the *Congressional Record* of July 10, 12, and 13.

Mr. Durborow: Well, it is no use to read that here. We are more familiar with that than you are yourself. What we are after is modifications of the existing law.

Mr. Jones: – Certainly.

Mr. Durborow: Now, if you will argue on the point of the modification of the law, the benefits why this law should be changed and modified in accordance with the resolutions that are before this Committee – that is what this Committee has these hearings for:

Mr. Jones: Well, that is what I am doing. I have given the Constitution as it provides, prohibiting this legislation, and when the Constitution prohibits it, then ought not the legislation to be undone?

Mr. Durborow: This is not the place to argue that question.

Mr. Little: I think you perhaps misunderstand the legislation that has already been taken. I agree with you as to the Constitution. But this legislation makes an appropriation and accompanies the appropriation with the condition that the Fair should be closed on Sunday. For instance, you have no right to say to a gentleman walking along the street, 'You shall not go into that saloon.' But if you give him five dollars you have the right to connect with it the condition that he shall not spend it in the saloon.

This is not admitted. For we have no right to bribe a man, even not to drink. And if Congress did this act upon this principle, as is here suggested, then it did add to the other evils of this legislation the element of bribery. And in fact this is precisely the view of it which has already been held by the American Sabbath Union. The President of the Sabbath Union has published that this act of Congress "puts a premium of $2,500,000 on doing right. It proves in a concrete way that 'godliness hath great gain.'" And this whole idea we repudiate with all the rest of the evil thing.)

Mr. Jones: I see your point. The argument has been made, and it was made when the legislation was before the Senate, that as Congress was appropriating the money, it had the right to put whatever restrictions it considered proper upon the use of the money.

Mr. Little: But they were not forced to take the money.

Mr. Jones: Certainly. But I deny that proposition. Congress had the right to put whatever civil restrictions she pleased upon the use of the money; Congress had no right under the constitution to put any *religious* restriction at all upon the use of the money.

Mr. Jones: Yes, sir. It is religious legislation entirely.

Mr. Houk: Do you believe that it would be right for Congress to say that the Fair should be closed one day in seven?

Mr. Jones: No, it would not be proper, for it all rests upon religious ground, and that is the only ground upon which Sunday observance or Sunday recognition rests. And the claim that the legislation was in the interests of the workingmen is contrary to the proceedings of the Senate. Senator Hawley said plainly, "Everybody knows what the foundation is; it is founded in religious belief." Senator Peffer said, "Today we are engaged in a theological discussion as to the observance of the first day of the week." So that they considered it as religious, and religious only. Now, I repeat, they had no right under the Constitution to put any religious restriction upon it. When they put that restriction there and said that the directors should sign an agreement to close the World's Fair on Sunday, on the "Christian Sabbath," as Congress declared Sunday to be, before they could receive any money, they had just as much right to say that the World's Fair directory should sign an agreement to submit to Christian baptism before they could receive any of the appropriation.

Voice: Or try Dr. Briggs.

Mr. Jones: Yes. When Congress put upon this appropriation the condition that the directory should sign an agreement to shut that Fair on the "Lord's day," as Congress declared Sunday to be, before they could receive any of the money, Congress had just as much right to require that the World's Fair Committee should observe the Lord's supper before they could get any of the money. Hence, if Congress can define what the Christian Sabbath is, they can require anything else in the Christian religion.

Voice: That is so.

Voice: Is not this a Christian nation?

Mr. Jones: No, of course not.

When they go beyond the Constitution in one point for religion's sake, they can go beyond it on every point. What Congress has done in this respect in favor of Sunday only opens the way to do whatever else may be demanded by those who have secured this. And it will be demanded, for the *Christian Statesman*, whose editor is in the hall, has said that "the great Christian majority has learned, by response to its great petition, and its host of letters with reference to the World's Fair, that it can have of national and State governments whatever legislation against immorality it will ask unitedly and earnestly." And a preacher in Pittsburgh, as soon as this bill had passed Congress, declared in a sermon: "That the Church has weight with great political or governing bodies has been demonstrated most effectually in the late World's Fair matter, when the United States Senate, the highest body in the country, listened to the voice of religion and passed the World's Fair five million appropriation bill with the Church-instituted proviso that the gates of the great Exposition should not be opened upon Sunday. That grand good fact suggests to the Christian's mind that if this may be done, so may other equally needful measures. The Church is gaining power continually, and its voice will be heard in the future much more often than in the past."

Voice: The statement of an individual.

Mr. Jones: No, not the statement of an individual only; it is representative, because those who secured the legislation, those who presented the petition – they did it as a grand combination, not as individuals, but as a combination. The National Reform Association, the American Sabbath Union, and the whole combination put together – they worked for it for religious reasons; they demanded it upon religious grounds only, and did it as religious. The basis of it was declared to be the fourth commandment, when Senator Quay sent up his Bible to the Secretary of the Senate to be read there. Here it is in the *Record*. Who will deny that the fourth commandment is religious? Who will deny that the fourth commandment as given in the Bible is religious and that the Bible itself is religious? I appeal to this Committee: Has the Congress of the United States a right to put that Bible into its legislation and to make *that* the basis of legislation in this government? No, sirs. THE CONSTITUTION is the basis of legislation by Congress, and not the Bible. And the Constitution has shut religious questions from the consideration of Congress. But the Bible was sent up that day, and this is the record:

Mr. Quay: On page 122, line 13, after the word "act," I move to insert:

"And that provision has been made by the proper authority for closing of the Exposition on the Sabbath day."

The reasons for the amendment I will send to the desk to be read. The Secretary will have the kindness to read from the Book of Law I send to the desk, the part enclosed in brackets.

The Vice President: The part indicated will be read.

The secretary read as follows: "Remember the Sabbath day to keep it holy."

Mr. Jones: You know the fourth commandment; I need not read it.

Voice: – Read it all.

Mr. Jones: "Six days shalt thou labor and do all thy work; but the seventh day is the Sabbath of the Lord thy God. In it thou shalt not do any work, thou, nor thy son, nor thy daughter, thy manservant, nor thy maidservant, nor thy cattle, nor thy stranger that is within thy gates; for in six days the Lord made heaven and earth, the sea, and all that in them is, and rested the seventh day: wherefore the Lord blessed the Sabbath day and hallowed it."

Voice: – Is that the seventh day or the first day?

Mr. Jones: The commandment says the seventh day; but in the face of this plain declaration of the Lord that the seventh day is the Sabbath of the Lord, the Senate has put its own interpretation upon that commandment, and has declared that the statement that "the seventh day is the Sabbath" means "the first day of the week, commonly called Sunday." Thus the Congress of the United States has taken the fourth commandment from the Bible and put it into its legislation, and has put its own interpretation upon that statute. If Congress can interpret the Bible on one point, it can interpret it on every other point. So that when it went beyond the Constitution of this country in this thing, it has put itself and the government in line with all the Church-and-State governments that have ever been and has assumed to itself to be the interpreter of the Bible for all the people in the land and for all who come into the land. That is what has been done.

Mr. Houk: Your argument is, then, that the quotation of that commandment by Senator Quay, and the insertion of that, incorporates the fourth commandment and the whole Bible into the legislation of this country?

Mr. Jones: In principle it does. [Laughter.] Why not? What is to hinder it? When they can incorporate one part of the Bible for this occasion, what is to hinder their incorporating every other part of the Bible as other occasions may be presented? And therefore it is true that the incorporation of this part of the Bible here, does in principle incorporate the whole.

Mr. Houk: That is a kind of general way to get God into the Constitution.

Mr. Jones: Exactly. And that is what these are rejoicing at who have wanted all these years to put God into the Constitution. And that is why they say now, "We can have all we want, when we ask unitedly for it." And this is true. This does give them all they wanted, for when congress can do that in one point, who will deny its right to do it in any other point? When the principle is once established, the thing is all done. But it did put the fourth commandment there as giving the reasons why the Fair should be closed Sunday and as forming the basis of the legislation upon this question.

> *Mr. Durborow:* Now was the reading of that commandment an organic act of the Senate, of Congress, in doing any such thing as that?
>
> *Mr. Jones:* It was the organic act of Congress, because it was an inseparable part of the legislation itself; it was given as the basis of the legislation, and as containing the reasons for it.
>
> *Mr. Houk:* Then anything that a member says incorporates it in the act?
>
> *Mr. Jones:* Oh no, not necessarily. But let us consider how this was brought in. Senator Quay proposed an amendment. The House had passed a bill to close the government exhibit, letting the Fair alone. when it went to the Senate, Senator Quay introduced an amendment to close the whole Fair. His amendment was "That provision has been made by the proper authority for closing the Exposition on the Sabbath day." That was the first step taken in Congress on the subject of closing the Fair, not the government exhibit, but closing the Fair. The Senate took that step, and in the taking of it, the fourth commandment was quoted by him who offered the amendment, and was adopted by the Senator as the basis, and as giving the reasons for the amendment. Now when this commandment was given by him, and read afterward by the secretary from the desk, as the basis of that amendment, and as containing the reasons for the legislation that was in the amendment, and when the Senate adopted that amendment by changing it to the first day of the week and calling it Sunday, and then the House confirmed their decision – then it is as plain as day that the fourth commandment is put there and embodied in the legislation of the country by the definite act of Congress.
>
> [The clock struck 12, the time expired.]
>
> Mr. Durborow announced that the time had expired and said, "This will bring the discussion to a close for this day."

That closed the hearing for that day. The Chairman had shut out the constitutional argument and refused to have that go before the Committee; but the questions that were asked brought all that out, until the time was consumed.

The American Sabbath Union knew that their cause was safe, and after the hearing was over, they simply stepped outside the door in the entry way and called a meeting of their Union and passed a vote of thanks to the Lord for preserving the American Sabbath.

They knew that when the constitutional argument was shut out, they had all they wanted.

The next day Elliott F. Shepard made the opening speech, and note how he started:

> The only thing that makes a congressman is the Constitution of the United States. He has no authority in this world but such as the Constitution gives him, and he has no right to listen to any argument that would not come within the Constitution.

But they shut that out, and now see what they did listen to in the first speech that followed:

OPENING REMARKS OF COL. E. F. SHEPARD

I approach this subject with great reverence. When we come to deal with heavenly things, we should put aside earthly things, and should do very much as the Jews used to do in the temple at Jerusalem. Before they made their offerings, before they entered upon the service, they prepared themselves by ablution and by prayer for the proper discharge of their duties. Now when we come to consider the Sabbath, that it rests upon the law of God, that it is a revelation to mankind which no one would have thought of, that we owe it entirely to our Father which is in heaven, we ought therefore to come with the same reverential spirit to its consideration ourselves. . .

We have resolved not [to] say one single word as to the constitutionality or unconstitutionality of this law before this Committee, for to claim that it is unconstitutional here would be a reflection upon the Committee, upon both Houses of Congress, and upon the President of the United States who approved this law. And you yourself very wisely took that last consideration entirely out from before the Committee when you stated that this was not the place to argue that question. Therefore we dismiss it without saying a single word.

Mr. T. A. Fernley, in his speech, told the Committee that there was no authority for reconsidering the question because there was no new evidence presented, that there was not a single new reason before the Committee for opening the Fair on Sunday. And he said that the only possible ground upon which you can reconsider that question is its unconstitutionality. So that confirmed the position that he had refused to hear from us so that everything they objected to from us they got from somebody else. They went on – not with heavenly arguments by any means – but they proposed to consider heavenly things, and they reined the Committee up before death and the Judgment, stating that when they came to die it would be a consolation to them to know that they had acted right on the maintenance of the Sabbath.

Others would bring up and threaten the wrath of God upon the nation if it did not preserve the Sabbath. A man was there from Asia Minor, and he wanted the world's Fair closed on Sunday as a stimulus to missions, and if the World's Fair should be opened on Sunday it would be the greatest set-back to the missionary cause that ever could happen to it. And thus they would bring the Judgment before the Committee and the presence of death and threaten them with the wrath of God and the Judgment of God if they did not do so and so. In an editorial in the Review not long ago there was a quotation referring to this point, that these men would go to Congress, speak for God, and threaten these things if Congress did not do so and so. (See *Review* of Oct. 25, 1892) That has been done.

Here is an argument from a lawyer, a judge, Judge S. B. Davis, of Terre Haute, Ind., that was sent up there and distributed by the hundreds and lying in quantities on the table of the Committee, in which is said:

> The Supreme Court of the United States says, "This is a Christian nation."

And goes on from this to argue for national and State recognition of Sunday. Yes, "this is a Christian nation." That was the grand chief argument of all. This is a Christian nation; the Supreme Court of the United States has said so. If there are any of the brethren here who doubt whether the decision of the Supreme Court means anything, I wish they had been there and seen what it meant there.

What is the situation now as the legislation stands tonight? As it stood then? What is the situation since? Here is an article from the Chicago *Herald* of Jan. 14, 1893, that gives the situation, and so I read it here:

> It is anything but an encouraging prospect which the friends of Sunday opening of the World's Fair have before them. . . . The hearings which have taken place during the last four days have greatly hurt the Sunday opening cause. Not that the advocates of closing have had the best of the argument, for they have not, but the publicity given to the matter throughout the country by this agitation has brought down upon Congress an avalanche of protests and appeals from religious people and church organizations all over the country.
>
> The churches and the ministers are at work again quite as earnestly as they were a year ago and with equal effectiveness. . .
>
> General Cogswell, who was counted upon till today, is now wavering. The Methodist Episcopal Church has brought some influence to bear upon him which he finds it difficult to resist. . . The trouble is that a large number of members who believe in Sunday opening on principle and as a matter of right are too timid to vote their convictions in the face of organized opposition from the churches and ministers. These statesmen argue that the men who want the Fair open on Sunday are reasonable men who will not permit their judgment or their votes to be affected by failure to get what they want. While on the other hand the Church people who are for Sunday closing will, if their wishes are thwarted, lose their tempers and at the next election make trouble for those who vote against them.
>
> This sort of cowardice or caution, combined with the fact that the ministers who are making Sunday closing a sort of stock-in-trade have no hesitancy about bulldozing their congressional representatives or anyone else they can get hold of, offers an explanation of the changed condition of affairs with reference to this question.

I read here the closing statement of Rev. Joseph Cook in his speech before the Committee:

> Sunday is the tallest of the white angels now entering foreign lands. Shall we consent to allow Chicago now to rise up and stab this angel in the back, in our country? And shall we call down the goddess of liberty from the Capitol to assist at the murder? God forbid.

In whose hands is the government of the United States? The churches. Who owns Congress? The churches. Who is using it? As that gentleman from Ohio said: "We have been able by our strength to use Congress as we choose." The churches. These are the facts.

These are some of the things that are taking place before us. Now the study will be what is soon to come upon us from what is now taking place before us. When we see that, as the testimony has said, we will see the necessity, recognize the necessity, that the Holy Spirit shall be recognized, received, presented to the people. And that is where we are, brethren, as Brother Prescott has said. The only question is, Shall we seek God for the power of His Holy Spirit? The country is sold into the hands of a religious hierarchy, and that is sold into the hands of the devil.

*Page 30.*

What I was going to read further was this:

> Was it not advertised and held as a mass-meeting? Had we not a perfect right to attend it? And had we not a perfect right to vote against any resolutions that might be offered? When we went to the meeting, as the masses were expected to go, were we to keep still when called upon to vote? And to remain silent when directly called upon, both by the gentleman who offered the resolutions and by the chairman, to explain our vote? In view of these facts, is it the fair thing for them to denounce us as "atheists," "religious anarchists," "brass interlopers," etc., as they have done? What kind of a mass meeting did they expect to hold, anyhow? More than this, what kind of a mass meeting is that wherein forty people can "mass their forces" and defeat the object of the meeting? In all their meetings they missed no opportunity to proclaim over and over that forty millions of the American people are on their side of the Sunday question. In the meeting that night Dr. George vehemently declared that on their side were forty millions, while there were only about twenty-five thousand of the Seventh-day Adventists in the United States. "Forty millions of us," he shouted, "and we are not afraid". Forty millions of us and we have the government on our side, and we are not afraid of anything that the Adventists can do. Now if the people were so overwhelmingly in favor of the work of the American Sabbath Union how would it be possible for a few, in proportion of only one in sixteen hundred, either to pack their meeting or defeat their resolutions? If their own representations were true, they would have had the house full and the galleries packed with people in favor of the work of the Sunday Union, and it would be literally impossible for all the opponents that could be "massed" to defeat the object of the meeting. But when the facts demonstrated that their own mass-meetings were so slimly attended that forty people could largely outvote them and kill their resolutions and "defeat the object of the meeting," this in itself demonstrates that their claim of an overwhelming majority of the people in favor of Sunday closing of the World's Fair is a downright fraud. And this is what hurts them. As long as they can go on unmolested and uncontradicted in their misrepresentations they are happy. But when an incident occurs that exposes the fraud in their claims it grinds them.

Sermon 3

January 31, 1893

I will take up the subject where we stopped last night and read just two sample statements of those we had in mind when the hour closed last night. Here is one:

> Mr. Chairman and gentlemen of the Committee and the friends and opponents of this measure: Allow me to call attention to one thing and that is a fact to which we all assent. None of this company will be here in 1993. At that time all of us shall be of one mind in regard to the value and sacredness of the Lord's day, for the sentence has gone forth against every man, "Set thine house in order."
>
> How fast they fall! Those we have known, As leaves from autumn branches grown, Are quickly seared. But while men die, the Nation lives.
>
> May the God of nations so guide us and our posterity that "America" may be sung until the end of time. –*From the speech of C. B. Botsford, before the House Committee on the World's Exposition.*

Another one:

> There is just one general reason, Mr. Chairman and gentlemen of the Committee, I would like to give why this Fair ought to be kept closed on the Sabbath. If these gates are open on the Sabbath it will be perilous to us as a nation and it will be perilous to Chicago and to the interests of the Fair. There is one thing we are to remember, and that is that God still reigns, God is still on the throne. God has not abdicated, and He has declared that the nation or the country that will not serve Him shall perish. And more than this, we are to remember that the ten commandments are the very basis of all our laws, National and State, which subserve our liberties and our rights. Take the fifth commandment, take the sixth commandment against murder and protection to life, protection to person; it is based on that sixth commandment. Take the seventh commandment. Now here is the fourth commandment in the very heart of these ten commandments, and that has never been repealed any more than has the fifth commandment or the sixth commandment or the seventh commandment or the eighth commandment. And therefore we are to remember that if we touch this commandment of God, standing thus in the very heart of these ten commandments, we touch the honor of God; we touch the law of God, for Christ has emphasized that fourth commandment. He said, 'The Sabbath was made for man.' What did He mean by that? He meant thereby that it was not made for the Jew only but for man everywhere in every age and in every condition. He said the Sabbath was made for man.

> It was made for man in all ages, in all time. He said the Sabbath was made for man; it was made for man's highest good in every age of the world, for his good morally and physically.
>
> And therefore it is, dear friends, if we touch that fourth commandment, which lies at the very root of all the other commandments, we touch the honor of God and the commandments of God. It has never been repealed, and *if we touch that God will bring a curse upon us as a nation,* because he distinctly told His people anciently that He would punish them for the profanation of the Sabbath day. And therefore it is, dear friends, that we as a nation cannot afford to touch this commandment. What it becomes us to do is, therefore, to set to the nations of the world a good example of the American Sabbath; set them an example of the Christian Sabbath; set them an example of the Sabbath as God has ordained it.
>
> A heathen prince once visited Queen Victoria, and desired the Queen to give him the secret of the government's greatness. Queen Victoria sent for a Bible, and handing that to him said, 'There is the secret of the nation's greatness.' And the secret of our greatness as a nation is the Bible that is enthroned in all the laws on the line of the Sabbath. That is the foundation of our laws.
>
> *From the speech of Rev. F. A. McCarrel, before the House Committee on World's Fair, Jan. 11, 1893.*

I read these simply as samples of the arguments that were presented to the Committee to persuade Congress to stand fast in the position where the government has been placed.

Now brethren, you remember I took a text last night that was to last a week. Tonight I want to read another passage in the same line. It is this:

> Brethren and sisters, would that I might say something to awaken you to the importance of this time and the significance of the events that are now taking place about us. I point you to the aggressive movements now being made for the restriction of religious liberty.

That is what we want to study tonight. And as I, with the help of the Lord, shall bring before your minds things that *are,* I want you to be as anxious to receive and see these things as God is that we shall, in order that we may see and meet His mind in this respect.

There are doubtless people in this house who were here about three years ago when a subject was given me, which was, I think, "The Present Crisis." Those who were here will remember that in referring to our work at that time, which was petitioning Congress and remonstrating against all this legislation, I called attention to the fact that that was our work at that time. It was to circulate these petitions everywhere through all the land, that by this means we might waken the minds of the people of the United States against that matter, and to have their petitions go to Congress in such abundance that Congress might see what the principle is and that we might perhaps delay that legislation. The idea was that of getting the truth before the people by that means. And you will remember that I called attention to this thought: that that work would continue only until Sunday had been adopted, until some Sunday law should be passed, and then all our petitioning would be past and our work in that direction would be stopped, because it would be of no use for us to protest against Congress doing a thing which was already done.

Well, we are there now. We are now in the place that I referred to that night about three years ago. From the evidence that was given last night, it is clearly seen that the government of the United States is now in the hands of a hierarchy and no longer in the hands of the representatives of the people. Government as our forefathers established it, is gone, irretrievably gone now. Government of the people, by the people and for the people is gone. The authority of the government from the people, expressed in the Constitution, and the government to be conducted according to the Constitution is gone. The constitution has been overridden, and now it is ignored. It was ignored by the Committee the other day; in fact shut out entirely, and a hierarchy heard upon hierarchical positions giving hierarchical arguments only. When that is so – when the Constitution itself is shut out from before, and from the consideration of, a committee of Congress, whose only authority is the Constitution, and this other matter is received instead – then where has the government gone? Do you know? Where has it gone?

[Answers from the congregation: "Into the hands of the churches."]

Well, from the extracts I read last night, it is confessed that Congress dare not act according to their own view, according to the principles which they themselves hold, for fear of what the churches will do and that they dare not act in a way that fair-minded men desire them to act, because of a fear of what the churches will do in creating more mischief and more trouble to the nation than if they acted the other way. That is precisely the reason that Judge Hammond gave in justifying his decision in an article which was printed afterward in the same paper in which his decision was printed, that when churches demand legislation of that kind it was correct statesmanship to grant it, because Protestants were a fighting people and if they did not give them what they wanted, they would cause such trouble in the nation that the State would perish. That is the thought. What is that but just simply saying that the principles that actuate the professed Protestant churches of the United States are identical with the papal principles from beginning to end? And the reason which they gave for the legislation at the first is simply papal principles outright. That resolution which the churches sent up to Congress demanding this legislation, is as follows:

> Resolved that we do hereby pledge ourselves and each other that we shall from this day henceforth refuse to vote for or support for any office or position of trust, any member of Congress either Senator or Representative, who shall vote for any further aid of any kind for the World's Fair, except on conditions named in these resolutions.

Richard W. Thompson of Indiana, who was Secretary of the Navy under President Hayes's administration has well said: "To allow any church to dictate beforehand what laws should or should not be passed is to deprive the people of authority of government which they ordained in their own hands and to transfer it to such church." And that is so. That has been done and from the words that they have spoken and the representations which we read last night, it stands as a literal fact before the world tonight that the government of the United States is no longer a "government of the people, by the people, and for the people," as our fathers made it, but the *subjection* of the people by the churches and for the churches. The Church rules the government; she has it in her hands, and she is holding it there, and she proposes to hold it there.

Now when that had been done, it was perfectly proper for us, or anybody else, and all the people, to demand that it should be undone. Having done it even for the reasons for which it was done, Congress could have undone it, could have opened its eyes and stepped back again precisely where it was before. Congress could have undone this thing and left it where they should have left it at the first, and then the churches would have had to make another effort to gain possession of the government. But instead of listening to that demand upon the only basis they have a right to consider any question – the basis of the Constitution – they shut out the Constitution and all argument upon the Constitution, openly refused to hear it, and played into the hands of the churches which had already secured this, and thus fixing indelibly in the legislation of the country that thing which has been done.

Then that is virtually the second step. When the first step was taken the next step could have been taken backward; that would have undone it. But instead of taking that step, what is being done is only to confirm what has been done, and then the thing never can go back.

Now what errand have we to Washington any more? What place have we in Washington any more with petitions or hearings protesting against religious legislation? None at all. We have no more such errands to Washington. There is no place for any of our petitions there any more. That is the situation as it is now.

Some have asked, "Well, suppose new legislation comes up; can't we send up a protest against that and go and ask a hearing upon that?" What would be the basis of our argument? What would be the basis of our protest? That it is unconstitutional? But the Constitution has been overridden in this; and we would be met with the reply that it has been cone already, and that this is constitutional. That has been declared. And when this is taken as constitutional, everything else follows.

When I presented the idea that they might have been mistaken in the representations which were made to them, I was met with, "Your argument is not respectful to Congress."

Elder Fifield: Suppose another National Sunday bill comes before another committee, might not that committee listen to a constitutional argument?

Elder Jones: Well suppose they did; what would be the force of it? The Constitution has been overridden already. This things is unconstitutional. Sunday legislation is all unconstitutional. But all that has been done. And what would be the force of any argument against any other Sunday bill; that is, on the ground of its unconstitutionality? Where is the force of it? There would be simply none at all.

So you can see that everything is gone, brethren. That is what I want you to think of; that the thing is gone. And the basis, the only basis which we ever had a right to go there upon – the Constitution – is taken from us. We had the right to go there upon that basis because the Constitution is God's idea in government. The principle of the government of the United States is God's idea for governments. And when we were holding up the Constitution and the principles of it as the idea of God, as we did every time, and as the right idea, that was the thing that we had to do. God had given that as an example to all the world and as a light to all the world, as the right ideas in government, and we had the right to appeal to it.

They wanted us to argue the other day against shutting the Fair on Sunday. You see we could not do that. And more than that, we can't argue against it being shut on Sunday for the reason that Sunday is not the Sabbath of the fourth commandment, because to argue that way would be simply allowing and admitting that Congress had properly incorporated the fourth commandment into legislation and that if they would only recognize the *day* of the fourth commandment instead of Sunday, we would not have anything to say. But we have everything to say against that. That would be only to give away everything. Consequently we could not leave our position on the Constitution. But when they shut us out, they shut out the Constitution. I say always we are in splendid company, for in being shut out by that committee from any constitutional argument, we are in splendid company, for we are in the company of the Constitution of the United States, and in order to get rid of us they had to shut out the Constitution. That is the company in which we belong.

So the sum of the whole matter is, we have no more errands to Washington such as we have had. Of course whenever there come up other such questions, that will be a good place to put our principles before Congressmen, as we spread the truth before all the people. But we have no more errands there with petitions or protests against religious legislation. That thing is gone. Well, in this work which is now past, what were we working against? Against something that was *done*, or against the *doing* of something? – Against the doing of something. Why did we protest against the doing of that thing? What did we say that the doing of that thing would be? – Forming a union of Church and State – Making an image to the beast.

Now that thing *is* done, and there is no more protesting against the *doing* of it. But is all our work done now? Have we nothing more to do in the world? Does all our work stop now, and we have nothing more to do in the world? No. Our work is *not* stopped. We have a work to do, but our work cannot be done in that way any more. Then what is our work? To warn against what is already done. But that which is done, is the making of the image of the beast. Then does not that bring us face to face with the third angel's message as it reads in words? Does not this bring you and me, and shut us up, to the third angel's message as it reads? There is no outlet but that, to speak the third angel's message as it reads in words against the thing that has been done. The third angel's message reads in words, "If any man worship the beast and his image and receive his mark in his forehead or in his hand." Then does not that show, in itself, that the image is there, and the mark is set up to be received?

I say again we cannot protest against the *doing* of the thing, because it has already been done. We cannot go to Congress and use constitutional arguments against religious legislation; we cannot protest against the making of the image to the beast. We cannot protest against the government recognizing the false Sabbath. That is set up, and it is put in place of the Sabbath of the fourth commandment by the definite act of Congress itself. Then that action has put the government of the United States into the hands of the churches. It has established the mark of the beast as the Sabbath of the nation and for all the world, and it has done it in place of the Sabbath of the fourth commandment in express words in the legislation.

What was the papacy? It was not simply the union of religion and the State; that was there in paganism. The papacy is the church ruling the State, the Church in possession of the State and the powers of the State and using them to enforce church decrees. It is a literal fact that the government of the United States is now confirmed in the hands of the professed Protestant churches, and that they are using it to enforce a church decree above all other decrees. That is what they did it for. That is what they are now doing. Is that like the papacy? Does that look like the papacy? Yes sir. So I say again, we are therefore shut up to the third angel's message. The facts are before our faces and we are shut up to that as our only work.

If we are to have any connection at all with public affairs we have got to have it in some other way than that in which we have had hitherto, and the only way in which we can have any connection with them at all is just simply to warn people against receiving or admitting the rightfulness of the thing that is done.

We are shut up to that one thing and there is no other way out. Every man from this day forth who professes to work in the third angel's message can carry that message or give that message in no other way than in the words which that message speaks, "If any man worship the beast and his image."

But never before 1892 had one of us the right to say that and warn the people against the worship of the image, because the image was not yet made. We have told the people that it was coming and that when certain things came, the image would be made, and the warning then would be, Do not you worship it. That has been our message, but that is not our message any more. We cannot tell them that now. We cannot protest against the making of it; we cannot do that now. That thing is done. We are shut up therefore to this one thing. I say again, There is no way out but to preach the third angel's message as it reads: "If any man worship the beast and his image." But there is a word there that comes just before that: "The third angel followed them, saying with a *loud voice*." What is that, then, but the loud cry of the third angel's message coming right in now. Does not that show us that when the time comes for the message to be given directly as it reads in words that the loud cry is right at that time? We have had enough before us in all these other things to show that, but is it not there in the words of the message itself, that when the message goes to the world in the words in which it is given, that is the loud cry? For it goes that way, with a loud voice.

Now another thought: How many of the nations of the earth besides this were there until this time that had no union of religion and the State? None. How many nations at all are there now that have it not? None. But a union of religion and the State, a union of Church and State, that is Satan's way of doing things. Paganism was Satan's way of doing things, and so was the papacy. And what is this now in our own nation? The image of the papacy.

Through what instrument did Satan make war against the church of God when Christ was born? -Through paganism. Through what instrument did he make war against the church in the wilderness? Through the papacy. Through what instrument does he make war against the remnant? Through the image of the papacy? See Revelation 12.

But until now the image was not made. Now it is made. Until now he did not have the government of the United States in his hands to wield against the truth of God. He has it now. How much then of the power of the world has Satan now in his hands to wield against the church and the Sabbath of God? He has it all. Hasn't he? Now you and I are pledged by years of profession to stand by the Sabbath of the Lord. We are pledged to that. But now opposed to this is every particle of power that this earth knows, with Satan the chief to wield the power. Then are we not brought face to face with this fact: That as certainly as we maintain our allegiance to the Sabbath of the Lord we shall have to do it in the face of all the power that this earth knows? Then does it not follow that in order to do that we must have with us a power that is greater than all the power that this earth knows? Can a man, of *himself*, stand successfully against all the power of earth? No, sir. Well, then, are we not shut up to this, that we must have a power working for us that is greater than all the power of the earth put together? Is it not time then, that that angel *should* come down from heaven having great power? That angel coming down and adding his voice to the other makes the loud cry. We therefore just now, at the point where that angel *has* come down with great power, and we need not be afraid. Though all the power of the earth be against the Sabbath of the Lord and against us for standing by it, the power of God is given to every one who will be faithful to Him.

Is not the message that the Saviour gave to His disciples precisely the message that is given to us? They were to go into all the world and preach the gospel to every creature. Here is our message. The everlasting gospel to preach "unto every nation, kindred, tongue and people." Revelation 14:6. It is the same thing. He said to them, "All power is given to me in heaven and in earth." Here Jesus Christ has a power *in the earth* that is greater than all the powers of earth. So if Jesus was only in the earth and was living on the earth, as He was once before, He would have more power than all the earth has besides anyway. "All power is given to me in heaven *and earth:* go ye *therefore.*" Why go? Because He has the power.

Go ye therefore and teach all nations these things, and lo *I am with you.* Is He? Is He with us, brethren? Let us stop saying he *will be* with us. He does not say it. Let us stop saying it; it is not faith at all. We say: "He says, 'I will be with you.'" And we ask Him to be with us, and then we wonder whether He is or not. He says, "Go ye; I *am* with you." Is He? Then thank Him that it is so. If you get into difficulties let Him help you out. It is Satan's office to present difficulties, to hedge up the way; but thank the Lord, when the Lord is with us, Satan cannot hedge up the way. He may put a Red Sea in front of us, and through we will go, for God can open the sea. The Lord *is* with us, and we want it a more personal thing than that He "will be," anyway. We want a power with us every moment, working with us, in us, and for us, and we want to be sure that it is so. How can we know it? He says so. Then let us say so, too.

There are two points that we have noticed thus far: One is that we are shut up to give the third angel's message as it reads; the other is that we are shut up to this one thing, that as certainly as we stand in our allegiance to the commandments of God, we have to do it in the face of all the power that this earth knows, with Satan using that power. And that shuts us up to this one thing, that we need therefore, in order to stand at all, in order to stand a minute, we need a power that is greater than all the power of this world put together. And the blessedness of it is, There He stands and says, "I am with you." Thank the Lord.

Now another thought, I think perhaps that will about fill the time for this evening, and these three points will be enough for tonight: Congress did take up the fourth commandment, did make it the basis and the reasons for that Sunday legislation. But it went further. It did not let that commandment stay there as it reads. It did not leave the commandment there as God gave it. It did not leave the commandment there as it is give in the Bible, and as it was put into the *Record.* It did not leave it there for the World's Fair Directory to interpret, each man for himself as to what it means.

Congress went beyond all that and interpreted the fourth commandment to mean "the first day of the week commonly called Sunday," as "the Christian Sabbath," "the Sabbath of the nation," and as that which should be observed and honored, for this nation and for the world, by shutting the Fair on Sunday. Then I ask, what is that but the government of the United States by a definite and decided act putting Sunday in the place of the Sabbath of the fourth commandment?

Let us look back a little now. The mystery of iniquity was working in Paul's day. The apostasy began; the apostasy went on; the church adopted Sunday, but could she compel anybody to keep it? No. Could she bring any restrictions, any force, to bear upon people who would keep the Sabbath of the Lord to compel them to put Sunday in the place of the Sabbath of the Lord, so long as the church stood alone? No. But she wanted to compel people to keep it instead of the Sabbath of the Lord. That apostate church wanted the Sunday sabbath kept instead of the Sabbath of the Lord and that people should recognize and observe it instead of the Sabbath. She could not do it alone.

What then did she do to accomplish her purpose? She took hold of earthly power. She seized the power of the State. How much power did that government represent in the world at that time? The Roman Empire was the world power then; so that Church then secured all the power of the world, and by that she compelled people to receive Sunday instead of the Sabbath of the Lord. Then was it not by that act that she succeeded in definitely putting the Sunday in the place of the Sabbath of the Lord? But what was that but making void the law of God? She took the seal of His law, the heart of His law, that which reveals Him, the seal showing that He is what He is; she by force took that away and put her own sign in its stead. What was that but supplanting God in the minds of the people of the world? And it was by that act that she succeeded in her purpose of making void the law of God. That was the beast. That made the beast. We have preached all these years that the papacy has made void the law of God. And that is correct.

Let us return now to our own time and the question that is before us. Have not the Protestant churches kept Sunday a long time? Have they not opposed the keeping of the Sabbath of the Lord a long time? But they could not compel anybody to keep Sunday instead of the Sabbath of the fourth commandment. In a measure, it is true, they could enforce the observance of Sunday in the States. But we know, and they have all confessed, that all efforts through State laws in this direction, we almost wholly nullified by the fact that the National Government was against it all, and we all know that one of the great reasons for their strenuous efforts to get the National Government committed to Sunday was to make the State laws effective. Then in order to make their purpose effective in exalting Sunday against the Sabbath of the Lord, these churches, professed Protestantism, had to seize the government of the United States, the power of this government, as the former apostasy seized the power of the Roman government. And now she has got it. And in the definite act by which she got it, she aimed at the Sabbath of the fourth commandment, to put it out of the way and to put the Sunday in its stead.

Then have not these by this definite act also made void the law of God? When the other was done that made the beast! What is this? It is the image. Is it not time, then, for the third angel's message to be given in its own words? "If any man worship the beast and his image and receive his mark in his forehead or in his hand."

Ah, and the Lord hath sent us a word just now, too. "It is time for thee, Lord, to work." Why? "Because they have made void thy law." Psalm 119:126. Then is not that word the prayer that God has put into our mouths at this time? Are you offering it? Are you living day by day and hour by hour in the presence of that terrible fact that it is time for God Himself to work, if His integrity is going to be maintained to all the world? It is a terrible fact; it is a fearful position. It brings us to the point of such consecration as not a soul of us ever dreamed of before; unto the place of such consecration, of such devotion, as will hold ourselves in the presence of God, with that fearful thought that "It is time for thee, Lord, to work, for they have made void thy law."

What is that but a confession, and a proper confession, too, "Lord what can we do? Here is all the power of the earth against us. What can we do against this great company?" Is not the prayer of Jehoshaphat our prayer now, "O our God, we have no might against this great company that cometh against us; neither know we what to do; but our eyes are upon thee." And they "stood before the Lord with their little ones, their wives, and their children."

"What does Joel tell us to do? "Sanctify a fast, call a solemn assembly, gather the congregation, assemble the elders, gather the children, and those that suck the breast: let the bridegroom go forth of his chamber and the bride out of her closet. Let the priests, the ministers of the Lord, weep between the porch and the altar, and let them say, Spare thy people, O Lord, and give not thine heritage to reproach, that the heathen should rule over them: wherefore should they say among the people, Where is their God?"

We stand pledged to the Lord and before the world that we depend upon God; that He loves His people; that He manifests Himself in behalf of those whose hearts are toward Him. Brethren, there is that fearful word also that touches that very thought, that came to us from Australia. It is in the testimony entitled, "The Crisis Imminent." What does that say? "Something great and decisive is to take place, and that right early. If any delay, the character of God and His throne will be compromised." Brethren, by our careless, indifferent attitude, we are putting God's throne into jeopardy. Why cannot He work? God is ready. Are not God's workmen ready? But if there is any delay, "the character of God and His throne is jeopardized." Is it possible that we are about to risk the honor of God's throne? Brethren, for the Lord's sake and for His throne's sake, let us get out of the way. Let us get out of the way. The only way to get out of the way of God is to flee to Him. That is the only way to get out of His way, and that is where He calls us now.

Here we stand. He has given us the prayer. O of all things when God has given us the prayer – how heartily and confidently can we present the prayer, and ourselves upon it.

He has given us the prayer, He has told us the word; "It is time for thee, Lord, to work, for they have made void thy law."

Then another thing; If we need anything to cause us to be sure that that is all so, there is that word that was read last Sabbath, from that last word that came from Australia:

> Brethren and sisters, would that I might say something to awaken you to the importance of this time, the significance of the events that are now taking place about us. I point you to the aggressive movements now being made for the restriction of religious liberty. God's memorial *has been* torn down, and in its place *a false sabbath stands before the world.*

Not, is going to be torn down. But "has been" torn down.

The testimony that came last winter – last year this time, said that a great move would be made "*to exalt* the false sabbath." What now? "God's memorial has been torn down, and in its place *a false sabbath stands* before the world." How fast God's word is fulfilled these days! One mail brings a testimony that such and such things "will be"; the next mail comes: "it is." One mail brings a word from the Lord that efforts are being made "to do" such and such things; the next mail brings words from the Lord, That thing "is done."

Brethren, should not we stand as minute men, ready to respond to God's word on the instant? There is no time, then, to lag for an instant. Brethren, let us seek God with all the heart. These testimonies that Brother Prescott read the past hour, bringing us face to face with this thought of calling upon God for His Holy Spirit – is not that the very evidence of all the work, of all the message, and everything else before us! Then is not the text applicable which I took last night:

> The people who will now see what is soon to come upon us by what is being transacted before us, will no longer trust in human inventions, and will feel that the Holy Spirit must be recognized, received, presented before the people.

I read that sentence complete now:

> God's memorial has been torn down, and in its place a false sabbath stands before the world; while the powers of darkness are stirring up the elements from beneath, the Lord God of heaven is sending power from above to meet the emergency by arousing His living agencies to exalt the law of heaven. Now, just now, is our time to work in foreign countries, as America, the land of religious liberty, *shall unite with the papacy* in forcing the consciences of men *to honor the false sabbath.*

Now not "to set up" the false sabbath, but to honor the false sabbath which has been set up, and which stands before the world.

Then this word came to us under date of August 30, 1882: After quoting the scripture from Revelation 3, it says this:

"Remember therefore from whence thou art fallen, and repent, and do the first works; or else I will come unto thee quickly, and will remove thy candlestick out of his place, except thou repent." The chosen people of God have lost their first love. Without this all their profession of faith will not save a soul from death. Suppose the attention should be turned away from every difference of opinion, and we should heed the counsel of the True Witness.

When God's people humble the soul before Him, *individually seeking His Holy Spirit* with all the heart, there will be heard from human lips such a testimony as is represented in this Scripture – "After these things I saw another angel come down from heaven, having great power; and the earth was lightened with his glory." There will be faces aglow with the love of God, there will be lips touched with holy fire saying, "The blood of Jesus Christ His Son cleanseth us from all sin."

Brethren, let that be a word that will come from every lip in this house, at this institute, in this church, before this institute and conference shall close. Has not God made the way plain enough? Has not He made it plain enough in the events that are standing before our faces, and from which we cannot hide our eyes? Then let us open our eyes and our hearts and bid the Lord come in and take full possession and use us just as He pleases.

Sermon 4

February 1, 1893

A question has been handed up.

Question: Can the States logically refuse to fall into line with the Supreme Court decision, defining the national constitution in its relation to religion?

Elder Jones: No sir. As a matter of fact the States do not need to do it. The Supreme Court of the United States has fallen into line with the States. That is the way the thing has already been done. That is the mischief of it.

I begin the lesson tonight by reading Revelation 14:9.

> And the third angel followed them, saying with a loud voice, If any man worship the beast and his image and receive his mark in his forehead or in his hand.

I need not present any other evidence tonight to show that we are in the time when that verse is fulfilled than merely to refer to the points we mentioned last night. Three distinct points that were noticed last night shut us up to that one thing. Now that is the warning which we are to give to the world. And no man can give the third angel's message without giving it just exactly as it reads. But what is the consequence of disregarding the message in that verse? The unmingled wine of the wrath of God. Then what is the next thing that comes in that respect? I mean in the fulfillment of this prophecy, what is the next thing we are to look for? [Congregation: "The wrath of God!"] Yes.

Now we have come to the loud cry, haven't we? That part of the prophecy is reached. We have come to the image of the beast; *that* part is reached; that prophecy is fulfilled. Now, of course, in the workings of the image of the beast there are many things to come in fulfillment of that, but all these things – persecutions, deceiving miracles, etc. – are simply the consequence of what has been done: simply the speaking and acting of the image that is already made. We are not to look now for any great, wondrous, marked movement in legislation or government to fulfill that part of the prophecy, because the image is made. That is fulfilled. What comes in the future in legislation and in the strifes and contentions and the rioting and warring, with the evil that will come, is simply the inevitable outcome and consequence of this. Then what next will there be in the line of this prophecy which is here before us? Rev. 14:9,10. [Congregation: "The wrath of God."] Yes.

I might put the question in another way now, to make it a little plainer. Is there any piece of legislation, any special move of this government for which we are now to look as the fulfillment of this prophecy in connection with the making of the image of the beast? What have we been looking for all the time? We have been looking for legislation – some move to be made or something to be done in or by the government that would make the image of the beast. That was what our eyes were upon all the time. But now do we look for that any more? [Congregation: "No sir."] Truth. Now then that having been done, isn't all that pertains to the image of the beast *in that*? and all that comes henceforth respecting the image of the beast and its work, is it anything more than the consequences of what is now here? Is not all that the image is to do, in the image when it is made to begin with? Then all that comes henceforth pertaining to the image of the beast being in that which is done, what great point in the words of the message stands next? [Congregation: "The seven last plagues."] Yes. The next thing that follows the working of the image of the beast in that prophecy is, The seven last plagues.

Now put the three things together. We *were* looking for the image of the beast, *then* the seven last plagues, and *then* the coming of the Lord. The image of the beast has come, hasn't it? The coming of the Lord is in the future, isn't it? But the seven last plagues are between them. Then what is the next great, marked thing in the history of this world and of mankind and of salvation? The seven last plagues. That being so, it becomes us to think very seriously *where* we are living, doesn't it? It becomes us also to think seriously *how* we are living.

Someone in the congregation: Is it necessary to amend the Constitution?

Elder Jones: The Constitution, nothing! No, we have no Constitution any more. It is set aside. It is taken clear out of the way. We can't use it any more. What could an amendment do more than has been done? Don't you see they have put aside the Constitution? What could anybody want with an amendment?

But the thought which I want just now to get before you is that the next great and marked event in the history of this world and in the work of salvation, is what is spoken of here in the text. This shows it on the face of it. Look at it again. We are to give this warning to the world: "If any man worship the beast and his image and receive his mark in his forehead, or in his hand." That is the warning we are to give. Well, in view of what is it that the warning is given? [Congregation: "The wine of the wrath of God."] What is the wine of the wrath of God? [Congregation: "The seven last plagues."] Rev. 15:1. Then doesn't it follow on the face of it, that the seven last plagues are the next thing after that warning? And that the warning will wind up with the seven last plagues? And we are now where that warning begins with a loud voice in its very words. Then doesn't that which is now begun and the work which is now in our hands, end with the bringing of us face to face with the seven last plagues? [Congregation: "Yes, sir."] When that work of warning is done, where will we be? [Congregation: "At the pouring out of the plagues."]

Now are you satisfied that this is so? Are you satisfied that the seven last plagues is the next thing that comes after we give this warning to the world? [Congregation: "Yes, sir."] Then as we go about to give that warning, isn't it in the nature of the case that we are to do it in view of the plagues that are to fall upon those to whom we speak of it? And that we must be faithful to that message ourselves, which we are giving, if we want to be shielded when the plagues do fall, of which that message speaks? But who will be shielded in that time? Those who have "the covering of the Almighty" drawn over them. And that covering of the Almighty is the covering that the prophet Isaiah spoke about, saying "I will greatly rejoice in the Lord, my soul shall be joyful in my God; for he hath clothed me with the garments of salvation, *he hath covered me with the robe of righteousness,* as a bridegroom decketh himself with ornaments, and as a bride adorneth herself with her jewels." Isa. 61:10. That is the covering that God draws over His people, which shields every one from the wrath of God, now and forever. Have you that robe of righteousness?

Now another thing right there. We are living in view of another fearful fact, that is, if that message which we are now to give, is not received, it has attached to it the fearful consequences that the wine of the wrath of God will be received; so that when that message finishes, the wrath of God succeeds it. I say we are living in the presence of that fact. And the work which is to bring all face to face with that fact, as it is there recorded, is now begun. Therefore, *will not that give a power to the health reform that it has not yet had?* When the health reform was given to the people of God, it was defined as that which is to fit the people for translation. That is the meaning of health reform. The leading thing, the great thing, that God intends health reform to do, is to prepare His people for translation. But we have to go through the seven last plagues before we are translated, and if a man's blood is impure and full of gross material will he be able to pass through that time, when the air is sick with pestilence? Indeed he cannot.

That brings us face to face with some more solemn experiences doesn't it? And some more solemn truth. A great many solemn questions have already been presented to us. And brethren, there are a great many more that are still to come to us. We are in the most solemn time we ever saw. Let us consider it.

Now let us take the points that have already been presented in the different lessons that have been given, the searching thoughts and solemn experiences in our religious profession to which we have been brought face to face. I want to know now how on earth it is ever possible for any one of us to meet these experiences without Jesus Christ in the full? I would like to have somebody tell. [Congregation: "We can't do it."] Of course we can't do it. Then brethren let us have Him come in in His fullness as quickly as possible. We need Him every moment, and each succeeding lesson brings to view more and more our need of Him.

Now as there are two other points that I want to present tonight, for the present purpose we will just sketch through what the further lesson of the plagues is.

When the first plague falls, it falls upon the men that "had received the mark of the beast, and them that worshipped his image" (Rev. 16:1,2) – the very people to whom the warning of this message is given. Then the plagues follow each other in direct succession, unto the sixth, under which the evil spirits gather "the kings of the earth and of the whole world," to the battle of the great day of God Almighty. Rev. 16:14-16. This battle is fought when the Saviour comes, for "I saw the beast and the kings of the earth and their armies, gathered together to make war upon him that sat upon the horse and against his army. And the beast was taken, and with him the false prophet that wrought miracles before him, with which he deceived them that had received the mark of the beast and them that worshipped his image." Rev. 19:11, 19, 20. And at that time the seventh angel pours out his vial in the air and there comes a great voice out of the temple of heaven from the throne saying, *It is done.* And there are voices, and thunderings, and lightnings; and there is a great earthquake, such as was not since men were upon the earth so mighty an earthquake and so great. Every island flees away and the mountains are not found. The heavens depart as a scroll and every mountain and island are moved out of their places. Rev. 16:17, 18, 20; 6:14. And the beast and his image "the Lord shall consume with the Spirit of his mouth and destroy with the brightness of his coming." 2 Thess. 2:8. And the remnant of the wicked world who went not up to the battle of Armageddon, "were slain with the sword of him that sat upon the horse, which sword proceeded out of his mouth." Revelation 19:21. The sword of Him that sits upon the horse is the brightness of the Lord's coming.

Then the events that are directly and inseparably connected with the end of the world are the events that follow the work, to the doing of which we are now completely shut up. That is the living fact now.

Brethren, do you believe that the seven last plagues are coming, just as certainly as the image of the beast has come" [Congregation: "Yes, sir."] Honest now? [Congregation: "Yes."] Now we looked for the image to the beast *to* come. It *has* come. Now what are we to look for? The seven last plagues. Do you believe that the end of the world is coming, with the seven last plagues, just as certainly as that the image to the beast is made? [Congregation: "Yes."] Do you believe that the end of the world comes when that seventh plague comes? [Congregation: "Yes."] Then brethren, these things mean something to us just now.

We will leave that point there now and take up another thought with reference to our government and what the consequences must be and can only be of what the government has now done; that is, the consequences to the government itself.

Let us begin with Acts 17:26, 27. Paul is calling the attention of the people to God and he says "And [God] hath made of one blood all nations of men for to dwell on all the face of the earth, and hath determined the time before appointed, and the bounds of their habitation." Then God made this nation of men to dwell on the earth, and He determined the bounds of the habitations of the people of this nation and how much space this nation should occupy. And He has given a portion of time to this nation. What did He do it for? The next verse reads: "*That they should seek the Lord,* if haply they might feel after him, though he be not far from every one of us!" If they might feel after Him and *haply* find Him? – No, there is no *hap* about that. If they feel after Him, what then? They would find Him. If anybody feels after Him, he will find Him.

In the fourth chapter of Daniel we learn that God rules in the kingdom of men and giveth it to whomsoever He will. God's idea concerning the nations is that they shall seek Him. Well then when a nation rejects the Lord what use has He for it? None. But will He reject a nation as long as the nation will seek Him? No, sir. Will He cut off a nation, so long as there are any people there to seek the Lord? He will not. He didn't before the flood. Neither did He in Sodom and Gomorrah. If He could have found ten people that would seek the Lord in Sodom and Gomorrah He would not have destroyed those cities. But He couldn't find them.

When He made the promise to Abraham, He said to him, "Know of a surety that thy seed shall be a stranger in a land that is not theirs, and shall serve them; and they shall afflict them four hundred years; and also that nation, whom they shall serve, will I judge: and afterward shall they come out with great substance. And thou shalt go to thy fathers in peace; thou shalt be buried in a good old age. But in the fourth generation they shall come hither again: *for the iniquity of the Amorites is not yet full.*" Gen. 15:13-16. Had God established bounds to their habitation? Yes. What did He do it for? That they should seek the Lord. As long as there was any possibility of their seeking the Lord, they held the place where God put them. And the Lord would not give the land to Abraham, His friend, nor to Abraham's seed as long as there were people there who would seek the Lord. The Lord's people could not occupy, because the iniquity of the Amorites was not yet full. But when the iniquity of the Amorites was full, there was no use for them any more.

When the Lord establishes a people on earth to seek the Lord and they will not seek Him, what then is the use of their staying any longer on the earth? To let them stay on earth after that was only to perpetuate iniquity for no possible use. So the Lord brought His people in there at that time and drove out the Amorites. He told His people not to do as the Amorites did lest the land spue them out as it had spued out the Amorites. But His people did the very thing He told them not to do. And the land did empty them out and He gave them into the hands of the king of Babylon.

He had established the kingdom of Babylon for a purpose; He set the bounds of their habitation. What was that for? It was that they should seek the Lord. Nebuchadnezzar sought the Lord in His day and He proclaimed the glory of the Lord, the honor of the Lord, and the existence of the Lord, to all the nations of the earth. You remember that proclamation He made in Daniel 4th chapter: "I thought it good to tell what the Most High hath done for me." And he told his experience. Let us read how far his proclamation reached:

> Nebuchadnezzar the king, unto all people, nations, and languages, that dwell in all the earth; peace be multiplied unto you. I thought it good to shew signs and wonders that the most high God hath wrought toward me. How great are his signs! and how mighty are his wonders! His kingdom is an everlasting kingdom, and his dominion is from generation to generation.

The Lord had said unto Nebuchadnezzar that He had given him all these lands round about and all the nations and that they should serve Him, and his sons and his son's son until the very time of his land came, and then what? Many nations shall serve themselves of him. God had determined the time before appointed as well as the bound of his habitation, so that when the time of his land came, many nations would serve themselves of Babylon.

Nebuchadnezzar's son succeeded him, then his grandson. Instead of Belshazzar seeking the Lord and honoring the Lord, he took the vessels of the house of the Lord and used them in his lascivious feasts, thus turning his back upon God completely. Then what use did the Lord have for him or his nation any more? He had no more use. That same hour there came the fingers of a man's hand and wrote upon the wall in the presence of the king. And the meaning of the words that were written is this: "God hath numbered thy kingdom and finished it. Thou art weighed in the balances and art found wanting. Thy kingdom is divided and given to the Medes and Persians."

Thus the Lord brought up the Medes and Persians. Did they seek the Lord too?

God had called Cyrus by name before he came up there. Cyrus did not then know the Lord. The Lord said: "I have surnamed thee, thou hast not known me." But Cyrus found the Lord and proclaimed his name to all the nations. God's prophet in Babylon took the word of God to Cyrus, and then see what Cyrus did. First chapter of Ezra, first verse to the third:

> Now in the first year of Cyrus, king of Persia that the word of the Lord by the mouth of Jeremiah might be fulfilled, the Lord stirred up the spirit of Cyrus, king of Persia, that he made a proclamation throughout all his kingdom and put it also in writing, saying, *Thus saith Cyrus,* king of Persia, *The Lord God of heaven* hath given me all the kingdoms of the earth; and he hath charged me to build him a house at Jerusalem, which is in Judah. Who is there among you of all his people? his God be with him, and let him go up to Jerusalem, which is in Judah, and build the house of the Lord God of Israel, (*he is the God*), which is in Jerusalem.

Cyrus found the Lord and proclaimed Him to all the nations of the earth. It had been done even before Cyrus came in. Darius succeeded Belshazzar. We read in Daniel 6:26, 27 what Darius did: "I make a decree, That in every dominion of my kingdom men tremble and fear before the God of Daniel: *for he is the living God,* and steadfast forever, and his kingdom that which shall not be destroyed, and his dominion shall be even unto the end. He delivereth and rescueth, and he worketh signs and wonders in heaven and in earth, who hath delivered Daniel from the power of the lions."

That is a splendid proclamation of God and His glory and His power. It sounds like the words of the prophet Daniel himself. Well, the Medes and Persians sought the Lord and found Him. But turn now to the 11th chapter of Daniel and there we read: "Also I [that is, the angel Gabriel] in the first year of Darius the Mede, even I stood to confirm and to strengthen him. And now will I shew thee the truth. Behold, there shall stand up yet three kings in Persia; and the fourth shall be far richer than they all: and by his strength through his riches he shall stir up all against the realm of Grecia. And a mighty king shall stand up, and shall rule with great dominion, and do according to his will. And when he shall stand up his kingdom shall be broken, and shall be divided toward the four winds of heaven."

That is Grecia. Now read in Daniel 10:20, "Then said he [Gabriel], Knowest thou wherefore I come unto thee? and now will I return to fight with the prince of Persia: and when I am gone forth, lo, the prince of Grecia shall come."

The angel would stay there as long as he could bear it, and when they had got so far along, that they would not seek the Lord, the angels would go, and when the angel went, Persia went too. And Grecia came. But what did the Lord establish Grecia for? That they might seek the Lord. Now read in the eighth chapter, verses 21-23:

> And the rough goat is the king of Grecia: and the great horn that is between his eyes is the first king. Now that being broken, whereas four stood up for it, four kingdoms shall stand up out of the nation, but not in his power. And in the latter time of their kingdom, *when the transgressors are come to the full,* a king of fierce countenance, and understanding dark sentences, shall stand up.

So you see every time, it is because transgression has come to the full that a nation falls, and transgressors come to the full when they set themselves against the Lord. It is because the measure of their iniquity is filled at last that another kingdom comes. So you can see the philosophy of the whole matter is contained in that verse, that God establishes nations that they shall seek the Lord, and when they refuse to do it and turn their backs upon Him, then the next thing is, that that nation leaves the world. There is nothing else for it.

The nation that followed Grecia was Rome. And Christ came in Rome's day, and the gospel of Christ was preached to Rome, although it was fearfully corrupt. And then that gospel of Christ was professed as an outward form by an apostate church, and she seized the power of the Roman government to compel people to recognize the Roman religion, to compel men to disobey the Lord. Then what became of the Roman government? It was swept from the earth.

As bad as the government was in the days of Tiberius, as bad as it was in the days of Claudius and in the days of Nero, yet God preached the gospel to Rome and brought multitudes of souls to the light and knowledge of His gospel. Even to Nero himself the gospel was twice preached by the apostle Paul, and there was opened to him the joys of heaven. But when the gospel was perverted as it was and made only a cloak to sanction ungodliness and instead of seeking the Lord indeed, perverted the very means that God offered for salvation. What could the Lord do for a people like that? The gospel is the only means that God has to save a person. But when that gospel is taken and used simply as a cloak for wickedness, how can the Lord possibly save the person who thus uses it? Then there is nothing that can touch him at all.

When that was done in the Roman empire by the power of an apostate church, then how could it stand any longer? It had to be swept away from the earth. And now this nation has been captured by the very same kind of iniquity. Here is an apostasy. The churches have turned away from God and have seized upon the power of this government. It has sold itself to them, and now compels people to dishonor God. Then what is the next thing for this nation? [Congregation: "Destruction."] Yes, but before the Lord overthrows it, He will send a message to whoever will be saved. What is that message? [Congregation: "The third angel's message."] Yes. Then does not that shut us up again tonight, face to face, to that one thing, that the third angel's message as it reads is the only thing to be given under the sun, and it is to be given to save such people as will be saved from the ruin that hangs over this devoted nation that has been inveigled and carried captive by an apostate professed Protestant church?

Well, then the end of the world is the next thing. Then are we not right now in the things that we are to preach; held, wrapped up, and concerned, daily and hourly, with the events that bring the end of the world? Is it any difficulty, brethren, to get people of the world even to see that? Is it any difficulty to get people of the world to see what has become of the nations that have gone before? Is there any difficulty in getting worldlings themselves to see that there is a union of church and State here, that the church has carried captive the government of the United States? Any difficulty to get them to see that? I tell you, brethren, when we go with the power of God and state the positive facts as they are before their faces and tell them what is to come out of these facts, they will begin to think. Brethren, there is more power, there is more convincing power, there is more moving power, in the plain declaration, by faith in God, and the consequences of these things as a literal fact before the people, than in tons of argument. You and I go with these things that are before the eyes of all people and call attention to them and show what is in the future, and tell them in the fear of God and by His grace and His power as He gives it to us, the things that are coming – tell them by actual facts and by our earnestness and devotion to God – show them that we believe the things ourselves and there will be more conviction than in tons of argument on doctrinal questions. Then let us preach the message as it is today.

Now another thought. God had a church in the world and a nation in old time, did He not? Christ came to that church and that nation. He preached the gospel of God, revealed in its living principles – the mystery of God, God with men, God in the flesh, God in men the hope of glory. He revealed that to them; they would not receive it. They rejected Him. They wanted to kill Him. They prosecuted Him for blasphemy, before Pilate, but Pilate could not take judicial notice of the offense of blasphemy, because that was an offense against Jewish law only. So Pilate said, "Take him, and judge Him according to your law." But they said, "We have a law, and by our law He ought to die." But they could not put Him to death without a decree from the Roman empire. Pilate said, "What shall I do with Him?" They said, "Crucify Him." Pilate: "Shall I crucify your king?" They replied: "We have no king but Caesar."

When they said that, did they not in that reject the Lord absolutely and join themselves to Caesar? They had to join themselves to Caesar to do against the truth of God what they could not do without it. When they turned their backs upon God, deliberately rejected Him and took Caesar for their king and allied themselves to earthly power in the face of the power of God, then what more could the Lord do for them as a people, as a church, as a nation? Nothing. There were individuals in the nation; there were individuals in the church, that feared God and had no part in this thing, but these, the representative men of the nation, the representative men of the church, they did that thing. They did join themselves, and in themselves they joined the nation and the church unto Caesar and turned its back upon God. Then the Lord could do no more for them as a church or as a nation. All He could possibly do, before its absolute and irretrievable ruin swept it out of the world, was to call out of it such as would receive Him. Then He sent His message, His gospel, to those people in that day, and there were many who came from that apostate church to the knowledge of God. He called out of them a people for His name. By the gospel which Christ sent to that apostate church, people were gathered out, such as would be saved, and then He gave them a warning that they were to flee when the whole combination would be destroyed.

Then the preaching of the gospel went on. But there are those prophecies – "The mystery of iniquity doth already work"; "of your own selves shall men arise speaking perverse things, to draw away disciples after them." In Romans 1:8 it is said that the genuine faith of the church at Rome, was "spoken of throughout the whole world." And so when she went in the way of apostasy she became famed for that throughout the world. The apostate church was opposed to the Sabbath of the Lord and was determined to destroy it and put the false sabbath in its place, but she could not do that of herself, and what did she have to do? In order to do it she had to join herself to Caesar. Just as the Jewish church did to get Christ, the Lord of the Sabbath, out of the way, so did the apostasy do to get the Sabbath of the Lord out of the way. Then that made her Mystery, Babylon the Great. That is the next thing that is said of her: "And upon her forehead was a name written, MYSTERY, BABYLON THE GREAT, THE MOTHER OF HARLOTS AND ABOMINATIONS OF THE EARTH." That is the church of Rome.

Then there came the Reformation; God called people out of Rome by Luther, others after him. But every one of those churches joined themselves to Caesar after the example of the mother, in every place where they had a chance, except the Baptist church in Rhode Island. All these others joined themselves to Caesar after the example of the mother, and thus became her daughters. Then arose the new republic and by its total separation of the church from all connection with the State established a new order of things, which is only the order of things prescribed by the Lord for government. Thus by her fundamental and constitutional principles this nation shut away all the churches from a union with the State. Thus it stood until 1892. But in A.D. 1892, the professed Protestant churches in the United States followed the example of the original apostasy of the church of Rome. And in order to get rid of the Sabbath of the Lord and exalt the false sabbath in its stead, these churches joined themselves to earthly power to the kingdom of men – to Caesar. They turned their backs upon the Lord; they forsook the Lord, and joined themselves to another; they turned away from the power of God and put their trust in the power of men and earthly government. These professed Protestant churches of the United States have turned their backs upon the Lord and joined themselves to Caesar, as certainly as did the Jewish church and the Romish church before them, and for the same reasons and for the same purpose. What then? This as certainly makes them the daughters of Babylon as certainly as the first great apostasy made Rome Babylon the mother. And they have even said it. "The Catholic Church the Mother of us all," and "the Protestant Episcopal church, the beautiful daughter of a beautiful mother" is what a leading Presbyterian paper published from the pen of a "Doctor of Divinity," some time ago, and not one of them has ever denied it so far as I have seen or heard.

They say it and it is so. Until now these churches had not joined themselves to the powers of the earth. They had many bad ways; they were doing many things that were out of harmony with the gospel; they had fallen away from Christ, but a woman may leave her husband and yet not be joined herself to another man. There is hope for her still to come back to her husband. But when she has joined herself to another man, what then? She is gone completely. She is an adulteress indeed. She cannot be brought back. Although they had wandered away from Christ, yet they had not joined themselves to another until 1892. Then they deliberately joined themselves to another – to the government of the United States and seized upon the power of this nation. They made this their husband, their dependence, and source of help, instead of the Lord. Are not these churches just as truly apostate as the Papal church herself when she did it? Is not Babylon the mother and daughters complete? What is she the mother of? "Harlots and abominations of the earth" (Rev. 17:4,5); and so they themselves are the daughters – it has been said for them and not one of them has disputed it.

Then what comes next? "I saw another mighty angel come down from heaven having great power, and the earth was lightened with his glory. And he cried mightily with a strong voice, saying, Babylon the great is fallen, is fallen, and is become the habitation of devils, and the hold of every foul spirit, and a cage of every unclean and hateful bird. For all nations have drunk of the wine of the wrath of her fornication, and the kings of the earth have committed fornication with her, and the merchants of the earth are waxed rich through the abundance of her delicacies. And I heard another voice from heaven, saying, *Come out of her, my people*, that ye be not partakers of her sins, and *that ye receive not of her plagues.* For her sins have reached unto heaven, and God hath remembered her iniquities."

And see the seventh plague. "And the seventh angel poured out his vial into the air, and there came a voice out of the temple in heaven, from the throne, saying, It is done. And there were voices; and thunders, and lightnings; and there was a great earthquake, such as was not since men were upon the earth, so mighty an earthquake, and so great. And the great city was divided into three parts, and the cities of the nations fell: *and great Babylon came in remembrance before God, to give unto her the cup of the wine of the fierceness of his wrath.*"

Then where are we in that line? What comes next upon Babylon? The judgments of God. Then by the direct work of the message, the next thing is the seven last plagues, after our work in that line is done.

By the direct line of the history of God's dealings with the nations, our nation stands today exactly where the other nations of the world have stood when they turned their backs upon God and refused to seek Him any longer. We knew what came upon them. And as certainly ruin awaits this nation. And the influence of this nation reaches all the world.

Therefore when ruin comes upon this nation, it comes also upon all the world. When these churches which should call the people and nations to seek the Lord, have followed the example of apostasy and forsaken the Lord and taught men to depend upon earthly power, then what is the use of them any longer in the world? None. Then what hangs over the churches? Destruction only, by the judgments of God. But there are people of God in them, and before the final fall and ruin God will call them out. But that which calls them out is the third angel's message, *the loud cry* of the third angel's message. Then where are we, brethren? We are in the loud cry. Oh, then let that loud voice be heard.

Then there are three more lines tonight just as distinct as the three we had last night, which shut us up to the third angel's message as it reads.

I will read a passage that belongs right with that one that we read last night:

> When God's people humble the soul before Him, individually seeking His Holy Spirit with all the heart, there will be heard from human lips such a testimony as is represented in this Scripture: "After these things I saw another angel come down from heaven having great power, and the earth was lightened with his glory."

Now I read the other one, which connects directly with this:

> Jesus longs to bestow the heavenly endowment in large measure upon His people. Prayers are ascending to God daily for the fulfillment of the promise, and not one of the prayers put up in faith is lost. [Prayers are ascending daily for it. Are your prayers amongst them?] Christ ascended on high, leading captivity captive, and gave gifts unto men. When after Christ's ascension, the Spirit came down as promised, like a rushing, mighty wind, filling the whole place where the disciples were assembled what was the effect? Thousands were converted in a day. We have taught, we have expected that an angel is to come down from heaven, that the earth will be lightened with his glory. Then we shall behold an ingathering of souls similar to that witnessed on the day of Pentecost.
>
> But this angel comes bearing no soft, smooth message, but words calculated to stir the hearts of men to the very depths. That angel is represented as crying mightily with a strong voice, saying, "Babylon the great is fallen, is fallen, and is become the habitation of devils, and the hold of every foul spirit, and a cage of every unclean and hateful bird." "Come out of her, my people, that ye be not partakers of her sins, and that ye receive not of her plagues." Are we indeed as human agencies, to cooperate with the divine instrumentalities in sounding the message of this mighty angel who is to lighten the earth with his glory?

Where are we? In the loud cry of the third angel's message. That angel's message is to go, to call God's people out of Babylon. But the angel comes down having great power. Then are we not brought face to face with the demand for that power that we must have to be clothed with power from on high, the power that is brought by God's Holy Spirit? Are we not there? [Congregation: "Yes."] Well, then, brethren, let us stay there. Let us stay there, calling for that power, and depending wholly upon it when it comes.

Sermon 5

February 2, 1893

I find that some are beginning to get a little perplexed by not doing what we agreed to the first night, or else they did not get here in time to agree to that. The first night, you know, we agreed to stand by that text of Scripture, and say it is so, that "If any man thinketh he knoweth anything, he knoweth nothing, yet as he ought to know." Some who have perhaps come in since these lessons began, and others who have not remembered fully to stick to the text, have begun to say like this: "Well now, all these things are plain that you have set forth, but I do not see how they are going to fit" such and such things that we have held before.

Don't be a bit afraid. If these things are plain – and they say they are – then look at them. If they are new – don't try to put new wine into old bottles. To all such who may think these things are new, I say, Do not try to put new wine into old bottles. You cannot do that. Do not get concerned about what you thought before. I am not talking at random on these things at all. I know what I am saying and I know some other things that are coming besides. If you have been thinking right before, this will fit; and if you have not been thinking right, it ought not to fit. Let us study these things together. Have I brought any matters before you that are not actual facts? [Congregation: "No"].

All we are studying this week is that one text we started with. Many other things are going to come that we have not yet taken a text for, but we are studying this week this text: "The people who will now see what is soon to come upon us *by what is being transacted before us,* will no longer trust in human inventions and will feel that the Holy Spirit must be recognized, received, presented before the people."

Now so far we have got along pretty well in seeing what is being transacted before us and some of the things that are soon to come upon us. Let us take what we have and make the most of it, and the rest will take care of itself when it comes.

Now to-night I am going to take up another study right in the same line – of what is being transacted before us. I will simply call attention to facts – things that you can see and things that everybody in the world can see who reads the common daily events as they appear in the daily papers of the world. You can see them, and everybody else can see them. Have we brought up anything in these lessons yet as to what is being transacted before us, that everybody cannot see? [Congregation: "No."] As to what is coming upon us, we can tell them. They may not believe what is soon to come, of course, but they cannot help seeing what is before them.

Four years ago last fall I was appointed to write a reading for the week of prayer on "Our present Standing and Work." In that I mentioned some of the thoughts that I referred to the other night, but I call attention to this one particular thought now for our study tonight. Here it is:

> Under our Constitution as it is, the total separation of Church and State and the perfect religious liberty thereby assured, have been a beacon-light of progress to all other nations for a hundred years. The American principle of the liberties and rights of men had an irresistible influence upon other nations in all parts of the earth. This is the genuine principle of Protestantism, which is, in short, the principle announced by Christ, that men should render to Caesar only that which is Caesar's and unto God that which is God's.
>
> Against this principle the papacy has constantly maintained that no State could exist without alliance with the church; in fact, that States exist only for the support and for the sake of the church. It is true that the American principle has not been adopted *in its clearness* by any other nation, but yet its influence has been untold in turning the minds of men from the influence of the papal theory. But just now, when the other nations in their perplexity are courting the support of Rome, the papacy takes advantage of this to reassert the papal theory and to claim that these things are an acknowledgement on the part of rulers and governors that her theory is correct.
>
> Now in view of all this, and just at this time, in fact this very year, 1888 [Here I mentioned the proposed Constitutional Amendment and the National Sunday Bill, which were then before the country, as proposed by Senator Blair, in which Christianity as the religion of the nation and Sunday as the sabbath were to be recognized and then continued as follows:] When this is done, its influence in favor of the papacy will be inestimable. Then it will be said that this nation, which has made such great pretensions to religious liberty and which has been set forth as the model for earthly governments, has been compelled to reverse that which was supposed to be the enlightened order and to adopt the principles which the church has all the time maintained.
>
> Then as this nation has been the model of liberty, enlightenment, and progress to all others, so when its principles shall have been reversed, when the liberties and rights of men are denied, when the nation is carried back to the principles of the papacy in the Dark Ages and persecution for conscience's sake is carried on, the reaction upon other nations will be such as will infinitely confirm and magnify the claims and power of the papacy.
>
> And so will be fulfilled the scripture: "All that dwell upon the earth shall worship him, whose names are not written in the book of life." In this way power will again be given to the papacy to make war with the saints of God, even as the scripture shows: "The same horn made war with the saints and prevailed against them, *until the Ancient of days came, and judgment was given* to the saints of the Most High, and the *time came that the saints possessed the kingdom.*" Dan. 7:21, 22.

I had not then found this passage, which I shall now read from Schaff's "Church and State." Dr. Philip Schaff, having been in Europe, being a born European himself, and not coming to this country until he was a man full grown, being a graduate of European universities and understanding European affairs better than any other person in the United States and then coming over here and understanding the affairs of the United States to a considerable extent, writes thus in his "Church and State in the United States," page 83:

> In conclusion we must briefly survey the influence of the American system upon foreign countries and churches.
>
> Within the present generation *the principle of religious liberty* and equality, with a corresponding relaxation of the bond of union of Church and State, *has made steady and irresistible progress* among *the leading nations of Europe,* and has been embodied more or less clearly in written constitutions. . .
>
> The successful working of the principle of religious freedom in the United States has stimulated this progress without any official interference. *All advocates* of the voluntary principle [in the support of churches and religion] and *of a separation of church and state in Europe* point *to the example of this country* as their *strongest practical argument.*

Elder Lewis Johnson: We know that is so in Scandinavia.

Yes, it is known in all Europe. But what we want to know is, that it is so in this country, that that is the influence our country has borne hitherto, and this, in order to see what its influence will be now that it has turned about and is going the other way.

Here is Dr. Schaff's statement as to the principles of the papacy in connection with the German Empire, in 1871:

> The Westphalia Treaty of 1648 confirmed the equal rights of the two contending churches. But the pope never consented to even this limited toleration and will always protest against it. The papal syllabus of 1864 condemns religious toleration among the eighty heresies of the age. The Roman Church acknowledges no other church, and cannot do it consistently. She knows no geographical and national boundaries and rallies around the common center of the Vatican 'vice-gerent of God on earth.' She must submit, of course, to hard necessity, but does it under protest. *Pp. 91, 92.*

So you see, according to that, the principles of the papacy are directly opposed to the principles of the United States Constitution.

I will read a few passages further concerning the papal principles. I read from a book by Gladstone and Schaff, entitled, "Rome and the Newest Fashions in Religion," page 113. It is declared to be an error and condemned as such by the Pope to say that–

> Every man is free to embrace and profess the religion he shall believe true, guided by the light of reason.

That is an error condemned by the church of Rome, but that is the doctrine of the government of the United States; that is the doctrine of the Constitution of the United States.

Another error condemned by Rome is to say that–

> The church has not the power of availing herself of force or any direct or indirect temporal power, p. 115.

That is an error condemned by the Catholic church. But that is the doctrine of the Constitution of the United States. It is a fundamental principle of the Government of the United States, that the churches shall have nothing to do with the affairs of the government.

Another error condemned by the papacy is to say that:

> The Church ought to be separated from the State and the State from the Church. p. 123.

All these are condemned as errors by the Catholic church. But all these express the very doctrine of the Constitution of the United States, as its makers established it and intended it to be. And nothing could show more plainly how directly antagonistic are the principles of the papacy and the principles of the Constitution of the United States government.

There is another word I will read. It is the statement of Leo XIII in 1891 as to what the authority of the church is, what her right is. Page 868 of "The Two Republics." He is writing to all the world about the condition of labor and the difficulties between labor and capital, governments and workingmen, etc., and says:

> It is the church that proclaims from the gospel those teachings by which the conflict can be put an end to, or at least made far less bitter; *the church* uses its efforts not only to enlighten the mind, but to direct by its precepts the life and conduct of men . . . and *acts on the decided view* that for these purposes *recourse should be had,* in due measure, and degree, *to the help of the law and of State authority.*

That is the very latest doctrine of the papal church, officially set forth and as in every other, in direct antagonism to the doctrine of the Constitution of the United States *as it reads,* and as it was *intended* to be, *not* as it *has been made to mean* by the Supreme Court of the United States, Feb. 29, 1892.

That is how it is that the influence which this government has had upon the other nations has been to carry them away from the doctrine of the papacy. And, as Dr. Schaff says, this influence has been "steady and irresistible." Well now in the Supreme Court decision, Feb. 29, 1892, and in the legislation of Congress recognizing and establishing Sunday as the Christian sabbath, the government of the United States has reversed that order. The Constitution has been disregarded and overridden entirely. The government of the United States stands tonight in the hands of a hierarchy here, which, in order to accomplish its purpose, joined hands with the papacy specifically.

Well now as to the influence that this will have upon the their nations, let me read from that testimony that is now in No. 1 of the Bulletin, top of page 16. It touches this question that is before us tonight and the Lord tells what is the consequence of this reversal of the original order of things in this government:

> As America, the land of religious liberty, shall unite with the papacy in forcing the consciences of men to honor the false sabbath, *the people of every country on the globe will be led to follow her example.*

How far then, brethren, is the influence of this nation to go, now that it has turned about? To every nation on the globe. What did the turning about of this nation do? That made the image of the beast. Well then as in view of that fact, other lessons that we have had bring us face to face with the giving of that message in its express words and terms, how far is that message to go? To every nation and kindred and tongue and people. Then as this nation, having turned about, will lead every nation on the globe in the wrong way, back to the principles of the papacy in fact, so it is time for the third angel's message to reach every nation on the globe.

That is the message now. Well then are you ready to go? That being the message that is to go, does it not become every professor of that message to hold himself in readiness to go to the ends of the earth, when God calls him to go? The influence of this is to lead every nation on the globe back to the papacy. The work of the third angel's message is to warn all nations of the earth against the worship of the papacy, and this image of it which brings us back to the papacy. Just as certainly as that influence reaches every nation on the globe, so certainly this warning must go to every nation on the globe. Then every man is unfaithful to the trust which God has given us in the third angel's message, if he holds himself back from the call of God to go anywhere on the globe, isn't he? Then that brings us again face to face with such a consecration as there has never been among Seventh-day Adventists. It brings us face to face with such a consecration that home, family, property, everything is surrendered into the hands of God to let Him call us and send us or such means as we have, where He pleases and do what He chooses with us. Are you ready? Isn't it time to get ready?

Elder C. L. Boyd: Yes, all are ready, Brother Jones.

Elder Jones: Good! But that is a thing we are to think of.

I was constrained to say today to one brother, while talking with him, that these things as they stand now, make a greater strain upon real, actual faith than we have ever had yet. For it is just to stand face to face with ourselves and tell ourselves and set it down as a convincing, actual fact that the seven last plagues are going to come pretty soon;

that we are working in view of that fact; and that the coming of the Lord follows the seven last plagues, in view of which we are working, and the coming of the Lord is the end of the world. And for me to face myself and talk to myself like that – I tell you it draws on a man. I find that it draws on me. Well, all I can say, brethren, is, Let it draw. I can't dodge it; I wouldn't if I could. I would not go back on it if I could. But it draws on the very vitals of a man's faith; that is a fact. Well, brethren, let it draw, until it draws us completely out of self and into Jesus Christ wholly.

> As America, the land of religious liberty, shall unite with the papacy in forcing the consciences of men to honor the false sabbath, the people of every country on the globe will be led to follow her example. Our people are not half awake to do all in their power with the facilities within their reach to extend the message of warning to the world. New churches must be built, new congregations organized. Let the light shine to all lands and all peoples.

I hope Brother Robinson will get all that he called for to build up the work in London, and I hope Sister White will get all she calls for to build that church in Australia and Brother Chadwick get all that he calls for and everybody else get all they call for. How long will our property be good for anything anyhow; when the seven last plagues are soon to fall? What will it be worth? What good is it going to do when the seven last plagues fall? What is the good of it?

But there is the point. When we come to say from real conviction and stand face to face with the fact as a fact, that the seven last plagues are indeed soon coming and that the Lord is coming right at the end of that – it is going to draw on the very vitals of our faith. It is going to bring out what is in us. If a person has real confidence in the message this is going to reveal it.

And there will be plenty of means. I am not a bit uneasy about the means. If Seventh-day Adventists who have means do not consecrate themselves to the Lord and let Him have their means the Lord will get means somewhere else. He will call up other people. Brethren, it is the worst thing that can happen to a Seventh-day Adventist who has means, when God has to pass him by and find somebody else that will give what is wanted. A Seventh-day Adventist left to himself is the worst-off man in this world. We have come to a place where God wants us to use all we have. And when we believe this, our means and ourselves will be for His use. And His work will soon be done and then we shall not need any more means. That is the situation now.

This government as it was drew the nations in its train *away from* the papacy. This government as it is, draws all in its train *back to* the papacy. *And the papacy knows it.* And knowing it she is working for that very thing now and has her – I was going to say her fingers – but no, she has got her whole arms in it and is beginning to wield the government in her own interests. All that Protestantism is today in the United States and all that these churches are that have worked for the Sunday law, is merely a tool in the hands of the papacy. How many of you have seen a Punch and Judy show? [Many in the congregation held up their hands.] Those little figures that work back and forth there, bobbing up and down and to and from above the curtain are manipulated by someone behind the curtain. You don't see him. Those little puppets that bob up there are exactly what these Protestant churches are today in the hands of the papacy. She is beneath; she sits behind the curtain; she works the wires; she touches the triggers. These Protestants, in their blindness, think they are doing great things for themselves, but they are simply the puppets in the hands of the papacy, working as she desires, upon this government and through this government for all the world.

And it is time to tell them so. But when the message goes that tells them so, it tells them that "Babylon is fallen," and that they must come out of her, if they would escape the plagues. and when they are called out of her, where can they go? All the world is under the control of the papacy – except the third angel's message, thank the Lord! All the world is under the control of the papacy and its principles. But when they are called out of it, where alone can they go? To the third angel's message as God gave it.

Brethren, we are in the grandest time this world ever saw. Oh, that we may consecrate ourselves to God as becomes us who are living in this grandest of times!

I shall read you at another time a statement from Vol 4, how that great numbers of ministers will turn to the truth of the third angel's message under the "loud cry." Many of the ministers who now think that this Sunday law work and all this is all right – they do not see what is under it – when the papacy begins to move a little more openly they will back out of the whole thing; they will cut loose from that thing. But where can they go? To the third angel's message. Thank the Lord! I tell you, brethren, the power of God is going to do something right away. Oh, that we may surrender all things to Him that He may!

Let me read here the aims of the papacy, as set forth in her own words. This is from the New York *Sun* of July 11th, 1892; and if there is an official Catholic paper in the United States, it is the New York *Sun*; don't forget that; not that the *Sun* is run professedly as a Catholic paper, but it is that. And *The Sun* has a correspondent in Rome, in the Vatican – a priest – I don't know what his name is. He doesn't sign his name but writes under a *nom de plume*. And you can bear in mind that dispatches to *The Sun* from Rome are always straight.

So I say that *The Sun* is virtually more representative of the Papacy, of the Catholic church in this country, than the most of Catholic organs even, unless perhaps Cardinal Gibbons's organ. This was the letter written directly by *The Sun* correspondent from Rome last summer. So I read it here. It is entitled "The Papacy and Nationality, Pope Leo and the United States." After speaking of certain classes in the Catholic church, bishops, archbishops, etc., and as to their aims in the United States it says:

> But Leo XIII has a still higher aim. His appeal for national unification is founded upon a traditional conception of the Holy See.
>
> In his view the United States have reached the period when it becomes necessary to bring about the fusion of all the heterogeneous elements in one homogeneous and indissoluble nation. Statesmen are preoccupied, and very properly, with the multiplicity of centrifugal forces which threaten the republic with disintegration. Enemies make use of this latent danger to accuse the foreign Catholics of having a tendency to form a State within the State. It is for this reason that the pope wants the Catholics to prove themselves the most enlightened and most devoted workers for national unity and political assimilation. Certain incidents have given a bad color to the loyalty of some foreign groups. All doubt upon this subject ought to disappear. The church has always been the able collaborator of all people in the work of national unity. It was she that constituted, through the efforts of popes and bishops the great political bodies and the great national organizations. The most united races and the most solid populations, politically and nationally, are those who have most profoundly felt the salutary action of the papacy and the church. France is the typical example of this law of history. If Italy in the middle ages did not take advantage of this incomparable benefit, was it not because the jealous States interfered with the work of unification of the church and of the Roman pontiffs?
>
> America feels the urgent need of this work of internal fusion. Formed of a mosaic of races and nationalities, she wants to be a nation, a collective being, one strong and united. What the Church has done in the past for others, she will do for the United States. . .
>
> That is the reason why the Holy See encourages the American clergy to guard jealously the solidarity and to labor for the fusion of all the foreign and heterogeneous elements in one vast national family. The American Church furnishes and must furnish at the present time the proof that Christianity is the school of patriotism and of national sentiment. By continuing to favor this work of unification it will form the grandeur of the United States and will demonstrate the degree to which religion and the Church are the generators of political and patriotic independence.
>
> As the approaching danger to the United States lies in fractionizing the republic into centrifugal and hostile parties, the Catholics will appear, through their cooperation in national concentration, the best sons of the land and the upholders of political unity. The pope will impose upon all the American motto, *E pluribus unum,* applied to the subject we are treating.
>
> Finally, Leo XIII desires to see strength in that unity. Like all intuitive souls, he hails in the united American States and in their young and flourishing church *the source of a new life for Europeans.* He wants America to be powerful, in order that Europe may regain strength from borrowing a rejuvenated type.

And I tell you another thing right here brethren, when things have come to that pass in the government of the United States that the papacy can afford to set forth her purposes and intentions as plainly as that – I tell you they are pretty far gone. The papacy doesn't speak openly until she knows she has the advantage. She always works underneath and secretly until the time comes to spring and she doesn't spring until she is ready.

And when the affairs of the United States are so under the control of the papacy that she can talk like that, openly to the people of the United States, then things are in a shape satisfactory to the papacy.

> *Europe is closely watching the United States.* Certain things there may frighten some people, but the general attraction is invincible. Bryce, Claudio, Fanet, Carlies, and all the historians and publicists have the inclusiveness of the record. Henceforth we will need authors who will place themselves upon this ground: "What can we borrow and what ought we to borrow from the United States for our social, political, and ecclesiastical reorganization?"

Until 1892 what could any European nation or any other nation borrow from this government for ecclesiastical reorganization? Nothing. What had this government to do with ecclesiastical affairs? The Constitution was absolutely pledged against the whole thing. But now since the Constitution has been overridden, the papacy can begin to ask: "What can we borrow from the United States for our ecclesiastical reorganization?" But the example has been set, and the thing has been done, which has put the United States into a place where the papacy can borrow from the United States example and influence for ecclesiastical reorganization in Europe and all other nations. And she is doing it. She is borrowing and using it for her purposes now.

> And from the pope's particular point of view, "What are the examples that these American Catholics are giving us?" The problem is difficult; but in its wanderings and its immense variety it captivates all strong and far-reaching minds.
>
> The answer depends in a great measure upon the development of American destinies. If the United States succeed in solving the many problems that puzzle us, Europe will follow their example, and this *outpouring of light will mark a date in the history not only of the United States, but of all humanity. Res vestra agitur* is what we might then say to Americans. "That is why the holy father, anxious for peace and strength, collaborates with passion in the work of consolidation and development in American affairs. According to him, the Church ought to be the chosen crucible for the moulding and the absorption of races into one united family. And that especially is the reason why he labors at the codification of ecclesiastical affairs, in order that this distant member of Christianity may infuse new blood into the old organism. . ."

Brethren, can anybody in the world shut his eyes to this that is taking place before us? This that is even taking place before the whole world? Can anybody see what is taking place before him? Do we know what is soon to come upon us by that thing that is taking place before us?

But the papacy not only proclaims her purpose – she follows it swiftly with a bold stroke to carry it into effect. That special representative of the pope that "permanent Apostolic Delegation which was established in this country only the other day, what does that mean? Monsignor Satolli came to this country as the pope's personal representative to attend the opening exercises of the World's Fair – a good excuse. Professedly he came as any other would come on a special mission. But when he got over here, then he was to stay awhile; temporarily as delegate of the pope. But there was an off-sided party in the Catholic church who began to say "We don't want him." Then the pope simply established him forever. This is the account of it in the New York *Sun*, of January 15, 1892:

> *ROME, Jan. 14* – The pope has decided to establish a permanent apostolic delegation in the United States, and has nominated Mgr. Satolli to be the first delegate. This decision the Vatican considers to be a sufficient reply to the opposition to Mgr. Satolli and his mission.
>
> The Propaganda will send by the Rev. F. Z. Rooker the documents authenticating the new power conferred upon Mgr. Satolli as permanent delegate.
>
> Pope Leo is said to be greatly interested in the situation in America, and desirous of putting an end to the ecclesiastical differences existing there. With this purpose the pope is preparing an encyclical to the American episcopate, advising harmony and union.
>
> *WASHINGTON, Jan. 14* – Mgr. Satolli, the papal ablegate, received at the Catholic University today the following cable message from Dr. O'Connell, the American Secretary of the Propaganda, who accompanied Mgr. Satolli to this country, and recently returned to Rome:
>
> Rome, Jan. 14, 1893
>
> *Mgr. Satolli*:
>
> The apostolic delegation is permanently established in the United States and you are confirmed as the first delegate.
>
> *O'Connell*
>
> Information was also received here confirming the announcement that the Rev. F. Z. Rooker of Albany had been formally appointed Secretary of the apostolic delegation, and stating further that he had left Rome for New York and was no doubt the bearer of the Papal bull creating the delegation and confirming all the powers of Mgr. Satolli.
>
> *ST. PAUL, Jan. 14* – When asked about the institution of an apostolic delegation in the United States, this afternoon, Archbishop Ireland said: "Yes, a permanent apostolic delegation has been established in the United States, and Mgr. Satolli has been named the first apostolic delegate. The decree was issued in Rome last evening. I have had myself a direct cablegram from the Eternal City to this effect. I am heartily glad. The controversies agitating American Catholics for some time past are over and peace will reign".
>
> Mgr. Satolli came to this country as a Papal Ablegate – a term which indicates a temporary mission and somewhat limited powers. Objections were at once raised in certain quarters against him, his authority was questioned or denied, his recall demanded, his mission declared a failure. To all clamorings of this nature the pope gives answer swift and effective. He declares that we shall have a permanent apostolic delegate in the United States. So well satisfied is he with the work accomplished by the ablegate that, as a perfect recognition of Mgr. Satolli's rights, he names him the first apostolic delegate.

> Leo XIII. is a man of firm character: opposition strengthens his resolve. All that has occurred since Mgr. Satolli's arrival demonstrates the more plainly the need of a representative of the pope clothed with well-defined and extensive powers. For Catholics Rome is the supreme tribunal; but Rome is rather far away. A hand near by is needed that will at any moment reach out and bid the sea be placid. If some men had been seeking the most effectual way to make evident to all eyes the necessity of a delegate in America, they could not have adopted in proof of their thesis more effective arguments than the method they have in fact been pursuing. God be thanked for all that has been done.
>
> The Catholic Church in America is now thoroughly organized and has put on the mantle of perfect stature. She has on her own territory a supreme court – a branch of the Appellate Court of Rome, deriving from this latter its life, but capable in itself of immediate action. This is home rule for American Catholics, so far as Catholics away from Rome can have home rule. In addition to our own energy and inspiration, we shall have in all our undertakings the direction and impetus, as directly as never before, of the sovereign head of the Church. Catholics will have a more practical realization of what Church unity and papal supremacy means. Remote authority dwindles at times into a speculative theory, or a beau ideal; present authority is a living test. It tests one's obedience, while at the same time adding new power for well doing.
>
> So far as the country at large is concerned, the American people will welcome the recognition that a religious element of the and so important as the Catholic has this new glory added to its record, this new strength infused into its life.
>
> Moreover, a closer acquaintance with the workings of the papacy will be interesting and salutary; it will dissipate many an old-time prejudice. The papacy will appear to all of us in its true light, harmonizing magnificently with the aspirations of modern democracy and accelerating the march of all that is useful, good, and elevating in modern progress. The clouds of old fogyism, said to hang around the throne of Peter, exist only in the befogged river of religious prejudice or the darkened recesses of narrow and blind-folded minds.
>
> They exist not in the Vatican. The most far-seeing, liberal mind in the world today is that of Leo, the most gentle and generous heart is his. Neither Catholics nor Protestants of America know him sufficiently. It is the duty of all to study him; it is the particular duty of Catholics to draw nearer to him and follow more loyally his spiritual guidance.

There are other things that have taken place in connection with the matter of public money to the churches. The Catholic church is getting nearly all of it now, because the Methodists, Baptists, and Episcopalians have refused to receive any more money from the government. And leading ministers of the Presbyterian church are trying to get that church to refuse to take any more money from the government.

Soon therefore the Catholic Church will be getting money, almost wholly alone, from the public treasury – nearly $400,000 a year. Then will Protestants stand by and allow the Catholics to have that money without raising a wonderful opposition against it? But it will do no good for them to protest against it. If they protest against it as unconstitutional, the Catholic church can simply reply:

This is a Christian nation: The Supreme Court has decided that this is a Christian nation. And to prove it, the Court has cited the decree of Ferdinand and Isabella, who were Catholics only, and who sent out Columbus, who was a Catholic, to discover new worlds, that they might bring them to God and to the Christian religion. And the only religion that Ferdinand and Isabella or Columbus meant or had anything to do with was *the Catholic religion*. When the Supreme Court cites that decree to prove that this is a Christian nation, that proves that it is a *Catholic* Christian nation. That is the argument the Catholic church may make, *and Protestants cannot successfully dispute it*. Protestants cannot deny the *constitutionality* of the argument, because they have used the Supreme Court decision for their own interests, for their own purposes in Sunday legislation. They have endorsed the decision as all right, and when they have used the decision for their own purposes, they can not go back on it, when the papacy uses it for *her* purposes. They are caught as firmly as ever anything was ever caught in a trap, and the only way they can ever get out of the trap is by having the Lord Jesus Christ deliver them from the iniquity of it by the third angel's message. Is it not time they were having that message?

The Catholics conducted the last campaign upon that very issue. President Harrison tried during all his administration to stop that appropriation of money to the churches. The Catholic church opposed his efforts all through his administration. She tried to prevent his nomination at Minneapolis, but failed; then when Cleveland was nominated, she threw all her influence for Cleveland, and he was elected.

(For particulars, see *Sentinel Library* No. 53, pp. 48-54.)

President Harrison tried to stop that appropriation but could not do it and was obliged to confess through Senator Dawes on the floor of Congress that he found it impossible to do it. Well, then, when it was impossible to break this off by an administration that was absolutely opposed to it, how can it possibly be broken off in an administration that was absolutely opposed to it, how can it possibly be broken off in an administration that began it, that is in favor of it, and that was supported by the Catholic church upon this sole issue?

Then in whose hands is the government of the United States tonight? In the hands of the Catholic church and she holds it there and she will hold it there in spite of all that the Protestants can do. But she never would have got it, if the Protestants had been Protestants indeed, and had not played into her hands. False Protestantism has betrayed the government of the United States, as established upon God's principles, into the hands of the papacy, and there it will stay in spite of them.

Here is a word that Brother Conradi gave today which is taken from a paper from Germany. It is the boast that the Catholic church is making respecting Germany now. Germany, you know, is the grand model Protestant nation of Europe. This is taken from a Catholic paper, so it is the voice of the Catholics on this question.

> The Catholic papers in Germany declare openly that soon the power will be in their hands and Germany return to the Catholic faith. As two and one half millions of dollars have been appropriated for a Protestant cathedral at Berlin, they said this was all right, as soon it would become Catholic anyway.

And these things are going on before the world, and the world sees them, and the world reads them. Brethren, has not God given us a word to say on this subject. Here is a word on that. Speaking of the papacy, in the chapter in *Great Controversy*, Vol. IV, on "The Character and Aims of the Papacy," page 579, it is said: "She can read what is to be." When she with the light only of the wisdom that Satan can give – the wisdom gathered from her wicked experience only, the wisdom gathered only from her own history – when she by this can see what is to be, does it not become a people to whom God speaks, to see also what is to be?

Here are the events and there is the word of God, that as this nation now has turned from the principles which God gave, the influence with which it irresistibly drew nations away from the papacy, will carry them all back to the papacy. Then that elevates the papacy to the highest place it has ever held on this earth. And in that place she fulfills, and in that place there is fulfilled the word which is spoken in Revelation 18:7: "She saith in her heart, I sit a queen and am no widow and shall see no sorrow."

The nations to whom she was wedded have in the past, one by one, from the time of Napoleon, one by one drifted off, drifted off, until not one remains and she sits desolate, a widow, not a single husband left to whom she had bound herself all these years. What them? Here stood the grandest nation, the youngest of all, standing before the world, standing in the vigor of the principles which God has established for nations, and was drawing all these nations in its train, leaving her more and more desolate. Then and therefore she turned her blandishments upon this nation to seduce it into her train, into fornication and adultery with her. And through a false and apostate Protestantism, she has succeeded. And now when she has gathered this nation to herself, in this she gathers all the others back to her, and then she is so glad of it all that she glorifies herself and lives deliciously, and joyfully congratulates herself, saying, "I sit a queen, and am no widow, and shall see no sorrow."

What then? "*Therefore* shall *her plagues come* in one day, death, and mourning, and famine; and she shall be utterly burned with fire: for strong is the Lord God who judgeth her."

Then these events, these things which the papacy is doing tonight, bring us face to face with the judgments of God upon the nations of the earth. And we see what is coming upon us, by what is being transacted before us. Is it not time that we began to tell the people who know not these things that these things are so? Is it not time? Some were saying, Well it seems to me I never could preach a sermon or give a Bible reading again in the way I have, about the United States in prophecy. Thank the Lord! Thank the Lord that you cannot. Thank the Lord that you know where the

United States is in prophecy indeed, and that you cannot use any old dried up stuff. We want the United States as it now stands in prophecy, and that is what is wanted. Can you not give it? [Congregation: "Yes."] And can not people see that that is so? Whether they will believe what is coming, that is not the question. But they will have to go back on their own reason and their experience in daily life, to deny that it is a fact.

"Therefore shall her plagues come in one day, death, and mourning, and famine; and she shall be utterly burned with fire: for strong is the Lord God who judgeth her." But what is the fire that burns her? "And then shall that Wicked be revealed, whom the Lord shall consume with the spirit of his mouth, and shall destroy with the brightness of his coming." "For our God is a consuming fire" to wickedness. Thank the Lord that He is. But brethren, He is a glorious salvation to those who are free from iniquity. Let Him cleanse us from iniquity now, that when His glory appears we will not be consumed but changed into His glorious likeness itself. That is what He wants. "And the kings of the earth, who have committed fornication and lived deliciously with her, shall bewail her, and lament for her, when they shall see the smoke of her burning, standing afar off for the fear of her torment, saying, Alas, alas, that great city Babylon, that mighty city! for *in one hour* is thy judgment come."

Whether that "hour" is prophetic time, fifteen days, or a short indefinite season, I do not know. But whether it be really prophetic time, or a short indefinite season is not material to this discussion tonight; for either way it shows that *the time is exceedingly short* from the time when she congratulates herself that all the nations have returned to her – the time is exceedingly short – till the judgments of God come upon her and upon all the nations. And when that comes then God's people are delivered.

Well, then, brethren, where are we? We are in the very presence of the impending judgments of God. Well, then, let us act as though it were so. Let us act as though we were there.

Sermon 6

February 3, 1893

To-night I propose to take up a kind of summary of what we have had through the week, and then a further lesson from that. The first night after the report of the hearing was given, which laid the foundation for all our following study – Tuesday night that was – we took up and noticed three particular points; on Wednesday night three more, and last night one more. The three points of the first night you remember shut us up to the giving of the third angel's message now as it reads in words. "If any man worship the beast and his image, and receive his mark in his forehead, or in his hand, the same shall drink of the wine of the wrath of God." And that of itself shows that the time has come when the image is there, and that the mark is to be received, because the warning is against the worship of the beast and his image, and receiving his mark in his forehead, or in his hand.

The first of the three points was that we are shut off now from work as we have been conducting it hitherto, and in the work of the message, are shut up to the preaching of that message itself, as it is in words. The second, that this shows that the image is made, and that that brings all earthly power into the hands of the enemy of the third angel's message and the cause of God, to be wielded against the people of God and the work of God. And therefore whoever would stand for God, must have a power greater than all the power of the world.

Then the third point was, that in citing the fourth commandment in the legislation, and interpreting that commandment to mean the first day of the week commonly called Sunday, thus putting Sunday in the place of the Sabbath of the fourth commandment, it is just as literally true that the Protestant churches of this country, by the power of this government, have made void the law of God, as far as earthly power can, as was the action of the papacy the original apostasy, in joining herself to the government to do the same thing. And when that is done, God has put into our mouths these words: "It is time for thee, Lord, to work, for they have made void thy law." And that brings to view the further thought, that as all the power of earth is set against God and His Sabbath and His people who keep it, that this people, in order to stand at all, must have a power that is greater than all the power of the earth, and that brought us to that verse, "It is time for thee, Lord, to work, for they have made void thy law." Therefore we need the power of God. Our daily prayer is, Lord, it is time for thee to work now; we cannot do anything at all.

Then the first point in the succeeding lesson was that this message is given in view of the fact that the plagues are to come upon those who reject the message, "If any man worship the beast and his image, and receive his mark in his forehead, or in his hand, the same shall drink of the wine of the wrath of God." The first plague is poured out upon those who receive the mark of the beast; and under the sixth plague the kings of the earth are gathered together to the battle of the great day of God Almighty. In the time of that battle the Lord comes and the end of the world. "And the seventh angel poured out his vial into the air; and there came a great voice out of the temple of heaven, from the throne, saying, It is done. And there were voices, and thunderings, and lightnings; and there was a great earthquake, such as was not since men were upon the earth, so mighty an earthquake and so great."

Then the next was that in the history of the nations that have gone before, when a nation would no longer seek the Lord, but would turn their backs upon God, and set themselves against God, then there was no more place for them in the world. Ruin was the only thing that followed. As this government has done that, ruin is the only thing to follow here.

By the way I was looking through *Special Testimonies* this evening, and there is a passage so expressive on this point that I turn and read it here. It is on page 16 of *Special Testimony to Ministers and Conference Committees*.

It is this:

> The Christian world has accepted the child of papacy, and cradled and nourished it, thus defying God by removing His memorial and setting up a rival sabbath.

When was that done? That was done when they removed His memorial; defying God by removing His memorial, and setting up a false sabbath. Now here is the word we read the other day:

> God's memorial has been torn down, and in its place a false sabbath stands before the world.

But that was done by the churches securing the power of this government to make their work effective. Then what has this nation been dragged into doing, by the apostate Protestant churches of this country? into defiance of God. When Belshazzar defied God by taking the sacred vessels of the house of God and prostituted them to his lascivious worship, then there was no more use for that government in this world. Then this government has been brought into the same place, and ruin is the next thing that comes here. But the ruin of this nation is the ruin of the world, because the influence of the nation affects the world, and that ruin is accomplished at the coming of the Lord, and the coming of the Lord is when that great battle is fought. And we are right in the presence of that.

And then the next was that the apostate Jewish church joined herself to Caesar in order to get rid of the Lord. The apostate Romish church joined herself to Caesar in order to get rid of the Sabbath of the Lord; and the apostate churches now have joined themselves to Caesar in order to get rid of the Sabbath of the Lord. And the only thing that God could do for the apostate Jewish church when she joined herself to Caesar was to destroy it. But before He destroyed it He called out all who would be His. The Jewish church was church and nation in one, so that when that was destroyed, the lesson was set before the world, for both churches and nations. It was the Jewish nation and the Jewish church both, turning the back upon God. When the Jewish church put God out of the way, that was the Jewish nation doing the same thing. Now when that was done, the nation was to be destroyed, but the church was to be destroyed too; and so the effect of this thing upon the church and the nation was the same thing; it was ruin.

When the Roman Church followed in the same way, that ruined the Roman Empire; and when this nation has gone in the same way the only thing that remains is ruin, and ruin for the nation is ruin for the church too. But before this impending ruin, the message goes, "Come out of her, my people, that ye be not partakers of her sins and that ye receive not of her plagues."

The last night we noticed the papacy, that her work is to get all nations back under her influence; and when she has got all nations there, and congratulates herself, saying, "I sit a queen, and am no widow, and shall see no sorrow," then what is it that comes right away? The plagues.

Then the same thing will happen to this nation that happened to other nations when they turned away from God; and we are right in the whirlpool of the events that bring all this. The same thing is soon to come, here, that came upon the other nations when they forgot God. There are seven distinct points, each one of which brings us to the events of the third angel's message, which is to save the people who will be saved before the world ends. They are not manufactured points either; not a single one of them is manufactured; each one of them is simply the consequence of things that stand before the eyes of everybody in this world. That was the text to start with, you know; "The people who will now see what is soon to come upon us by what is being transacted before us, will no longer trust in human inventions and will feel that the Holy Spirit must be recognized, received, presented to the people." So all I have attempted to do in these lessons that we have had, is to take what stands before us in the world, and see what is soon to come upon us; not simply what is to come upon us, but what is *soon* to come upon us and it is bound to do it. There is no escape from the things that everybody in the world can see, and must see, whether their eyes are open, or not; whether they believe what is coming – that is not the question; they can not help seeing what they see. There is no escape for them but by the third angel's message.

Now let us follow that a little further, as to what it means to us. We have found that all the power of this earth is now under the influence of the papacy. You see that it is. But who is running the papacy? Who is working against the church of God? Satan. By whom did he work when Christ was on the earth? The dragon. By whom did he work when the church was in the wilderness? The beast. by whom does he work against the remnant? By the image. By the dragon, by the beast, and by the false prophet, the image. These are the three instruments through which he makes war against the church of God, from the birth of Christ until the end of the world.

Then all the powers of this earth are in the hands of Satan to wield against the church. Then how long do you suppose it is going to be before that verse is fulfilled, in which it is said that Satan works with all power? He has got it, hasn't he? All the power that earth knows, all the power that is in the realm where Satan is, all the power that is in this earth, this is now in his hands. He is going to work with all power. "Even him, whose coming is after *the working of Satan with all power* and signs and lying wonders, and with all deceivableness of unrighteousness." What has he that power for? Is it not to use it? Then do you suppose he is going to stand idle very long, especially when God's people are calling upon God and consecrating themselves to Him? That is what makes Satan so mad; the commandments of God are kept, and the testimony of Jesus Christ is manifested.

Then there is that power in his hand to wield against the church of God, against God, His Sabbath, and those who respect the Lord and His Sabbath, because that is the sign of allegiance to the Lord.

Well then anybody who is going to be faithful to God, I say again, has got to do that in the face of all the power that there is in the world, all the power that the world knows of every possible kind. Then, brethren, the thing for you and me to decide right now is, whether we are going any further, or not. We are to decide, whether we are going any further or stop right here. Just as certainly as we decide to stand by the profession we have made, just as certainly as we decide to stand by the law of God and faithfulness to our profession, we have to decide it in the face of all the power that this world knows, with Satan in possession of this power and using it. Then we are to maintain our allegiance to God and His law, against all consideration of any earthly support or protection. Does it not become the people who are to stand by the law of God, that they depend alone upon God, for there is nothing else under the sun to depend upon.

We are to warn the people of the world against this power, and against the working of it, and to draw them away from it unto God. Now can I do that with any force at all, if I have any connection with the world or worldliness? [Congregation: "No."] If I may partake of a worldly spirit, and a worldly disposition and inclination, I want to know how I am going to warn the people to separate from the world utterly? How is there going to be enough force in my words to get anybody to do it? Can you tell?

Can you tell how you can do it? I do not care whether you are a minister or not, if you are only a Seventh-day Adventist, or even only a *professed* Seventh-day Adventist; you need not be a minister but only a *professed* Seventh-day Adventist to answer this question. I want to know how you are going to make the profession worth anything, or have any power at all upon people of this world, if you are in any way connected with this world in spirit, in mind, in thought, in wishes, in inclinations? No sir. A hair's breadth, a connection with the world as thin as a hair, will rob you of the power that there must be in this call that will warn the world against this evil power of the world, so that they shall be utterly separated from it.

Then, brethren, if there is going to be any power to our message from this time forth, what are we to do? We are to just cut loose from everything that this world knows. Are you ready? Nor is it enough to ask if you are *ready*? but I want to ask, Is it done? Is it done? [Congregation: "Yes."]

That is a splendid picture that Brother Porter read awhile ago; that the prophet looked for those who give this message, but looked *too low*. Said the angel, "Look higher." Thank the Lord, they are above the world. That is where they belong. Above the world, upon a foundation which God has established for them to walk upon. And every one who is down so low that any one has to look to the world to see them – such as these cannot give the third angel's message. We are to be above the world. Then cut loose, brethren.

Then, brethren, the time has come as never before in this world when there must be a separation from the world. "I have chosen you out of the world," says Jesus. Now that He has chosen us, Oh let us seek Him day by day that He may ordain us. Christ said to His disciples, "I have chosen you, and ordained you." Now He has chosen us. Let us see that He has ordained us to the work that He has for us; and the work is, to carry the word of God against all the power that this world knows, and to separate a people from the world, so entirely separated unto God, that they will disregard utterly the power of this world and all its connection.

That brings us to consecration again doesn't it? Thank the Lord that it does. And we can hold to the third angel's message, we cannot stand by that, we cannot have the spirit of it or do the work of it without just that consecration.

Now there is another thing. The people who stand by the law of God are not going to be thought very well of, all the way through. No, sir. They are not going to be praised and petted and made much of and courted and palavered over. No, sir. Perhaps I had better read a passage here on that. I will read from *Great Controversy*, Vol. IV, p. 590:

> The great deceiver will persuade men that those who serve God are causing these evils. The class that have provoked the displeasure of Heaven will charge all their troubles upon those whose obedience to God's commandments is a perpetual reproof to transgressors.

> It will be declared that men are offending God by violation of the Sunday-sabbath, that this sin has brought calamities which will not cease until Sunday observance shall be strictly enforced, and that those who present the claims of the fourth commandment, thus destroying reverence for Sunday, are troublers of the people, preventing their restoration to divine favor and temporal prosperity. Thus the accusation urged of old against the servant of God will be repeated, upon grounds equally well established. 'And it came to pass, when Ahab saw Elijah that Ahab said unto him, Art thou he that troubleth Israel? And he answered, I have not troubled Israel; but thou, and thy father's house, in that ye have forsaken the commandments of the Lord and hast followed Baalim.' As the wrath of the people shall be excited by false charges, they will pursue a course to God's ambassadors very similar to that which apostate Israel pursued toward Elijah.

Again we read on page 592, as follows:

> Those who honor the Bible Sabbath will be denounced as enemies of law and order, as breaking down the moral restraints of society, causing anarchy and corruption, and calling down the judgments of God upon the earth. Their conscientious scruples will be pronounced obstinacy, stubbornness, and contempt of authority. They will be accused of disaffection toward the government. Ministers who deny the obligation of the divine law will present from the pulpit the duty of yielding obedience to the civil authorities as ordained of God. In legislative halls and courts of justice, commandment-keepers will be misrepresented and condemned. A false coloring will be given to their words, and the worst construction will be put upon their motives.

In *Testimony* No. 32, p. 208, I read a testimony that was given in 1885 – seven years ago:

> While men are sleeping, Satan is actively arranging matters so that the Lord's people may not have mercy or justice.

How could it be expected that we should have mercy or justice when all the power of the governments on the earth is in the hands of the papacy and being run by Satan? How could you expect justice? And how could you expect justice when all the power of this earth is set against the people of God by Satan himself? That is not justice. We could not expect it. That brings us to the point that we are to be so utterly cut loose from this world that we will not expect any protection; we will not expect any justice, any mercy even, from it. If it comes it will be only the mercy of God that draws it in spite of themselves. When we are in a position that the only mercy that we can expect of the earth, is what God draws from them, then where is our dependence? In God only. We are not going to be petted and made much of at all. Then, this being so, every kind of reproach will be manufactured and spread against us. I want to know how anybody is going to stand faithful to the third angel's message and do the work of that message who cares particularly what people say about him and has much respect for reputation or puts his dependence upon reputation? He cannot do it. But thank the Lord, God has something *a great deal better* for us to depend upon, and that is *character*. Let us not forget that Jesus, our example in this world, "made himself of no reputation."

Now then that settles it that the people who are to give the third angel's message and to stand faithful to God in the world are to do it with respect to *character* only and no question of reputation can ever come into the calculation. No question of reputation, as to how or what men may think or say, can ever come into our calculations any more. Never. Because reputation will not save a man. If he is going to have any respect to reputation, if that is going to come into his mind at all, then he would better give up the whole thing because he cannot have it if he stands by the third angel's message.

Then right now, tonight, brethren, is the time to give up all such professions, because in doing that you will be a relief to your brethren. If you are going to compromise with this thing at all, you had better do so right now, because the farther you go, and then compromise, the harder you will make it for your brethren. Therefore, unless you are going clear through, just stop tonight and go the other way and be done with it and let the others that are going straight ahead be free. We have come to the parting of the ways and let every one decide in view of no dependence on anything that is in this world that no consideration that this world can present, can come into the calculation. No question of reputation or of what men will think, ever comes into the calculation. When all the power of the world stands against those who will maintain their allegiance to God, then the *character of Jesus Christ* is worth ten thousand times ten thousand *reputations* that anybody can manufacture anyway.

But reputation is a big thing in the eyes of the world: with God a reputation does not amount to anything. A reputation is all that Satan has to offer. It is all he has to build on. And that statement that is often quoted is correct enough from the man into whose mouth it is put by the writer who preached it: "The dearest treasure that mortal times afford is spotless reputation." That was well enough for him, for reputation was all he had. Then he went on to say he had lost his and he was very much grieved, saying: "O my reputation, my reputation! I have lost my reputation." And when he had lost that, of course, he had nothing to support him. He was out entirely. He did not have *character* you see, but only reputation to depend on. That sentiment comes from him very properly, from the character into whose mouth it was put by him who write it; but it is a lie; it is a lie. The dearest treasure that mortal times afford is not *spotless* reputation: the dearest treasure that either mortal or immortal times afford is spotless *character*, and the only spotless character that ever appeared in this world is the character of Jesus Christ. And that character He comes and gives to you and me, a free blessed gift from Him who made it.

Then brethren, let all questions of reputation go to the winds; that is where they belong. For reputation is as unstable as the winds, while character is as fixed as eternity. Then let all questions of reputation go. Let us have character; let us have that character that will fit us for the judgment. Then, though Satan with all his power might succeed in saddling upon us the worst reputation he can invent, thank the Lord we have got a character that will stand in the judgement. Then we can afford to let the world and reputation both go. In Jesus Christ we have something better.

That is not all. There is another phase of it. The time is coming when anybody who stands by the third angel's message, the Sabbath of the Lord, and maintains his allegiance to that, cannot buy anything or sell anything in this world. Then every one who professes to be a Seventh-day Adventist, who has a profession of the third angel's message, needs to decide now as to whether he is going to stand by that message against all questions and considerations of property or possessions in this world.

No question, no calculations as to property, or business interests in this world, can come into our calculations or into our work, now. No question of that kind can enter into the calculations of any Seventh-day Adventist from this time on. If it does, he might as well stop right here; for if I am going to let questions as to whether I can have so much or how this business affair is going to come out and whether I am going to lose by that means or gain by this, if I stand by the Sabbath – if I am going to let such questions come into my calculations, then I had better let property interests have full place and go with it and be done with it. But where is that business, this property going, that I am questioning and hesitating about? It is all going to destruction. Then if there is any string that binds me in sympathy with that thing, when it goes, where will I go? I will go with it, of course. Suppose that string is only the size of a silken hair, will it take me with it? Yes. Then, brethren, it is time to cut loose. So we have come to the parting of the ways again.

Henceforth he who stands in allegiance to the third angel's message must do it and he *will* do it with no calculation at all that any question of profit, money, or property, or anything of the kind will ever bear the weight of a feather or the weight of a hair as to how he is going to act with respect to the third angel's message. That is so. That is in it. For there is the statement that "No man might buy or sell, save he that had the mark, or the name of the beast, or the number of his name." "If *any man* worship the beast and his image, and receive his mark in his *forehead* or in his *hand*." He need not believe in it at all. But the law says, "Keep Sunday", and if he does, then what? He has compromised with Satan and he has accepted the sign of Satan, instead of Christ. He has put Satan above Christ and is obeying the power of the world and not the words of Christ. And how much power over the world is that man going to have to save him?

The man who compromises with Sunday laws to the extent that he will stop work and observe Sunday because the law says so, while still thinking that he is keeping the Sabbath, has put Satan above Christ. He is putting dependence upon earthly power; but in whose hands is that power? In the hands of Satan. Then is he not, according to his own profession and actions, depending on Satan just as much as upon Christ? Are they partners? No sir. Well then let us not let him come into the partnership, brethren.

No man who holds his allegiance to the third angel's message will allow Satan to come into such a partnership as that.

Isn't the Sabbath a sign of what God is to a man? Isn't it a sign of the true God, and is not God *what* He *is?* Then is it not a sign of *what* God is as well as *that* He is? Then the Sabbath being a sign of *what* God is as well as *that* He is, what is He? Oh, He is the Lord, the Lord God, merciful and gracious, long-suffering and abundant in goodness and truth, keeping mercy for thousands, forgiving iniquity and transgression and sin. He is our life.

Good. Then the Sabbath is the sign of what God is to the man who believes Him.

But where do we find God? Where alone can anybody find God? In Jesus Christ. "No man knoweth the Father save the Son and *he to whomsoever the Son will reveal him.*" Then to us Christ is God. To this world and to all intelligent creatures, Christ is God. Then is not the Sabbath the sign of what Christ is to a man? Then when we observe it, it is the sign of what Christ is to us. Then for me to keep Sunday because the law says so is to say that Sunday is just as much to me as the Sabbath is: Oh well that is only to say that Satan is as much to me as Christ is. And when that is so, Christ does not amount to much to me. When Christ is so little to me that I will put the sign of the power of the papacy, which is only the sign of the power of Satan, on a level with the sign of what Christ is to me, *then Christ isn't anything to me.* If Christ is not all, what is He? "He is all and in all." If He is not all to me, then what is He to me? He is nothing. That brings us again to the fact that now, brethren, we have got to stand to this sign against every consideration that earth can mention.

That is not all yet. There is another thought in that verse:

> And he had power to give life unto the image of the beast, that the image of the beast should both speak, and cause that as many as would not worship the image of the beast *should be killed.*

Then, the time will come when he who stands to his allegiance to the third angel's message will have the penalty of death pronounced upon him; his life will be forfeited and declared forfeited by the powers of this earth in whose reach he is. Then can any question of life come into our calculations now? Can it, brethren? shall a man weigh up what his life is worth now and have that to weigh anything in his calculations in the third angel's message, as to whether he is going to stand by it or not? These things are worth thinking of. That is what they mean. If I am going to allow my life to weigh anything at all in my calculations of allegiance to the third angel's message, then what is the use of my going any farther with this message? Why not stop right here tonight? The fact is as stated there, that this life will be forfeited if I stand by the message. So, if we are to let that question weigh anything with us, we had better stop right here and be done with it.

And don't you know that the penalty of death is, in itself, in every step, even the first step, that is taken in persecution? It is certainly there. It is not there in words – it is not there in a pronounced penalty – but it is there, because when the government undertakes to enforce religious laws, it is always to save the government, always for the salvation of the government – this Sunday act of Congress has already been declared to be for that purpose. Now, people who do not obey the Sunday laws, of course, are fined and they don't pay their fine – Sabbath-keepers don't of course. They have to go to prison to satisfy the fine, and they serve out the time and they are tuned out. Then they go to work on Sunday again. And then they are fined again, and are imprisoned to serve out the fine, and then turned out again. They go to work on Sunday again, of course, when it comes, then the fine is made heavier, and that makes the imprisonment longer. But none of it stops the Sunday work, which is the one thing aimed at. Therefore don't you see that as heavier penalties are laid on without reaching what the government is after, it will simply have to reach the heaviest penalty at last, and that is death. Then the penalty of death is in every Sunday law that was ever made on this earth, in itself, just as certainly as the law is to be enforced and carried into effect. For this reason the historian Gibbon told the world more than a hundred years ago that:

> It is incumbent on the authors of persecution previously to reflect whether they are determined to support it in the last extreme. They excite the flame which they strive to extinguish, and it soon becomes necessary to chastise the contumacy, as well as the crime, of the offender. The fine, which he is unable or unwilling to discharge, exposes his person to the severity of the law, and his contempt of lighter penalties suggests the use and propriety of capital punishment.

Therefore the historian called the attention of nations and rulers everywhere that before they entered into the line of persecution they should consider whether they were ready to support it with capital punishment. If they were not, they had better not start with it. That is so in the nature of things and there stands the record that that is going to be so in the practice of things.

Then is it not plain from these words that the people who will stand faithful to the third angel's message, faithful in allegiance to the law of God andHis Sabbath, will have to do it without any calculations of life itself coming into their account? Isn't that so? [Congregation: "Yes."]

Another thing: When all earthly support and protection are taken away, when all questions of reputation, which the world think so much of, are taken away; when all questions of property or business of any kind are taken away and when all questions of life are taken away, how much is left? How much of worldly things or worldly interests is there connected with that man? When he has reckoned up the account and has set aside all considerations of earthly protection, even of mercy or justice; when he has reckoned up the account and set aside all questions as to what men think or say upon the subject; reckoned up the account and set aside all questions as to whether property can be had or whether he can buy or sell or do this, that, or the other; reckoned up the account and set aside all questions of calculation as to whether his life shall be dear unto him or whether it shall come into the account in any way – when all these things are cast out of the account, then how much of the world is in that man's calculations? [Congregation: "None."]

Then has not the Bible, the word of God, brought every Seventh-day Adventist face to face with that reckoning and called upon him to make that calculation and that decision? [Congregation: "Yes."] Then it is time for every one of us to begin to think very seriously indeed. But thank the Lord, we need not be a bit afraid of our enemy. The Lord will never allow you or me to be shut up in a place where he does not expect to take us out a great deal more gloriously than if we had never got in there. The Lord does not call upon you or me to enter upon a course that calls for the forfeiture of anything but that in the place of that which is forfeited He will give us that which is worth infinitely more. When He calls upon us to stand in allegiance to His truth, which shuts off from us all considerations of earthly support or protection, then He simply says, "Here is all the power of heaven and earth for you." "All power is given to me in heaven and earth" and "I am with you"; here is the covering of the Almighty drawn over you. Come with me. "The eternal God is thy refuge, and underneath are the everlasting arms"; "Be not afraid." That is His word, is it not?

Let us read it a little more fully so as to get the direct reference upon it. In Isaiah 51 we find a prayer that the Lord tells us to speak to Him:

> Awake, awake, put on strength, O arm of the Lord; awake, as in the ancient days, in the generations of old. Art thou not it that hath cut Rahab [Egypt], and wounded the dragon? Art thou not it which hath dried the sea, the waters of the great deep; that hath made the depths of the sea a way for the ransomed to pass over? Therefore the redeemed of the Lord shall return, and come with singing unto Zion, and everlasting joy shall be upon their heads. They shall obtain gladness and joy, and sorrow and mourning shall flee away.

How are they going to go to Zion? With singing. Then let us begin it now. Why the Lord doesn't want us to go with our heads bowed down and skulking around as though we were afraid to be seen and had no place in the world. "Look up, and lift up your heads, for your redemption draweth nigh!" said Jesus. We belong in this world, every one of us, until God is done with us, and Satan himself cannot do us any damage until the Lord is done with us, and even then he cannot do us any damage. Let us go on our way with singing then. Let us be glad of it.

> I, even I, am he that comforteth you; who art thou that thou shouldest be afraid of man which shall be made as grass?

And we profess to believe in God! We are standing by the law of God and we have the Sabbath of the Lord and that reveals to us who God is, that He is the true God, He is the living God and everlasting King. At His wrath the earth shall tremble, and by His word He can bring worlds into existence, and by His word shake them to pieces, and here are some men that are just like grass and will vanish in a little while, and *they* say that if you do that you shall go to prison, and if you persist in it to the last you shall be put to death. And we get scared at that! Why, isn't the Lord right in asking just such a question as that? "Who art thou that thou shouldest be afraid of a man that shall die?" That is what He wants to know. Is not that a fair question? "I, even I, am he that comforteth you; who art thou that thou shouldest be afraid of a man that shall die, and of the son of man which shall be made as grass?" Don't you see the very insult of the idea that any one who professes to believe in the Lord should act in that way? The Lord says that isn't depending on Him.

Let us read some more.

"And forgettest the Lord, thy Maker, that hath stretched forth the heavens, and laid the foundations of the earth, and hast feared continually every day because of the fury of the oppressor, as if he were ready to destroy? And where is the fury of the oppressor?" Thank the Lord. Just now it is so that the fury of the oppressor is about to break forth. Well, why should we fear before him as though he were able to destroy? Was not Elijah attacked and driven out and had to flee for his life? But when he had gone a long journey and was weary and lay down to rest and fell asleep from weariness, behold an angel of the Lord stood by him and touched him and said, Arise, Elijah, and eat. And he found a cake baken on the coals and a cruse of water at his head. Thank the Lord.

Was not Elijah perfectly safe? Brethren, isn't it worth being driven out, in order to have an angel do that? Which would you rather, not be driven out or not have the angel come and stand by you like that? Let us not be afraid then. Elijah laid down and went to sleep again, just like Peter when he was condemned to be killed. Well, why not? What was the use of worrying? Elijah laid down and went to sleep, and the angel came and awakened him the second time, and ministered to him. Again he said, Arise, Elijah, and eat, for the journey is too great for thee!

Brethren, God will give us bread for the journey. If the journey is too great, He will give us bread twice before we start. I tell you, brethren, it is time to begin to trust the Lord. Let us do it now. He says so. In another place He says, "Bread shall be given him; his waters shall be sure." It is so.

> The captive exile hasteneth that he may be loosed, and that he should not die in the pit nor that his bread should fail. But I am the Lord thy God, that divided the sea, whose waves roared: The Lord of hosts is his name. And I have put my words in thy mouth, and

I have covered thee in the shadow of mine hand, that I may plant the heavens, and lay the foundations of the earth, and say unto Zion, Thou art my people. Isa. 51:14-16.

Then brethren, let us receive it. And then we need not be afraid of oppression or difficulties, or whether we can buy or sell anything at all, because the Lord has something so much better.

Then about the reputation. Let that go. He gives a character – a character which He Himself wove from infancy to the grave – that is complete in every respect; and He says, "Take it and put it on, and you shall come to my wedding supper." That is the character, and that is the covering that he draws over His people so that the plagues cannot touch them, and no power of the enemy can overcome or defile it. "I will greatly rejoice in the Lord, my soul shall be joyful in my God; for he hath clothed me with the garments of salvation, he hath covered me with the robe of righteousness." Isa. 61:10. Thank the Lord.

And about the life. When He calls upon you and me to take a position in allegiance to His law, which will forfeit our lives, that will put our lives in jeopardy so that some earthly power would deprive us of it. what then? Well, He simply says, Let that life go. It will vanish away in a little while anyway. Here is one that will last through all eternity. When He asks you and me to take a course of allegiance to His law that will put into jeopardy and forfeit this vapory, vanishing, mortal life, He says, "Here is eternal life to begin with." "He that believeth on the Son, hath everlasting life." "This is the record, that God hath given to us eternal life, and this life is in his Son." Has He given it to us? "He that hath the Son" is going to have life some time? [Congregation: "No."] "He that hath the Son *hath* life." How in the world can we have the Son without it? Is Christ dead? No. He is alive. So, when we have Him, we have the life that is in Him. Just see what it brings us to, when a man who professes to have Christ, does not believe that He has the life which is in Christ, which is eternal life. What kind of Christ is He? A Christ with no life in Him? No. Christ isn't dead. Is not that what has been rung in our ears over and over for years by the voice that has been speaking so long for the Lord? "Brethren, Christ is not in Joseph's new tomb with a great stone rolled at the door of the sepulcher. No. He is risen! He lives! He lives! Tell it with tongue and pen."

Then as He lives and does nothing but live forever more, when I have Him, I have a living Saviour. "He that hath the Son hath life." what kind of life is in Him? Eternal life only. Then when I have Him, I have the life which is His, and that is eternal life, just as He says. But, as Brother Haskell has brought before us in his lessons, we cannot have that life without yielding up this one. In doing that we meet Jesus Christ. That was the lesson today, don't you see? Yield up this life and you will get one that is a great deal better. Now is the time. But if I cling to this life, when it is gone, what have I left? [Congregation: "Nothing."]

Therefore the man or woman who has only this life to start with, need not start with the third angel's message, because when the test comes that this life is at stake, he will stick to it. That's the danger. A man can't go through what the third angel's message is to go through, with only this life that he has. He can't do it. Because it is all he has, and he will stick to it, when it is brought into jeopardy. But he will let this life go, count it worth nothing and take that life that measures with the life of God, that life which is the life of God, will have a life that can never get into jeopardy. That man is safe. He can go wherever the message calls him. For He who is the life of the message is the life of him who will maintain his allegiance to this message.

Then, "Always bearing about in the body the dying of the Lord Jesus, that the life also of Jesus might be made manifest in our body. For we which live are always delivered unto death." Is not that so from this time forth? Is it not a living truth from this time forth, that those who stand by the third angel's message are always "delivered unto death," just as certainly as the apostles were themselves? Always "delivered unto death," and that is in all our calculations. We live face to face with it all the time.

Then brethren, instead of the power of earth that we cannot depend upon, and which is decidedly set against us, God gives us *the power of God.*

Instead of reputation God gives us *character.*

Instead of earthly things – earthly riches, houses, lands, property, business considerations or anything of the kind, God gives us Jesus Christ, in whom are hidden all the treasures of wisdom and knowledge, and "Ye are complete in Him." God hath appointed Him to be heir of all things, and we are heirs of God and joint heirs with Jesus Christ if so be that we suffer with Him that we may be glorified together. He is heir of all things, and we are joint heirs. Then how much belongs to us? [Congregation: "All things."] Then what have we? all things that God has. Then are we not rich?

Instead of this life which the powers of earth would take away God gives us His life. When He asks us to take a position in allegiance to Him and His cause, the Lord simply says, "Here is eternal life to start with."

Then brethren has not the Lord fully armed us? O, then let us have on the armor of God now. That is what is wanted – to be strong in the Lord and the power of His might. "For we wrestle not against flesh and blood, but against principalities, against powers, against the rulers of the darkness of this world, against spiritual wickedness in high places. Wherefore take unto you the whole armor of God, that ye may be able to withstand in the evil day, and having done all, to stand." That is where the Lord wants us to stand, and that is what He wants us to do. And He says, "I will never leave thee nor forsake thee." That's where we are. Now what are you going to do? "Choose ye this day whom ye will serve," and which course you will take.

Sermon 7

February 5, 1893

Some of the folks wondered last Friday night whether I was not making things rather strong; but I think after what Brother Porter read from the "Testimonies" just now all will agree that it was just straight. I do not want you to think, brethren, that I am making up things to say here just because it is you. If I had been preaching since last Monday night to a people who never heard of a Seventh-day Adventist, nor the third angel's message, I would preach to them just exactly what I have to you, because I do not know what else to give now than the third angel's message. I do not know what else to do to people wherever I do preach than to bring them face to face with their need of the power of God. So I am not saying anything to you yet that I would not have said to anybody. It might come after a while that I shall say something to you that I would not to other people, because maybe some of us have been doing things that other people would not do, but that is the only reason.

Now let us glance again at a summary of the lessons we have had. We have found that there is nothing that will hold us up in this time but the *power* of God. We have found that nothing will satisfy us, nothing will do for us, but the *character* of God. We have found in the matter of means and business affairs so far as this world is concerned, that we cannot depend upon any of these any more, but only upon *the things that God* gives. We have found that as to life itself, we cannot count on that anymore; the only thing that will satisfy, the only thing that we can depend upon, the only thing that will meet our demand – the demand of the people who will now stand for the Lord – is *that life* that is better than this one – the life that is eternal, the *life of God*.

Well, then, first, nothing will support us but the power of God. And where do we find the *power* of God? In Jesus Christ. "Christ the power of God and the wisdom of God"; that is what He is. Where do we find the *character* of God? In Christ. Where do we find all things, the great things of God? In Christ. Where do we find a better life than this? The life of God, in Christ.

Well, then, what in the world have we to preach to the world, but Christ? What have we to depend upon but Christ? Then what is the third angel's message but Christ? Christ the power of God; Christ the unsearchable riches of God; Christ the righteousness of God; Christ the life of God; Christ is God! That is the message that now we are to give to the world. Is it not? Then what does the world need? Christ. Do they need anything else? No. Is there anything else? No. "In Him dwelleth all the fullness of the Godhead bodily, and ye are complete in Him."

As I said a while ago, if I had been preaching to a people that had never heard anything about the third angel's message, if I had been preaching to them since Monday night, I would preach just as I have, and bring them face to face with Jesus Christ just as we have. And by the way, there is a whole congregation of infidels that are just in that place, waiting now to give me an invitation sometime to come and speak the next time, and that is what I am to tell them. A whole congregation – profess to be nothing but infidels – have given me the opportunity to speak to them three times already, and I have spoken on these things just as they are right before men's faces; and they have already asked, "What are we to do?" And one of them said, "Well, he has told us all these things, and it is all plain, but he has not told us what to do." "Well," said I, "I did not have time to tell you what to do tonight. Give me a chance, and I will tell you what to do." They said, "All right" and I will do it.

When that time comes I propose to tell them just what to do. I propose to set before them just what I have set before you, that if they are going to oppose this Church and State movement, they have got to set aside all ideas of earthly dependence, they have got to set aside all thoughts of riches or possessions or anything of that kind and all ideas or thoughts of life. And they can see it. And then I shall tell them they cannot afford to do that unless they get something better, and the thing better is Jesus Christ, and they must have Him or else they cannot stand at all. Why, brethren, the world is ready to hear the message, *when we get the message;* the world is ready to hear it, and they will hear it.

Well, then, Christ the power of God; Christ the wisdom of God; Christ the unsearchable riches of God, and Christ the life of God. That is what we are to preach. Well, what is that all summed up in one thing? What expresses it? The Gospel. What is it to preach the gospel? It is to preach the mystery of God, which is Christ in men the hope of glory. What has God given to us to give to the world but "the everlasting gospel to preach unto every kindred and nation and tongue and people"? Rev. 14:6. Is not that what the message starts with? And then, when men will not receive the everlasting gospel nor worship Him who made heaven and earth and the sea and the fountains of waters – whom did they worship? The beast and his image. "Babylon is fallen, is fallen"; and then the third angel's message says they will worship the beast and his image. So that now, men worship the beast and his image, or else they will worship God. That is settled. According to the message as it is, and the time in which we are, the only thing that people in this world can worship is Him that made heaven and earth, the sea and the fountains of water, or else the beast and his image; there is no half-way place. The three messages are simply one three-fold message. In the special testimonies, is one that is addressed, "To Brethren in Responsible Positions," we read on page 15:

> While you hold the banner of truth firmly, proclaiming the law of God, let every soul remember that the faith of Jesus is connected with the commandments of God. The third angel is represented as flying through the midst of heaven, *symbolizing* the work of those who proclaimed the *first*, *second*, and *third* angel's messages; *all are linked together.*

So that the opening thing, and the one thing of all, that which covers all of these messages, is the everlasting gospel.

Now we have referred a time or two to the Jewish Church, as an illustration of the situation in which we are. We found there that that church turned its back upon God and joined itself to Caesar in order to put Christ out of the way and to execute their mind concerning Him. Then the Lord called out of that church and nation all who would obey Him, all who would serve Him, before the nation was destroyed and He did that work by those few disciples that believed in Jesus when He ascended to heaven. They had been with Jesus three years and a half; they had preached. They had even performed miracles in His name. He had sent them to preach, saying "The kingdom of heaven is at hand"; and so important was their message that if the place did not receive them, they were to shake the dust off from their feet before they left.

Yet before they could preach the gospel which He gave them to preach, when He ascended to heaven He said, "Tarry ye at Jerusalem until ye be endued with power from on high." Would not we have thought that their being with Christ three years and a half, hearing Him, loving Him, studying Him and with Him, having been taught by Him this length of time, and having even preached – it would naturally be supposed that they were fitted to carry the gospel to the world? But no, said He. "Tarry ye at Jerusalem." "Behold I send the promise of my Father upon you, but tarry ye at Jerusalem until ye be endued with power from on high." Luke 24:49.

How much power was there enlisted against them and the message they were to preach? All the power of the world. For the church of God, the professed church of God, that whole nation, had joined itself to Caesar, whose power filled the world. All the power of the world was allied against them. The professed church and nation of God had allied themselves to power and had arrayed it against God and the name of Christ. And yet this Christ whom they had crucified and whom they had done their best to take away from the world and the minds of men – His disciples were to go and preach that very name and that very person, and that faith only in Him could save them. And they had to preach this in the face of all the power that the world then knew.

Well, not very long before that, only about twelve days or two weeks before Jesus told them this, Peter got scared at a girl and denied that he knew Christ. There was a girl that began to say, "I saw you with that Galilean." "No, you did not; no. I don't know Him." He came closer to the fire and she got a better look at Him, and she said, "You are one of them." No, I am not. No. I never knew Him." And then to prove it, he cursed and swore.

Was he prepared to face all the power in the world? No. He needed to be acquainted with a kind of life and have hold of something that a girl could not scare him out of before he could face the world. Did he not? and Jesus has told them all, "You will all forsake me and flee this night." "No, we will not," they all said, and Peter said, "Though they all forsake you, I will not." Jesus said, "Before the cock crow you will deny me three times, Peter." "Though I should die with thee, I will not deny thee." "And so likewise said they all." But they did forsake Him, didn't they? Matt. 26:31-35.

Well, then, we see that so far as themselves and their work was concerned and so far as the power that was opposed their work was concerned, we stand exactly in the situation in which they stood at that time when Jesus ascended to heaven. We stand exactly in that place where all the power of this earth is allied against the message which we are to give to the world, and therefore we need, just as they, to be endued with power from on high. So it is a literal fact that we stand exactly where they did when Jesus ascended to heaven and told theme to tarry until they got that power.

So when He ascended, He said, as recorded in Acts 1:8: "Ye shall receive power after that the Holy Ghost is come upon you." Then what were they to tarry for? For the Holy Ghost. What was He to bring to them? The power. What was to endure them with power? The Holy Ghost. Now I do not need to read the references from the little special testimonies and from Gospel Workers that Brother Prescott read here, which are on the same things; how that the words of the Lord tell us that just as the disciples were doing that, so we now should be doing the same thing. How we should be gathered in companies praying for the Holy Spirit, and how it required ten days of seeking God to bring them into the place where they could offer effectual prayer and receive that which they asked because they asked in that abiding faith that would receive what was asked.

Nor do I need to read again those passages that I read from Testimonies in manuscript, that when the people of God individually seek for His Holy Spirit with all the heart, there will be heard from human lips the testimony that fulfills that word, "I saw another angel come down from heaven, having great power, and the earth was lightened with his glory," and "Prayers are ascending daily for the fulfillment of this promise" of being endued with power." Then we have the word of the Lord that prayers are ascending daily. Are yours amongst them? Are mine amongst them? Now the day is going to come when the last prayer that will be necessary to bring that blessing will have ascended. Then what? It will come. The flood will burst, and out will pour the Holy Spirit, the day of Pentecost. Now, notice, the word is, as "Prayers are ascending to God daily" for this promise, "not one of those prayers put up in faith is lost." There is the blessedness of that promise, you see. Yes, when God tells us to pray for a thing, why, that opens the door wide for us to pray for that thing with the most perfect confidence that we shall receive it. When He tells us to pray for a thing, that throws open the door wide, and there is not a single thing to hinder that prayer from finding a lodgment there. What is His word to us? That not one of those prayers put up in faith is lost.

Well, one of these days the last prayer needed will be lodged there, and out the blessing will be poured. And who will receive it? Those whose prayers have ascended to God for it. I do not care whether that man is in the center of Africa and that outpouring is here in Battle Creek; he will receive it, because by our prayers for it, the channel is opened between us and the source of the blessing and just as certainly as we keep that channel open by our prayers, when the Spirit is poured out it will reach the place where the prayers start from just as sure as can be, because the channel is open.

Then brethren, could we possibly have more encouragement for the prayers which we see by everything around us, we must offer? Could there possibly be more encouragement for us to offer those prayers with all the heart and with perfect confidence?

There is a word in *Gospel Workers* that I want to read, which speaks plainly upon this question, page 370, 371.

Speaking about the apostles, it says:

> They were waiting in expectation of the fulfillment of His promise, and were praying with special fervency. This is the very course that should be pursued by those who act a part in the work of proclaiming the coming of the Lord in the clouds of heaven; for a people are to be prepared to stand in the great day of God. Although Christ had given the promise to His disciples that they should receive the Holy Spirit, *this did not remove the necessity of prayer.*

Why, of course not. That opens the way to prayer. When God has not promised a thing, am I free to pray for that thing? No, because we are to ask according to His will. But when God has promised, should I do anything else than pray? That is the beauty of it.

> They prayed all the more earnestly. They continued in prayer with one accord. Those who are now engaged in the solemn work of preparing a people for the coming of the Lord, should also continue in prayer. The early disciples were of one accord. They had no speculations, no curious theory to advance as to how the blessing was to come.

Now the thought I am after is this: "They had no speculations, no curious theories to advance as to how the promised blessing was to come." That means us now. We are to have no curious theories as to just how it is going to come. If any one begins to say, "O it is coming as on the day of Pentecost. The sound of it as the rushing mighty wind will be just so and so; the tongues of fire will look just so, etc., etc." And so settle it thus and say, "That is the way it is going to come the next time, and thus I shall know when it comes." The one who measures up this matter is any such way, will never receive it. What they needed was to get their hearts right before God, and it was none of *our* business how the Lord would fulfill His promise. He does not propose to have us dictate to Him and say, "The Holy Spirit must come in such a way or else it will not be the Holy Spirit." Then if you have had any theory about it, just annihilate that theory tonight, and let your theories always stay annihilated. We have no right to fix up in our minds the way the Lord is going to do things. That was their situation; that is our situation; and, brethren, just as certainly as the promise was fulfilled to them, so certainly it will be fulfilled now to those who are praying for the same thing. We do not know how long it will take.

Another thing, – They were to preach, what? The gospel. And Paul defines the gospel over and over to be the mystery of God which had been hid from ages and generations, now made manifest to His saints. They preached that gospel, that mystery of God, and what is that? "Christ in you the hope of glory"; "Christ the power of God and the wisdom of God"; "The unsearchable riches of God." "Christ and Him crucified." That is what it was; nothing but that.

And Paul defined it in the 6th chapter of 2 Cor., you remember, "as having nothing and yet possessing all things." Verse 10. Don't you see the poor, poverty-stricken condition of the man that holds to what he has in his hands in this world? Don't you see the poor, poverty-stricken condition of that Seventh-day Adventist that will now hold to what he has in this world? He must have more than that or he will never get through the time of trouble. But when we let everything go and count ourselves as having nothing, then what? Then what will we have? "All things." Then they cannot take anything away from us. The people who are in that condition, nothing can be taken from them. Now is that so? [Congregation: "Yes."] Of course, it is. They cannot take power from us, can they? They cannot take the character from us. Then they cannot take our riches from us. And they cannot take our life from us, for *Christ* is our life, and they cannot take Him from us. So when we are in this position we have the victory over the world and all its power, to start with.

Now another phrase in that same connection, "Having nothing and yet possessing all things; *as poor yet making many rich.*" That is our work in the world, to make people rich. As Jesus became poor that we might be made rich, so we become poor that many others may become rich. And so when we have Christ, Christ only, nothing but the unsearchable riches of Christ, we can make everybody rich who will take the free gift of the riches.

They preached the mystery of God – "Christ in you the hope of glory." But there arose another mystery. It began to appear while they were preaching. This mystery that they were to preach "had been hid from ages and generations"; now it was manifested as never before in the world. But while they were preaching that mystery, there appeared the working of another mystery, and that mystery of iniquity arose and hid again the mystery of God – after the apostles died that mystery of iniquity arose and spread over the world and hid again the mystery of God from ages and from generations. Didn't it? But when we come to the 10th chapter of Revelation an angel is there represented as standing with one foot on the sea and the other on the land, and crying with a strong voice, "and sware by him that liveth forever and ever, who created heaven, and the things that therein are, and the earth, and the things that therein are, and the sea and the things which are therein, that there should be time no longer. But in the days of the voice of the seventh angel, when he shall begin to sound, the mystery of God should be finished."

I have wondered lately whether that is not intentional that it is put in that way, that the mystery of God *should* be finished, instead of *shall* be finished. It should have been finished long ago. The Testimonies have told us that. But by our dilatoriness, our slackness, our slowness to believe God, it is not finished. Yet He said it *should* be finished. *Now,* thank the Lord it is to be finished indeed. If He would speak now He would say, it "shall be," of course. But the point is, that when the voice of the seventh angel shall begin to sound, the mystery of God stands forth to the world. What is that? "Christ in you the hope of glory." That is the everlasting gospel. That is the third angel's message. Then don't you see how it is that God has settled it that the third angel's message, the mystery of God, shall triumph over the mystery of iniquity, and that as certainly as the mystery of iniquity has held the attention of the world and has attracted the gaze of the nations, and the wonder of men, just so certainly the mystery of God will attract the attention of nations and the wonder of men? It will do it.

Now let us turn to the book of Joel and read that second chapter again. There are some things that we want to study. The first part of it you remember, up to the twelfth verse, not including the twelfth, is a picture of the coming of the Lord. If you turn to that Testimony (Vol. 1, p. 180) that tells about "The Shaking," you will find this chapter there given by the Spirit of the Lord as the reference on which is based that idea. It applies to the time of the shaking, and the shaking prepares for the loud cry.

> Blow ye the trumpet in Zion, and sound an alarm in my holy mountain: let all the inhabitants of the land tremble, for the day of the Lord cometh, for it is nigh at hand; a day of darkness and of gloominess, a day of clouds and of thick darkness, as the morning spread upon the mountains; a great people and a strong; there hath not been ever the like, neither shall be any more after it, even to the years of many generations. A fire devoureth before them; and behind them a flame burneth. The land is as the garden of Eden before them, and behind them a desolate wilderness; yea, and nothing shall escape them. The appearance of them is as the appearance of horses; and as horsemen, so shall they run. Like the noise of chariots on the tops of mountains shall they leap, like the noise of a flame of fire that devoureth the stubble, as a strong people set in battle array. Before their face the people shall be much pained: all faces shall gather blackness. They shall run like mighty men; they shall climb the wall like men of war; and they shall march every one on his ways, and they shall not break their ranks; neither shall one thrust another; they shall walk every one in his path: and when they fall upon the sword, they shall not be wounded. They shall run to and fro in the city; they shall run upon the wall, they shall climb upon the houses; they shall enter in at the windows like a thief. The earth shall quake before them; the heavens shall tremble; the sun and the moon shall be dark, and the stars shall withdraw their shining: and the

> Lord shall utter his voice before his army: for his camp is very great: for he is strong that executeth his word: for the day of the Lord is great and very terrible; and who can abide it?

The parallel is Revelation 19:11-18.

> Therefore also now, saith the Lord, turn ye even to me with all your heart, and with fasting and with weeping, and with mourning: and rend your heart, and not your garments, and turn unto the Lord your God: for he is gracious and merciful, slow to anger, and of great kindness, and repenteth him of the evil. Who knoweth if he will return and repent, and leave a blessing behind him: even a meat offering and a drink offering unto the Lord your God?

Who *here* knows that when a person seeks the Lord with all the heart, whether or not the Lord will return and leave a blessing behind Him? If we know He will, then let us go at it. There is all the encouragement in the world; just as certainly as we know He will do that, there is nothing to hinder us from seeking Him with all the heart, because we know He will give the blessing. Let us have it.

> Blow the trumpet in Zion, sanctify a fast, call a solemn assembly: Gather the people, sanctify the congregation, assemble the elders, gather the children and those that suck the breasts: let the bridegroom go forth of his chamber, and the bride out of her closet.

How many people in Zion does that include? The people, the congregation, the children, the elders, the babies, the bridegrooms, and the brides. How many does that call? [Congregation: "All."] Yes, all What does it call us to? To seek the Lord with all the heart. Then let us do it. We are in the time.

> Let the priests, the ministers of the Lord, weep between the porch and the altar; let them say, Spare thy people, O Lord, and give not thine heritage to reproach, that the heathen should rule over them: Wherefore should they say among the people, where is their God?

Have not the heathen got things in their own hands, so that they propose to rule over us? And they propose to blot out the Sabbath of the Lord and to rule over the world.

I think I have a word here that I had better read on that, perhaps. On page 17 of the testimony entitled, "To Brethren in Responsible Positions," I read these words: "The false sabbath is to be enforced by an oppressive law.

Satan and his angels are wide awake and intensely active, working with energy and perseverance through human instrumentalities to bring about *his purpose of obliterating the knowledge of God.*"

What is the Sabbath a sign of? That He is the Lord our God, and the Lord that sanctifies His people. Well, then, when that sign by which He is known to the people, is taken out of the way, they take *Him away* from *the knowledge of the people.* That is what they are after. And that thing is now done. I read before, "God's memorial has been torn down, and in its place a false sabbath stands before the world." All the power of the earth is now enlisted in that business. So they propose to blot out the knowledge of God from the world. Therefore we *need* to seek the Lord with all the heart, that the heathen shall not rule over us. Now let us see what He is going to do:

> Then will the Lord be jealous for His land, and pity His people. yea, the Lord will answer and say unto His people, Behold, I will send you corn, and wine, and oil, and ye shall be satisfied therewith.

What is that that He will send? What is the "oil"? "The oil of joy for mourning," "joy in the Holy Ghost." What is the "wine"? Jotham told us "wine that maketh glad the heart of God and man." Gladness, then, He will give. And what is the "corn"? The wheat, the grain, from which comes our bread, to sustain life and supply *strength*. Strength, then, also, will He give. Oh, then, thank the Lord. He will send us strength, and gladness and joy.

But to whom will He send it? When will He send it? When the people are gathered and the congregation assembled and the children and the babies, the elders, the bridegrooms and the brides, and the ministers – when we are gathered together as the testimony says, "in companies" seeking God with all the heart – *then it is,* that He will do what He says. Let us go at it as never before. It is a wonderful thing when the Lord promises that we *shall be satisfied* with what He is going to give. It is not according to our measure. How much is God satisfied that we should be satisfied with? Nothing short of everything He has, for He gave just that in Jesus Christ, and He does not want us to stop short of everything He has. Just as Brother Haskell read in that blessed testimony this morning – you remember what wonderful thing that was – that when we come as beggars, having no deserts of our own, then all is ours in one everlasting gift.

> And I will no more make you a reproach among the heathen: But I will remove far off from you the northern army, and will drive him into a land barren and desolate, with his face toward the east sea, and his hinder part toward the utmost sea, and his stink shall come up, and his ill savor shall come up, because he hath done great things.

The margin of this verse says, "He hath magnified to do great things." Who is it that "has magnified to do great things"? Who has all the power of the world in his hands? Satan. It is he who thinks he is going to do great things. Now let us see what the Lord will do just then.

> Fear not, O land; be glad and rejoice; for *the Lord will do great things.*

Why, brethren, we ought to be the gladdest people in the world that Satan *has* to do great things; for it follows inevitably that when Satan has got to do great things God is doing such great things, that Satan has to exert himself to save his credit. But even then he cannot save his credit, even though he has boasted before the world and the nations that he has all the power, his case gets so desperate at last that he has got to come himself. But we can be gladder than ever, because then *Jesus* comes *Himself*. But when is it that the Lord will do great things? – When this one, Satan, has magnified himself to do great things.

> Be not afraid, ye beasts of the field: for the pastures of the wilderness do spring, for the tree beareth her fruit, the fig tree and the vine do yield their strength. *Be glad then, ye children of Zion,* and rejoice in the Lord your God!

Why should we be discouraged? what is the use of it? What is the sense of it? Jesus said, "Lift up your heads!" and this says, "Be glad – and rejoice" And then says it over again. "Be glad then, ye children of Zion, and rejoice in the Lord your God." Let us do it. Brethren, I just tell you I don't know how to do anything else than be glad, for the Lord tells me to. And this is just as much the word of God as any other part of the word of God. And the creative power is in these words just as much as any other to put the gladness there and to put the rejoicing there, and it is gladness – it is rejoicing in the Lord.

"For he hath given you the former rain moderately, and he will cause to come down *for you* the rain, *the former rain, and the latter rain,* in the first month," or, as at the first, as some versions read.

Was that at Pentecost a moderate thing according to what God is going to do? Yes. He gave the former rain moderately.

But there is going to be a double portion at this time. If that was moderate, what do you suppose this is going to be? We can't imagine what that was. Let me read you a word in Vol. IV, p. 611:

> The Advent movement of 1840-44 was a glorious manifestation of the power of God, and the first angel's message was carried to every missionary station in the world, and in some countries there was the grandest religious interest which has been witnessed in any land since the Reformation of the sixteenth century, but *these are to be far exceeded by the mighty movement under the last warning of the third angel.*

Another testimony that has never been printed says, that this will come as suddenly as it did in 1844, and with "ten times the power."

But now about the Pentecost, we read from the same (611, of Vol. IV) as follows:

> The prophecies which were fulfilled in the outpouring of the former rain at the opening of the gospel, are again to be fulfilled in the latter rain at its close.

Now you see there are prophecies pertaining only to the latter rain, but the prophecies pertaining to the former rain are to be fulfilled *too,* in the giving of the latter rain. Then you see it is going to be double.

> Here are the times of refreshing to which the apostle Peter looked forward when he said, "Repent ye therefore and be converted, that your sins may be blotted out (in the investigative judgment), when the times of refreshing shall come from the presence of the Lord, and he shall send Jesus."

Does that mean that *we* shall repent and be converted? "Well," says one, "I was converted twenty years ago." All right, be converted now, too. I was converted nearly nineteen years ago, but it does not amount to that [the snap of the fingers] if I am not converted right now. It is no good to look 'way back there. Says one, "Do you mean to say that I was not converted?" Oh no, I do not mean anything of the kind. But I mean that if you depend upon that conversion 'way back there, it does not amount to anything. If you do not know how to repent any more, just take Jesus Christ and you will know. Any man who received the Lord Jesus Christ is a new creature.

> And the floors shall be full of wheat, and the fats shall overflow with wine and oil. And I will restore to you the years that the locust hath eaten, the cankerworm, and the caterpillar, and the palmerworm, my great army which I sent among you. And ye shall eat in plenty, and be satisfied, and praise the name of the Lord your God, that hath dealt wondrously with you: and my people shall never be ashamed.

Then praise the Lord. They will reproach us; they will call us names; they will make us as the filth and the off-scouring of the earth, and the despised of the despised; but God has said, "My people shall never be ashamed." And it means just that. But it does not stop there.

He says it over:

> And ye shall know that I am in the midst of Israel, and that I am the Lord your God, and none else: and my people shall never be ashamed.

Why I tell you, brethren, what is it that the Lord has not put into that chapter for us? See the encouragement, the blessedness, the promises! And when it is necessary for Him to repeat that "we shall never be ashamed" that means on the face of it that it will be the purpose of everything on earth to put us to shame.

But God has pledged His word that it shall not be done, and we shall never be ashamed.

> And it shall come to pass afterward, that I will pour out my Spirit upon all flesh; and your sons and your daughters shall prophesy, your old men shall dream dreams, your young men shall see visions!

Thank the Lord, He is not going to be content much longer with one prophet! He will have more. He has done a wonderful work with one. And having done such a great work with one, what in the world will He do when He gets a lot of them?

> And also upon the servants and upon the handmaids in those days will I pour out my Spirit. And I will show wonders in the heavens and in the earth, blood, and fire, and pillars of smoke. The sun shall be turned into darkness, and the moon into blood, before the great and terrible day of the Lord come. And it shall come to pass, that whosoever shall call on the name of the Lord shall be delivered: for in Mount Zion and in Jerusalem shall be deliverance, as the Lord hath said, *and in the remnant whom the Lord shall call.*

Where is going to be deliverance? "In the remnant whom the Lord shall call." But who is Satan making war against? The remnant. Who has Satan rallied all the powers of earth against? The remnant. Where is he directing all his force and efforts? Against the remnant. And right there is deliverance. Brethren, the best place in the world to be, is right where the devil is spending all his efforts, because there is deliverance. That is where the grace and power of Jesus Christ are, and Satan has got to rally all his hosts to make any show at all. That is the best place on earth to be, because Christ is there; God is there; and "my people shall never be ashamed."

Brethren, I am *awfully* glad of these things. I am just as glad as I can be of what the Lord says in that chapter, because it is all present truth you see. Every verse is right now, and tells such wondrous things. He is going to do such wondrous things; and all He asks of us is to seek Him with all the heart that we may have it all. If we seek Him with half the heart we cannot have it all. We want to seek Him with *all* the heart to get *all* He has. Let us do what the Lord says, and "Be glad and rejoice, ye children of Zion"; for "the Lord will do great things" and ye shall never be ashamed" and there is deliverance "in the remnant" that the devil is warring against with all his might.

Sermon 8

February 6, 1893

THE evidences have been given to us showing over and over that we stand in the very presence of the events that bring the end of the world. Over and over evidences have been presented from the Bible and the direct statements of the Lord, in testimony, that now is the time when we must have the power by which alone the message may be given to the world, to save such as will be saved from the ruin that comes from the events that are about us. Brethren, the dangers that threaten us as to the end of the world, persecutions, and those things from without are, and always are, very little compared with the dangers that hang over each individual in his individual experience. [Voices in the congregation: "That is so."] The greatest danger that there is about this congregation and with our people everywhere, is that they will not see the things which concern them individually, but will look more at the things that are without, and at the evidences of those things, than they will to see that their own hearts are right with God. They will look more at these things as a sort of theory than they will to have a living Christ within, in order that all those things may be living realities without, and that we may be prepared to meet them in the fear of God and the salvation of God. That is the greatest danger, as I said, that there is with this congregation who are here, and we may spread the congregation to take in every professed Sabbath-keeper in the world.

And now we have come, in the study of this subject, to the study of that part of it that comes right down to you and me as individuals – the things that you and I need to do, and the things that we need from God; to look at these things, and act upon them, in view of the salvation of God that is concerned in these things to you and me. To me, from what I know, and what I know that I know – to me this lesson and the next one are the most fearful of all that I have been brought to yet. I have not chosen them, and I dread them; but, brethren, as Brother Prescott brought before us the other night, it is no use to slight anything; it is no use for us to tamper with these things; it is no use for us to view these things lightly; it is no use for us to walk these days with our eyes shut and not knowing what our situation is. It is no use for us to have our expectations raised by the truth of God, as it does raise men's expectations, and we be expecting things to come, and yet difficulties in our own hearts and lives prevent those things doing us a particle of good when they do come. It is no use for us to do that, is it?

I say again that the lessons to which I have come, and which will have to be given – that is settled – are to me the most fearful, in the realities of the things which they tell, the situation in which they place us, of any that I have had anything to do with yet in my personal teaching. Then I can say again, I dread it; I dread it because of some of the consequences that I fear it will have, because of its not being received as it should be – with the heart and mind subdued before God, asking Him alone whether these things are so. Some things may not be pleasant for all to hear, as they are not pleasant for me to relate. They apply so personally to us as individuals. But, brethren, where we stand, and in the situation in which we stand, and in the fear of God, it has to be done.

And as it shall be done, I ask you, now to start with, do not place me up here as one who is separated from you and excluding myself from the things that may be presented. I am with you in all these things. I, with you, just as certainly, and just as much, need to be prepared to receive what God has to give us, as anybody else on earth. So I beg of you not to separate me from you in this matter. And if you see faults that you have committed, I shall see faults that I have committed, and please do not blame me if things are brought forth that expose faults that you have committed; please do not blame me as though I were judging you or finding fault with you. I shall simply state facts, and you who have a part in these things will each one know that it is a fact for himself; as when it concerns me and myself in these things, I shall know that it concerns me as a fact. What I want, brethren, is simply to seek God with you with all the heart, [Congregation: "Amen."] and to have everything out of the way, that God may give us what He has for us.

I shall not try, and you need not expect me to try, to go very fast, because I shall be willing to go just as slow as it may be, that we may consider all these things carefully. It will take these lessons to present what is in my mind, to be presented. So let us simply study these things together.

I will begin with the thought where we stopped last night. The thought was before us that the time has come when God has promised to give the early and latter rain. The time has come when we are to ask for it and to expect it. And we may keep in mind the lesson and the testimony that Brother Prescott brought before us the other night on the same subject.

I read tonight that passage that I referred to last night but did not have the book here. It is in *The Ministry of Peter and Conversion of Saul*, page 9. After telling about the outpouring of the Holy Spirit and the day of Pentecost and the results in the conversion of souls, etc., it says:

> This testimony in regard to the establishment of the Christian church is given us, not only as an important portion of sacred history, but also as a lesson. All who profess the name of Christ should be waiting, watching, and praying *with one heart. All differences should be put away,* and unity and tender love one for another pervade the whole.

> *Then* our prayers may go up together to our Heavenly Father with strong, earnest faith. *Then* we may wait with patience and hope for the fulfillment of the promise.

When does that "then" come in? When we are waiting, watching, and praying with one heart, and all differences put away, unity and tender love one for another pervading the whole.

Therefore, brethren, if there are any differences at all between you and any of the people on this earth, whether they are at this institute or not, it is time for you and me to get them out of the way. If the person is not here, so that you can go to him and talk it over, you write to him and tell him all about it, and tell him your position and what you are doing. You have no responsibility any further for him, whether he receives it or not. You have acted in the fear of God in what He tells *you* to do. [Question from someone in the congregation: "Do you mean people of the world, everybody?"] Yes, I say everybody, because if there are sins between me and people that are outside, they know it, and those differences will hinder our approach to them when we go with the message, though God should even give to us His Holy Spirit in the outpouring of the latter rain. Any difference, any enmity, anything of that kind that is between me and anybody of the world don't you see that will hinder me from approaching him with the message?

If we have cheated people, and have not been honest in our deal with the people and have not been honest in our transactions before the world, why for our soul's sake, brethren, let us straighten up.

And here in Battle Creek, perhaps there are people that have things of that kind to do toward the people of this city – I mean our own people, toward the people of this city. Our meetings are going on in this city for the people of this city, and it was told us here in the institute that it is expected that when the blessing of God would come upon this meeting, it was to be taken to the people of this city, and they are to share with us in this thing. Then I would say to the Seventh-day Adventists in this city, Straighten up where there are crooked things, for your own soul's sake and for the sake of souls whom God wants to save in this city, straighten up. If you have been cheating people, go and confess it to them and give back what you stole. If in your business transactions you have not been straight, if you have got anything in a grasping way, undo the wickedness. Stand straight in the sight of God.

Here is the word to us:

> All differences should be put away and unity and tender love one for another pervade the whole.

That is what the disciples were doing when they sought the Lord those ten days. They put away all differences.

Now don't you suppose that in those ten days that the other disciples who were so envious of James and John when they went and asked, by their mother, the Saviour to let them sit one on one side and the other on the other side of Him in the kingdom of God and the rest of the disciples did not like it – don't you suppose they put away all that thing, and confessed it and talked it over with one another and saw, themselves, how mean it all was?

The Saviour took that little child and said, Whosoever will be greatest in the kingdom of heaven shall become as this little child and shall become the servant of all. These things they were putting away, those differences and those envyings for fear that one would be greater in the kingdom of God than some of the other disciples were all put away. And we have the word here that those things are amongst us – ambition for place, jealousy of position, and envy of situation – those things are amongst us. Now the time has come to put them away. Now the time has come for each one to find how low he can get at the feet of Christ and not how high in the Conference or in the estimation of men or how high in the Conference Committee or General Conference Committee. That is not the question at all.

> All differences should be put away, and unity and tender love one for another pervade the whole.

As this pertains particularly to us, as brethren and sisters in the church, it becomes us if we know of any difference between us and anybody in this world to get it out of the way. No difference what it costs. That has nothing to do with it. It cannot cost our life if we do it; it *will* cost our life if we do not do it. That is settled. And when that is done, "then our prayers may go up together to our heavenly Father with strong, earnest faith." Yes, sir. When you know that you are clear in the sight of God, so far as anything is possible for you to get out of the way between you and your brethren and everything confessed to God that He has shown and we hold ourselves before Him as the erring, helpless, undone sinners that we are and see our need of what He has to give, THEN there are all His promises and they are for us and we know that they are *our* promises; THEN we can depend upon them and "THEN our prayers may go up together to our heavenly Father with strong, earnest faith. THEN we may wait with patience and hope the fulfillment of the promise."

That is what there is now to do. When that thing is done, when all those differences are put away, and unity prevails, and each one is seeking unity of heart and mind, then God has promised that we shall see eye to eye. The time has come; let us do it.

Again I read on page 9:

> The answer may come with sudden velocity and overpowering might; or it may be delayed for days and weeks and our faith receive a trial. But God knows how and when

to answer our prayer. It is our part of the work to put ourselves in connection with the divine channel. God is responsible for *His* part of the work.

Just as the thought came before us last night, when the channel is open and our prayers are ascending as they are described, then the channel is open, and when the Spirit of God is poured out, it will reach to the full length of the channel that is open.

> It is *our* part of the work to put ourselves in connection with the divine channel. God is responsible for *his* part of the work. He is faithful who hath promised. The great and important matter with us is to be of one heart and mind, putting aside all envy and malice and as humble supplicants to watch and wait. Jesus, our Representative and Head, is ready to do for us what He did for the praying, watching ones on the day of Pentecost.

Here is another thought that is worthy of our deep consideration:

> Jesus is as willing to impart courage and grace to His followers today as He was to the disciples of the early church. None should rashly invite an opportunity to battle with the principalities and powers of darkness.

We need to go into that thing carefully, with deliberation. We need to be sure and not go into that contest until we know God is with us, with the power and grace of God to give courage and strength to meet those powers with which we are to deal. This contest that is before us is no light thing.

> When God bids them engage in the conflict it will be time enough; He will then give the weak and hesitating, boldness and utterance beyond their hope or expectation.

So what the Lord wants us to do is to seek Him, and then when He sends us, we go with His power and grace only.

On page 11, I read:

> The disciples and apostles of Christ had a deep sense of their own inefficiency, and with humiliation and prayer they joined their weakness to His strength, their ignorance to His wisdom, their unworthiness to His righteousness, their poverty to His inexhaustible wealth. Thus strengthened and equipped, they hesitated not in the service of their Master.

What an equipment that is, though! Think of that equipment! Strength, wisdom, righteousness, wealth! Those are the very things that we need in the face of the things that are against us, for we cannot make any calculations upon any power of earth nor reputation that men will give nor upon any wealth that this world might furnish or any considerations of it or of life. So here are almost the very things enumerated that we considered in a previous lesson.

But how was it that they obtained strength? By acknowledging their weakness, confessing their weakness. How did they get wisdom? By confessing their ignorance.

How did they get righteousness? By confessing their unworthiness. How did they get wealth, inexhaustible wealth? By confessing their poverty. Now then that is the situation in which we are to be: inefficient, ignorant, poor, unworthy, and blind. Is not that just what the Laodicean message tells us – that we are wretched and miserable and poor and blind and naked and do not know it? Someone was reading that the other day and he touched upon that word "blindness," and immediately my mind ran to the ninth chapter of John and the last verse. All turn to that, if you will. John 9:41. It is at the end of the account of that man's healing from the blindness and restoration of sight to the man that had been born blind. What does that verse say?

> Jesus said unto them, If ye were blind, ye should have no sin; but now you say, We see. Therefore your sin remaineth.

When Jesus tells you and me we are blind, the thing for us to do is to say, "Lord, we are blind." He told those folks *they* were blind and they *were* blind, but they said it was not so. It *was* so. If they had confessed their blindness they would have seen God in that man's healing from his blindness. Well, then, brethren, the thing for us to do is to come square up to that Laodicean message and say that every word He says is so. When He says you and I are wretched, tell Him, "It is so, I *am* wretched; miserable; it is so, I *am* miserable; poor, it is so; I *am* poor, a perfect beggar, I shall never be anything else in the world; blind, I *am* blind, and shall never be anything else; naked, that is so; and I do not know it; that is so, too. I do not know it at all, as I ought to know it." And then I will say to Him every day and every hour, "Lord, that is all so. But, oh, instead of my wretchedness, give me thine own satisfaction. Instead of my misery, give me thine own comfort. Instead of my poverty, supply all thine own riches. Instead of my blindness, be thou my sight. Instead of my nakedness, oh, do thou clothe me with thine own righteousness. And what I know not, Lord, teach thou me." [Congregation: "Amen."]

Brethren, when we come with one heart and one mind to that place, we shall have no difficulty at all in repenting. It will not be difficult to repent and there will be no lack of repentance. That next verse will be fulfilled: "As many as I love, I rebuke and chasten. Be zealous therefore and repent."

The difficulty about our not being able to repent is that we have not confessed that what the Lord has told us is the truth. When I know that I am wretched then I know that I need something that will satisfy me. And I know that nothing but the Lord can give that, and I depend upon nothing but Him to give it. And if I have not Him, why it is only wretchedness. Any moment that I have not Him it is only wretchedness, and any moment that I have not His comfort it is only misery. Any moment that I have not absolute dependence upon His unsearchable riches – the unsearchable riches of Christ – I am utterly poor, a complete beggar. And every moment that I do not see and confess that I am blind and have Him as my sight, I am in sin. He says so.

"But now you say, you see; therefore your sin remaineth". And every moment that I do not see my nakedness and depend only and absolutely upon Him and His righteousness to clothe me, why so certainly I am ruined, utterly ruined, and every moment that I begin to say, "Now I know so much," no, I do not know that at all. Well, then, the thing that I am to do is to say, "Lord, I do not know it. I depend upon thee to teach me everything, even to teach me that I am wretched and miserable and poor and blind and naked and that I need all these things. And when I tell Him all that He will give all I need. He will do it. That is our situation.

Here is a passage in Volume I, of the regular edition of the *Testimonies for the Church* p. 353, which brings before us a wonderful thing:

> At the transfiguration Jesus was glorified by His Father. We hear Him say, "Now is the Son of man glorified and God is glorified in Him." Thus before His betrayal and crucifixion he was strengthened for His dreadful sufferings. As the members of the body of Christ approach the period of their last conflict, "the time of Jacob's trouble," they will grow up into Christ and will partake largely of His Spirit. As the third message swells to a loud cry and as great power and glory attend the closing work, the faithful people of God will partake of that glory. *It is the latter rain which revives and strengthens them to pass through the time of trouble.* Their faces will shine with the glory of that light which attends the third angel.

What is the loud cry for? To strengthen us for the time of trouble. Where are we? [Congregation: "In the loud cry."] Has the loud cry begun? [Congregation: "Yes."] What has it begun for? To do a work for us, to enable us to stand in the time of trouble. Now a little further in regard to that demand for unity. This that is before us – this call for the Loud Cry – the latter rain – it is this that strengthens us for the time of trouble. And it has already begun. There is the word. This is the one important thing – to be of one heart and mind.

Now from this testimony that has not yet been published, I will read a few passages:

> It is sin in some form that brings variance and disunion. The affections need transforming, a personal experience of the renewing power of Christ must be obtained. "In whom we have redemption through His blood, the forgiveness of sins, according to the riches of His grace." The apostle, speaking to Christian believers, called by God's grace, says: "If we walk in the light, as He is in the light, we have fellowship one with another, and the blood of Jesus Christ His son, cleanseth us from all sin." Here are conditions plainly stated. If we walk in the light as He is in the light, the sure result will follow; we shall have fellowship one with another. All jealousies, and envyings and evil surmisings will be put away. We shall live as in the sight of a holy God.

That is, we shall live now, today, each day, we shall live as in the sight of the holy God, because our prayers are going up to Him to bring His presence by the outpouring of

His Holy Spirit. And can we go carelessly on in this slip-shod way, knowing that there are envyings and jealousies and evil surmisings?

"It has become altogether too common to indulge our hereditary tendencies and natural inclinations, even in our religious life. These can never bring peace and love into the soul, for they always lead us away from God, away from His light. 'He that followeth me shall not walk in darkness but shall have the light of life.' When differences arise among brethren as to the understanding of any point of truth, there is one Bible rule to follow. In the spirit of meekness and love for God and one another, let brethren come together, and after earnest prayer, with sincere desire to know God's will, study the Bible with the spirit of a little child, to see how closely they can draw together and not sacrifice anything but their selfish dignity. They should regard themselves as in the presence of the whole universe of God, who are watching with intense interest as brother tries to see eye to eye with brother, to understand the words of Christ, that they may be doers of the word, and not hearers only."

What is the universe of God doing, brethren? They are watching to see you and me be brethren. They want to see us be brethren. That is what they are doing. They are watching to see you be brethren in the church – be brethren and sisters indeed. They are watching to see us see eye to eye. Now, brethren, let us not let them watch in vain.

> When you recall the prayer of Christ, that His disciples may be one as He was one with the Father, can you not see how intently all heaven is beholding the spirit you manifest toward one another? Are those who claim to be saved by the righteousness of Christ, seeking with all their entrusted capabilities to answer the Saviour's prayer? Will they grieve the Holy Spirit of God by indulging their own unconsecrated feelings, struggling for supremacy, and standing as far apart as possible? . . . The solemn important hours intervening between us and the judgment are not to be employed in warfare with believers.

Brethren, what have we to do to backbite and war against one another? The devil is making war against our brethren. Let us leave that for him. Let us love our brethren. Let us stand by our brethren. When a Seventh-day Adventist, even, attacks one of our brethren, let us defend him. Let us defend him in the fear of God. My brother's reputation is important to me, because if one will attack my brother's reputation to me, he will attack mine to my brother. If I listen to tales and all these things about my brethren, then why should not other people listen to them about me? No, sir, brethren, we have a care for the reputation of our brethren. Let us stand by our brethren one with another. We have a right to rebuke this tale-bearing that comes to you and me and wants to tell this, that, or the other, about the brethren. We have a right to rebuke it as the spirit of Satan, that it is. "The solemn, important hours." Important what? Days or years? No, sir. "The solemn, important *hours*." The days are gone. We are in hours, and it will not be long if we have not even now reached the time, when the *hours* will be gone and the *minutes* will begin to drop.

> The solemn, important hours intervening between us and the judgment are not to be employed in warfare with believers. This is Satan's work. He began it in heaven, and he has with unabated energy kept it up ever since his fall. "But if ye bite and devour one another, take heed that ye be not consumed one of another." Let there not be in any of you an evil heart of unbelief. The time has come when the cry of the faithful watchman is to be heard, calling to his fellow-watchman, "What of the night?" to be answered, "The morning cometh, and also the night."

The answer is not to be "I do not know what of the night." The answer is not to be, "Well, I think you are going too far ahead"; "I think you are going too fast"; "I think you are extreme." That is not to be the answer. When the call is, "Watchman, what of the night?" the only answer that God will accept is, "The morning cometh, and also the night"; then let us get ready for it.

> Would it not be well for us individually to examine closely our own position before God in the light of His holy word and see our own special peril?

Not see how good we are, not see how much better we are than our brethren, but "see our *own* special peril." What is *my* peril? That is enough for *me* to see, to watch for my own deviltry, and not watch for other people's.

> God does not separate from His people, but His people separate themselves from God by their own course of action. And I know of no sins greater in the sight of God than those of cherishing jealousy and hatred toward brethren, and turning the weapons of warfare against them.

How could there be any greater sins? Is not that Satan's own action?

> I point my brethren to Calvary. I ask you, What is the price of man? It is the only begotten Son of the infinite God. It is the price of all the heavenly treasures.

That is the price of man. Then can you and I set lightly by, one whom God prizes like that? One for whom God has given all the treasures of the universe. Can I set him lightly by and set him at naught and count him as of little worth? No, sir. He is worth all that God paid for him. That is what God paid for you. Am I going to count you little and mean and cheap? No, sir. I ask grace from God to enable me to count you worth all He paid for you. And I am not going to have Seventh-day Adventists, even, belittling you in my estimation. I am not going to do it. No, sir. I am not. How can I, if I love Christ who paid the price? Brethren, what is wanted is the love of Christ in our hearts, and then we will love all whom He loves as He loved them at the first.

> Evil is ever warring against good. And since we know that the conflict with the prince of darkness is constant, and must be severe, let us be united in the warfare.

Yes, sir. I need the support of every one whom Christ has bought. I need it in the warfare.

I need it to be successful in the warfare. I need it. And, brethren, I pledge myself before God that by His grace you shall have my support in your warfare. If you are overcome, I will lift you up. If you fail, I will say, "Be of good courage, brother." If you fall, I will say, "There is lifting up." Brethren, what God wants is for us to love one another as He has loved us, and we *shall* love one another as He has loved us. When we have *Him* – His love in our hearts – we *cannot* do anything else, and we wouldn't if we could.

> Cease to war against those of your own faith. Let no one help Satan in his work. We have all that we can do in another direction.

Brethren, let us stand together today, for it is God's work that He wants to do with us.

> A passive piety will not answer for this time. Let the passiveness be manifested where it is needed, *in patience, kindness, and forbearance*. But we must bear a decided message of warning to the world. The Prince of Peace thus proclaimed His work, "I came not to send peace on earth, but a sword." Evil must be assailed. Falsehood and error must be made to appear in their true character. Sin must be denounced. And the testimony of every believer in the truth *must be as one*. All your little differences which arouse the combative spirit among brethren, are devices of Satan to divert minds from the great and fearful issue before us.

Shall we allow Satan to cheat us? Brethren, you know that in the things of this world it is bad to be cheated, but when a man cheats you in the meanest little infinitesimal way, you feel worse about it than if he had done it in any other way, don't you? [Congregation: "Yes."] Now Satan stirs up these little differences that have not a particle of merit or principle in them, if they were carried out to their extreme. And yet he will get our eyes on these things and make a great commotion in the church and by that turns our minds off from these fearful issues that are hanging over our heads. Now, it is bad enough to be cheated at all, but when we allow ourselves to be cheated in such a mean, little, insignificant way as that, it is worse. Then let us quit.

> The true peace will come among God's people when through united zeal and earnest prayer the false peace, that exists to a large degree, is disturbed... Those who are under the influence of the spirit of God will not be fanatical but calm, steadfast, free from extravagance. But let all who have had the light of truth shining clear and distinct upon their pathway, *be careful how they cry,* Peace and safety. *Be careful* how you make the first move to suppress the messages of truth. *Be careful* what influence you exert at this time. Those who profess to believe the special truths for this time need to be converted and sanctified by the truth. As Christians we are made depositaries of sacred truth and we are not to keep the truth in the outer court but bring it into the sanctuary of the soul. Then the church will possess divine vitality throughout. The weak shall be as David and David as the angel of the Lord.

Then let us confess our weakness and find out as quickly as possible that we are weak. "The weak shall be as David," and their weakness is united to Christ's strength.

> One question will be all absorbing, – Who shall approach the nearest to the likeness of Christ.

That is the one thing, not who shall be greatest in the Conference, or who shall be greatest in the church or who shall have this or that position in the church or the Conference Committee. That is not it. But, "Who shall approach the nearest to the likeness of Christ?"

> Who shall do most to win souls to righteousness? *When this is the ambition of believers, contention is at an end; the prayer of Christ is answered.*

Brethren, that is where we are.

> When the Holy Spirit was poured out upon the early church, "The whole multitude of them that believed were of one heart and of one soul." *The Spirit of Christ made them one.* This is the fruit of abiding in Christ. But if dissension, envy, jealousy, and strife are the fruit we bear, it is not possible that we are abiding in Christ.

Then that passage that I have read a time or two:

> Jesus longs to bestow the heavenly endowment in large measure upon His people. . . How great and widespread must be the power of the prince of evil which can be subdued only by the mighty power of the Spirit. Disloyalty to God, transgression in every form, has spread over our world. *Those who would preserve their allegiance to God, who are active in His service,* become the mark of every shaft and weapon of hell.

That brings us right to the lessons we have had the previous evenings, – that we cannot stand at all if we have not Christ.

> If those who have had great light have not corresponding faith and obedience, they soon become leavened with the prevailing apostasy; another spirit controls them. While they have been exalted to heaven in point of opportunities and privileges, they are in a worse condition than the most zealous advocates of error.

"Those who have had great light," if they "have not corresponding faith and obedience," "are in a worse condition than the most zealous advocates of error." That is you and I. Judgment begins at the house of God. When those messengers went through the city to smite and slay utterly, he was counseled to begin at the ancient men before the house (Eze. 9:5-7), and if we are in a worse position "than the most zealous advocates of error," then the judgment *must* begin with us.

> There are many who have thus been preparing themselves for moral inefficiency in the great crisis.

We will stop right here with this lesson and take it up just there at the next lesson, as the time has expired.

Sermon 9

February 7, 1893

SOME have said they cannot see how a man can acknowledge himself to be wretched and miserable and poor and blind and naked, and don't know it and at the same time be rejoicing in the Lord. Well, *I* would like to know how anyone else can. I would like to know how a man is going to rejoice in the Lord when he thinks he is all right himself. Can you tell? I can't imagine. But when a man knows that he is what the Lord says he is, and acknowledges that, and then finds that the Lord is so good that He will take him just as he is and fit him to stand in the presence of God through all eternity, then that man has something to rejoice for. He can't do anything else.

Why, brethren, the Lord does not save us because we are so good, but because *He* is so good. Do not forget that. He does not save us nor bless us in the work of God at all because we are so good but because *He* is good and we are bad. And the blessedness of it is that He will bless us so much when we are so bad. And the rejoicing of the whole thing is that He saves us and makes us to reflect His own image, as bad as we are. *That* is where the rejoicing comes in.

Well, about understanding that – I cannot understand it, but I know it is so, and that is all I care for. It will take eternity to explain it so we can understand it, but as long as I know that *it is so,* I am not going to trouble myself and worry about *how* the Lord can do it or whether I can understand it. Are you? [Congregation: "No."]

There is another point right here that we may bear in mind – those who can't see that that is so. Brethren, you tell the Lord over and over that it is so, and then you will see it. You will not understand it then, but you will see it. You can't see *how* it can be, but you can see that it is a fact, and that is the only way you can. Can I see it as long as I keep myself from it? No. It is a thing that pertains to the heart, and you can't see it with your eyes. You must see it with your heart, and it is only the Spirit of God who gives the eyesalve that you can see it. Here is something that will – not *explain* it, but it will perhaps help you to get the idea a little better. In "*Testimony* No. 31," page 44, I read these words:

> Are you in Christ? Not if you do do not acknowledge yourselves erring, helpless, condemned sinners.

That is what some of the brethren say they can't see. They say, "I can't see how, if I am in Christ, I am to acknowledge myself a helpless, undone sinner. I thought if I was in Christ, then I could thank the Lord I was good, sinless, entirely perfect, sanctified, and all that." Why, no. He is. When you are in Christ, *He* is perfect; *He* is righteous; *He* is holy and never errs, and *His holiness is imputed to you* – is given to you. His faithfulness, His perfection *is mine,* but I am not *that.*

Perhaps you can get this thought a little more clearly by that word with which we are all familiar in 1 Cor. 1:30: "Who [Christ] of God is made unto us wisdom and righteousness and sanctification and redemption." Then where is my righteousness? –In Christ. Where is my wisdom? –In Christ. Where is my sanctification? –In Christ. Where is my redemption? –In Christ.

O yes, *but* when I come to Him for wisdom and ask Him for wisdom and He gives it to me, then can't I boast and say, "*I* am wise"? Why, no. Just the moment that I say that, I'm a bigger fool than I ever was before in this world. Because by yielding to the Lord He has deigned to stand by me, and so give me *His* wisdom, that it may lead me and guide me in wisdom's ways and that I should walk in the way that is right. His having done that, can *I* then pride *myself* upon it and say, "Now *I* am wise"? Don't you see, in the nature of things, that would be the biggest piece of foolishness that ever struck me. *He* did it; He helped me. He gave me *His* wisdom; *He was* my wisdom. When I did not walk wisely, He gave me His wisdom. His wisdom guided me. His wisdom took hold of my mind and heart and led me and kept me in wisdom's ways. Then *He* is my wisdom and *I* have no wisdom at all but *His* wisdom. Don't you see? Now you just get it that way and then you will know that it is a fact.

"I will guide thee with *mine* eye." When He says He guides me with *His* eye, I shall answer, it is His *eye* that guides you and me, and not our own eyes. Then the only thing to do is to just let ourselves go, utterly, completely, and let ourselves be His, utterly and completely, that He may be all, and in all of us.

Therefore *He* is our wisdom, our sanctification, our redemption, and our righteousness. Then He is my satisfaction where I am wretched. He is my comfort where I am miserable. He is my sight where I am blind. He is my riches where I am poor. And He is my knowledge where I do not know.

And now about that thought last night – some thought that I was going entirely too far. They could say, it is well enough when he says, "You are wretched," I say I am wretched. When He says, "You are poor," I say, I am poor. When He says, "You are blind," I say, I am blind And when He says, "You don't know it, then I am to say, "I *know* it"? No, no. When He says, "You don't know it," I am to say, "I *don't* know it." Do not go to putting constructions upon His way. When I say I am wretched and miserable and poor and blind and naked and on top of it He says that I don't know it, I say, "Lord, I don't know it."

That brings us right to the text we started with that night, "If any man *thinketh he knoweth anything,* he knoweth *nothing yet* as he ought to know it." I do not know yet, as long as I have been acknowledging that thing, yet, I know not how wretched and miserable and poor and blind and naked I am, if He should show myself just as I am. Just as certainly as we take that Laodicean message as He speaks it, we shall receive all He has in it. Then, brethren, that is what it is intended for. That is just what the Laodicean message is intended to do. Let it do its own work in *His* own way. Look here. Let us notice this testimony in Vol. 1, pages 186 and 187. This was given in 1859:

> I was shown that the testimony to the Laodiceans applies to God's people at the present time, and the reason it has not accomplished a greater work *is because of the hardness of their hearts*. But God has given the message time to do its work. The heart must be purified from sins which have so long shut out Jesus. *This fearful message will do its work*. When it was first presented, it led to close examination of heart.

That is what it is going to do at this time. Let it do its work then. But there has been an intervening time since it was first presented. I read further:

> Sins were confessed, and the people of God were stirred everywhere. Nearly all believed that this message would end in the loud cry of the third angel. But as they failed to see the powerful work accomplished *in a short time,* many lost the effects of the message.

They gave it up, as this testimony that has not yet been published says:

The sins of Israel must go to judgment before hand. Every sin must be confessed at the sanctuary. *Then the work will move;* it must be done *now*. The latter rain is coming on those that are pure – all, then, will receive it as formerly. None receive the latter rain but those who do all they can. Christ will help us. All could be overcomers by the grace of God through the blood of Jesus. All heaven is interested in the work. Angels are interested.

> God can make them a host against their enemies. *Ye give up too quick. Ye let go* too soon, that arm! The arm of God is mighty. Satan works in different ways to steal the mind off from God. Victory, victory! We must have it over every wrong. A solemn sinking into God. Get ready. Set thine house in order.

But when it was first presented, because it didn't do the work "in a short time," they said, "The time hasn't come," and so they gave up and missed it. Again I read from *Testimony*, Vol. 1, page 186:

> I saw that this message would not accomplish its work in a few short months. It is designed to *arouse* the people of God, to *discover to them their backslidings,* and to lead to *zealous repentance, that they may* be favored with *the presence of Jesus* and *be fitted for the loud cry* of the third angel. As this message affected the heart, it led to deep humility before God. Angels were sent in every direction to prepare unbelieving hearts for the truth.

That is where we are. While that message is preparing us for the loud cry, God is sending angels everywhere to prepare people for the truth. And when we go forth from this Conference with this message as it is now, the people will hear it.

> The cause of God began to rise, and his people were acquainted with their position. If the counsel of the True Witness *had been fully heeded,* God would have wrought for His people in greater power. Yet the efforts made since the message has been given, have been blessed of God, and many souls have been brought from error and darkness to rejoice in the truth. God will prove His people.

The particular point I wanted to read is this, that it is to prepare us that we "may be favored with the presence of Jesus, and be fitted for the loud cry of the third angel." Then what is it that fits us for the loud cry of the third angel? the Laodicean message.

Now, brethren, that place where I was reading last night gives us the reason why it is so important that we should have this anointing of the eyes with eyesalve *just now.* I had merely read the passage last night. I will read it again now for further use:

> If those who have had great light have not corresponding faith and obedience, they soon become leavened with the prevailing apostasy; another spirit controls them. While they have been exalted to heaven in point of opportunities and privileges, they are in a worse condition that the most zealous advocates of error. There are many who have thus been preparing themselves for moral inefficiency in the great crisis.

Have you "been preparing" yourself "for moral inefficiency" at this time? Have *I* been at that?

> They are wavering and undecided. Others who have not had so great light, who have never identified themselves with the truth, will under the influence of the Spirit respond to the light when it shines upon them. Truth that has lost its power upon those who have long slighted its precious teaching, appears beautiful and attractive to those who are ready to walk in the light.

What we want to study just now is the point, that *many* have "been preparing themselves for moral inefficiency in this great crisis." We want to inquire what that "moral inefficiency" amounts to, what the danger is, and how we got into it, don't we? If I am in that place, then don't I want to know what that means, that "moral inefficiency," what the danger is that is involved and how I got into it? The difficulty is, to get the people where they will see what they need. The Lord will take us out every time. He shows us the way. But the first thing we want is to understand the danger, and then how we got into that. Let us study that. Let us go at it, and we want to go at it in the same spirit that we studied this lesson last night, for it is all one lesson.

In Special Testimonies, "Danger in Adopting Worldly Policy in the Work of God," page 5 [see Testimonies to Ministers, pp. 460-471 – Publisher], I read these words:

> As far back as 1882, testimonies of the deepest interest on points of vital importance, were presented to our people, in regard to the work, and the spirit that should characterize the workers. Because these warnings have been neglected, the same evils that they pointed out have been cherished by many, hindering the progress of the work, and imperiling many souls. Those who are self-sufficient, who do not feel the necessity of constant prayer and watchfulness, *will be ensnared.* Through living faith and earnest prayer the sentinels of God must become *partakers of the divine nature,* or they will be found professedly working for God, but in reality giving their service to the prince of darkness.

Now that is a fearful position to be in. For a person to be thinking that he is "working for God" and yet his whole service is for the enemy! Who will be in that position? Those who have not earnest faith, who have not surrendered all and have not Christ. In other words, those who have not heeded the Laodicean message.

Further:

> Because their eyes are not anointed with the heavenly eyesalve, their understanding will be blinded, and they will be ignorant of the wonderfully specious devices of the enemy.

Brethren, we are in the time, and we shall be in it from this time to the end of the world, when we may be brought at any hour or any day to a place where if we wait to reason, we are lost. We will take the wrong side, just as certainly as we wait to reason, we will take the wrong side. We can discern it only by that heavenly eyesalve by which "Ye shall know the truth," and as soon as the thing is suggested you can see the way all before you.

We will be in places where the cause of God will hang upon what you or I shall say, and advantages that the enemy may have over us, will depend upon what you or I say. And in these times which are all the time, if you and I do not see and have the heavenly Spirit to give us the right word to say, we shall say the wrong word, and it will throw every one of our brethren on the defensive, and every soul of us will be at a disadvantage, because the enemy is getting to that place where he is scrutinizing every position we take.

The enemy is now watching every position we take, for the sole purpose of perverting it and to put us at a disadvantage. You and I need something more than human wisdom or our own reason to know how to take the right position. We will be in places where the honor of the cause will depend upon us. Questions will be asked that you never heard in your life before. Before a committee, legislature, or something of that kind – in some place where God has called us and given us an opportunity to spread the light and the truth – a question may be asked that you never heard in your life. You will have to know at that *instant* what answer to make, you will not have time to think or reason about it. Questions will be asked which, if you take time, and pause to reason about it, the probabilities are that the reasonableness of the thing would appear directly the opposite to what the Spirit of God would say about it, because His ways are not our ways.

And, brethren, I am not talking at random. Some of these things have actually been done, and today you and I are at a disadvantage, and there are burdens which have been put upon you and me that we shall have to bear, because of this very blindness of some Seventh-day Adventists. That is where we are. And when our enemies get hold of these things, if unfortunately, they shall, and bring them against you and me to compromise our position when we stand for the truth as it is in Christ, we shall simply have to repudiate the whole thing and declare that it is not the truth, although it came from a Seventh-day Adventist. It is a fearful position in which to be placed. I do not want to place you there, and I do not want you to place me there. Well, then you and I both need the heavenly anointing that we may know what to say and what to do at a moment's notice. "Anoint thine eyes that thou mayest see."

Here, on page 7, is the word:

> Those who believe the truth must be as faithful sentinels on the watchtower, or Satan will suggest specious reasonings to them, and they will give utterance to opinions that will betray sacred, holy trusts.

But what sacred, holy trusts have we? Is not the cause of God, the work of the third angel's message, is not that the only trust that we have? Then when you and I betray sacred, holy trusts, what are we betraying? We are betraying the third angel's message. And we are betraying every brother that we have, putting him at a disadvantage, selling him into the hands of the enemy. I would like to know why you and I do not need to walk straight.

A voice: Isn't there a passage where it says the Spirit of God will tell us what to say?

Elder Jones: Exactly, and that is the very point. This exhortation is that we should depend upon the Spirit of God and be sure we have that, not slight the teachings of the Spirit of God, nor the way of the Spirit of God. On page 13 a reference is made to Elijah:

> Does Elijah weaken before the king? Does he cringe and cower, and resort to flattery in order to mollify the feelings of the enraged ruler? Israel has perverted her way, and forsaken the path of allegiance to God, and now shall the prophet, to preserve his life, betray sacred, holy trusts? Does he prophesy smooth things to please the king and to obtain his favor? Will he evade the issue? Will he conceal from the king the true reason why the judgments of God are falling upon the land of Israel?

What does that mean to us? Are not we in the time of Elijah? Are not we to be driven out as Elijah was? Is not fire to come down from heaven *against* the truth as it came down there for the truth of God? Are not we to be driven out and to be protected by angels as was he? and to be translated as was he? Do we not stand as did he? Then do we not need to have the *faith* that he had? There is a very important word for us on this subject in *Testimony* No. 32, p. 139:

> Is Satan always thus to triumph? Oh, no! The light reflected from the cross of Calvary indicates that a greater work is to be done than our eyes have yet witnessed.
>
> The third angel, flying in the midst of heaven, and heralding the commandments of God and the testimony of Jesus, represents our work. The message loses none of its force in the angel's onward flight; for John sees it increasing in strength and power until the whole earth is lighted with its glory. The course of God's commandment-keeping people is onward, ever onward. The message of truth that we bear must go to nations, tongues, and peoples. Soon it will go with a loud voice and the earth will be lighted with its glory.

Now the word comes, not that it is soon to go, but that it is "begun" and "goes" with the loud voice.

> Are we preparing for this great outpouring of the Spirit of God? Human agencies are to be employed in this work. Zeal and energy must be intensified; talents that are rushing from inaction must be pressed into service. The voice that would say, "Wait. Do not allow yourself to have burdens imposed upon you," is the voice of the cowardly spies. We want Calebs now, who will press to the front – chieftains in Israel who with courageous words will make a strong report in favor of *immediate action.*

Who went into the land of Canaan? [Congregation: Caleb and Joshua.] The men who said they could go in. And because God was with them they went into the land when all the rest fell in the wilderness. They went with their perishing brethren, as they wandered because of their unbelief all the thirty-eight years. But God had promised, "You shall go in." Who will go into the land now? Has not the testimony been read to us that as Israel was on the borders of Canaan, so are we? Who shall go in? Those who "make a strong report in favor of immediate action." They will go in. God says so. It may be that the doubting, fearful ones will linger, and cause the cause of God to linger, but do not be afraid. God has promised that we shall go in; the Calebs shall go in. That is settled.

> When the selfish, ease-loving, panic-stricken people, fearing tall giants and inaccessible walls, clamor for retreat, let the voice of the Calebs be heard, even though the cowardly ones stand with stones in their hands, ready to beat them down for their testimony.

What are we here for? We have had in our lessons hitherto that we are not to be afraid of all the powers in this world and the powers of the enemies that will stand against us and against the cause of God. We have seen that in the lessons here. Now this brings us to the point where we are to stand faithful to the message of God and not be afraid of cowardly Seventh-day Adventists even. That is where God wants us to stand. He wants us to know what the message is now. He wants us to give the message as it is now, and if there are those who would beat you down with stones and clubs in their hands, and revile you or anything of the kind, thank God that now is the time for "immediate action."

Another word or two from this *Special Testimony*, p. 6:

> I was shown that the follies of Israel in the days of Samuel will be repeated among the people of God today, unless there is greater humility, less confidence in self, and more trust in the Lord God of Israel, the ruler of the people.

In the same chapter, I read again:

> They must be hewed by the prophets with reproof, warning, admonition, and advice, that they may be fashioned after the divine Pattern.

On page 4, I read again:

> The world is not to be our criterion. Let the Lord work; let the Lord's voice be heard. Those employed in any department of the work whereby the world may be transformed, must not enter into alliance with those who know not the truth. The world know not the Father or the Son, and they have no spiritual discernment as to the character of our work, as to what we shall do, or shall not do. We must obey the orders that come from above. We are not to hear the counsel or follow the plans suggested by unbelievers. Suggestions made by these who know not the work that God is doing for this time, will be such as to weaken the power of the instrumentalities of God. By accepting such suggestions, the counsel of Christ is set at naught.

What is that warning for? Is there any danger of our following worldly ways? If there were no danger, God would not have told us that there is. Is there any danger of our allying ourselves with, or taking up the pattern of, worldly organization and gets *himself* or *herself* at the head of it, and then because they have a little show of success because of "temperance" or "morality" or something of that kind, we think we have to copy after them and take up their plans.

God has something better than that. He wants us to listen to the plans that come from above. He has told us long ago that although some of these organizations might have things that were in themselves good enough – temperance he has mentioned as one of them – but as long as they are allied to the mark of the beast, Sunday institutions, working for that, and for laws to compel people, and to force the conscience, we cannot join with them. That testimony has been there all these eight years that I know of – nine years now nearly. What the Lord wants is us, and the question now is, at this time, Shall He have us? Shall He have us to use us? Shall we be fully submissive to His will? and listen for orders from above, and obey these orders?

There is a word on this point in Vol. I of the *Testimonies for the Church*, p. 183, speaking of the cause when the loud cry begins:

> All seemed to have a deep sense of their unworthiness and manifested entire submission to the will of God.

On page 2 of the Testimony, "Danger of Adopting Worldly Policy in the Work of God," I read these words:

> I have somewhat against thee, because thou hast left thy first love. Remember therefore from whence thou art fallen, and repent, and do the first works; or else I will come unto thee quickly and will remove thy candlestick out of his place, except thou repent. He who wept over impenitent Israel, noting their ignorance of God and of Christ their Redeemer, looked upon the heart of the work at Battle Creek. [But, brethren, *we* are in Battle Creek now and this means us. This same Redeemer is now looking upon us.] Great peril was about the people, but some knew it not. Unbelief and impenitence blinded their eyes, and they trusted to human wisdom in the guidance of the most important interests of the cause of God.

And from the Testimony entitled "To Brethren in Responsible Positions," p. 10, I read these words:

> The original apostasy began in a disbelief and denial of the truth. We are to fix the eye of faith steadfastly upon Jesus. When the days come, as they surely will, in which the law of God is made void, the zeal of the true and loyal should rise with the emergency, and should be the more warm and decided, and their testimony should be the more positive and unflinching.

And on page 12 we read:

> There are those who have prided themselves on their great caution in receiving "new light," as they term it, but they are blinded by the enemy and cannot discern the works and ways of God. Light, precious light, comes from heaven, and they array themselves against it. What next? These very ones will accept messages that God has not sent, and *thus will become even dangerous to the cause of God* because they set up false standards.

And again,

> They need the heavenly anointing that they may comprehend what is light and truth.

That means you and me. That means me especially. I tell you, a good thing to do if you have not done it yet, is to read that first-page article in the *Review* of February 7. It speaks quite fully on this subject. I will read a few sentences:

> To place ourselves in a position where we have an appearance of yielding, is a new position for this people. It is a new experience, a departure from the principles to which we have adhered, which have made us what we are today, a people whom God has prospered, a people who have the Lord of hosts with them. . . You who have a connection with sacred things, God bids you to be careful where you put your feet. He holds you accountable for the light of truth, that it shall shine forth in clear and distinct rays to the world. The world will never help you by its devices to let your light shine. . . All who hold the truth should hold it in righteousness and appreciate its value and sacredness. . . We need divine wisdom and skill that we may improve every opportunity that the providence of God shall prepare for the presentation of truth.

Improve the opportunity, not betray it, nor fail when the opportunity is offered because you are not prepared. What are we here for if we are not prepared? What are you and I as ministers – as Seventh-day Adventist ministers, ministers to carry the third angel's message – what are we here for, if we are not prepared, when God calls us and give us an opportunity?

> Let not the fear of man, the desire for patronage, be allowed to obscure a ray of heaven's light. Should the sentinels of truth now fail to sound the warning, they would be unworthy of their position as light-bearers to the world, but should the standard fall from their hands, the Lord would raise up others who would be faithful and loyal.
>
> It will require moral courage to do God's work unflinchingly. Those who do this can give no place to self-love, to selfish considerations, ambition, love of ease, or desire to shun the cross. . . Some may not apparently engage in the conflict on either side. They may not appear to take sides against the truth, but they will not come out boldly for Christ, through fear of losing property or suffering reproach. *All such are numbered with the enemies of Christ.*

The time has come when Christ's friends should be known. And if it is a Seventh-day Adventist that is called in question for his standing in Christ and the message, let your friendship in Christ be known by standing by Him.

Now we have a few minutes to talk upon how we got into this position, how these dangers came upon us.

You remember the other evening when I was reading that second chapter of Joel, that one of the brethren, when I had read that 23rd verse – Brother Corliss – called attention to the margin. Do you remember that? And I said we would have use for the margin at another time. Now all of you turn and read that margin. The 23rd verse says: "Be glad, then, ye children of Zion, and rejoice in the Lord your God: for he hath given you *the former rain,* moderately." What is the margin? "A teacher of righteousness." He hath given you "a teacher of righteousness." How? "According to righteousness." "And he will cause to come down for you the rain"; then what will that be? When He gave the former rain, what was it? "A teacher of righteousness." And when He gives the latter rain, what will it be? "A teacher of righteousness." How? "According to righteousness." Then is not that just what the testimony has told us in that article that has been read to you several times? "The loud cry of the third angel," the latter rain has already begun, "in the message *of the righteousness of Christ.*" Is not that what Joel told us long ago? Has not our eye been held that we did not see? Did not we need the anointing? Brethren, what in the world do we need so much as that? How glad we ought to be that God sent His own Spirit in the prophets to show us, when we did not see! How infinitely glad we ought to be for that!

Well then the latter rain – the loud cry – according to the testimony and according to the Scripture, is "the teaching of righteousness," and "according to righteousness," too.

Now brethren, when did that message of the righteousness of Christ, begin with us as a people? [One or two in the congregation: "Three or four years ago."] Which was it, three? or four? [Congregation: "Four."] Yes, four. *Where* was it? [Congregation: "Minneapolis."] What then did the brethren reject at Minneapolis? [Some in the congregation: "The loud cry."] What is that message of righteousness? The Testimony has told us what it is; the loud cry – the latter rain. Then what did the brethren in that fearful position in which they stood, reject at Minneapolis? They rejected the latter rain – the loud cry of the third angel's message.

Brethren, isn't it too bad? Of course the brethren did not know they were doing this, but the Spirit of the Lord was there to tell them they were doing it, was it not? But when they were rejecting the loud cry, "the teaching of righteousness," and then the Spirit of the Lord, by His prophet, stood there and told us what they were doing – what then? Oh, then they simply set this prophet aside with all the rest. That was the next thing. Brethren, it is time to think of these things. It is time to think soberly, to think carefully.

On page 8 of "Danger of Adopting Worldly Policy in the Work of God," I read the following:

> As man's Intercessor and Advocate, Jesus will lead all who are willing to be led, saying, "Follow me upward, step by step, *where the clear light of the Sun of Righteousness shines.*" But not all are following the light. Some are moving away from the safe path, which at every step is a path of humility. God has committed to His servants a message for this time; but this message does not in every particular coincide with the ideas of all the leading men, and some criticize the message and the messengers. *They dare even reject the words of reproof sent to them from God through His Holy Spirit.*

You know who it was. I do not mean for you to look to somebody else. You know whether you yourself were at it or not. And, brethren, the time has come to take up tonight what we there rejected. Not a soul of us has ever been able to dream yet the wonderful blessing that God had for us at Minneapolis and which we would have been enjoying these four years, if hearts had been ready to receive the message which God sent. We would have been four years ahead, we would have been in the midst of the wonders of the loud cry itself, tonight. Did not the Spirit of prophecy tell us there at that time that the blessing was hanging over our heads? Well, brethren, you know. Each one for himself. We are not to begin to examine one another, let us examine ourselves. Each one for himself knows what part he had in that thing, and the time has come to root up the whole business. Brethren, the time has come to root up the whole thing. I will read another passage upon that presently.

Again I read:

> What reserve power has the Lord with which to reach those who have cast aside His warnings and reproofs and have *accredited the testimonies of the Spirit of God to no higher*

> *source than human wisdom? In the Judgment, what can you who have done this offer to God as an excuse for turning from the evidence that He has given you that God was in the work? "By their fruits ye shall know them." I would not now rehearse before you the evidences given in the past two years of the dealings of God by His chosen servants.*

This testimony was given in the fall of 1890, on the 3rd of November. Two years from that takes us back to the fall of 1888 in the month of November, and that was at Minneapolis at the very time when this thing was done. There are a half a dozen brethren in this house, yes, perhaps a dozen of them, who, at another time, after Minneapolis, in an institute, heard the Spirit of God reprove and rebuke in open words that Minneapolis spirit that was in that Institute where we were and said plainly it was "the spirit of Satan." That was the next spring after Minneapolis had passed.

But I continue:

> But the present evidence of his working is revealed to you, and *you are now under obligation to believe.* You cannot neglect God's message of warning, you cannot reject them or treat them lightly but at the peril of infinite loss. Caviling, ridicule and misrepresentation can be indulged in only a the expense of the debasement of your own souls. The use of such weapons does not gain precious victories for you, but rather cheapens the mind, and separates the soul from God. Sacred things are brought down to the level of the common, and a condition of things is created that pleases the prince of darkness, and grieves away the Spirit of God. Caviling and criticism leaves the soul as devoid of the dew of grace as the hills of Gilboa were destitute of rain. Confidence cannot be placed in the judgment of those who indulge in ridicule and misrepresentation. No weight can be attached to their advice or resolutions. You must bear the divine credentials before you make decided movements to shape the working of God's cause.
>
> To accuse and criticize those whom God is using, is to accuse and criticize the Lord, who has sent them. All need to cultivate their religious faculties that they may have a right discernment of religious things. Some have failed to distinguish between pure gold and mere glitter, between the substance and the shadow.

Before I read the next paragraph I want to read two paragraphs from this testimony that has not yet been published:

> The false ideas that were largely developed at Minneapolis have not been entirely uprooted from some minds. Those who have not made thorough work of repentance under the light God has been pleased to give to His people since that time will not see things clearly and will be ready to call the messages God sends a delusion.

Brethren, what greater danger could there be before us than that into which we have been brought by the course here pointed out and against which it warns – the danger of our betraying sacred, holy trusts, the danger of betraying our brethren and bringing them into places and positions where they will have to bear fearful burdens that the enemy will lay upon us and persecute us with?

There is another statement on the same subject, that I will read:

> We should be the last people on the earth to indulge in the slightest degree the spirit of persecution against those who are bearing the message of God to the world. This is the most terrible feature of unchristlikeness that has manifested itself among us since the Minneapolis meeting. Sometime it will be seen in its true bearing with all the burden of woe that has resulted from it.

Brethren, God is getting in earnest about that thing. It is time for you and me to seek the Lord now, while mercy yet lingers that we may be able to see the burden of woe in all its enormity, while yet there is mercy to free us from it. God calls us to Himself.

Now this additional paragraph in the Special Testimonies:

> The prejudices and opinions that prevailed at Minneapolis are not dead by any means; the seeds sown there in some hearts are ready to spring into life and bear a like harvest. The tops have been cut down, but the roots have never been eradicated, and they still bear their unholy fruit to poison the judgment, pervert the perceptions and blind the understanding of those with whom you connect, in regard to the message and the messengers. When by thorough confession, you destroy the root of bitterness, you will see light in God's light. *Without this thorough work you will never clear your souls.*

Brethren, will you thus clear your souls and open the way for the Lord to send His Spirit in the outpouring of the latter rain?

> You need to study the word of God with a purpose, not to confirm your own ideas, but to bring them to be trimmed, to be condemned or approved, as they are or are not in harmony with the word of God. The Bible should be your constant companion. You should study the Testimonies, not to pick out certain sentences to use as you see fit, to strengthen your assertions, while you disregard the plainest statements given to correct your course of action.
>
> There has been a departure from God among us, and the zealous work of repentance and return to our first love, so essential to restoration to God and regeneration of heart, has not yet been done. Infidelity has been making its inroads into our ranks, for it is the fashion to depart from Christ and give place to skepticism. With many the cry of *the heart* has been, "We will not have this man to reign over us." Baal, Baal, is the choice. The religion of many among us will be *the religion of apostate Israel,* because they love their own way and forsake the way of the Lord. *The true religion,* the *only religion of the Bible,* that teaches forgiveness only through the merits of a crucified and risen Saviour, *that advocates righteousness by the faith of the Son of God,* has been slighted, spoken against, ridiculed, and rejected. It has been denounced as leading to enthusiasm and fanaticisms. *But it is the life of Jesus Christ in the soul; it is the active principle of love imparted by the Holy Spirit,* that alone will make the soul fruitful unto good works. The love of Christ is the force and power of every message from God that ever fell from human lips. What kind of future is before us, if we shall fail to come into the unity of the faith?

That was the question that was before us last night – the unity of the faith. When the early disciples came together as one and prayed as one, and saw eye to eye, then the Holy Spirit came upon them and that is the thing that is set before us now.

Brethren, I do not say these things to find fault, or to condemn, but I say them in the fear of God, that each one of us may know where we stand. And if there be any of those roots from Minneapolis lingering these four years or any caught from this and have been crops of this four years' standing, let us see that we here and now root up the whole thing and prostrate ourselves at the feet of Christ with only that one plea – "I am wretched, and miserable, and poor, and blind, and naked, and I do not know it." That is where we are.

I know that some there accepted it. Others rejected it entirely. You know the same thing. Others tried to stand half way between and get it that way, but that is not the way it is to be had, brethren, that is not the way it is received. They thought to take a middle course and although they did not exactly receive it or exactly commit themselves to it, yet they were willing to go whichever way the tide turned at the last, whichever way the body turned they were willing to go.

Since that time others have seen that God is moving the body of the cause forward in this very line and they have proposed to go along with the body as they see it moving that way. Brethren, you need to get that righteousness of Jesus Christ nearer to your heart than that. Every man needs to get the righteousness of God nearer to him than simply weighing up things and compromising between parties or he will never see or know the righteousness of God at all.

Others have apparently favored it and would speak favorably of it when everything was that way, but when in the fierceness of this spirit – this spirit described there as the persecuting spirit – when that spirit would rise up in its fierceness and make war upon the message of righteousness by faith, instead of standing nobly in the fear of God and declaring in the face of that attack, "It is the truth of God and I believe it in my soul," they would begin to yield, and in an apologetic way offer excuses for those who were preaching it, as though it were a matter only of men's persons, to be held in advantage because of admiration.

Brethren, the truth of God needs no apology. The man who preaches the truth of God needs no apology. The truth of God wants your *faith;* that is what it wants. All that the truth of God needs is that you and I shall believe it and receive it into our hearts and stand by it in the face of all the attacks that can be made upon it and let it be known that you do stand by the messengers whom God sends to preach, not because they are certain men, but because *God sends them* with a message.

That, however, is but a sample. There will be things to come that will be more surprising than that was to those at Minneapolis, more surprising than anything we have yet seen. And, brethren, we will be required to receive and preach *that* truth. But unless you and I have every fiber of that spirit rooted out of our hearts, we will treat that message and the messenger by whom it is sent, as God has declared we have treated this other message.

I will read the balance of this testimony in Volume 1 of the *Testimonies for the Church*, pages 186-7, and then close for tonight:

> God will prove His people. Jesus bears patiently with them and does not spew them out of His mouth in a moment. The angel said, "God is weighing His people." If the message had been of as short duration as many of us supposed, there would have been no time for them to develop character. Many moved from feeling, not from principle and faith, and this solemn, fearful message stirred them. It wrought upon their feelings and excited their fears but did not accomplish the work which God designed that it should. God reads the heart. Lest His people should be deceived in regard to themselves, He gives them time for the excitement to wear off, and then proves them to see if they will obey the counsel of the True Witness.

So, do not let us be weary of seeking God in this Conference and if the blessing does not come in a day, or a week or a month, let us keep on in the way, for God has said it shall come.

Again I read on page 187:

> God leads His people on, step by step. He brings them up to different points calculated to manifest what is in the heart. Some endure on one point but fall off at the next. At every advanced point the heart is tested and tried a little closer. If the professed people of God find their hearts opposed to this great work, *it should convince them that they have a work to do to overcome,* if they would not be spewed out of the mouth of the Lord. Said the angel, "*God will bring His work closer and closer* to test and prove *every one* of His people." Some are willing to receive one point, but when God brings them to another testing point, *they shrink from it and stand back,* because they find that it strikes directly at some cherished idol.

All this I myself have seen in individual cases, over and over, since the Minneapolis Conference.

> Here they have opportunity to see what is in their hearts that shuts out Jesus. They prize something higher than the truth and their hearts are not prepared to receive Jesus. Individuals are tested and proved a length of time to see if they will sacrifice their idols and heed the counsel of the True Witness. If any will not be purified through obeying the truth and overcome their selfishness, their pride, their passions, *the angels of God have the charge,* "They are joined to their idols; let them alone." And they pass on to their work, leaving these with their sinful traits unsubdued to the control of evil angels. Those who come up to *every point,* and *stand every test* and overcome, *be the price what*

> *it may,* have heeded the counsel of the True Witness and *they will receive the latter rain,* and thus be fitted *for translation.*

Brethren, that is where we are. Let us act like it. Let us thank the Lord that He is dealing with us still, to save us from our errors, to save us from our dangers, to keep us back from wrong courses, and to pour upon us the latter rain, that we may be translated. That is what the message means – translation – to you and me. Brethren, let us receive it with all the heart, and thank God for it.

Sermon 10

February 9, 1893

> I counsel thee to buy of me gold tried in the fire, that thou mayest be rich; and white raiment, that thou mayest be clothed, and that the shame of thy nakedness do not appear, and anoint thine eyes with eyesalve that thou mayest see. As many as I love, I rebuke and chasten: be zealous therefore, and repent. Behold, I stand at the door and knock: if any man hear my voice and open the door, I will come in unto him and will sup with him and he with me. Rev. 3:10-20.

This is the counsel we want to study tonight. I counsel thee. Who is this? [Congregation: "Christ."] What is He called in the 14th verse? [Congregation: "Faithful and True Witness."] He will make quite a good counselor will He? the faithful and true witness, the beginning of the creation of God, comes and counsels you and me. Isn't that a good deal of condescension, considering the place from whence the Counselor comes? That which we have been studying during the several lessons that are past, that which has come before us so constantly and so fully a few days past now, that word sent to the Laodicean church as to what we are and how we do not know it – that has come to us from every point of the compass, hasn't it, the last few days? It has come from every side and from every mouth that has spoken and the Lord with all the rest has spoken direct to us in the word that was read yesterday upon that very thing. Well, I suppose that all now are ready to confess that what He says is so. So I will not repeat any of that to-night.

He has told us that, and now if we confess that that is so, we shall be ready to take His counsel and appreciate it and will profit by His counsel, because it is only those persons whom He counsels. Those who receive His testimony, those who are spoken of just before this, He counsels those who are poor, wretched, miserable, blind and naked and do not know it – those that are lukewarm. That is the people to whom this counsel is given. Well, having been brought to that place by the word and testimony and in every way the Lord has dealt with us these days that are past, in all the lessons that have been given us, then He stoops down and counsels us. Isn't that so? Then, brethren, let us not be so slow to take this counsel as we were the other. Let us not be so slow to come to a place where we can adopt this, as we were to get into a place where we could adopt the other.

Well, then, He comes as a counselor from this time henceforth. Isn't that so? [Congregation: "Yes."] Then when you want to know whether you shall sell out your property I suppose you will go ask your brother what to do? [Congregation: "Ask the Counselor."] When you want to know what to do, you are going to ask some other man what to do, are you? Why, when I want to know what to do, how is any man to tell me, when, if he were in my place he would have to ask the same question as to what *he* would do? How am I going to get any help from him, when he himself does not know what he would do unless he were in the place where I am, and even then he would have to ask counsel for himself?

Perhaps this is the way I would do: I am only a common member of the church and I must go to the elder of the church or some one of more prominence and ask him what to do. But suppose he wants to know for himself, I suppose he must asks the president of the conference what to do.

Elder Boyd: Isn't there safety in the multitude of counselors?

Elder Jones: But suppose the president of the conference wanted to know and needed to ask, then he would have to ask the president of the General Conference, I suppose. But suppose the president of the General Conference wants to know – who shall he ask? [Congregation: "Ask the Lord."] Oh, well, you can ask the Lord, can you? So, then, we common people can get our knowledge from the Lord without straining it through half a dozen persons like the other Catholics? Can we? [Congregation: "Yes."] Is that so? [Congregation: "Yes."] In the Catholic church the common people cannot get at the Lord except through the priest and the priest through the bishop and the bishop through the archbishop and the archbishop through the cardinal and the cardinal through the pope? Is that the way the Lord's people are to do? No, sir. That isn't God's method. When you want to know a thing, you ask the Lord. He is your Counselor, and He is my Counselor. And when He is your Counselor, *then,* Brother Boyd, "in the multitude of counselors there is safety," and *not until then* either, because then we have counsel of the Master of Assemblies. And when He is the Counselor of each one and then we counsel together and *He* is in the midst, then there is safety in the multitude of counselors.

You will find a sentence in *Gospel Workers*, like this:

> "We are to counsel together and to be subject one to another, but *at the same* time we are to exercise the ability God has given us in order to learn what is truth. Each one of us must look to God for divine enlightenment." "After you have received counsel from the wise, the judicious, *there is yet a Counselor* whose wisdom is unerring. Fail not to present your case before Him and entreat His directions. He has promised that if you lack wisdom and ask of Him, He will give it to you liberally and upbraid not." *pp.* 129, 257.

Then I ask again from this night henceforth, Is He your counselor? Is He individually our counselor? [Congregation: "Yes."] And the word that we heard from Brother

Underwood on this same subject, especially in the selling of property, "if there were more of this seeking the Lord for His guidance, there would be more of His direction." We would have more of Him in our work and in our counsels. What in the world did He make Himself our Counselor for, if He did not expect we should have His counsel? Then let us have it.

What is His name? [Congregation: "Wonderful Counselor."] The way it is printed is, "Wonderful, Counselor, Mighty God, Everlasting Father, the Prince of Peace." That is the name whereby He shall be called. What is the first part of His name? [Congregation: "Wonderful."] The second part? [Congregation: "Counselor."] What the next part? [Congregation: "Mighty God."] Next part? [Congregation: Everlasting Father."] And the last? [Congregation: "Prince of Peace."] He is "Wonderful" and Counselor"; then isn't He a wonderful counselor? [Congregation: "Yes."] I should say so. You will also remember that other passage, "wonderful in counsel." And what else? "Excellent in working." Don't forget that when He comes as a counselor He is there as a worker, too, and the counsel which He gives is as a worker and as an excellent worker, who will perform the work, "for it is God which worketh in you, both to will and to do of His good pleasure."

So now we have this counselor, the faithful and true witness, the wonderful counselor, wonderful in counsel and excellent in working. Then when we have sought this counsel and obtained it, He is to go right with us in the execution of the counsel as well as be there to give it at first. Isn't that so? If we have not learned that, there is no use for us to go any further at all, unless we do depend fully upon His power, His character, His righteousness and His life. Because if there be any other consideration and any other way which we are to take, we might just as well give up right now and stop. That being so, we could not go any further without Him. Very good then, He is the Wonderful Counselor; wonderful in counsel and excellent in working, and He says, I am with you to counsel; I am with you to execute.

"I counsel thee to buy of me gold tried in the fire." Other scriptures besides this passage show that nothing will satisfy us but that gold which will stand the test of the fire. You will remember 1 Peter 1:4,5, speaking of the living hope unto which God has begotten us by the resurrection of Jesus Christ from the dead, and how we are kept by the power of God through faith unto salvation. How are we kept? [Congregation: "By the power of God."] Through what? [Congregation: "Faith."] Unto what? [Congregation: "Salvation."] When? [Congregation: "Ready to be revealed at the last time."] We might now read, "Ready to be revealed," and could stop right there, and it would be so, for we have come to the "last time." But this hope. How are we kept? [Congregation: "By the power of God."] Through what? [Congregation: "Through faith."] Wherein ye – do what? [Congregation: "Greatly rejoice."] Do you now? I want to know now, is that so? [Congregation: "Yes, yes."] "Wherein ye greatly rejoice." Do you? Then why do you go moping around with your face drawn down? The time has come for us to believe the Scriptures.

Abraham believed God and it was counted to him for righteousness. The Lord said it, and he greatly rejoiced that it was so. Is that so tonight, that we greatly rejoice? [Congregation: "Yes."]

"Wherein ye greatly rejoice though now for a season if need be we are in heaviness through manifold temptations." what is manifold? [Congregation: "Many fold."] We are in many fold temptations and greatly rejoice all that time. How can that be? It can be because God says so. And it is so, is it? That is the only way I know it can be, because He says it is so. Now what is this for? "That the trial of your faith being much more precious than gold that perisheth, though it be tried with fire" What is tried? [Congregation: "Faith."] Are you to expect your faith to be tried as with fire? Are you to expect your faith to endure that test as gold passing through fire? [Congregation: "Yes."]

We will study this further. What care men take in this world of the gold that perisheth! Many hoard a great deal of gold, and great buildings are erected – safe deposits, then they have a little box, and lock it, put it in a bigger box, and lock that, and put it in a great safe with lots of boxes, and that is locked again, and then a great steel gate shuts up the whole thing, and that is locked, and a guard walks around it all night to see that it is safe. Hundreds of people in these large cities are thus caring for the gold that perisheth. Let me say to you, my brethren and sisters, the trial of your faith, I care not how weak it may be, is more precious in the sight of our Wonderful Counselor, is more precious in the sight of God, than all the gold and jewels in all the safe deposit vaults that are on earth.

Do not be afraid that He is going to forget it. What does He call it? More precious than gold that perisheth. Who is it that says that? The Wonderful Counselor, the Lord Himself. Let us then thank Him that He regards our weak, trembling faith like that. Well then, brethren, haven't we right there one of the greatest possible encouragements that the Lord can offer? Why people bewail their weak faith, I do not know. Sometimes you say, "I haven't any faith." Well, the Lord says you have, and I say, Thank Him for what you have. I do not care how little you have, though it be like the mustard seed, thank Him that you have it and thank Him that it is more precious to Him than all the gold and wealth of this earth. That is the way the Lord regards your faith.

You are not to question whether you have faith or not. God says you have it, and it is so.

Let us read Romans 10:6-8: "But the righteousness which is of faith speaketh on this wise, Say not in thine heart, who shall ascend into heaven? (that is, to bring Christ down from above) Or, Who shall descend into the deep? (that is, to bring up Christ again from the dead.) But what saith it? The word is nigh thee, even in thy mouth, and in thy heart: that is, the word of faith, which we preach."

Then it is right to bewail and wonder whether we have faith or not? Not so. God has planted faith in every heart that is born into this world, by that Light which lighteth every man which cometh into the world. God will cause that faith to grow exceedingly and He will reveal His righteousness unto us as it grows, "from faith to faith." Where does faith come from, anyway? God gave it to us. Who is the Author of faith? Christ, and that light which lighteth every man which cometh into the world is Jesus Christ. This is the faith that is in every man's heart. If each one uses the faith which he has, he will never have any lack of faith, but if he will not use the faith that he has, how in the world is he going to get any more?

Then we have faith, have we not? And the trial of your faith is "more precious" than all the gold that ever was on this earth. Mark you, it is more precious in the sight of God. Not that gold is precious in His sight – that is not the thought at all. It is more precious in the sight of God than all the gold would be *in the sight of a man.* How precious would all the gold be if a man had it all? Would not he think himself rich? would not he pride himself upon it wonderfully? Then do not forget that the trial of that faith which you have – no matter how small it may be – is more precious in the sight of God than all the gold of this world would be in the sight of a man. So then "the trial of your faith, being much more precious than of gold which perisheth, though it be tried with fire," is precious in the sight of God. Who is the most interested in that process? [Congregation: "The Lord."] Assuredly! For I cannot express how precious it is in His sight. My idea of how precious it is in His sight is just as far from the reality of it as my thoughts are from His thoughts.

Consequently He is the most interested person in all the universe in the trial of our faith, in the working of our faith, and all the process of it. Isn't it a gift from Him? Isn't it to His interest? This is the true light, in which we should view this matter.

Then we read further: "Though it be tried with fire, might be found unto praise and honor and glory at the appearing of Jesus Christ, whom having not seen, ye love." Do we not? He says we do, and it is so. "In whom, though now ye see him not, yet believing, ye rejoice with joy unspeakable and full of glory." Is not that so? Assuredly it is. But, brethren, I often think of that verse "Whom having *not seen,* ye love," and believing it is so, I wonder what in the world it will be when *we see Him?* And the blessedness of it is, we will not have to wait long for that now. [Congregation: "Praise the Lord."]

There is another passage I will refer to, found in the 12th verse of the 4th chapter of 1 Peter: "Beloved." Who? "Beloved." Is that so? Why, brethren, how can we be anything else than the gladdest people on the earth, when God talks to us like that? He comes and makes Himself the Wonderful Counselor and wants to counsel and talk with us and the first word He says is, "Beloved." Now we have thought many a time that when the angel came to Daniel directly, and said, "O man greatly beloved," that that was quite a personal statement. It can be no more personal than this is to you and me. He comes Himself and says, "Beloved."

Then, "think it not strange concerning the fiery trial which is to try you, as though some strange thing happened unto you." The word to us now, brethren, is, "beloved." Let us use the word in that way. Beloved, we are to treat the fiery trials as strangers henceforth? There is nothing strange about it. Then it will not surprise us when we meet them. You know a great many people are somewhat diffident and bashful and when they meet a stranger suddenly face to face they are quite out of countenance. Now if you and I are going to be diffident and bashful about the trials – we are going to come face to face with some of them one of these days, a brawny one – and then if we are diffident and bashful at all, we will be put out of countenance. But just as certainly as anybody is put out of countenance by a trial, just so certainly the enemy has got the victory there. That is the way he wants to catch us off our guard, so that we will be startled and put out of countenance for even a moment, and he will get in his fiery darts and wound us.

The Lord comes and counsels us like this: "Think it not strange." So then when we meet these fiery trials we are not going to meet a stranger. Do you see? We will be acquainted. We will know them. I do not care how bashful or diffident a person is, when he meets an acquaintance he is not astonished at any sudden meeting. He will not be put out of countenance, but he is glad to meet his acquaintance.

Then the Lord wants us to be so well acquainted with fiery trials that, no matter how suddenly we meet them, we can say, "All right, glad to meet you, sir. I know you, come along." Then when he tells us this, let us not think it strange concerning the fiery trials "as though some strange thing happened" unto us. We are not to meet them and deal with them as strangers, but as acquaintances. Not only that, but we are to meet them as helpers on to Zion.

James told us long ago, "My brethren, count it all joy" when we fall into divers temptations. What did he call us there? "My brethren." James 1:2. He calls us "My brethren" here, and other places we are called "Beloved." What does "divers" mean? Different. What does Peter call it? "Manifold." Then, my brethren, count it all joy when we all into "divers," diverse, different, and various kinds of temptations. So we see by these different definitions that the thought it, count it all joy when we fall into *all* kinds of temptations, and we will count none of them strange, because we are to regard them all as acquaintances.

We read further: "But rejoice, inasmuch as ye" – shall be partakers? Oh no, but "rejoice, inasmuch as ye *are* partakers of Christ's sufferings." That is the point. In James he says, "My brethren." Now let us read a text that will connect both of them. Heb. 2:10-12:

> For it became him, for whom are all things and by whom are all things, in bringing many sons unto glory, to make the captain of their salvation perfect through sufferings. For both he that sanctifieth and they who are sanctified are all of one: for which cause he is not ashamed to call them *brethren*.

This is why He calls us brethren, and why we are to count it all joy when we fall into divers temptations; for He has been there. He has met every one of them. He has met each temptation to its fullest extent. He has passed through all these things *for* us. Then He comes back and says to us, I will pass through them *with* you. He passed through them alone *for* us first; now He passes through them *with* us. "I have trodden the winepress alone, and of the people there was none with me." But thank the Lord, God was with Him, for "the Father hath not left me alone." Thank the Lord that He had the royal courage to do it alone, trusting only the father to be with Him. And oh, how good He is, not to ask us to try it alone. No. He comes and says, I will go with you through all these trials. My brethren, He will go with you. So then this is why we are not to count them strange. He calls us His brethren, and He has passed through every one of these trials and is well acquainted with them, and therefore we are not to count them strangers.

Is Christ a stranger to trials? No. How many trials did He meet? All. How many trials that you will ever meet, did He meet? Every one of them. To what extent did He bear the contest upon each one of the temptations? To the fullest extent on each point. With whom was He contending on these things? Satan. Satan knows more tricks and trials and temptations than any man would ever be obliged to meet alone, doesn't he? And he tried every one of them on "my Brother," did he not? He tried every temptation on Jesus. To what extent of his effort did he have to try each of them on Jesus? To the fullest extent. Did he not have to exert all the power he knows on each single point in the temptations and trials of Jesus? He did. Did not Satan try everything that he knows in every way that he could possibly invent, on him? And did not he try it to the fullest possible extent that he could try it? Yes. Well, then, has not all his reservoir of trickery, of temptation, and trial, been exhausted on Christ? And has he not exhausted all the power that he has to use in any of these trials and temptations? Yes. Well, then, when I am in Jesus, and when He is in me, how much power has Satan left to affect me with? [Congregation: "None."] How many remaining tricks does he know to play on me? There are none. Do you not see, then, that when we are in Christ we *have* the victory; we have it *now*. Victory is not the only word; we have the triumph, and we have it now.

Now 2 Cor. 2:14: "Now thanks be unto God." When? Now. "Which always causeth us to triumph." When? Always. Is that so [Congregation: "Yes."] "Always causeth us to triumph in Christ, and maketh manifest the savor of his knowledge." How? By us. Is that so? And maketh manifest the savor of his knowledge by us." Where? [Congregation: "In every place."] Think of it. When is it? Now and always, that is when. How? By us. Where? Everywhere. Then I would like to know what in the world is the reason we have not the victory in Christ. I would like to know what in the world is the reason we are not conquerors now. "This is the victory that overcometh the world, even our faith." Is it? Yes, that is the victory. Christ is our victory. His victory is my victory, isn't it? Yes. Well, then, when we are in Him we are perfectly safe, are we not? Are we safe as long as we are in Him? Yes.

Do you not remember way back in olden times they had cities of refuge and when some accident happened, as when an ax flew off the handle and struck a man and killed him, and there was another man present as a friend standing by, who perhaps might not take time to think deliberately but would fly into a passion and would go about to take revenge in that matter right off. What was the man to do? He was just to strike out with all his might for the city of refuge and perhaps the other man after him with all his might. But if he got in there, then what? He was safe and the other man could not touch him, and he was perfectly free. Suppose he went out of town? Just as certain as he went out and that other man found him, his blood was upon his own head. He was responsible. But he was safe there as long as he stayed in the refuge. And he was to stay there until the high priest died. When the high priest died, the man was perfectly free, and he could go out anywhere and the other man could not touch him at all, no matter how much he wanted to.

Speaking of Abraham, it is said, "By two immutable things in which it is impossible for God to lie, we might have strong consolation who have fled for refuge." We have done mischief. We have sinned. What are the wages of sin? Death? Death. Then who is after us? Death. Who had the power of death? Satan. Then who is after us? Satan. And we fled for refuge to lay hold on that hope set before us. Where is that hope? [Ans: "In Christ."] Who is our refuge? [Ans.: "In Christ."] Who is our city of refuge? [Ans.: "Christ."] Who is our enemy? [Ans.: "Satan," "death."] Now then, when we are in Christ, our refuge, can Satan touch us? He cannot. How do you know? It says so. Suppose we go out before the priesthood closes, what then? Satan can, and he will smite us, and our blood will be on our head. If we go out before the priesthood closes, we have no protection and he will take us. If that man would remain in the city ten or fifteen years he would have grown strong enough to meet his enemy, wouldn't he? He would have got experience there, and therefore he could say, "I am strong enough now I am not afraid of any enemy; now I can go out. I can go out now, I am all right. That other fellow has gone away now and forgotten all about this." But he is not able to meet the enemy, is he? Where is he able alone to meet the enemy? In the city. And in the city he does not have to meet him at all, does he? [Voice: "The city meets him."] The walls of the city meet the enemy. That shield of faith that quenches all the fiery darts of the wicked – that shield of faith which is Jesus Christ, is the walls of our city of refuge, and the fiery darts of the enemy cannot get past it at all.

Well then our strength and our safety forever, is only inside of our refuge, isn't it? And then when the priesthood closes, we can go everywhere in this universe – but not outside of Christ. Then we can go everywhere, and can the enemy do us any damage? No, sir. Let us stay in the City, brethren; let us stay in the refuge to which we have fled, where our safety is. And when we are there haven't we the victory? Yes, sir. In Him we have the victory. We can meet the temptation then with joy. Why, we have the victory before we meet temptation, haven't we? Then cannot we be glad? Wouldn't you rather have a battle when you know you have a victory before you start in, than to have no battle at all? Then let us do some of that kind of fighting. Come on, what is the use of being afraid? The victory is ours.

Of course if we go in, calculating to be whipped, we had better not fight. The one who goes in expecting to be whipped had better run before he begins. The Lord does not want us to make such a fight as that. Our Brother did not make such a fight as that. No, sir. And He doesn't propose that we shall. He wants us to know our victory. He wants us to know our confidence. He wants us to know our strength; He wants us to know the power that is ours and He wants us to know our duty. And then, when the contest comes, we will know how to meet it. We meet it in Him. We meet it by Him. We meet it with the shield of faith and the fiery darts of the enemy are quenched, and there is no question about it. Then it is in suffering, where we meet the power, the victory, and the elevating presence of Christ. When the trials come we stand with Him and we know that we cannot stand without Him. "Count it all joy"; let us do it. Think it not strange when the fiery trials come as though some strange thing happened unto you, but rejoice. "Rejoice forasmuch as ye are partakers of Christ's suffering, that when His glory shall be revealed in you, ye shall be glad also with exceeding joy."

Then we need gold tried in the fire, to meet these trials, do we not? We need something that will stand the tests that will come, and this is what we have learned before. "Those who bear every test have heeded the testimony of the True Witness, and will receive the latter rain that they may be translated." Brethren, is there not a lot of good cheer in the thought that it is for that, that the latter rain is to prepare for translation? No, where is the latter rain to fall, and when does it? Now is the time for the latter rain: and when is the time for the loud cry? [Voice: "Now."] What is it to prepare us for? [Voice: "For translation."] It brings good cheer to me that the tests that the Lord is giving us now, are to fit us for translation. And when He comes and speaks to you and me, it is because He wants to translate us, but He cannot translate sin, can He? Then the only purpose that He has in showing us the depth and breadth of sin is that He may save us from it and translate us. Then, shall we become discouraged when He shows us our sins? No. Let us thank Him that He wants to translate us and He wants to do this so much that He wishes to get our sins out of the way as soon as possible. Brethren, let us believe the Lord right along, all the time.

Then we need something that will bear as severe a test when tried, as gold is required to bear in purifying it in the fire. What does the Counselor tell us to get? What does He tell us to buy? [Voice: "Gold tried in the fire."] That very thing is needed right now in order to meet the trials that are coming. No, the trials that *are here*. We do not care for what is coming, we need that now. We need that to meet the trials that are here, and that is the very thing that the Counselor says: "Buy of me, I have a supply." He has a supply, for He has manufactured it. He has the thing that will bear the test, for it has already borne the test. It has borne every test that will ever be required of anybody again.

The test was born in His sufferings. Through sufferings the gold is purified, made white, tried and perfected and proven to be the genuine article. We have the definition of that by the Spirit of the Lord. Gold tried in the fire is love, it is "faith and love." Read Gal. 5:6: "for in Jesus Christ neither circumcision availeth anything nor uncircumcision, but *faith* which worketh *by love.*" In other places it is expressed "faith and obedience." What is obedience? [Voice: "The expression of love."] In Steps to Christ, p. 64: "*Obedience is* not a mere outward compliance, but *the service of love.*" Then, when the testimony speaks of faith and obedience, it is simply "faith which works by love." The expressions in the testimony of "faith and obedience" and "faith and love" mean the same thing as the expression of the Scripture "faith which worketh by love." They are simply different modes of expressing genuine, spiritual faith, for in Christ nothing availeth but "faith which works by love."

Obedience is the service of love, and Jesus tells us to buy of Him gold tried in the fire, which is faith and love, the faith which works by love, the genuine article of faith. What is it that is to be tried with severe fiery trials? Your *faith* which is more precious than gold, though it be tried in the fire. Then, you see, as every man's faith is to be so tried, he needs the faith that has stood the trial. Then we have the testimony: "Here are they which keep the commandments of God and" – *have faith in Jesus?* No. The *have* is not in there. They keep the commandments of God and [keep] the faith of Jesus.

That is the genuine article; that is the faith which, in Him, endured the test. That is the faith which met every fiery trial that Satan knows, and all the power that Satan could rally, that faith endured the test. So then, He comes and says to us, "You buy of me that faith that has endured the test, "gold tried in the fire." So, in the expression "buy of me that faith that has endured," is not that the same line of thought that we have learned in "Let this mind be in you that was also in Christ Jesus"?

When that mind is in me that was in Him, will not that mind do in me precisely what it did in Him? How is it that we serve the law of God, anyhow? "With the mind I serve the law of God." Rom. 7:25. Christ in this world, every moment served the law of God. How did He do it? With the mind. By what process of the mind did He do it? By faith. Then, does He not tell you and me to buy of Him the faith of Jesus? Did not the faith of Jesus keep the commandments of God perfectly, all the time? And is not that the faith that works by love? Love is the fulfilling of the law. Then is not that the third angel's message, when He says, "Come and buy of me gold tried in the fire, (love and faith) and white raiment (righteousness of Christ) that thou mayest be clothed, that the shame of thy nakedness do not appear"? So, we see how it is now that the mind that was in Christ will stand all of the trials that this world can bring. Is not the mind of Christ the same yesterday, today, and forever? Will the mind of Christ in Him do differently from the mind of Christ in me or in any other man? No. The mind of Christ was whose mind? [Voice: "The mind of God."] God was in Him in the flesh.

How shall we buy? Read Isa. 55:1: "Ho, everyone that thirsteth." Brethren, have we not become pretty thirsty by all that the Lord has said in the last few days? I know brethren who have come to me and talked and they were just about perishing of thirst, they were almost ready to drop of thirst. Then these words are to you and me. "Ho!" Just think, He wants to call the people's attention, so He calls loudly: "Ho! Everyone that thirsteth! Come ye to the waters." "Come."

When He said to Peter: "Come," could Peter come? Yes. What, come on the water? [Voice: "On the word, Come."] Yes, by that word Peter walked on the water. Then, when he forgot the word and thought he was about to sink, he said, "Lord, save me." He could not get to Him, could he? He started, but forgot the power of the word, the faith slipped, and he thought he could not get to Him, and he cried, "Lord, save me." And the Lord put forth His hand. He did not wait for Peter to get to Him, but put forth His hand and lifted Him up. My brother or my sister, if you have mustered up courage to start on the word, "Come," and have forgot the power of it, and your faith has slipped because of the storm that was about you, you can say, "Lord, save me," and He reaches out His hand, and will save.

"Come ye to the waters, and he that hath no money, come." He tells us to buy, and whoever has no money, He will attend to the buying, He will see that we get the article. And that is also what He said to those who thought they had money, and did not know they had none. But that means us; that means you and me. And He comes with those words, "beloved" and "brethren." "Without money, buy and eat; come buy wine and milk without money and without price." The same thing is in Isa. 52:3, "For thus saith the Lord, Ye have sold yourselves for nought, and ye shall be redeemed without money." How in the world can we get back when we have sold ourselves? What did we get? Nothing. Now if He should ask anything for us to get back, how in the world can we do it? We sold ourselves for nothing, and if it costs us anything to get back, that means everlasting ruin, does it not? So then, we must settle down on that one thing that it does not cost anything for us to get back. "Ye have sold yourselves for nothing, and ye shall be redeemed for nothing." It cost *the Lord* something, however. It cost Him everything. But all this He gives us, so that it costs us nothing. The price was paid, but not by us.

"Wherefore do ye spend money for that which is not bread, and your labor for that which satisfieth not? Hearken diligently unto me, and eat that which is good, and let your soul delight itself in fatness. Incline your ears and come unto me. Hear and your soul shall live." What is it that you are to do that your soul shall live? [Voice: "Hear."] Do you *hear,* brethren? Have you heard the invitation? Do you live? You have heard of the creative power and the wonder-working power of Jesus Christ; having heard it, do you live by it? Do you live in Him and by Him and to Him?

Back there in the wilderness Moses lifted up a serpent, and what were they to do? "Look and live." And as the serpent was lifted up in the wilderness, and they were to live, so the Son of Man was lifted up that whosoever should look to Him should live. But here it is stated, *Hear,* and ye shall live. God had the plan fixed that we should *speak* and live, but Moses spoiled it.

In the 20th of Numbers we read that the Lord told Moses there when the people were murmuring for water, to go and "*speak* to the rock," and it should bring forth water. Moses went up and said, "Hear, now, ye rebels; must we fetch you water out of this rock?" And he *smote* the rock twice.

It was then that he spoiled God's splendid figure, that He would have set up, that all we were to do was to speak. For the rock *had been smitten* when they entered the desert.

The record says, when the people were thirsty the Lord told Moses to go up to Horeb and that He would stand before him on the rock. He told him to smite the rock with the rod that was in his hand, that the people might drink. He did that, and the water flowed out. What was that rock? [Voice: "Christ."]

Then why did he smite the rock the second time? Christ is not to die the second time for you and me. The Lord wanted to show us this in that splendid figure that He was about to set up, but Moses forgot His word. He did not believe Him, and thought that He was to do as he did before. He forgot that the Lord said, Go and *speak* to the rock, so he *smote* it, and spoiled the figure. Then God said unto him, "Because ye believed me not, to sanctify me in the eyes of the children of Israel, therefore ye shall not bring this congregation into the land which I have given them." Brethren, the Lord Himself cannot keep us from sinning when we do not believe Him. Do not forget that. The Lord did not intend that Moses should do as he did, but Moses did not believe the Lord. Why did not the Lord keep him from sinning? He could not, when Moses did not believe Him. Then it becomes you and me, whenever God speaks to us, to take Him just as He says. Then He will keep us from sinning.

Christ told His disciples that night that they would all forsake Him and flee. They said, No, we will not. No, sir. You are mistaken. Peter said, Though all forsake thee, I will not. Before the cock crew, he denied Him three times, although he had said, "Though I should die with thee, yet will I not deny thee." Who was right? Christ. And they all said the same thing, but they all fled, because of their unbelief. If they had believed what He had said, would they have fled? Wouldn't He have saved the flock?

Brethren, what we want to do is to believe the Lord. Undoubtedly Moses thought when the Lord told him to speak to the rock, that he *meant* to say as he did before – to go and *smite* it. He should have listened to what the Lord *said.* That is for you and me. "Consider what *I say* and the Lord give you understanding of all things."

So then, what we are to do is to *look* and live; *hear* and live; *speak* and live; let us do it. The rock has been smitten; speak, and He will give forth the water of life. Brethren, that is from our Counselor. "Hear and your souls shall live, and I will make an everlasting covenant with you, even the sure mercies of David."

And we have it further,

"Buy of me gold tried in the fire, and white raiment that thou mayest be clothed." And you remember the description that we have already had of that raiment. The figure is, it is, "that garment that is woven in the loom of heaven, in which there is not a single thread of human making." Brethren, that garment was woven in a human body. The human body – the flesh of Christ – was the loom, was it not? That garment was woven in Jesus; in the same flesh that you and I have, for He took part of the same flesh and blood that we have. That flesh that is yours and mine, that Christ bore in this world – that was the loom in which God wove that garment for you and me to wear in the flesh, and He wants us to wear it now, as well as when the flesh is made immortal in the end!

What was the loom? Christ in His human flesh. What was it that was made there? [*Voice:* The garment of righteousness."] And it is for all of us. The righteousness of Christ – the life that He lived – for you and for me that we are considering tonight, that is the garment. God the Father – God was in Christ reconciling the world to Himself. "His name shall be called Immanuel" – that is, "God with us." Now then, He wants that garment to be ours, but does not want us to forget who is the weaver. It is not ourselves, but it is He who is with us. It was God in Christ. Christ is to be in us, just as God was in Him, and His character is to be in us, just as God was in Him, and His character is to be woven and transformed into us through these sufferings and temptations and trials which we meet. And God is the weaver, but not without us. It is the cooperation of the divine and the human – the mystery of God in you and me – the same mystery that was in the gospel and that is the third angel's message. This is the word of the Wonderful Counselor.

[*Voice*: "Was not the character woven without us?"]

Yes, but it will not become ours without us. So we are led through these fiery trials and temptations to be partakers of the character of Christ, and these trials and temptations that we meet reveal to us our characters and the importance of having His, so that through these same temptations that He passed through, we become partakers of His character, bearing about in the body the righteousness of the life of the Lord Jesus Christ.

Of course the garment was woven without us, and the beauty of it comes in that we are to have that garment as complete as He is. We are to grow up into Christ, until we all come in the unity of the faith. It is the same message still, until we all come in the unity of the faith, and of the knowledge of the Son of God unto a perfect man, "unto the measure of the stature of the fullness of Christ."

How tall are we to be in character before we leave this world? As tall as Christ. What is to be our stature? That of Christ. We are to be perfect men reaching "unto the measure of the stature of the fullness of Christ."

Who is the weaver? [*Voice*: "God."] In whose eye is the pattern? God's. Many times, brethren, the threads seem all tangled when we look at them. The meshes seem all out of shape, and there is no symmetry at all to the figure; there is no beauty at all to the pattern as we see it. But the pattern is not of our making. We are not the weaver. Although the threads become tangled and the shuttle as it goes through gets all clogged and we do know how it is all coming out, who is sending the shuttle? God sends the shuttle, and it will go through. You need never mind, if the threads get tangled and you can see nothing beautiful in it. God is the weaver; can He untangle the threads? Assuredly He will untangle them.

When we look for the symmetry of the pattern and see it all awry and the colors intermingled and the threads drawn through this way and that and the figure seems spoiled, who is making the figure anyhow? God, of course. Whose loom contains the pattern of the figure in its completeness? And who is the pattern? Christ is the pattern, and do not forget, "no man knoweth the Son but the Father." You and I cannot shape our lives on the pattern. We do not know Him. We cannot see clearly enough to discern the One who shapes the pattern or to know how to shape it right even if we were doing the weaving. Brethren, God is doing the weaving. He will carry that process on. God sees the pattern in its completeness before it is done. It is in His eye perfected, when to our eye it all seems tangled and awry.

Brethren, let Him weave away. Let Him carry on His blessed plan of weaving through all our life and experience the precious pattern of Jesus Christ. The day is coming and is not far off when the last shuttle will be shot through, the last thread will be laid on, the last point in the figure will be met completely and sealed with the seal of the living God. There we shall wait only for Him that we may be like Him because we shall see Him as He is.

Brethren, is He not a wonderful Counselor? Oh, let us take His counsel tonight. Let us take the blessed faith that has been tried and all that He tells us, for it is all our own. God has given it. It is mine. It is yours. Let us thank Him and be glad.

> Beloved, now are we the sons of God, and it doth not yet appear what we shall be: but we know that, when He shall appear, we shall be like Him; for we shall see Him as He is. And every man that hath this hope in Him purifieth himself, even as He is pure.

Sermon 11

February 13, 1893

The place where we were in the Scriptures, you remember, in this series of lessons, is that counsel of the True Witness, the second thing that He tells us to buy. We studied the first the other night. "I counsel thee to buy of me gold tried in the fire, that thou mayest be rich." That was our study the last lesson. Our study tonight begins with the next thing: "I counsel thee to buy of me white raiment, that thou mayest be clothed, and that the shame of thy nakedness do not appear."

What is that raiment? [Congregation: "Righteousness."] Whose righteousness? [Congregation: "Christ's."] Whose is that? [Congregation: "The righteousness of God."] Whose are we to seek? [Congregation: "The righteousness of God."] What is righteousness? [Congregation: "Right doing."] Is righteousness right doing? [Congregation: "Yes."] [Voice: "All thy commandments are righteousness."] What are they to us? What do they say? [Voice: "Do."] Do they? The commandments require doing, do they? [Congregation: "Yes, sir."] The first of all the commandments is, "Thou shalt love the Lord thy God with all thy heart and with all thy soul and with all thy mind and with all thy strength," and the second is like unto it. "Thou shalt love thy neighbor as thyself. On these two commandments hang all the law and the prophets." Righteousness is right doing, then; that's plain enough.

Whose righteousness are we to seek? [Congregation: "God's righteousness."] Whose are we to have? [Congregation: "God's."] Whose right doing are we to have? [Congregation: "Christ's."] But whose right doing is in Christ? [Congregation: "God's."] Christ did not do anything of Himself. He says, "Of mine own self I can do nothing." John 5:30. Whose right doing do we find in Christ? [Congregation: "God's."] "God was in Christ." 2 Cor. 5:19. Whose right doing are we to have? [Congregation: "God's."] Now is that so? [Congregation: "Yes, sir."] Will you stick to that for a week? [Congregation: "Yes, sir." Elder Wm. Hutchinson said: "For life."] All right. But if some people in this audience will stick to that for a week, I shall be happy. And so will they, because there are some here who are not sticking to it at all. They haven't it, they don't know it, and there are a good many of them, too, and for that reason we want clearly to understand as we start, what kind of raiment it is that we are to buy – what we are after. Whose right doing is it that we are to have? [Congregation: "God's."] Whose righteousness are we to seek? That is what we are to find out in this lesson.

Now calling attention again to a thought that we have studied before, with which to begin this study tonight directly, that is, what this righteousness is to us now, let us turn back to that passage in Joel, the second chapter, and 23rd verse, and notice also the marginal reading. "Be glad then, ye children of Zion, and rejoice in the Lord your God, for he hath given you the former rain moderately and he will cause to come down for you the rain, the former rain and the latter rain."

Our study on that was in Bulletin No. 7, p. 183. What is the margin? "He hath given you the former rain?" What is that? "A teacher of righteousness." "Given you the former rain moderately." What is that, moderately? What was the former rain at Pentecost? "A teacher of righteousness." "He hath given you a teacher of righteousness according to righteousness." Was that the former rain? And He will give you "the rain, the former rain, and the latter rain," as at the first. What will the latter rain be? "A teacher of righteousness" again. According to what? [Congregation: "Righteousness."] But what is another expression for the latter rain? [Congregation: "The outpouring of the Spirit."] What is another one? [Congregation: "The times of refreshing."] What is the latter rain to the third angel's message? [Congregation: "The loud cry."] What is the latter rain in connection with the fall of Babylon? It is the bestowal of that power and that glory with which the angel of Revelation 18 comes down and lightens the earth.

Now let us read a few passages of those that we have had already to get the connection here definitely. On page 58 of the Bulletin in Brother Haskell's lesson, we had, as it was read from the Review of November 22nd, these words:

> The time of test is just upon us, for the loud cry of the third angel has already begun in the revelation of the righteousness of Christ. . . This is the beginning of the light of the third angel, whose glory shall fill the whole earth.

Another passage on page 16 of the Bulletin, in that Testimony that was read:

> Yet the work will be cut short in righteousness.

What "work will be cut short in righteousness"? [Congregation: "God's work."]

> The message of Christ's righteousness is to sound from one end of the world to the other. *This is the glory of God* which closes the work of the third angel.

What is this message of Christ's righteousness as we read here before in these other places? "This is the beginning of the light of the third angel, whose glory shall fill the whole earth." Now, "This is the glory of God which closes the work of the third angel." Then, when we have come to that time what time have we reached? [Congregation: "The loud cry of the message."] We have reached the time when God is going to close it up. That is the glory that closes the work of the message.

Now another thing: What is that first expression which we have just read? "He will cut it short in righteousness." Then when that message of God's righteousness – the righteousness of God, which is by faith of Jesus Christ, God's right doing – when that is received and is allowed to be carried on and is held by His people, what does that mean about the work of God on earth? It will be but a short time until the whole thing is done.

Then, when we reach the time of the latter rain, the loud cry, the angel coming down from heaven having that great power, all these things coming together, as thus stated by the words of the Lord, we are simply brought to the same point where we were brought by the study of the things which are before us and which led us to view what is coming upon us. That line of study that we had – studying the things that are before us to see what is soon to come upon us – led us face to face with six or seven different events that shut us up to this very thing, that now is the time that the work will be closed up shortly, and we are in the midst of the scenes that close up this world's history. Here are these different expressions in the Testimony of the Spirit of God, when put together, that show that it is the same thing from that side.

Well, the latter rain is the loud cry of the third angel's message; it is the beginning of that message of glory that lightens the earth. But the latter rain is the teaching of righteousness. When did that message of the righteousness of God, as such, come to us as a people? [Congregation: "Four years ago."] Where? [Congregation: "At Minneapolis."] Yes. This point was brought up the other night and can be read again in Bulletin No. 7, p. 183. I do not know that we can state it any more clearly than we did that night.

Now that message of the righteousness of Christ is the loud cry. It is the latter rain. We have been praying for the latter rain here at this Conference already, haven't we? Have you? [Congregation: "Yes, sir."] What were you looking for when your prayer was answered? Are you ready now to receive the latter rain? We have been praying here for the latter rain. Now there is the connection.

The testimonies tell us what it is and Joel tells us what it is. I simply ask now, are you ready to receive the latter rain? That is, are you ready to receive God's message of righteousness, according to righteousness? Let us look at that a little further. Joel says, according to the margin, that it is a teacher of righteousness, that which brings the teaching of righteousness *according to righteousness.* Whose idea of righteousness? [Congregation: "God's."] No, mine. [Congregation: "No."] Yes, mine will do! [Congregation: "No."] Why? If I receive the righteousness of Christ according to my idea, is not that enough? Is not that receiving the latter rain? Is not that receiving the righteousness of Christ? [Congregation: "No, sir. It is your own righteousness."] But that is what is the matter with a good many people who have heard this message of the righteousness of Christ. They have received the message of the righteousness of Christ *according to their own idea* of what His righteousness is, and they have not the righteousness of Christ at all.

Now, let us ask again, how are we to receive that? How is that to be given? "According to righteousness." How, then, is it to be received? "According to righteousness." It is given "according to righteousness," and we must receive it "according to righteousness." We must receive it as it is given.

But let us dwell further upon that thought, and I am in no hurry to get away from it either. When we receive the teaching, that teaching of righteousness "according to righteousness," we must receive it according to God's idea of righteousness and not according to our own measure of it. And he who thinks of receiving that message of Christ's righteousness according to his own idea of it will miss it entirely. We are to receive it according to God's idea of it and nothing else than God's idea of righteousness, nothing else than that, is righteousness.

There is a thought again that we had the other night that when it was presented four years ago and all along since some accepted it just as it was given, and were glad of the news that God had righteousness that would pass the judgment and would stand accepted in His sight. A righteousness that is a good deal better than anything that people could manufacture by years and years of hard work. People had worn out their souls almost, trying to manufacture a sufficient degree of righteousness to stand through the time of trouble and meet the Saviour in peace when He comes, but they had not accomplished it. These were so glad to find out that God had already manufactured a robe of righteousness and offered it as a free gift to every one that would take it, that would answer now and in the time of the plagues and in the time of judgment and to all eternity that they received it gladly just as God gave it and heartily thanked the Lord for it. Others would not have anything to do with it at all but rejected the whole thing. Others seemed to take a middle position. They did not fully accept it, neither did they openly reject it. They thought to take a middle position and go along with the crowd, if the crowd went that way. And *that* is the way they hoped to receive the righteousness of Christ and the message of the righteousness of God. Others deliberately discounted the message about fifty percent and counted *that* the righteousness of God. And so, all the way between open and free deliberate surrender and acceptance of it, to open, deliberate and positive rejection of it – all the way between – the compromisers have been scattered ever since, and those who have taken that compromising position are no better prepared tonight to discern what is the message of the righteousness of Christ than they were four years ago.

Some of these brethren, since the Minneapolis meeting, I have heard, myself, say "amen" to preaching, to statements that were utterly heathen and did not know but that it was the righteousness of Christ. Some of those who stood so openly against that at that time and voted with uplifted hand against it and since that time I have heard say "amen" to statements that were as openly and decidedly papal as the papal church itself can state them. That I shall bring in here in one of these lessons and call your attention to the Catholic church's statement and her doctrine of justification by faith. I shall bring that in at some future lesson and will let you see what the doctrine of the Catholic church is as to justification by faith. "Why," says one, "I didn't know that the Catholic church believes in justification by faith." Oh, yes, she does. Yes, indeed she does. You can read it out of her books. Says one, "I thought they believed in justification by works." They do and they do not believe in anything else, but they pass it off under the head of justification by faith. And they are not the only people in the world that are doing it (I mean the members of the Catholic church.). They are not the only ones that are doing it.

So I appeal to all to just let us come together now and let us lay aside everything, every preconceived notion, every thought of just how this or that opinion is or should be, and come together now to hear the message of the righteousness of Christ and study it in the fear of God, praying with all the heart that He may in this Conference give us the Teacher of righteousness according to His own idea of righteousness. That is what we want.

And brethren, as certainly as we pray for Him to do that, that is what He will do. And then when He sends to us, by His Spirit, the teaching of the message of His righteousness, let us take it exactly as He gives it, and do not discount it a particle, no difference if it takes away all that we ever thought was the right idea in that connection. We have nothing to do with that. We agreed at the beginning of this institute when we came here to study, to stand upon this platform, that if anyone of us thought we knew anything, we knew nothing as we ought to know it. That is applicable to this subject, to those who have received it, just as certainly (though not in the same degree perhaps) as those who have not received it. Because those who have received it cannot boast now, and stand up and say, "I am all right now. I do not need to learn anything now." If anyone gets into that position, he is the one who needs most to learn of anyone.

So what you and I want to do is to lay aside every thought of this kind, every deduction we have made upon it, every discount we have put upon it, every shape we have given to it – drop all these, and let us come, as Christ said, "as little children," asking what is the kingdom of God, for the kingdom of God is righteousness and peace and joy in the Holy Ghost.

These that will not receive the kingdom of God as little children, Jesus Himself says, cannot enter into it. And if we come with what we have already learned, and try to frame it upon that, it will not fit upon that. If we come and try to mould everything else that He will give us now, upon our conception of what we have, we will spoil the whole thing, and just shut ourselves out from it all. Therefore that text abides with us still: "If any man thinketh he knoweth anything, he knoweth nothing yet as he ought to know." That belongs to us.

Now taking that thought a little further. The latter rain, this message, is the righteousness of God, which is by faith of Jesus Christ. That is the loud cry, but that message is the teaching of righteousness *according to righteousness,* and that means God's idea of righteousness and not our own. Is *my idea* of God's righteousness – my idea at its broadest stretch – is that God's idea of righteousness? [Congregation: "No."] Then when I get the broadest idea I possibly can of God's righteousness, and am satisfied with that and say that that is to save me, then whose righteousness is it that is to save me? [Congregation: "Your own."] Of course it is. Because when I measure up His ideas and mine and make Him like myself, I confine Him within my comprehension and I am my own saviour, because that makes Him no greater than I am. Do you see that? [Congregation: "Yes, sir."]

Yes, indeed. We are to receive this message, this latter rain, this righteousness of God, according to His own ideas and in His own way and when He says it, when He gives it, we are to take it up and thank Him for it, not to question how it comes, or anything of the kind, but to receive it as He speaks it, as He gives it, and let Him do just as He pleases in carrying it forward in the world. Because, what is righteousness? Right doing. Whose righteousness is it that we are to have? [Congregation: "God's."] Then it is God's right doing that we are to have. It is not our own right doing. It is His idea of His right doing and not our idea of right doing. It is not our idea of His right doing. It is His own idea of His own right doing. It is, in fact, His own right doing when He does things. Therefore that calls upon you and me to yield up everything of ourselves to Him and let Him do the doing as He pleases with this which is His own. He is to do the doing. We are to be instruments. "Yield yourselves as instruments of righteousness." Your members as instruments of righteousness. Yield them to whom? To God. He uses the instruments. Rom. 6:13. Will you let Him? [Congregation: "Yes, sir."] Will you stick to that for a week? [Congregation: "Yes, sir."]

Now another thought that leads us thus. We know it is God's idea only. That is the true idea of this righteousness of God. Then can I grasp His idea of righteousness with *my own mind?* [Congregation: "No, sir."] Can I have a mind that will grasp it, and that can grasp it? Yes. Is there any mind in the universe that can grasp God's idea of righteousness? Yes. Whose? Christ's. Then does not that shut you and me up to that fact, that without the mind of Jesus Christ we have not and cannot have the righteousness of God? I care not how much of a theory a man may have of the righteousness of God; I care not how much he may say he believes in the righteousness of God. I care not how much he may say he believes in justification by faith, if he has not the mind of Christ itself, he does not understand God's idea of justification by faith, and he cannot tell it.

No man can grasp the righteousness of God without the mind of Jesus Christ, which alone of all minds in the universe can grasp it or comprehend it or know it. No is that so? [Congregation: "Yes, sir."] But I can have my mind turned into the mind of Christ?

Can't I? Re-made, re-vamped, and transformed into the mind of Christ? [Congregation: "No, sir."] [Someone in the congregation quoted the text: "Let this mind be in you which was also in Christ Jesus."] All right, will you let it? Will you do that? Is that what you have made up your mind to do? [Congregation: "Yes, sir."] That is the thing to start with, then, is it not? Let us get that clear and I think that by that time the hour for the study this evening will be expired. That the only possible way in which anybody in this world can know the righteousness of God, can receive the righteousness of God, can receive the teaching of this righteousness according to righteousness . . . the only way, the only possible way, that any man in this world can receive it or know it is by having the mind of Christ itself.

Here is an expression we will give, correct enough in itself, that the commandments of God are the reflection, the transcript, the expression, of God' righteousness. The ten commandments are the manifestation in writing, in letters of the will of God. Rom. 2:17, 18: "Behold, thou art called a Jew, and restest in the law and makest thy boast of God and knowest His will and approvest the things that are more excellent, being instructed out of the law." Then the law being the expression of God's will, that expresses what is God's will that shall be done in the way of right doing. Will the ten commandments accept any doing from anybody that comes short of God's own idea of what is right doing? No. Then the ten commandments simply require such a measure of right doing as God's own mind measures, as His will expresses. Well then, when the ten commandments require just that, and will accept nothing short of that, how in the world are the requirements of the ten commandments to be met in any man's life in this world who has not the mind of God? It cannot be done.

Where do we get that mind? [Congregation: "In Christ."] Then is it possible for any man, by any possible means, to render to the ten commandments what they require and what only they will accept, without having the mind of Jesus Christ itself? [Congregation: "No, sir."] Well, can I have the mind of Christ without the rest of Him? No, I cannot. Therefore as I cannot have the mind of Christ without the rest of Him, it follows that I must have the personal presence of Christ Himself.

What is it that brings to you and me the personal presence of Jesus Christ? The Spirit of God. Turn to two texts, one in John and one in Ephesians, and I think that will be all we will have time to read tonight. John 14:18, "I will not leave you comfortless; I will come to you." He does not leave us comfortless, that is without a comforter. So He says, I will come to you, but when He comes to us thus, we are not without a Comforter. Then He does come to us by the Comforter, which is the Holy Ghost.

Now turn to Eph. 3:16, 17. Let us read that carefully together.

This is the prayer:

> That he would grant you, according to the riches of His glory, to be strengthened with might by his Spirit in the inner man; that Christ may dwell in your hearts.

[Some one quoted the words of the text, "by faith."] Of course faith belongs there. But there is a double attachment to the middle statement: First, strengthened with might by His Spirit in the inner man, that Christ may dwell in your hearts, but He dwells in the heart by faith.

We *receive* the promise of the Spirit through faith; but what *brings* it? The Spirit of God; and when we have that, Christ dwells in the heart. Then it is the Holy Spirit that brings the personal presence of Jesus Christ, and in bringing His personal presence to us, He brings Himself. Then it is the mind of Christ, by which we may comprehend, investigate, and revel in, the deep things of God which He reaches down and brings forth to our understanding and sets them before us in their plainness. That is what we must have, in order to have the presence of Christ, in order to have the righteousness of Christ, in order that we may have the latter rain, in order that we may give the loud cry.

Sermon 12

February 14, 1893

LAST night we came to this: that in order to have the righteousness of God – which is the latter rain, which is the preparation for the loud cry – we must have the mind of Christ only; it cannot come in any other way. This is precisely the advice that is given to us in the Scriptures: "Let this mind be in you which was also in Christ Jesus." Phil. 2:5,6. What is the thing that that text shows that the mind of Christ does? What did it do in Him? It "emptied himself." When that mind is in us, what will it do there? The same thing. It will empty us of self. Then the first thought that that text gives is that the mind of Christ empties of himself the one in whom it is.

When that mind that was in Christ emptied Himself, then what came? God filled Him. When that mind that was in Him is in us and does in us what it did in Him – empties us of self – what then will fill the place? God in Christ will fill us. Then God in Christ dwells in us. But that takes self out of the way.

Now what mind is in us to start with? The mind of self. What does that mind do? It exalts self. What kind of mind is it we have to start with? The natural mind. A man has a natural mind, and he must have another mind. He must have the mind that was in Christ, but that mind that is in Christ only empties of self the one in whom it dwells. Therefore as we have a mind to start with and *must* have *another* than that, while that other empties of self the one in whom it is, does it not follow inevitably that the mind which we have to start with, *is a mind only of self*?

God made man to start with, at the real start in Eden. Did God put in that man the mind of self? [Congregation: "No, sir."] Whose mind was it in that man? The mind of God. Brother Haskell has read to us in his lessons the wonderful wisdom that was in Adam and that wisdom was of God that was reflected in the life of Adam – his mind, his thoughts, his whole make-up reflecting the Maker. When God said, "Let us make man in our image," it meant a great deal more than the *shape;* it meant that if you and I could have seen Adam and Eve as they came from the hand of God, we would have seen the image of God reflected and would have been caused to think of somebody back of them, far back of them and far superior to them. Who is that? God.

But they did not stay as God made them. Satan came into the garden. God had said to them certain words, *His* words, the expression of *His mind,* His *thought* concerning them. If they had received those words, had retained those words and the thoughts of God in those words, whose *mind* would they have retained? God's. When this other one, Satan, came and told them other words, expressing his thoughts and the product of his mind and they accepted that and yielded to that, then whose thoughts did they receive and whose mind did they receive? [Congregation: "Satan's."]

We need not go back into the depths of Satan's experience; we all know what it was that caused his fall. What was that? [Congregation: "Pride."] But self was the root of the pride; self is the root of everything;; pride is the fruit of self only. Satan looked at himself before he got proud of himself. If he had looked into the face of Him who sits upon the throne he never would have become proud. He would have reflected the image of Him who sits upon the throne, as that image is manifested in Jesus Christ. But when he turned His look from the face of Him who sits upon the throne and turned it upon himself, then it was that he became proud of himself. Then it was that he considered how beautiful he himself was, and his heart was lifted up because of *his* beauty, and he began to give *himself* credit for what *he* was. What he was came from God. But Lucifer gave *himself* credit for all that he was and for what he was. Did he not in that count himself as self-existent – in fact put himself in the place of God? But it all came from self, and that is the thought of it all. He said, "I will be like God. I will be like the Most High." He would be in the place of Christ, and anyone who puts himself in the place of Christ puts himself in the place of God, because God is in Christ.

Then that being so, that being Satan's mind, when he came to our first parents and they received of that mind, what mind was that? The mind of self, because it is the mind of Satan who is self, and the same ambition was set before them that he set before himself that made himself what he is himself. "Ye shall not surely die, for God doth know that in the day ye eat thereof, then your eyes shall be opened, and ye shall be as gods, knowing good and evil. And when the woman saw that the tree was good for food and that it was pleasant to the eyes and a tree to be desired to make one wise." To be desired to do what? To make one wise. Wise as what? Like God. "Ye shall be like God," knowing more than you know now. Knowing such and such things. O yes, then that tree is a tree to be desired to bring to me that knowledge, to give me that wisdom, and this tree is the channel through which I can accomplish that object of being like God. That is it. Then what is the mind that is in us? [Congregation: "Self."] The natural mind is the mind of Satan. That is self always.

Now the Lord did not leave it there alone. The Lord did not stop right there. If He had stopped there, there never could have been in any man's mind in this world any impulse other than that of Satan himself, because the whole natural mind is of self and Satan only. But God said, I will break that up. "I will put enmity between thee and the woman and between thy seed and her seed." God put the enmity there, the hatred against Satan's power, the hatred against the things that are in that mind even. God has planted that hatred there, and that is the source of every impulse to good, or to right, or anything of the kind that ever comes into any man's mind in this world.

But when God put that hatred of evil there, it also begets the *desire* for something better than this evil which we hate. But what is that better thing? What is the object of that desire? [Congregation: "Jesus Christ."] Because Jesus Christ and His presence, God's mind, comes back to the place whence it has been taken away. God's image comes back to the place from whence it has been banished by this deception of Satan. Christ is the image of God, the express image of His person, and when we receive Jesus Christ in His fulness the image of God is returned to the place where it belongs. Therefore His putting that enmity sets the will – the choice – free, so that man can choose this other mind. This is that Light that lighteth every man that cometh into the world. If a man will follow that light he will find Jesus Christ, as Abraham did, as Cornelius did, as everyone does who will follow that ray of light. So He is the Desire of all nations. Haggai 2:7. Christ is that.

The man who finds that hatred of evil, that desire for something better, that will to do good, is that the doing of good? [Congregation: "No."] Can He do the good that He is drawn to, by that impulse? [Congregation: "No."]

Let us read in Romans and see what is done. Rom. 3:10, "As it is written, There is none righteous, no, not one." And the 12th verse: "They are all gone out of the way; they are together become unprofitable; there is none that doeth good, no, not one." Is that so? [Congregation: "Yes, sir."] Then how can we talk about a heathen doing good? *Does* he do good? "There is none that doeth good, no, not one." [A voice: "If a man has Christ, he can do good."] But if he has Christ, he is not a heathen. What we are talking about is the heathen.

No, even this need not be. We need not go to the heathen to inquire. All we need is to go to the Jews. Here is one that was a Jew, like you and I. Romans 7:14, "For we know that the law is spiritual, but I am carnal, sold under sin." The carnal mind is the natural mind. Whose mind is the natural mind? Satan's, that is the mind of self; that is the mind of Satan. Well, let us read further. "For that which I do, I allow not." What is the reason I do not allow what I do? What is the matter with it? Why can't I allow it? Because I know it is wrong. It is not good. If it were good could I not allow it? "That which I do, I allow not." What is actually done then? The good? No, the *not good*. The bad. The wrong.

"For what I would, that I do not." What would he do? [Congregation: "Good."] That which I would I do not. What *would* he do? [Congregation: "Good."] What *did* he do? [Congregation: "Wrong."] Then on both these points what was done? The evil.

"But what I hate, that do I." What did he hate? Sin. He hated the evil, the wrong, the bad. But what did he *do*? The evil. He did the evil; he did the wrong; he did the bad.

Then how much *good* does the natural man do? None. Although he hates the *bad,* how much *good* does he do? None. He *would* do the good, but how much of the good that he *would* does he actually do? None. Now is that so? [Congregation: "Yes."] It is so, for the Bible says so. Then what in the world is the use of anybody's talking about the heathen doing good or even a Jew doing good or any man doing good, who has only the natural mind and *is* only the natural man? This is not saying anything as to what he *knows;* that is not saying whether he has impulses to good or not; that is not the question. He had these impulses all the time, didn't he? He had the knowledge of good, so much that he hated the bad things that he was doing.

Now think of that. There was the natural man: there was a man like you and I and every other man born into this world. He had impulses to good; he had the knowledge of good; he hated the evil; but what did he *do?* Not what did he think? Not what did he know? But what did he *do?* He did the *evil.* It is not a question of what he *knew.* Did he *do* anything else than evil? No. He *knew* something else; he knew better, didn't he? [Congregation: "Yes, sir."] Then let us not pass off our right *knowing* for right *doing.* Let us not pass off our right knowledge for right deeds. *Knowledge* of right is not *doing* right. So he did not do any good. Who is that? It is you and I – the natural man. Is that I? Yes. Without the mind of Christ itself is that I? Yes. Then though I profess to believe in Christ, if the mind of Christ itself is not there is that I? Yes. Is it you? [Congregation: "Yes, sir!"] All right, then, let us go together.

"If then I do that which I would not, I consent unto the law that it is good. Now then it is no more I that do it." No. I said I *would not* do it. I said that I hated it and declared that I would never do it again. But I did do it. Then when I hated it and resolved and re-resolved and determined that I would never do it again and yet *did* it, what in the world was the matter with me? I had the *knowledge* but did not have the *power.* Now the gospel of Christ, "which is Christ in you," that is *power.* It is the power of God to every one that believeth.

Well, then, the natural man is not free, is he? [Congregation: "No, sir."] He is not in a condition where he can *do* what he *would,* even with the bedimmed intellect and the obscured mind that he has. He cannot live up to his own standard. But is what he would do *as he sees it,* is *that* as God would *have* him do it? [Congregation: "No."] Or as God would do it? [Congregation: "No."] Whose *right-doing* are we to have? [Congregation: "God's."] Yes, for God's righteousness is what we are to have. and righteousness is right doing. So that it is God's right doing that we must have. Then our understanding is exceedingly low, even with the light which God has let shine into our hearts. Then where is the *good doing* of any man in this world who has not the mind of Jesus Christ?

"For I know that in me (that is, in my flesh) dwelleth no good thing: for to will in present with me; but how to perform that which is good I find not." What is it that is present with us? To *will* to do good. Then what did that putting of enmity there against

Satan – what was that the doing of? Is not it setting the man free to will? Yes. Was it anything more than that? [Congregation: "No."] Now think carefully of this; I mean on this point. There are other things in it, of course, but did that do any more for the man to enable him to *do* right things, and glorify God, did it do any more for him than to set free his *will,* that he might *choose* which master he would have? [Congregation: "No."] It put the hatred there, and gave him the knowledge of something better. It gives the hatred of evil, leads him out towards the good, but does it enable him to *do* the good? [Congregation: "No."]

Now just another thought there. He hates the evil and declares he never will do it, and yet against his will and against all his being for that matter, it is done. But what is it, and who is it, that actually does it? [Congregation: "'Sin that dwelleth in him.'"] And who rules that? [Congregation: "Satan."] Who is the master of that man? [Congregation: "Satan."]

Now when the man is set free from that carnal mind, that mind of self and Satan, who controls that man? Who then is his master? [Congregation: "Christ."] Yes. He who sets him free. It is Christ Jesus. Then when we are free from Satan's mastery we become bound to another Master. Satan's mastery is slavery and ruin; Christ's mastery is freedom and everlasting life, everlasting joy, and everlasting prosperity.

Now carry that thought a little further. When we had the mind of Satan and he was ruling, we said we would not do those evil things, but just those were done. Who did it? [Congregation: "Sin that dwelleth in us."] We said we will do so and so. We did not. Who kept us from it? [Congregation: "Satan."] But now in Christ we are free from him: we have the other mind. We say we will do that. Who does it? [Congregation: "Christ."] While in the natural mind we *refuse* and who *does* it? [Congregation: "Satan."] And when in the mind of Christ we *choose* and who does it? [Congregation: "Christ."] Is that so? [Congregation: "Yes."] It is God that worketh in you both to will and to do, of His good pleasure.

This thought will come more fully at another time, but we want to get the thought before you tonight.

> For the good that I would, I do not, but the evil which I would not, that I *do.* Now if I do that I would not, it is no more I that do it, but sin that dwelleth in me. I find then a law, that, when I would do good, evil is present with me. For I delight in the law of God after the inward man: But I see another law in my members, warring against the law of my mind and bringing me into captivity to the law of sin which is in my members. O wretched man that I am! Who shall deliver me from the body of this death?

What is the condition of the man who has only the natural mind? [Congregation: "Wretched."] Yes, and in captivity. And the more intense the hatred of the evil the more wretched the condition, because there is no deliverance from it in anything the man can do for himself. Well, then, who shall deliver? "I thank God through Jesus Christ our Lord." "There is therefore now no condemnation to them which are in Christ Jesus, who walk not after the flesh but after the Spirit."

Now Romans 8:6,7: "For to be carnally minded is death." What is the condition of that man who has only the natural mind? [Congregation: "Dead."] "But to be spiritually minded is life and peace. Because the carnal mind [the natural mind] is" AT enmity with God [Congregation: "No. *is* enmity against God."] No, it is not *at* enmity with God, but *it* itself *is* enmity. It "*is* enmity against God: for it is not subject to the law of God," until the man is converted? [Congregation: "Neither indeed can be."] Can't be? Cannot God make that mind subject to His law? [Congregation: "No."] Now, can't the Lord make that mind that is in you and me – the natural mind – can't He make that subject to His law? [Congregation: "No."] what is that mind? It is enmity against God. Cannot the Lord make that which *is* enmity *against* Him – can't He make it love *for* Him? [Congregation: "No."]

There is the point: If it were *at* enmity, then it might be reconciled, because the thing that would make it *at* enmity would be the source of the trouble. And therefore take away the source of the trouble, then the thing that is at enmity would be reconciled. *We* are *at* enmity, but when He takes the enmity away, *we* are *reconciled* to God. In this matter of the carnal mind though, there is nothing between; *it* is the *thing itself*. That is the root.

Then it *cannot be* subject to the law of God. The only thing that can be done with it, is to *destroy* it, *uproot* it, *banish* it, *annihilate* it. Whose mind is it? [Congregation: "Satan's."] It is the mind of self, and that is of Satan. Well then, what can a man do in the way of righteousness? What can be done in him, even, in the way of righteousness, until that other mind is there? [Congregation: "Nothing."] Well, that is the mind that is in all mankind. Now let us see how this carnal mind, this natural man, works in the matter of righteousness in the matter of justification.

Romans, first chapter, tells us this, verses 20-22: "For the invisible things of him from the creation of the world are clearly seen, being understood by the things that are made, even his eternal power and Godhead; so that they are without excuse: because that, when they knew God, they glorified Him not as God, neither were thankful; but became vain in their imaginations, and their foolish heart was darkened. Professing themselves to be wise, they became fools." Who was the first inhabitant of this world that professed to follow wisdom at the suggestion of self, at the suggestion of Satan? Eve. She was the first one that reached out after wisdom in this way. What did she get? [Congregation: "Foolishness."] She became a fool. And *we are all there*. Who leads the natural mind? Satan. Who works it? Satan. Then when those that he is speaking of here, had gone away from God, became fools; "and changed the glory of the uncorruptible God into an image made like to corruptible man, and to birds, and four footed beasts, and creeping things" – that is heathendom.

Fifteenth chapter of Gibbons' *Decline and Fall of the Roman Empire*, paragraph 17; he says of the heathen in the inquiry after the immortality of the soul:

> In the sublime inquiry, their reason had been often guided by their imagination, and their imagination had been prompted by their vanity.

Mark it. Reason of what kind of a mind? [Congregation: "the carnal mind."] Guided by the imagination of what kind of a mind? [Congregation: "The carnal mind."] And the imagination prompted by the vanity of what kind of a mind? [Congregation: "The carnal mind."] Is not that exactly the mind of Satan? Vanity the root of the inquiry, and self the root of the vanity. This is the best comment upon that verse of Scripture you will find in this world. I read on:

> When they viewed *with complacency* the extent of *their own mental powers,* when they exercised the various faculties of memory, of fancy, and of judgment, in the most profound speculations, or the most important labors, and when they reflected on the *desire of fame,* which transported them into future ages, far beyond the bonds of death and of the grave; they were unwilling to confound themselves with the beasts of the field or to suppose that *a being, for whose dignity they entertained the most sincere admiration,* could be limited to a spot of earth and to a few years of duration.

What is that but the description of Satan's career when he started. His reason prompted by his imagination; his imagination guided by his vanity, and viewing with complacency the extent of his own mental powers; the desire for fame beyond that of God, and unwilling to allow that a person for whose dignity *he* entertained the most sincere admiration could be properly confined to a subordinate place in the universe of God. Is not this an exact description of mankind in a heathen condition, written by a philosopher, looking only at the question from man's side of it? Could there be a clearer description of the working of Satan in his original career?

Well, what then?

> With this favorable prepossession they summoned to their aid the science, or rather the language, of metaphysics. They soon discovered that as none of the properties of matter will apply to the operations of the mind, *the human soul* must *consequently be a substance distinct from the body,* pure, simple and spiritual, incapable of dissolution, and susceptible of a much higher degree of virtue and happiness *after the release from its corporeal prison.* From these specious and noble principles, the philosophers who trod in the footsteps of Plato deduced a very unjustifiable conclusion, since *they asserted,* not only the future immortality, but *the past eternity of the human soul,* which they were too apt to consider *as a portion of the infinite* and *self-existing* spirit, *which pervades* and *sustains the universe."*

What is that but the mind of Satan? Self-existing, like God. Equal with God. What is that then but the action in man of that very mind which in Lucifer in heaven, aspired to be equal with God? The mind that would exalt self to equality with God. That is the natural mind. That is the mind that is natural in every man in the world. That is the mind of Satan. And that is the working of this natural mind in open, bold heathenism. Then does not every such one need another mind – even the mind of Jesus Christ, that thought it not a thing to be seized upon to be equal with God, but emptied Himself? Wherefore God hath highly exalted Him.

Well, there we have seen the heathen idea openly, broadly, and rawly, just as it is. Now let us see what this same thing is, as it stands before the world, professing to be justified by faith. And that is as it is manifested in the papacy. For the papacy is the very incarnation of Satan and this mind of self. For he "opposeth and exalteth *himself* above all that is called God or that is worshipped." And all this under the name and form of Christianity; all this as a counterfeit of the truth.

I have here a book entitled, *Catholic Belief.* It bears the *imprimatur* of John Cardinal McCloskey, Archbishop of New York, and Henricus Eduardus, Card. Archiep. Westmonastery; written by the "Very" Rev. Joseph Faa Di Bruno, D. D., Rector-General of the Pious Society of Missions; Church of SSmo Salvatore in Onda, Ponte Sisto, Rome, and St. Peter's Italian Church, Hatton Garden, London, E.C.; edited by Rev. Louis A. Lambert, author of "Notes on Ingersoll," etc., etc., and comes into this country with the approval of the hierarchy in this country.

I shall read some from it. And, that you may have the two things – the truth of justification by faith and the falsity of it – side by side, will read what this says, and then what God says in Steps to Christ. It is in the Testimonies also and all through the Bible, of course. I want you to see what the Roman Catholic idea of justification by faith is, because I have had to meet it among professed Seventh-day Adventists the past four years right straight through. These very things, these very expressions that are in this Catholic book, as to what justification by faith is and how to obtain it, are just such expressions as professed Seventh-day Adventists have made to me as to what justification by faith is.

I want to know how you and I carry a message to this world, warning them against the worship of the beast, when we hold in our very profession the doctrines of the beast. Can it be done? [Congregation: "No."] And so I call your attention to this tonight so you may see just what it is, and so that, if possible, knowing what it is to start with, knowing that it is papal, knowing that it is the beast, you will let it go because it is that, even if you are not ready to believe in justification by faith, indeed, even if you cannot see that, as some are unable to, as God gives it. Now, if we find out that it is papal, I hope those who have held that, or expressed it at any rate, whatever they have held, will be willing to let it go any way. On page 74 of this work I read as follows:

> In the case of grown-up persons, some dispositions are required on the part of the sinner in order to be fit to obtain this habitual and abiding grace of justification.

He has got to prepare himself for it. He has got to do something to make himself fit to receive it. As I read each statement from this book, I shall then read the opposite of it. So now, on pages 26 and 27 of *Steps to Christ*, I read as follows:

> If you see your sinfulness, do not wait to make yourself better. How many there are who think they are not good enough to come to Christ. Do you expect to become better through your own efforts?. . . There is help for us only in God. We must not wait for stronger persuasions, for better opportunities, or for holier tempers. We can do nothing of ourselves. We must come to Christ just as we are. (And Romans 4:5).

This is justification by *faith*. That other thing is justification by works. This is of Christ; that is of the devil. One is Christ's doctrine of justification by faith; the other is the devil's doctrine of justification by faith. And it is time that Seventh-day Adventists understood the difference. [Congregation: "Amen!"]

Again from the Catholic work:

> A man can dispose himself only by the help of divine grace, and the dispositions which he shows do not by any means effect or merit justification: *they only serve to prepare him for it.*

"No, I don't believe in justification by works, but we have got to do something in order to be prepared for it. We have got to show our good intentions any way. We have got to make some good resolutions before we start, any way; something to prepare us for it."

What does God say? On page 33 of *Steps to Christ* I read:

> He is wooing by his tender love the hearts of his erring children. No earthly parent could be as patient with the faults and mistakes of his children, as is God with those he seeks to save.

He does what? "*Seeks* to save." This is God's way. Oh, no, He waits until men prepare themselves to be saved. That is Satan's way.

I read on from *Steps to Christ*:

> No one could plead more tenderly with the transgressor. No human lips ever poured out more tender entreaties to the wanderer than He does. All His promises, His warnings, are but the breathing of unutterable love. When Satan comes to tell you that you are a great sinner, look up to your Redeemer and talk of His merits. That which will help you is to look to His light. Acknowledge your sin, but tell the enemy that "Jesus Christ came into the world to save sinners," and that you may be saved by His matchless love. (And John 3:16).

This is justification by faith. *That* is justification by works. *This* is Jesus Christ. *That* is Satan.

Then in this Catholic work it goes on to tell a lot of things that you must do in order to have these dispositions: "An *act* of faith . . . an *act* of fear of God, an *act* of hope . . . an *act* of repentance . . . a *resolution* to approach the Sacrament of *Penance*."

These are things that will prepare you to be justified to be saved. On page 76 of this same work, I read:

> We stand in continual need of actual graces to perform good acts, *both before* and *after* being justified.

Good acts must be performed before we are justified, in order to fit us for it.

> The good acts, however, done by the help of grace before justification are not, *strictly* speaking, meritorious, but serve *to smooth the way* to justification, to *move* God.

They "serve to move God." That is just the hard, iron spirit the devil asserts was in the Lord when He started, in heaven; that God was a tyrant, that God does not want His people to be free, His creatures to be free, that He sits there and wants everything to go just so without any reason, judgment, freedom, or anything of the kind. He has to be "moved" by His creatures. That is the doctrine that Satan has put into the idea of sacrifice from that time until now. God appointed sacrifices to show to man, to convey to man, what God is willing to do for man, that God is making sacrifice for him. But Satan whirled it around and man has got to do this in order to get God into good humor, that the Lord is angry with him and the Lord wants to punish him and now we have got to sacrifice to pay Him off so He will not hurt us, and we have to "move" Him to justify us.

Let us read what the Lord says on that, *Steps to Christ*, pages 57 and 58. Speaking of the parable of the prodigal son and how that, when the wanderer was yet a great way off, the father had compassion on him and ran and fell on his neck and kissed him, it says:

> But even this parable, tender and touching as it is, comes short of expressing the infinite compassion of the heavenly Father. The Lord declares by His prophet, "I have loved thee with an everlasting love; therefore, *with loving-kindness* have I *drawn* thee." While the sinner is yet far from the Father's house, wasting his substance in a strange country, the Father's heart is yearning over him and every longing awakened in the soul to return to God is but the tender pleading of His Spirit, wooing, entreating, drawing the wanderer to His Father's heart of love.
>
> With the rich promises of the Bible before you, can you give place to doubt? *Can you believe* that *when* the poor sinner *longs to return,* longs to forsake his sins, the Lord sternly withholds him from coming to His feet in repentance? *Away with such thoughts!* Nothing can hurt your soul more that to entertain such a conception of our heavenly Father.

Who wants to hurt our souls? [Congregation: "Satan."] Who wants most to hurt the soul? Satan. What could more hurt the soul than that doctrine there in that book that we must put ourselves into dispositions, into frames of mind, and make good resolutions and all these things in order to "move" God to take pity on us and save us. What could more hurt the soul than to think that God sternly holds off the sinner until the poor lost soul does something to move Him? What more hurtful thing could a person believe? The Lord's answer is: "There is nothing can hurt your soul more than such a conception." Then, where alone can that doctrine come from? [Congregation: "Satan."] Yet *that* is passed off under the title and under the idea of justification by faith! There is no faith in it. Away with it, saith the Lord. And let all the people say, Amen.

Again I read from "Catholic Belief":

> But if with the assistance of actual grace, good works are done by a person who is in a state of justifying grace, then they are acceptable to God and *merit* an *increase of grace* on earth and an *increase of glory in heaven.*

What saith the Lord? Page 61, *Steps to Christ*. And this is in the chapter entitled "The Test of Discipleship." It is talking to those who are disciples; it is talking to the same persons to whom that other book talks. What does it say?

> While we cannot do anything to change our hearts or to bring ourselves into harmony with God, while *we must not trust at all to* ourselves or *our good works,* our *lives will reveal* whether the grace of God is dwelling within us.

You see then, God's idea is that when He is there, He will show Himself through us. The other, Satan's idea, is that after we have got the Lord converted, then we do some good work that is "meritorious," and we will be safe in this world; we will have "an increase of grace" on this earth, "and an increase of glory in heaven." That is the very foundation of the merits of the "saints," from which the pope draws indulgences to give to those who have not enough merit of their own.

Now that which I have just read from this Catholic work is in a chapter on justification, preaching the straight doctrine on justification. Here (page 365) he reviews the doctrine of justification by faith, *in condemnation of Protestants who believe it.* Let us see, brethren, whether we shall be Protestants or Catholics. Let us see whether we shall believe in Jesus Christ or Satan. That is what we need to understand now, and now we understand it, before we start in to give the third angel's message.

I read:

> As in revolutions the leaders try to gain the people over by the bait of promised independence, so at the time of the so-called reformation – which was a revolution against church authority and order in religion – it seems that it was the aim of the reformers to decoy the people under the pretext of making them independent of the priests, in whose hands our Saviour has placed the administering of the seven Sacraments of pardon and of grace.

> They began, therefore, by discarding five of these Sacraments, including the Sacrament of Order, in which Priests are ordained, and the Sacrament of Penance, in which the forgiveness of sins is granted to the penitent. . . They then reduced, as it appears, to a mere matter of form, the two Sacraments they professed to retain, namely, Holy Baptism and the Holy Eucharist. To make up for this rejection and *enable each individual to* prescribe for himself, and *procure by himself* the pardon of sins and divine grace, *independently of the priests.*

Elder Jones: Is this true doctrine? Is it true that a man can approach God by himself, independently of the priests? [Congregation: "Yes."] What saith the Lord? *Steps to Christ*, p. 117:

> The relations between God and each soul are as distinct and full as if there was not another soul for whom He gave His beloved Son.

Thank the Lord. Now I read on in the Catholic book:

> Independently of priests and of the sacraments, they invented an *exclusive means*, never known to the Church of God, and *still rejected* by all the Eastern Churches and *by the Roman Catholics throughout the world,* by which the followers of Luther ventured to declare that each individual can secure pardon and justification for himself, independently of priests and sacraments.
>
> They have framed a new *Dogma, not to be found in any of the Creeds,* or in the Canons of any General Council; I mean, the new dogma of *Justification by Faith alone, or by Faith only.*

That is the "new dogma" that is condemned by the papacy; that is not in any of the creeds which she has. On page 366 I read again:

> By adding the word *alone*, Protestants profess to exclude all exterior, ceremonial, pious, or charitable works, works of obedience or of penance, and good moral acts whatever, as *means of apprehending* justification, or as *conditions to* obtain it.

"Oh, yes, you have got to do something to pave the way; you have got to do something to get out of that place where you are," so that you can be justified. You must lift yourself up part of the way, and then the Lord will be moved and will receive you and justify you. That is Satan's doctrine. Shall we be Protestants or Catholics? That is the question. [Congregation: "Protestants."] Shall we proclaim the third angel's message against the worship of the beast and his image? or shall we be a part of the beast and his image ourselves? That is the question. For the image is the image of the beast in this point as well as in all else, even though it profess to be Protestant. It is apostate Protestant. On page 367 of the Catholic book I read the following:

> To do these acts with the view of being justified is, they say, like giving a penny to the queen to obtain from her a royal gift.

What saith the Lord? Page 51, *Steps to Christ*:

> This is the lesson which Jesus taught while He was on earth, that the gift which God promises us, we must believe we *do* receive, *and it is ours.*

Then which is Christianity? [Congregation: "The last."] But the Catholic Church says that this is Protestantism. It is true. Thank the Lord!

But we continue reading from this Catholic work:

> Come as you are, they add; you cannot be too bad for Jesus.

Thank the Lord that this is not Catholic doctrine. Thank the Lord it is no part of the beast or his worship nor the image and his worship. Let us put them together. What saith the Lord? Page 27, *Steps to Christ*:

> We can do nothing of ourselves. We must come just as we are.

Again on page 55, *Steps to Christ*:

> Jesus loves to have us come *just as we are, sinful.*

What is "sinful?" [Congregation: "Full of sin."] Does Jesus love to have us come to Him just as we are, *full of sin?* [Congregation: "Yes."] Does He? [Congregation: "Yes, sir."] Let us be Protestants. Let us have the third angel's message, which is the gospel of Jesus Christ.

> Jesus loves to have us come just as we are, sinful, helpless, dependent. We may come with all [how much? "All."] our weakness, our folly, our sinfulness, and fall at His feet in penitence. It is His glory to encircle us in the arms of His love and to bind up our wounds, to cleanse us from all impurity. . . None are so sinful that they cannot find strength, purity, and righteousness in Jesus, who died for them.

That is the gift of God. That is His gift – a free gift without money, without price, and I take it gladly and everlastingly thank Him for it. This is the Lord's idea of justification by faith. The other is Satan's idea. Let us read from the Catholic book again:

> Through *faith alone* in His promise, *they* [Protestants] *assert,* you can and should accept Christ's merits, seize Christ's redemption and His justice; appropriate Christ to yourself, believe that Jesus is with you, is yours, that He pardons your sins, and all this without any preparation and without any doing on your part.

Good! Thank the Lord, that is Protestantism! and Catholics know that it is Protestantism. Do you know it?

On page 53, *Steps to Christ*, let us see what the Lord says:

> It is the will of God to cleanse us from sin, to make us His children, and to enable us to live a holy life. So we may ask for these blessings, and believe that we receive them, and thank God that we *have* received them. It is our privilege to go to Jesus and be cleansed and to stand before the law without shame or remorse. Eph. 1:3.

[Congregation: "Amen!"] Without any need of doing penance? [Congregation: "Yes."] Thank the Lord.

Now the Catholic book again:

> In fact, that however deficient you may be in all other dispositions *which Catholics require,* and however loaded with sins, if you only trust in Jesus that He will forgive your sins and save you, you are by that *trust alone* forgiven, personally redeemed, justified, and placed in a state of salvation.

Now let us read on page 33, *Steps to Christ*, again:

> When Satan comes to tell you that you are a great sinner, look up to your Redeemer, and talk of His merits. That which will help you is to look to His light. Acknowledge your sins, but tell the enemy that "Jesus Christ came into the world to save sinners, and that you may be saved by His matchless love". Jesus asked Simon a question in regard to two debtors. One owed his lord a small sum, and the other owed him a very large sum, but he forgave them both, and Christ asked Simon which debtor would love his lord the most. Simon answered, "He to whom he forgave most." We have been great sinners, but Christ died that we might be forgiven. The *merits of His sacrifice* are *sufficient* to present to the father in our behalf.

Are they, in fact? [Congregation: "Yes sir."] Good! There is a great deal more in this Catholic work that I will not take time to read now. It goes on to define what *faith* is.

Now think carefully, because I have met people all the way along who think that this very thing is faith which this Catholic book calls faith.

I read page 368:

> The word "faith" in the Scripture sometimes means *confidence* in God's omnipotence and goodness, that He can and is willing to cure or benefit us by miraculous interposition. Mostly it refers to revealed truths, and signifies *belief* in them as such. *No one has a right* to give to the word faith a new meaning, *and take it,* for instance, *to signify reliance on Jesus* for being *personally saved* through this very reliance alone, unless Jesus Christ or the Apostles had, in some instance *clearly* attributed such a meaning to the word faith and taught the doctrine of *trust in Christ for personal salvation* as the only requisite for justification. No one should attach a particular meaning to the word *faith,* without having a good warrant in Scripture or in divine tradition.
>
> Now in many passages of Holy Scripture in which *saving* faith is plainly spoken of, by *faith* is not meant *a trust in Christ for personal salvation,* but evidently a firm belief that

> Jesus is the Messias, the Christ, the Son of God, that what is related of Him in the Gospel is true, and that what He taught is true.

On page 370, it defines faith, and I will read that before reading the opposite.

> These texts, all of which refer to saving faith, prove beyond a doubt that *not trust in Christ* for *personal salvation* but *the faith of the creed,* the faith in revealed truths.

Now what is faith according to that? "The faith of the creed."

They simply draw up a statement of stuff that they call the doctrine of God and then you *believe* that and *do your best* and that passes for justification by faith. Whether the creed is drawn up in actual writing or whether it is somebody's idea that they want to pass off by a vote in a General Conference, it makes no difference in principle, the creed is there and subscription to it is just that kind of faith. And there are people here who remember a time – four years ago; and a place – Minneapolis – when three direct efforts were made to get just such a thing as that fastened upon the third angel's message, by a vote in a General Conference. What somebody believed – set that up as the landmarks and then vote to stand by the landmarks, whether you know what the landmarks are or not, and then go ahead and agree to keep the commandments of God and a lot of other things that you are going to do, and that was to be passed off as justification by faith.

Were we not told at that time that the angel of God said, "Do not take that step; you do not know what is in that"? "I can't take time to tell you what is in that, but the angel has said, 'Do not do it.'" The papacy was in it. That was what the Lord was trying to tell us and get us to understand. The papacy was in it. It was like it has been in every other church that has come out from the papacy; they would run a little while by faith in God and then fix up some man's idea of doctrine and vote to stand by that and vote that that is the doctrine of this church and then that is "the faith of the creed," and then follow it up with *their own doing.*

Is there anybody in this house who was there at that time that cannot see now what that was back there? Then, brethren, is it not time to cut loose, if it takes the very life out of us? It will take the very life out of us; it will crucify us with Jesus Christ. It will cause such a death to sin as we never dreamed of in our lives before. It will take all that papal mind out of us, all that iron spirit out of us, and it will put there the divine, tender, loving mind of Jesus Christ, that wants no creed, because it has Christ Himself.

Well, let me read that again and then the contradiction of it here. It seems as though one book was written for the other. Brethren, which of the books shall we follow? Ah, *Steps to Christ*. That is what it is, and then it is steps *with* Him; when we have stepped *to,* then it is steps *with* Christ.

Now, I will read that over again and then read the opposite:

> Now, in many passages of Holy Scripture in which *saving* faith is plainly spoken of, by *faith* is not meant *a trust in Christ for personal salvation,* but evidently a firm belief that Jesus is the Messias, the Christ, the Son of God, that what is related of Him in the gospel is true, and that what He taught is true.

That is Catholic "faith." Now what is the Lord's definition, His idea of faith?

Page 69, *Steps to Christ*:

> When we speak of faith, there is a distinction that should be borne in mind. There is a *kind of belief* that is *wholly distinct from faith.* The existence and power of God, the truth of His word, are facts that even Satan and his hosts cannot at heart deny.

Did not the evil spirits tell Jesus that He was Christ? [Congregation: "Yes."] Then the devils, Satan and his hosts, do believe in the existence and power of God, that His word is true, and that Jesus is the Messias, the Christ, the Son of God. Satan and his hosts believe all that. But that is not faith. How much power is there in their belief to work good in their lives? None at all. They have no faith. But just this is the Catholic faith, isn't it? What kind of faith is that then? That is satanic faith. That is all it is, satanic belief, as this puts it; but yet the papacy passes it for faith. And whoever passes that for faith is a papist even thou he profess to be a Seventh-day Adventist.

But I read on from *Steps to Christ*:

> The Bible says that "the devils also believe and tremble," but this *is not faith.* Where there is not only a belief in God's word, but a *submission of the will* to Him; where the *heart is yielded* to Him, the *affections fixed upon Him,* THERE IS FAITH.

That is the truth of justifying faith; that is righteousness by faith; that is a faith that works, thank the Lord – not a faith that believes something away off, that keeps the truth of God in the outer court, and then seeks by his own efforts to make up the lack. Not that. No, but faith that *works*. It itself is working; *it* has a divine power in it to manifest God's will in man before the world. That is righteousness by faith – the righteousness which faith obtains, which it receives, and which it holds – the righteousness of God.

I continue reading from *Steps to Christ*:

> Faith that works by love and purifies the soul. Through *this faith* the heart is renewed *in the image of God.*

I do not need to read any more, as this is enough to show the contrast and the time is far gone. This is enough to show that the papal doctrine of justification by faith is Satan's doctrine; it is simply the natural mind depending upon itself, working through itself, exalting itself and then covering it all up with a profession of belief in this, that, and the other, but having *no power of God*. Then, brethren, let it be rooted up forever.

In paganism Satan led the mind of man to put itself on an equality with God, without any covering at all. Then Christ came into the world, revealing the true gospel as never before – Christ in man, man justified by faith in Him, and faith alone – a faith which has divine life in it, a faith which has divine power in it, a faith which lives and works, a faith that brings all things to him who has it, and restores the image of God in the soul. Then Satan took that same carnal mind which in paganism had made itself equal with God and now he covered it with his own idea of faith and passed it off as justification by faith and exalted the chief representative of it, above all that is called God or that is worshiped, so that as God he sitteth in the place of worship of God, showing himself that he is God.

Oh, that we may have the mind of Christ and not the carnal mind! Oh that we may have the mind of Christ and not the mind of Satan! Oh that we may have the Lord's idea of justification by faith and not Satan's idea of it! Oh that we may receive the Lord's idea of righteousness by faith and not Satan's! Then shall we indeed receive the latter rain, "the teaching of righteousness, according to righteousness."

Brethren, let us believe the third angel's message. Now I hope that the way is clearly open before us to study as it is the righteousness of God which is by faith of Jesus Christ unto all and upon all them that believe. Then let us go at it in the fear of God, seeking for His Holy Spirit to make it plan to us, so that that Teacher of Righteousness may teach us righteousness according to righteousness.

Sermon 13

February 20, 1893

The last study we had here was an effort to get as plainly as possible before this people, the difference between satanic belief and the faith of Jesus Christ; the difference between justification by works under the heading of justification by faith – the difference between that and justification by faith as it is. That was the effort; that was the aim. And you will remember how it was done. And that brought us to the subject that is ever before us now: that we must have the teaching of righteousness according to righteousness. And this can be, as we have found, only according to God's idea of righteousness and not our own, and in order to have God's idea of righteousness instead of our own, we must have the mind that can comprehend it, and that alone is the mind of Jesus Christ. Whoever has not the mind of Christ itself, whoever has not yielded up himself and all that he has and is and received the mind of Christ instead, does not know, and he *cannot* know what righteousness by faith is; he cannot know what justification by faith is. He may profess it; he may assent to it; he may claim it, but he cannot know it, for no man can know it with the natural mind. Let us turn now and read from the Bible where it says so.

1 Cor. 2:14:

> But the natural man receiveth not the things of the Spirit of God: for they are foolishness unto him.

That is just the way the righteousness by faith has been treated by hundreds of people who profess to believe it.

Elder Lewis Johnson: The priests of the State church in Scandinavia preach it that way.

Yes, the Catholics all preach it that way. With the natural mind it belongs that way. And it will always be that way with the man who has not the mind of Christ. But the man who has not that mind does not know it. He thinks he is straight; he thinks he has got the righteousness of God which is by faith. And yet what he has is not so good but what he has to do ever so much himself in order to patch it up and complete it; but yet he thinks that that is righteousness by faith. "But the natural man receiveth not the things of the Spirit of God, for they are foolishness unto him: neither can he know them, because they are spiritually discerned."

How can a man then know the righteousness of God with the natural mind? Now, I just appeal to you. I do not care who you are, whether you have ever heard of Christ before in your life. Now just take that verse as it reads; how can a man know the righteousness of God for himself with the carnal mind – the mind of Satan, for that is what the carnal mind is. Now, can that man do it? [Congregation: "No."] Can the mind of Satan know the righteousness of God?

Again: the righteousness of God as expressed in letters, in words, in the ten commandments is the law of God. Now all agree with that; there is not a Seventh-day Adventist that will not agree with that. The difficulty is, so many people try to get the righteousness of God out of the law *by* the law. Some try to get it – No. They *actually get* it without the law, by the faith of Jesus Christ, which is "unto all and upon all them that believe: for there is no difference." "For now . . ." (and that means *now*!) "Now the righteousness of God without the law, is manifested, being witnessed by the law and the prophets, even the righteousness of God which is by faith of Jesus Christ unto all and upon all them that believe: for there is no difference." Rom. 3:21, 22.

He who obtains it in that way has it, but I say we all agree, every Seventh-day Adventist will confess, that the ten commandments express in letters, in words, the righteousness of God.

Now, then, "The carnal mind is enmity against God: for it is not subject to the Law of God, neither indeed can be." How then can the carnal mind know the righteousness of God? How can the carnal mind be subject to it? It *cannot* be, says the Lord. Then the man who has only the carnal mind, who knows only the natural birth and has not the mind of Jesus Christ, the man who has not had the natural mind of Christ there, cannot know the righteousness of God which is by faith of Jesus Christ. And now, just now, when the Lord wants to reveal to us the righteousness of God according to righteousness, to give to us the teaching of righteousness according to righteousness, now as never before on earth, it is that we need and must have the mind of Jesus Christ alone.

Now, "the carnal mind is not subject to the law of God, neither indeed can be." Is the mind of Christ subject to the law of God? [Congregation: "Yes."] Was it ever anything else? [Congregation: "No."] The mind of Christ was subject to the word of God always. The whole Bible, of course is simply the drawing out of the law of God as it is in Christ. Well then, was not the mind of Christ always subject to the law? to the whole word of God just as it is? [Congregation: "Yes."] There was never any hitch upon that. Wherever the word of God was read, how did the mind of Christ receive it? It instantly received it. He would not say, "Now how can that be, I wonder." Don't you suppose He said, "Well now I think that means this way." Didn't He say, "Are not you a little too strong about reading that text?" "Can't you modify it just a little?" Did He ever get troubled over what the Bible said about anything or what the Lord would say? No. Whenever the word of God was spoken, the mind of Christ instantly responded.

Brethren, I know that you can know and that any man in this world can know and can have just that kind of a mind. I know that you can have just such a mind, that whenever the word of God speaks the response is instantaneous, and there is no question or doubt or sign of rejection. Now you can see upon this very thing, that if you and I have such a mind as that, then when the word of God is read, there is no rising up, or objection, or dissent – is that the mind of Christ? [Congregation: "Yes."] Then it is easy enough to know whether we have the mind of Christ or not.

If your mind or my mind, if your disposition or my disposition or yourself or myself is not in that surrendered condition – that position of surrender unto God – that whenever He speaks in the word there or by His prophets and there is anything in that mind or in that heart that raises up any objection or dissent, then whose mind have we? [Congregation: "The carnal mind."] That is the mind that started out to object in the first place. The time has come to get rid of that thing.

But I say that a man can have just that kind of a mind whenever and whatever the word of God speaks there is instant response. There is nothing in that mind or about it in the world that can rise up in objection against it. That mind is not natural to a man, but a man can have it, and can know that he has it and that is the mind that we are to have. That is the mind to which the Lord can reveal His righteousness according to righteousness; because it is the mind that receives from God just what God has to give in God's own way and not in any way that I would fix up or modify or discount it.

So then the man who receives the idea, *the truth,* of justification by faith or righteousness by faith, according to *his own idea* or his own view of it, simply cannot do it; he simply has not got it; that is all. It is just that same satanic idea of righteousness by faith; it is simply the same Roman Catholic system of justification by works, passing it off for Justification by Faith. And the time has come now in a great deal more serious sense than nine-tenths of us dream of, when we need to know that we have the righteousness of God and Justification by Faith in another sense than the Roman Catholics use it. That is settled.

I will read a passage or two that will connect with what we had the other night. In *Testimonies for the Church*, Vol. 1, page 186, I read the passage about the Laodicean message: what it is designed to do:

> It is designed to arouse the people of God, to discover to them their backslidings, and to lead to zealous repentance, that they may be favored with the presence of Jesus and be fitted for the loud cry of the third angel.

Who will be fitted for the loud cry of the third angel? Those who have the presence of Jesus Christ. Those to whom the Laodicean message has brought by its working and its intent the presence of Jesus Christ. This means the *personal* presence too –

not imaginary, a way off presence; it is not that at all. Let us read the explanation of it here in *Steps to Christ*, pages 82-85:

> When Christ ascended to heaven, the sense of His presence was still with His followers. *It was a personal presence,* full of love and light. Jesus, the Saviour, who had walked and talked and prayed with them, who had spoken hope and comfort to their hearts, had while the message of peace was still upon His lips, been taken up from them into heaven, and the tones of His voice had come back to them, as the cloud of angels received Him – "Lo, I am with you alway, even unto the end of the world." He had ascended to heaven in the form of humanity. They knew that He was before the throne of God, their friend and Saviour still; that His sympathies were unchanged; that He was still identified with suffering humanity. He was presenting before God the merits of His own precious blood, showing His wounded hands and feet, in remembrance of the price He had paid for His redeemed. They knew that He had ascended to heaven to prepare places for them, and that He would come again, and take them to Himself. As they met together, after the ascension, they were eager to present their requests to the Father, in the name of Jesus.

That was a fine prayer meeting, wasn't it? Where there were 120 people, each one *eager* to present his requests to the Father in the name of Jesus.

> In solemn awe they bowed in prayer, repeating the assurance "Whatsoever ye shall ask the Father in my name, he will give it you. Hitherto have ye asked nothing in my name: ask, and ye shall receive, that your joy may be full." They extended their hands of faith higher and higher, with the mighty argument, "It is Christ that died, yea rather, that is risen again, who is even at the right hand of God, who also maketh intercession for us." *And Pentecost brought them the presence of the Comforter,* of whom Christ had said, *He "shall be in you."* And he had further said, "It is expedient for you that I go away; . . . for if I go not away, the Comforter will not come unto you; but if I go away I will send him unto you." Henceforth through the Spirit, Christ was to abide continually in the hearts of His children. Their union with him was closer than when He was personally with them.

That is what He wants us to have now. He wants us to have now what they got at Pentecost – the personal presence of Jesus Christ, and if we have that, He will be closer to us than if He was here in the body. He wants to come closer to you and me than He would be if He should come to the meeting here every night and sit down with us. That is what He wants now.

> The light, and love, and power of the indwelling Christ shone out through them, so that men beholding, "marveled; and they took knowledge of them, that they had been with Jesus."

Here is a statement in *Testimony* No. 31, page 156:

> The message borne in the love of Christ, with the worth of souls constantly before us, would win even from worldlings the decision, "They are like Jesus."

The time has come when He wants that message borne that way, and He is going to have it borne that way. If those who profess His name now will not let Him come in in His fullness, so they can bear the message that way, He will find a people that will. That is where we are now. We cannot dally any longer.

> All that Christ was to the first disciples, He desires to be to His children today, for in that last prayer, with the little band of disciples gathered about Him, He said, "Neither pray I for these alone, but for them also which shall believe on me through their word."
>
> Jesus prayed for us, and He asked that we might be one with Him, even as He is one with the Father. What a union is this! The Saviour had said of Himself, "The Son can do nothing of Himself," "The Father that dwelleth in me, He doeth the works." Then if Christ is dwelling in our hearts, *He will work* in us.

The man that is so anxious and so dreadfully afraid that you will not let him have any works to do and that you are going to destroy all his works – if Christ is dwelling in His heart, he will find works to do. Brethren, don't be so anxious about works; find the Lord Jesus Christ and you will find work, more than you can do. [Congregation: "Amen!"] But the difficulty is, when the people get their minds on works and works and works instead of upon *Jesus Christ* in *order* to work, they pervert the whole thing. Satan does not care how much a man professes justification by faith, and righteousness by faith, so long as he keeps his mind on works. That is just the thought that is before us here in this definition of faith that we read the other night. Let me read it again. page 69, *Steps to Christ*:

> When we speak of faith there is a distinction that should be borne in mind. There is a kind of belief that is wholly distinct from faith. The existence and power of God, the truth of His word, are facts that even Satan and his hosts cannot at heart deny.

They believe that, but what power does their believing it bring to them to make them righteous, or to enable them to do good works? What power is there in their belief? What power does that give to them? [Congregation: "None."] No, it is away off there, simply as a theory, held off to look at, held as a theory, held as a creed; and so, a spirit even, can believe in the existence and power of God; he can believe the truth of the Bible; he can believe that Jesus is the Messiah, the Son of God, the Holy One of God, and be a devil. And in the form of a papist he can believe all this is this way and profess justification by faith at the same time, and he can be a great stickler for what they call "good works" at the same time. Yes, he can work the very skin off his bones in order to be good, in order to be righteous, in order to move God, as we read the other night. You know they do it. You know they make pilgrimages and do penances, and fairly wear themselves out, and in addition to these things they will shut themselves off from every earthly comfort.

But who is doing the work? Who in these things does the work? Self does the work in order to be righteous, in order to have that treasure of merit that will give an increase of grace in this world and an increase of glory in heaven. That is what it is for, is it not? [Congregation: "Yes."] Who is doing it then? [Congregation: "Self."] Yes, sir. Has the mind, as the heart been yielded to God? Are the affections fixed upon Him? Is the surrender of all to Him? No. And therefore it is still self in all.

Who then is to do the work in order that it may be good works always? Let us read again: "If Christ is dwelling in our hearts, *He will work in us* 'both to *will* and *to do* of His good pleasure.' *We* shall *work* as *He* works; we shall manifest *the same spirit*. And thus, loving Him and abiding in Him, we shall 'grow up into Him in all things, which is the head, even Christ.'" Now, then, that is what the Lord wants, that is what the mind of Christ is. As we had the thought the other evening – I cannot have the mind of Christ separate from Him. I cannot have the mind of Christ without having Him personally. But the personal presence of Jesus Christ is just what He wants to give us by the Holy Spirit in the outpouring of the latter rain just now. The personal presence of Christ is what He wants to give us.

Then the rest of that definition of belief: A person may believe in the existence and power of God; he may believe the truth of the Bible; he may believe and say that Jesus Christ is the Messiah, the Son of God, the Holy One of God, and yet be a devil. But that *is not faith*. There is no power in that kind of belief to help anybody. Is not that the secret of all these exhortations that have come to us in the Testimonies all these years, that the truth must not be kept in the outer court, but must be brought into the inner sanctuary of the soul; is not that what this means? [Congregation: "Yes."] Is not the idea there that men will hold the truth away off and look at it as a theory and put their own construction upon it and their own interpretation into it and then go about of themselves to do what they believe? That is not faith.

Here is faith: "Where there is not only a belief in God's word, but *a submission of will to Him;* where *the heart is yielded to Him,* the affections fixed upon Him." Now these are weighty expressions; they are worth considering. "The submission of the will to Him," is it done? Is *your* will submitted to Him never to be taken back, or exercised in your own way or for yourself? Is your will surrendered to Him? Yours? Yours, I mean? Has He *your* will? Says one, "I think He has." Well, you want to know it. "Well," says another, "I have been trying to submit my will to Him." Well, stop your trying and submit your will to Him and be done with it and know it.

"The submission of the will to Him," is your will submitted to Him? Is it gone so that you know it is gone, and that you have no wish or impulse or any inclination ever in any situation to use it yourself? Is it gone? You *can know* it. You can *know* whether that is done. [Voice: "How?"] How? Why by doing it, telling the Lord it is done and it is so. Of course a man knows it is so when it is done. [A voice: "If he does not know it, it is not done."] Exactly.

If a man does not know it, that is the strongest possible evidence that he could have that it is not done. And when it is done, ah! He knows it. That is the very thing. When it is done he becomes a spiritual man, and he knows what he never knew before in his life. The natural man cannot receive it, he cannot understand it, he never can. How in the world can I understand what there is in the doing of a thing I never did? Here is something that you have done, you know how it goes, but I never did it, and yet I want you to explain it all to me so that I will understand just how it is done, without the *doing* of it myself. Brethren, that is not straight, and much less is it straight in this thing, for this is to be known, and can be known only between God and the individual himself. "They shall be all taught of God." One can tell another that it is a fact; one can tell another that he knows that it is a fact. But no one can give it to another, so that my brother can get it from me. I can tell him it is a fact, and that he can know it, but *he* must learn it from God. You do it simply by yielding to God. That is the only way any man can do it or know it. Lots of people do not understand how, but the worst difficulty is *they will not do it* when you tell them how.

Now I ask again, Is your will submitted to Him? Is that thing done? Have you gone over that barrier and stand where you know that you stand there and that you know that your will is surrendered to Him, for Him to use in His way, and that there is no further question about it, and no dissent from it in any way? Now is your will submitted to God for Him to use as He pleases and you have no objection to raise at all; you have no thought or inclination to use it your way; you want Him to do His way, and that is all you care for? Is that so? Is your will there? [Congregation: "Yes."]

Are any here in whom it is not so? You just go and tell the Lord all about it. Tell Him, "Lord, I submit everything to thee; everything goes; nothing stays; I do not retain a single thing; all is gone; everything, will and all – to thee, that thou mayest use it both to will and to do." [Congregation: "Amen."] Brethren, we every one need to do just that, here, each day. The Lord wants to come in here in just the way that that will let Him in.

But as long as I reserve some of my will, I will go my way in spite of myself, I cannot have God use me fully. He cannot come in fully, Christ cannot come in fully, unless there is a full submission to Him. Let there be some dying here. Let there be some actual dying to self. That is what it means; it means death: and of course people never struggle to die. They struggle to stay alive, if there are any struggles.

Bear in mind that it is not enough to "want" to die. Go ahead and die; that is what the Lord wants. Says one, How shall I do that? He tells how: "Reckon ye also yourselves to be dead indeed." Dead indeed. Brother Durland read to us here yesterday, "He that is dead is freed from sin." It is so. "Reckon ye also yourselves to be dead indeed unto sin," and God will furnish the fact. The point is, brethren, we need to get acquainted with the Lord. The trouble is, people are not personally acquainted with the Lord and do not know how these things are with Him.

"Where the heart is yielded to Him." How much of it? [Congregation: "All of it."] Is it done? [Congregation: "Yes."] The whole heart is gone? Everything is gone? Well, says one, I have yielded all I know. Well, now just take the other step, and yield all you *do not* know.

Elder O. S. Ferren: When a person does that, is he poor, and miserable?

Elder Jones: Yes, sir.

Elder Ferren: And naked and blind?

Elder Jones: Yes, sir.

Elder Ferren: And does not know it?

Elder Jones: I say, Yes, of course he is. But, thank the Lord, he has riches that embrace the universe. Says one, I cannot understand that. I cannot either, but I know it is a fact.

Why, brethren, let us bear this in mind to start with and never try to forget it, because the further you go the more you will see it is a fact, that when we get hold of the gospel of Jesus Christ just as it is, we find at every turn and in every phase of it, the *mystery of God*. At every point and in every turn, you find a place and a situation in which nothing can explain it but God, and all you can do is to believe that God is there. It is so and you will know the fact, and let Him go ahead and explain it. It will take eternity to do that. What He wants you and me to do is to be glad that we have eternity before us in which for Him to explain it to us. I am going to be glad that I have eternity to live in – not bother about whether I understand this, that, or the other. No. God forbid that we should throw away eternal life because we cannot understand all that God understands. But, ah! There is the same spirit again that Satan had – to be equal with God and not submit to any unless we can understand all. Let that mind be put away. And let us believe the Lord and let Him take His own good time to explain it.

Well, then, is your heart yielded to Him? Now that thought I had a moment ago. Many say, "I have surrendered to the Lord all I know." That is not enough. What you want to do is to surrender to Him all you know and all you *do not* know. Because when I surrender to Him only what I know, there are a good many things left that I *do not* know, a good many situations where I will meet myself, and good many things will come up, and I will meet something that will be very attractive and desirable to me, and if I have not surrendered all, what then? There will be a contest, whether I will surrender that or not. So I am kept constantly in hot water to know whether I am surrendered to the Lord or not. The Lord wants you to get out of the hot water and stay out. Surrender everything you know and everything you do not know. Let everything go to Him, with no reservation now or evermore. Then you are not afraid of anything; you do not care if you drop into the bottom of the sea the next minute. It is all surrendered; You are in His hands – and then you have got something. That man has got something; he has something never had before, and he has something that he cannot get until he does just that thing.

"The affections fixed upon Him." Are your affections fixed there, so that He takes precedence of everything? So that He is first before everything? Nothing at all coming into the account anywhere or at any time? Is that so? When a man does that he has got something; he has indeed, and he knows it. Well, says one, is not a man to care for his wife and children? Why, they are all surrendered to the Lord too and cannot the Lord care for them a great deal better than you can without being surrendered to Him? They are surrendered too, and instead of the situation being this: that when my affections are fixed upon Him they are severed from those who are dear to me, it is the other way; when my affections are fixed upon Him, they are *intensified* and *deepened* and glorified, upon those who are tenderly connected with me. Why, people miss it all when they think that to fix the affections on God is going to separate them from somebody they like while on the earth; it is the only way they can love properly those whom they think they like on the earth.

Well, now, is it so? Is the will submitted to Him? Is your heart yielded to God, so that your affections are fixed upon Him? Is it done, so that you can stand before Him and thank the Lord that it is so? I do not mean to stand up in the congregation and say that it is so but just tell it over *to the Lord* that it is so. People will get up in the congregation and say things there that they will not say to the Lord. You tell it to the Lord. Tell Him that your will is given up bodily to Him. Submit the whole thing without a particle of reservation now or evermore, and just tell Him that your heart is yielded up to Him, for it is good for nothing and you want His heart instead of yours. And after that your affections are fixed upon Him, and that there they stay. And they will stay there. Tell Him that all the time, every day; tell Him wherever you go. Live with Him, brethren; live with Him; live with Him; that is what He wants. Why He is raised from the dead, and we are raised up with Him that we may live with Him. Romans 6:8. His personal presence is to be with us. That is what the Laodicean message is to do for us; it brings the presence of Christ to live in us.

This you can do alone for yourself and nobody else can do it for you. Brethren, let us go to doing that. Let us get into that place. When a man is there, then he simply waits the direction of the Lord; waits the time of the Lord. When the Lord gets ready to pour out His Holy Spirit there is nothing to hinder. If there be something that he does not know, Oh well, that was surrendered long ago.

It may be as dear as the right eye, but that went long ago. It is gone, thank the Lord, and so there is nothing between you and Him and He can pour out His Spirit whenever He pleases. That is where He wants you and me to stand in this Conference, waiting for Him to give us that teaching of righteousness according to righteousness.

Now how much of Christ are we to have? When the personal presence of Christ comes to us He will be closer to us than if He would come in here to meeting with us every day. Is that so? [Congregation: "Yes, sir."] Well, then, that is the gospel, is it not? That is the righteousness of God, which is by faith of Jesus Christ. That is the gospel, "for therein is the righteousness of God revealed from faith to faith." Romans 1:17. Oh, no! From faith to *works*! The righteousness of God is revealed from faith to *works*! "the righteousness of God is revealed from *faith* to FAITH." Thank the Lord.

The presence of Christ, the personal presence of Christ – "Christ in you the hope of glory" – that is the gospel, isn't it? Now, see here – and there is not any need of their being a particle of misunderstanding about this question of faith and works, or a particle of hesitation about it – see here: Christ was in the world once, wasn't He? [Congregation: "Yes."] He did not do anything of Himself. "Of mine own self I can do nothing." The Father dwelt in Him. He did the works. "The Father that dwelleth in me He doeth the works." John 14:10. "As my father hath sent me, even so send I you."

As God was in Christ, Christ is to be in us. Is that so? [Congregation: "Yes."] Is Christ the same yesterday, today and forever? [Congregation: "Yes."] How did He act when He was on earth, in our flesh that He had? How did He act in that, when He was here before? He went about doing good; He cared for the sick, sympathized with them. "He hath borne our griefs, and carried our sorrows." Bears our sickness. His sympathy with the sick was so close that when He went to minister to them He actually entered into their feelings. He actually bore their sicknesses. How will He act when He is in our flesh now? [Voice: "He will act the same way."] How will He act when He is in your flesh? When He is in the flesh now? [Voice: "As He acted then."]

Don't you see then how that the works take care of themselves in Him who has *faith* in Jesus Christ. I do not mean that satanic belief. I mean the man that has *faith*. Then don't you see what those people miss who get their minds on works more than on Christ? They miss the very incentive and the very power that alone can do the things that are good, to reach and minister to the sick in the right spirit, to visit the poor and minister to them in the right spirit. Have not you seen people that have ministered to the poor and the sick, in a way that makes those people feel worse than if they had not gone there at all? That is not the kind of ministering that Jesus Christ does. That is not the kind of ministering He does. No, sir. It is Christ in you. And when He goes with you and in you there stands the testimony, "It will win even from worldlings the statement, 'They are like Jesus.'"

What does He want the world to see in us? [Congregation: "Christ."] He wants the world to see in our lives, Jesus Christ – the life of Christ, Christ in you the hope of glory – and they will know it, and you will know it. Be sure that Christ is there, and the Spirit of the Lord will convey to peoples' minds that He is there. But as certainly as you and I appear instead of Christ, that is all that will appear, and the world will see only that.

Now brethren, is there any real need of anybody getting any misunderstanding of having any hitch at all about whether righteousness by faith, justification by faith carries with it in itself the very living virtue of God to work in God's way? Is there any need of it? No. Not the least. And it will never be done by any mind that is submissive to God. It will not be done by the mind that is yielded to God and wanting to have God's way, Christ first and last, and through all and in all and over all. Because then he becomes so acquainted with Christ that he knows that faith in Jesus Christ brings that divine presence and that divine power and that divine virtue and that divine grace that will so make him who receives it, so move upon him, that he who has the most faith will be the one of all the world that will do the most work. Why you cannot separate it. The divine life is in it; the divine power is in it; the divine word is in it.

Did not Paul strive, says one, and does not the Saviour say, "Strive to enter in at the strait gate"? Yes, he does, and Paul tells us how. Let us turn and read that. It is right upon this very line, and then we will quit for tonight. It is in the first chapter of Colossians, the 25th verse and onward: The gospel "whereof I am made a minister, according to the dispensation of God which is given to me for you, to fulfill the word of God, even the mystery which hath been hid from ages and generations but now is made manifest to his saints: to whom God would make known what is the riches of the glory of this mystery among the Gentiles." What is it that God wants to make known, at this time, to you and me? He wants to make known "what is the riches of the glory of this mystery." That is a great deal, is it not? How great are the riches of the glory of the mystery of God? How great? As great as God. Then how can we know them except by the mind of Christ, which is brought to us by the Holy Spirit bringing His presence?

Now, then: "Which is Christ in you, the hope of glory: whom we preach, warning every man, and teaching every man in all wisdom; that we may present every man perfect in Christ Jesus: whereunto I also labor, *striving* according to *his working, which worketh in me* MIGHTILY."

How can I strive when I have nothing to strive with? "Without me ye can do" – How much? [Congregation: "Nothing."] Is that so? [Congregation: "Yes."] Then without Christ I want to know how you are going to strive. Without Him how are you going to strive? I want you to think of that. "Without me ye can do nothing." "Dead in trespasses and sins." Is that so? How can a dead man strive? " When we were without strength." Rom. 5:6. Were we without strength? [Congregation: "Yes."] That is so. Then how can a man strive who has no strength? Don't you see, then, that it is an utter satanic perversion of the divine idea, to go to striving and working and wearing the life out *in order* to get to Christ *to obtain* this gift of justification. No. It is the *free* gift of God to every man, and every man who receives it, receives Jesus Christ Himself indeed. The gospel is the power of God unto salvation unto every one that believeth. Then he who surrenders all, yields all, and obtains that power of God, that living Saviour – to whom is given all power in heaven and earth – he has *something to strive with;* he has *strength* that he can put to a good purpose; he has *power* with which he can do something.

Then where does the striving come in? to find the Lord? or to *use the power* which the Lord gives, which He puts into us? Which is it? [Voice: "To use the power."] Assuredly. Then do not let us get it on the wrong side, brethren; let us have it on the right side.

"Striving according to his working, which worketh in me mightily." As he says in that other place: "The love of Christ constraineth us." 2 Corinthians 5:14. Constrains, impels, drives on with an irresistible force. That is the idea that is in the word striving. Other translations give it, "agonize" to enter into the strait gate. And they do really and bodily agonize and wear themselves out, doing penance, just like any other Catholic – and they will do it all in order to move the Lord, so that He will have pity on them. That is not the thought.

It *is* agonizing, but everybody who is acquainted with it, knows that the word is taken from the Greek games, the Greek races. One who entered the games was an *agonistes.* They started out to run a race. Now what does he do? He just strains every nerve to win the race; every faculty of his being is devoted to the object before him, isn't it? [Congregation: "Yes, sir."] Now that is bodily exercise; that is bodily striving, agonizing. Is this that kind that Christ is talking about? [Congregation: "No."] What kind is this? Spiritual. Yes, of course. Then carrying that thought from *bodily* exercise, that *bodily* straining of every nerve, carrying that into the spiritual realm, what does it signify? Doesn't it signify that complete surrender of the will to Christ, that surrender of the heart, and the affections to Him, that makes no reserve? And there is no reservation; it yields everything to Him, every fiber of the being is devoted to the one object and the glory of God. Is not that so? Then His power moving us, His divine power urging us on, don't you see? I say again that in all cases he who believes in Jesus Christ most fully will work most for Him.

Now let us have this word, and that will be the best close I could make to the whole thing tonight. *Steps to Christ,* page 79: "The heart that *rests most fully* upon Christ will be the *most earnest* and *active* in *labor* for Him." Amen. [Congregation: "Amen."] Do not forget that now. Do not think that the man who says that he rests wholly upon Jesus Christ is either a physical or a spiritual loafer. If he shows this loafing in his life, he is not resting on Christ at all but on his own self.

No, sir, the heart that rests most fully upon Christ will be most earnest and active in labor for Him. That is what real faith is. That is faith that will bring to you the outpouring of the latter rain; that is faith that will bring to you and me the teaching of righteousness according to righteousness – the living presence of Jesus Christ – to prepare us for the loud cry and the carrying of the third angel's message in the only way in which it can be carried from this Conference.

Sermon 14

February 22, 1893

We have seen the manifestation of the natural mind – the carnal mind – in two of its ways: paganism and papacy. But there is another one that is modern. There is one that has arisen nowadays, another trick that the author of the carnal mind is playing and by which he will deceive lots of people if they have not the mind that is in Christ. Now whose mind is the carnal mind? [Congregation: "Satan's"] What is the thing that the carnal mind does mind? [Congregation: "Self."] In Satan it is self; in us it is self. We have seen how that in paganism, open, bold, naked paganism, it put that in the place of God, equal with God, in the immortality of the soul. Then we have found how that when Christianity came into the world this same carnal mind got up a counterfeit of that and covered itself – the same carnal mind – with a form of Christianity, and called it justification by faith when it was all justification by works – the same carnal mind. That is the papacy, the mystery of iniquity.

Now there is another development in Satan's working in the last days, separate from paganism as it was in itself, and separate from the papacy as it was in itself, and as it has been manifested so far. Is that so? [Congregation: "Yes."] In what form does that come? In what form does Satan work in the last days? [Congregation: "Spiritualism."] Yes, and this will exalt self. But will spiritualism always work in the name of Satan? [Congregation: "No."] The nearer we come to the second coming of the Saviour the more fully spiritualism will be professing Christ. Who is it that comes before the Saviour comes, many of them? [Congregation: "False Christs."] There will be many coming and saying, "I am Christ"; and at last Satan himself comes – as Satan? [Congregation: "No. As Christ."] He comes as Christ, he is received as Christ. So then the people of God must be so well acquainted with the Saviour that no profession of the name of Christ will be received or accepted where it is not the actual, genuine thing. But when false Christianity is presenting itself to the world, when every kind of a false Christ appears, then how alone can a person be safe? How shall a man know that these are false? Only by Him who is the true; only by having His mind itself.

Now I want to read you an expression of this last phase of the carnal mind. We have read the other two; we have read the pagan and the papal. Now when we read this last then we will have all three of the stages; we will have before us the dragon, the beast, and the false prophet. And then there will be no shadow of an excuse for any one of us after that, taking any position but that which is openly and itself alone the mind of Jesus Christ and the righteousness of God according to His idea of righteousness. Will there? No excuse. When we see before us the direct expression of the false way in all three of its forms, then, even though we be not able to understand or see the other, we will know that well enough to let it alone, and take the other whether we see it or not. Would not we rather let the devil go that we see, and accept the Lord that we cannot see as we would like to? Which would you rather? I would rather take the Lord with my eyes shut, than the devil with my eyes *open*.

This is a monthly publication – I will tell you what it is presently; but I will read a passage or two from it first. This is a discipline for the week – a course of training for each day of the week.

> Let Thursday be your day for declaring your faith.

See what the faith is.

> Say, "I do believe that God is now working with me and through me and by me and for me." Say it with a sure certainty, for it is true.
> On Friday be courageous and strong and powerful; overcome all obstacles by your word; say, "I can do all things through Christ that strengtheneth me." Say this with all the strength of your being, and I tell you that you can do just whatever you want to do, even to the working of miracles.

Now that is a lie. That you all may see that it is a lie, I read Wednesday's discipline:

> On Wednesday use the affirmations; not only the affirmations of science, but affirm all good things *in yourself*.

[*Voice from the congregation*: "That proves it is a lie."]

Don't they say God is working in me, and by me, and for me, and through me? When we have come to Jesus and have His righteousness and His goodness, then can't we affirm that *we* are good? [Congregation: "No."] What is the reason? [Congregation: "It is in Christ; it is not in us."] You are willing to admit then, that when you have found Jesus and all the wealth and the honor and power and the riches that there is in Him, that even then we cannot boast that we are good? Are you willing to admit that? are you? [Voice: "Yes, sir."] Are you? [Voice: "Yes, sir."] All right. That is not near all.

I read more:

> Affirm all good things *in yourself*. Praise *yourself* that you are so kind and loving, and that you are so honest in your intentions of serving the good; praise *yourself* that you are so steadfast in these same intentions; praise *yourself* because you are so strong and healthy.

Yes, perhaps praise *yourself* because you live up so strictly to the health reform so that you have good health. You have done it; praise *yourself* for it?

> Praise *yourself* because you have such a sweet charitable disposition.

You can do that, can't you? [Congregation: "No."] Not when your sins are forgiven, and you are free from all these things by the power of Christ. Can't you praise *yourself* then for *your* sweet charitable disposition, that *you* have got such a good one? [Congregation: "No, sir."] But I read more:

> Praise *yourself* because you see only the good in everybody and everything in all the world. Praise *yourself* for every good thing that you do see *in yourself* and for every good thing that you *want* to see in *yourself*. . . You must praise for the good characteristic that is there to strengthen it, and praise for the good trait that seems lacking to compel it to appear, for you know that the fruit of your lips will be created for you.

Now that is what is called "Christian Science." You can read the title (holding up book). A brother handed me a copy of that thing the other day. The title is "Christian Science," and on the cover is a quotation of Scripture: "My words shall not pass away." Now, brethren, is it not about time that we began to believe the scriptures and the Testimonies? Isn't it about time we had the mind of Jesus Christ? [Congregation: "Amen!"] The mind that will confess that this from the Testimony is so, that has bothered so many of the brethren every time that it has been read. Now let us read it again and see whether you will say it is so, whether you believe it or not. It is time. Testimony No. 31, page 44:

> Are you in Christ? Not if you do not acknowledge yourselves erring, helpless, condemned sinners.

You are not in Christ unless you acknowledge yourself to be that. Now is that so? [Congregation: "Yes."] Are you willing to stick to that now whether you understand *how* it is so or not? [Congregation: "Yes."] Will you stick to it in the face of paganism, the papacy and spiritualism, in all their phases? Then I want to know why in the world it is not time for you and me to have a mind that will not say "Amen" to any such stuff as that which I read from that anti-Christian Science thing? I read on again from the Testimony:

> Are you in Christ? Not if you do not acknowledge yourselves erring, helpless, condemned sinners. Not if you are exalting and glorifying self.

Then although these folks quote the words of Christ, it is all counterfeit. You know that "Vol. IV" tells us that when Satan himself comes with the gracious words that the Saviour uttered, he will talk them with much the same tone and will pass it off on those who have not the mind of Christ. Brethren, there is no salvation for us, there is no safety for us, there is no remedy for us at all, but to have the mind of Christ.

And it goes through all our works, too. It is not simply for the minister. It is for everyone. Don't you remember the other day in the talk that Dr. Kellogg gave us on the medical missionary work, how that he saw, and had seen for a long time, the lack in the systems of medicine, to reach and make easy *the mind*? Don't you remember that he told us that he realized this lack in all medical practice? He had found in their practice all the way through that there was a defect in the medical systems, and that there was nothing that would reach and relieve the mind and turn it off from the diseased souls, that the body might go ahead and get well by the treatment that the physicians would give it.

Brethren, has not Christ supplied just that lack that is in all medical systems, in His own medical system that He has given us by His own Spirit? The mind of Christ, for the nurse, for the physician, to carry to the distressed and the diseased and the suffering and the perishing and get the mind of the sufferer upon Jesus Christ and have His mind, taking it away from self. Then the patient being at rest, the physician can go ahead and doctor the body and it will get well, while the patient is enjoying the blessings and peace of Jesus Christ and the mind which He gives. Don't you see how it goes through all your work, and it is the one thing everywhere? This part is not new to the doctor either. But as he was telling us about the defect in the medical systems, I want you to see that the mind of Christ will supply the defect. I read on from the Testimony:-

> You are not in Christ, if you are exalting and glorifying self.

Now mark:

> If there is any good in you, it is wholly attributable to the mercy of a compassionate Saviour.

Now mark this:

> Your birth, your reputation, your wealth, your talents, your virtues, your piety, your philanthropy, or anything else in you or connected with you, *will not form a bond of union between your soul and Christ.*

Now, is that so? [Congregation: "Yes."] Elder Underwood: "Please read that over again."

> Your birth, your reputation, your wealth, your talents, your virtues, your piety, your philanthropy, or *anything else in you or connected with you* [even your good works] will not form a bond of union between your soul and Christ.
>
> Your connection with the church, the manner in which your brethren regard you, will be of no avail unless you believe in Christ.

Now mark this emphasis:

> It is not enough to believe *about* Him [the word "about" is italicized]; but you must believe *in* Him.

"*In* Him." What does that mean?

> You must rely wholly upon His saving grace.

That is Christianity. That is the mind of Christ. There is no devilism about that at all; and it can't get in there, either. Why, you find it also in *Steps to Christ*. Not stated exactly as that. I will read a passage or two from *Steps to Christ*, beginning on page 67 and reading to page 71:

> The condition of eternal life is now just what it always has been – just what it was in Paradise before the fall of our first parents – perfect obedience to the law of God, perfect righteousness.

And if you and I have not that, we will never have eternal life. We can't have it now or at any other time. If you and I have not "perfect obedience to the law of God" *from the first breath we ever drew until this one, now, tonight,* and it must be *until the last one we ever draw,* then eternal life does not belong to us. But just as certainly as you and I have "perfect obedience to that law of God," then eternal life is ours that very moment. But that "perfect obedience" must read, I say, from the first breath we ever drew until this one, now, tonight, and it must be until the last one we ever do draw, even though it be ten thousand years from now, in the depths of eternity. I am not asking whether you understand this, brethren; believe it, and you will understand it. "Well, doesn't this contradict something he has been preaching before?" It does *not* contradict what I have been preaching; it is what I have preached all the time, and what every other man preaches who preaches the gospel.

> The condition of eternal life is now just what it always has been – just what it was in Paradise before the fall of our first parents – perfect obedience to the law of God, perfect righteousness. If eternal life were granted on any condition short of this, then the happiness of the whole universe would be imperiled. . . *We have no righteousness of our own* with which to meet the claims of the law of God.

That is so. Then how in the world are we ever going to have eternal life? [Congregation: "Through Christ."] Ah! "the gift of God is eternal life through Jesus Christ our Lord." But we have got to have "perfect righteousness" before we can have that gift, don't you see? Oh then, just like the Lord, He comes and says, "Here, in Christ, is perfect righteousness; here is perfect obedience to the law of God from birth to the grave; you take that and that will fully meet the condition on which alone anyone can have eternal life."

All right. Are you not glad of it? [Congregation: "Yes."] I am so glad of it that I don't know what else to do than to be glad. Oh, He wants me to have eternal life. I haven't a thing to merit it; I haven't a thing that will meet the condition upon which alone it can be granted. Everything that I have would ruin the universe if He should grant me eternal life upon it. Well, He can't do that; but He wants me to have eternal life; He wants me to have it so bad that He died that I might have it. [Congregation: "Amen!"] And oh, then again I say, it is just like God, who is love, as He is, He comes and says, "Here, in Christ, is perfect obedience from the first breath you ever drew, until the last one, and you take Him and His righteousness and then you have got the other." That is the condition. Good! Good! Yes, sir.

> We have no righteousness of our own with which to meet the claims of the law of God. But Christ has made a way of escape for us.

Thank the Lord!

> He lived on earth amid trials and temptations such as we have to meet. He lived a sinless life. He died for us and now he offers to take our sins and give us His righteousness.

What a trade! What a trade! Brethren, isn't it awful that men will so hesitate and linger and dally before they will surrender up everything and make that blessed trade? Isn't it awful?

> If you give yourself to Him, and accept Him as your Saviour, then, *sinful as your life may have been,* for *His sake* you are *accounted righteous.* Christ's *character* stands in place of *your character* and you *are accepted before God* just *as if you had not sinned.*

Yes sir, you and I, when we have done that, you and I stand before God, just as though we had never committed a sin in this world – just as though we had been angels all the time. Brethren, God is good! He is good! Oh, our Saviour is a wonderful Saviour! [Congregation: " Amen!"]

Brethren, That is so. Let us let *Him* have His own way.

> More than this.

Could there be any more, think ye? Why the Lord says so:

> More than this, Christ *changes the heart;* He abides in your heart by faith.

That is the blessedness of it. What good would eternal life do me with such a heart. No, He does not stop at that; He changes the heart.

> You are to maintain this connection with Christ *by faith* and the *continual surrender* of your *will* to Him;

That is the thought we had last night; it is the same lesson right along.

> And so long as you do this, He will work in you to will and to do according to His good pleasure. So you may say,

You may say – God has given us permission to say, He has told us that we may say. . .

> "The life which I now live in the flesh, I live by the faith of the Son of God, who loved me and gave Himself for me." So Jesus said to His disciples, "It is not ye that speak, but the Spirit of your Father which speaketh." Then with *Christ working in you,* you will manifest the same spirit and do the same works,

You can't do otherwise. Christ is the same yesterday, today and forever. He is the same here in our flesh now, as He was when He was here before in the flesh.

> Works of righteousness, obedience. *So* we have *nothing* in *ourselves* of which *to boast.*

Thank the Lord. Do not begin to boost yourself up and to boast of yourself, and say, "I am rich now, and increased in goods; now I am wise; now I am all right." No. Isn't the man that will say that at such a time as that, isn't he the worst creature in this universe? How *could* he be worse? When he was entirely lost, helpless and undone, and he confessed it and said so, and then the Lord has such wonderful compassion that He gives him everything He has in the universe, and then that man stands up and begins to boast of how good he is and how great he is; what greater reproach could he possibly put on the goodness of the Lord? No sir. "Let him that glorieth glory in the Lord." [Congregation: "Amen!"] Let us do it then.

> So we have nothing in ourselves of which to boast. We have no ground for *self*-exaltation.

The man that takes Jesus as He is, will always be humble. It makes a man humble to take Christ by faith. But if he does not take Him by faith but earns it, of course he has something to boast about.

> Our *only* ground *for* hope is in *the righteousness of Christ imputed* to us and in

What now, suppose you?

> Our only ground for hope is in the righteousness of Christ imputed to us and *in that wrought by His Spirit* working *in* and *through* us.

Our only ground for hope is Christ's righteousness imputed to us and this righteousness wrought in us by the Holy Spirit is the works we do. Then the very next paragraph is that about the satanic belief and what genuine faith is, which we studied in previous lessons. It is all one subject.

Now then, page 71:

> The closer you come to Jesus, the more faulty you will appear in your own eyes; for your vision will be clearer, and your imperfections will be seen in broad and distinct contrast to His perfect nature. This is evidence that Satan's delusions have lost their power.

What is the condition of that man then who begins to think *himself* pretty good? And praises himself? Satan's delusion is upon him. Even if he has lived with the Lord fifteen or twenty years, if he begins now to think he is quite good – what is the condition of that man? He is deluded by satan. He is under satanic delusions. That is all. There was a man that lived with Jesus Christ thirty years. When he first began, in the earliest years of his life with Christ, he said, "I am crucified with Christ: nevertheless I live: yet not I, but Christ liveth in me; and the life which I now live in the flesh I live by the faith of the Son of God who loved me and gave himself for me." And nearly thirty years after this near the close of his life, he said this: "This is a faithful saying and worthy of all acceptation, that Christ Jesus came into the world to save sinners of whom I" *was* chief? [Congregation: "Am chief."] No, *was* chief. [Congregation: "No, '*Am* chief.'"] Oh, no. When he was Saul of Tarsus, persecuting the saints, *then* he *was* the chief of sinners. [Congregation: No. "*Am* chief."] Amen. Exactly.

"Christ Jesus came into the world to save sinners of whom I *am* chief." When? [Congregation: "Now."] When he had lived thirty years with Jesus Christ? [Congregation: "Yes."] Yes. "I am chief." Oh, he had such a view of the Lord Jesus, of His holiness, of His perfect purity, that when He looked at Himself, considered Himself, as separated from Christ, he was the worst of all men. *That* is *Christianity*. That is the mind of Christ. The other is the mind of Satan.

So then:

> This is evidence that Satan's delusions have lost their power; that the vivifying influence of the Spirit of God is arousing you. No deep seated love for Jesus can dwell in the heart that does not realize its own sinfulness. The soul that is transformed by the grace of Christ will admire his divine character; but if we do not see our own moral deformity, it is unmistakable evidence that we have not had a view of the beauty and excellence of Christ. The less we see to esteem in ourselves the more we shall see to esteem in the infinite purity and loveliness of our Saviour.

That is Christianity, brethren.

Now let us go to studying the Bible for just what it says. What do you say? Brethren, we are in a fearful position here at this Conference, at this meeting. It is just awful. I said that once before, but I realize it tonight more than I did then. I can't help it, brethren. I can't help it. We are in a fearful position here. Not a soul of us ever dreams what fearful destinies hang on the days that pass by here. [Elder Olsen: "That is so."] That is so. Brethren, as the days go on, is our earnestness in seeking God deepening? Is it? Is it? or is it rather coming to a lull?

The first lessons, when we started in here, they were fresh; they were new; they brought truth in strong, plain, positive lines so we could see, and they had an effect. Hearts were moved as the Scripture says, "as the trees of the wood are moved with the wind."

But, brethren, has the breeze slackened up? What now? If our impressions, our sense of need, our earnestness is not found deeper, brethren, as these meetings go on, then there is something the matter with each one of us. I am not talking about us as a whole class merely in a general way; the only way we can get at this is each one individually for himself; if I am not doing that, if you are not doing that, there is something wrong.

Now, brethren, another thought. We have been obliged, by the Spirit of God, we have been obliged to look at the workings of the carnal mind, and what it will do for man and how it will deceive him in every way – paganism, papacy, and the image of the papacy, the dragon, the beast and the false prophet – we have seen it and the Lord means a lesson in it to us. Now as we have seen it, brethren, just let each one of us let go all holds, let the soul drop right out of everything into just that childlike readiness to receive what God has to give. [Congregation: "Amen!"] Let the searching of heart go one, and the confession of sin. Did not Jesus say to us, "Be zealous therefore, and repent"? "Be zealous therefore and repent." What does that "therefore" mean? For this reason; for these reasons. Let us see what He said before that.

I know *thy works,* that thou art neither cold nor hot: I would thou wert cold or hot. So then because thou art lukewarm and neither cold nor hot, I will spew thee out of my mouth. Because *thou sayest,* I am rich, and increased in good, and have need of nothing; *and knowest not* that thou art wretched, and miserable, and poor and blind, and naked: I counsel thee to buy of me gold tried in the fire, that thou mayest be rich; and white raiment, that thou mayest be clothed, and that the shame of thy nakedness do not appear; and anoint thine eyes with eyesalve, that thou mayest see. As many as I love, I rebuke and chasten: be zealous therefore and repent."

How much does that "therefore" cover? All of it? [Congregation: "Yes, sir."] The first thing He says is, "I know thy works", and the last, "Be zealous therefore, and repent." Are you ready to repent of your works now? Are you? Are you ready to admit that your works that you have done, are not as good as Jesus Christ would have done them if He had been here Himself and done them instead of you? [Voice: "Yes, a thousand times."] Good. How much good are these works going to do you? Are they perfect? Are they righteous works? "Whatsoever is not of faith is sin." Are there, or have there been, any works about you that have not been of faith? that have had self in them?

Do not forget that garment that we are to buy – that garment "woven in the loom of heaven, and not *one thread of human invention*" in it. Then if you and I have stuck up a single thread of our invention in that life that we have professed to be living in Christ, we have spoiled the garment. Brethren, do you suppose you and I have gone on these fifteen or twenty years so absolutely perfect that we have never got a thread of human invention into our character by our deeds? [Congregation: "No."] Then we can repent of that, can't we? [Congregation: "Yes."] I simply call attention to that, that part tonight.

And now for the few minutes that remain let us read a few passages of Scripture. Isaiah 59:6. What chapter does this 59th chapter follow? [Congregation: "The 58th."] Where does the 58th chapter apply? [Congregation: "It applies now."]

> Their webs shall not become garments, *neither shall they cover themselves with their works;* their works are works of iniquity, and the act of violence is in their hands.

Then what has that people been trying to do? What has that people been trying to do with their works? [Congregation: "Cover themselves with their works."] When He says, *"they shall not* cover themselves with their works," that shows on the face of it that they have been trying to cover themselves with their works. Now does He tell the truth? [Congregation: "Yes."] Then when He says to you and me that we have been trying to cover ourselves with our works, then does not He say in that that we have been really – whatever we profess – trusting in righteousness or justification *by works?* [Congregation: "Yes."] Then is not that what the Laodicean message says, "I know thy works." And what have our works done for us? Made us wretched, and miserable, and poor, and blind, and naked. What does He want us to have? "White raiment, that thou sayest be clothed, and that the shame of thy nakedness do not appear."

What is our condition? You know well enough that our efforts at that have not accomplished much. Every one has tried to do his very best – you know yourself that it was the most discouraging thing that you ever tried to do in this world. you know yourself that you have actually sat down and cried because you could not do well enough to risk the Judgment. [voice: "Could not do well enough to satisfy ourselves."] No. We ourselves were able to see our nakedness when we had tried our best to cover ourselves. You know that is so. Now, brethren, the Lord said so, didn't He? [Congregation: "Yes, sir."] Is it not time that we said, "Lord, that is so?" I quote it: "Neither shall they cover themselves with their works: their works are works of iniquity, and the act of violence is in their hands."

Now the Lord wants us to be covered; He wants us to be covered, so that the shame of our nakedness shall not appear. He wants us to have His perfect righteousness according to His own perfect idea of righteousness. He wants us to have that character that will stand the test of the judgment without a hitch or a question or a doubt. Let us accept it from Him as the free blessed gift it is.

Now brethren, in the next lesson, my thought is now that we will enter directly upon the direct straightforward Scripture, exactly what it says to you and me, as to how we can have Jesus Christ and all His righteousness and everything that He has, without a particle of discount. What do you say? [Congregation: "Amen."]

Sermon 15

February 23, 1893

We shall begin tonight just where we stopped the other evening, with the thought that was before us, that we would now proceed to study this subject as it is in the Bible. I could take the time and read it all from the *Testimonies* and *Steps to Christ*. I could preach from them as well as from the Bible on this. But I find this difficulty: The brethren seem so ready to be content with what we read in these and will not go to the Bible to find it there. That is what the *Testimonies* and *Steps to Christ* are for; they are to lead us to see that it is in the Bible and to get it there. Now I shall avoid these purposely, not as though there was anything wrong in using them; but what we want, brethren, is to get at it in the Bible and know where it is there. And that is the Lord's own way as pointed out in the Testimonies. Let me read it here:

> The word of God is sufficient to enlighten the most beclouded mind and may be understood by those who have any desire to understand it. But notwithstanding all this, some who profess to make the word of God their study are found living in direct opposition to its plain teachings. Then to leave men and women without excuse, God gives plain and pointed testimonies, *bringing them back to the word* that they have neglected to follow.
>
> The word of God abounds in general principles for the formation of correct habits of living and the Testimonies, general and personal, have been calculated to *call their attention* more especially *to these principles.* . . .
>
> You are not familiar with the Scriptures. *If you had made God's word your study* with a desire to reach the Bible standard and attain to Christian perfection *you would not have needed the Testimonies.* It is because you have neglected to acquaint yourselves with God's inspired Book that He has sought to reach you by simple, direct testimonies, calling your attention to the word of inspiration which you have neglected to obey.
>
> Additional truth is not brought out; but God has through the Testimonies simplified the great truths already given and in His chosen way brought them before the people to awaken and impress the mind with them, that all may be without excuse. . . . The Testimonies are not to belittle the word of God, but to exalt it and attract minds to it, that the beautiful simplicity of truth may impress all.

There is another reason also why we want to get this and see that it is in the Bible. That is because we, from this Institute and this Conference, are to go forth to preach nothing else but just this one thing; and we are to preach to people who do not believe the Testimonies. And the Scriptures have told us that prophesyings are not for them that believe not but for them which believe. Tongues are a sign to them that believe not; prophesyings are a sign to them that believe. 1 Corinthians 14:22. Now when we go and preach this message to people who do not know anything about the Testimonies, we have to teach them that the Bible says it, and we have to teach from that alone. If we were preaching to our own people, to use the Testimonies and all these other helps would be all well enough, but even then, if their minds were turned to these and not brought by these to the Bible itself, then *that* use of the Testimonies is not what is intended by the Lord as the right use of the Testimonies.

Now I have seen this same thing working another way. There is that book that a great many make a great deal of, The Christian's Secret of a Happy Life. I have seen people who have read that book and got a considerable good out of it, as they thought, and what was to them great light, encouragement and good, but even then they could not go to the Bible and get it. Brethren, I want every one of you to understand that there is more of the Christian's secret of a happy life in the Bible than in ten thousand volumes of that book. [Congregation: "Amen!"] I did not see that book for a long time. I think it was about five or six years ago when I first saw it. Somebody had it and was reading it and asked me if I had seen it. I said, "No." I was asked, if I would read it. I said, "Yes I will read it," and I did. But when I did read it, I knew that I had already got more of the Christian's secret of a happy life out of the Bible that there is in that book to begin with. I found that I got more of the Christian's secret of a happy life in the Bible than she has in that book. I wish people would learn to get out of the Bible what is in it, direct. [Congregation: "Amen!"] If that book helps people to get that secret in the Bible, with a good deal more of it, all right. But I knew that that book has nothing like the Christian's secret of a happy life that every one can get in the Bible.

Oh I did hear once, I did get the news once, that *I* got *my* light out of that book. There is the Book where I got my Christian's secret of a happy life (holding up the Bible), and that is the only place. And I had it before I ever saw the other book or knew it was in existence. And I say again, When I came to read the other I knew I had more of the Christian's secret of a happy life than there is in that book to begin with. And so will every one else, who will read the Bible and believe it.

Now I want to ask a few questions on what we have gone over. What is the latter rain? [Congregation: "The teaching of righteousness according to righteousness."] What is the loud cry? [Congregation: "The message of the righteousness of Christ."] The loud cry has already begun in the message of the righteousness of Christ. Where does the latter rain come from? [Congregation: "From God."] All of it? [Congregation: "Yes."] What is it? [Congregation:"The Spirit of God."]

Now let us just put two things together. The teaching of righteousness according to righteousness – the message of righteousness – that is the loud cry; that is the latter rain; that is the righteousness of Christ. Is that so? [Congregation: "Yes."] The latter rain comes down from heaven. How much of that latter rain comes out of me? [Congregation: "None of it."] How much of it can I manufacture? [Congregation: "Not any."] Now is that so? [Congregation: "Yes."] I cannot manufacture any of it? None of it springs from me at all? Where does it come from? [Congregation: "Heaven."] Will you take it that way? Will you receive it from heaven? [Congregation: "Yes."]

Now that is where we came to the other night. Are you ready to take it from heaven? [Congregation: "Yes."] Is everybody in this house tonight willing and ready to take righteousness from heaven? [Congregation: "Amen!"] According to God, without asking that God shall get some of it from us? Are you? [Congregation: "Yes."] Whoever is willing to take righteousness from heaven can receive the latter rain [Congregation: "Amen!"]; whoever is not, but wants the Lord to get some of it out of him, he cannot have the latter rain; he cannot have the righteousness of God; he cannot have the message of the righteousness of Christ.

What is the latter rain? [Congregation: "Righteousness."] Are we in the time of the latter rain? [Congregation: "Yes."] What are we to ask for? [Congregation: "Rain."] What is it? [Congregation: "The teaching of righteousness according to righteousness."] Where is it to come from? [Congregation: "Heaven."] Can we have it? [Congregation: "Yes."] Can we have it now? [Congregation: "Yes."] Then the latter train being the righteousness of God, His message of righteousness, the loud cry, it all being that, and that to come down from heaven: we are now in the time of it, we are to ask for it and receive it. Then what is to hinder us from receiving the latter rain now? [Congregation: "Unbelief."]

I will read a passage from this little book to start with. We have read it once before; it is found on page 8 of "Danger in Adopting a Worldly Policy":

> As man's Intercessor and Advocate, Jesus will lead all who are willing to be led, saying, "Follow me upward, step by step, where the clear light of the Sun of Righteousness shines." But not all are following the light. Some are moving away from the safe path, which at every step is a path of humility. God has committed to His servants a message for this time. . . I would not now rehearse before you the evidences given in the past two years [four years now] of the dealing so God by His chosen servants; but the present evidence of His working is revealed to you and you are now under obligation to believe.

Believe what? What message is there referred to that God has given to His servants for this time? [Congregation: "The message of righteousness."] The message of the righteousness of Jesus Christ. This is a testimony that had been despised, rejected, and criticized for two years, and two years have passed since that time. But now the present evidence of His working is revealed, and now what does God say to every one of us? "You are now under obligation to believe" that message. Then whoever does not believe it simply has to answer to God, does he not? That is all. Well, then, let us begin.

There is, however, another word to which I wish to call attention. You will remember that I read Isaiah 59:6 in the last lesson; it was about those people who were trying to cover themselves with their works. In the fourth verse we have these words: "None calleth for justice." After the lesson Brother Starr called my attention to the German translation, and that, he says, is: "None preacheth righteousness." I looked at the revised version and that has it: "None sueth for righteousness," or the margin, "None calleth for righteousness." I looked at Young's literal translation and that likewise reads: "None calleth for righteousness." So you see the thought as expressed in this verse, "None sueth," that is too say, to court, to ask for, to beseech, "for righteousness." None calleth for that. The same idea is conveyed in the German, only it is put in other words, "None preacheth righteousness." Well, is not that what the Lord says? They are trying to cover themselves with their works and that is not righteousness.

Isaiah 54, last sentence of the chapter: "This is the heritage of the servants of the Lord and their righteousness is *of me,* saith the Lord." Their righteousness is of whom? of themselves? [Congregation: "Of the Lord."] Their righteousness is of their works? No, "their righteousness is of me, saith the Lord." What do you say? [Congregation: "Of the Lord."] Their righteousness is of their works? No. "Their righteousness is of me, saith the Lord." What do you say? [Congregation: "Amen."] Then any man who expects, looks for, or hopes for, any righteousness that does not come from God, what then? What has he? [Voice: "Filthy rags."] It is no righteousness at all. Even those who want to get it out of their own works, will it work that way? [Congregation: "No."] Is that of God? [Congregation: "No sir."]

The only way that God can get into our works is by having Him to start with, and having His righteousness to begin with and our only ground of hope is in the righteousness of Christ imputed to us, and in that wrought in us by His Holy Spirit. This takes up the subject exactly where Brother Prescott stopped. Do you see it is Christ in us, that living presence that does the righteous work and that is by the Holy Spirit? That is what the Holy Spirit brings; that is the outpouring of the latter rain, is it not? You see we cannot study anything else. That is the message for us now. Shall we receive the message? When we receive the message what do we receive? [Congregation: "Christ."] When we receive Him what have we? [Voice: "The Holy Spirit. The latter rain."] This will come more fully afterward.

Now another thing, brethren. I do not want you to put off until after the meeting, your receiving of it. You do not need to do that at all. What the Lord wants is for you and me to come here each evening and sit down and receive that just exactly as he gives it. Just exactly as he says it. You just open your mind and heart to the Lord and say, "Lord, that is so." [Congregation: "Amen."] Don't wait until you go out of the house. "Well," says one, "are we to sit down here and take everything that is said without any question at all?" No, not in that sense. But we are to sit down here and have such a measure of the

Spirit of God that we can see what He gives through that word which is the truth and then take it because it is the truth of God. [Congregation: "Amen."]

Elder D. C. Babcock: Brother Jones, please read Job 29:23.

Elder Jones: Very good. "And they waited for me as for the rain; and they opened their mouth wide as for the latter rain." All right. What shall we do? What does the Lord want us to do? Wait for His Spirit as for rain. Open your mind; wait as for the latter rain. What did He say by David? "Open thy mouth wide and I will fill it." Brethren, let us sit down here and open our mouths just like little birds; you know how they do. It looks as though the mouth was all the bird there was. That is what He wants us to do.

Can we not trust God to give to us what He wants us to have? Brethren, there is a question in that that I want to ask: When we come into a place like this, come with hundreds of people who are seeking the Lord, come asking the way to Zion, with our faces thitherward, do we need to sit here suspiciously looking cross-eyes at the Lord as though we did not dare to trust Him for what He would give? Is that honest? [Congregation: "No."] Is that fair? [Congregation: "No."] No, sir. I believe this much in the Lord, that when we come together with our hearts seeking Him, every one that lays His heart wide open to receive what the Lord has to give, will not receive anything but what God gives. And the man who comes into such a place as this, with His suspicions aroused and with a readiness to look askance at the Lord – that man is not treating the Lord as a person ought to treat the Lord: he is treating the Lord just as a person might fairly treat the devil. Is he not?

Now brethren, let us treat the Lord honestly; let us be honest with Him and He will be honest with us. "To Him that showeth Himself forward the Lord will show Himself forward." If you and I treat the Lord honestly, He will treat us just exactly like God treats people. So I say, we need not come into this house with a particle of suspicion as to whether the Lord is going to give us things straight. He will do it, and I am going to expect He will do it, and so I am going to receive lots of blessing out of this thing. That is settled.

Now Romans 5:17: "For if by one man's offense death reigned by one; much more they which receive abundance of grace *and of the gift of righteousness* shall reign in life by one, Jesus Christ." What is righteousness in that verse, then? [Congregation: "A gift."] Is it? [Congregation: "Yes, sir."] "Their righteousness is of me, saith the Lord." It is a gift of righteousness. How does it come to us, then? [Congregation: "It is a gift."]

Now put those two things together: "Their righteousness is of me" – it is a gift. He who receives it, what does he receive? [Congregation: "A gift."] He who receives it as the gift that it is, receives what? [Congregation: "Righteousness."] According to what? God's idea of righteousness. Will He give us anything than that which is righteousness in His own sight and according to His own mind? [Congregation: "No."] Do you see that point?

Then he who does not receive the righteousness of God as the free gift of God, does He have it? [Congregation: "No."] And He cannot so have it, you see, because it is a gift. It is of God. It comes from God by the precious gift that it is. And therefore it being of God, and He giving it of His own gift, it is left to me to get it in His own way. He gives what is His own and He gives it according to His own idea. That is the genuine article; that is the righteousness of God alone.

Then don't you see in that there can be no room for a single thread of human invention? We cannot get it in there at all. Don't you see what ample provision the Lord has made that we may have the perfect robe which He Himself hath woven, which is the righteousness of God itself and which will make us complete now and in the time of the plagues and in every other time and throughout all eternity? Brethren, I am glad that that is so. I am just as glad as I can be.

A sister told me not long ago that before that time four years ago she had just been lamenting her estate and wondering how in the world the time was ever going to come for the Lord to come if He had to wait for His people to get ready to meet Him. For she said the way she had been at it – and she had worked as hard as anybody in this world, she thought – she saw that she was not making progress fast enough to bring the Lord in any kind of reasonable time at all, and she could not make out how the Lord was going to come.

She was bothered about it, but she said when the folks came home from Minneapolis and they said, "Why the Lord's righteousness is a gift; we can have the righteousness of Christ as a gift, and we can have it now." "Oh," said she, "That made me glad; that brought light, for then I could see how the Lord could come pretty soon. When He Himself gives us the garment, the clothing, the character, that fits us for the judgment and for the time of trouble, I could then see how he could come just as soon as He wanted to." "And," said she, "it made me glad, and I have been glad every since." Brethren, I am glad of it too, all the time.

Now there is sense in that thing today. You know we have all been in that same place. You know the time was when we actually sat down and cried because we could not do well enough to satisfy our own estimate of right doing; and as we were expecting the Lord to come soon, we dreaded the news that it was so near; for how in the world were we going to be ready? Thank the Lord He can get us ready. [Congregation: "Amen."] He provides the wedding garment The master of the wedding feast always provided the wedding garment. He is the Master of the wedding supper now, and He is going to come pretty soon, and He says, "Here is the clothing that will fit you to stand in that place." Now there will be some folks that cannot attend that feast, because they have not on the wedding garment, but the Lord offers it as a free gift to all and as to the man who does not take it, who is to blame?

Another thing: Do you believe now – let us have that settled before we go any further. I want to know how many people in this house actually believe, right down honestly in their hearts, that God is able to say what He means when He says it? [Congregation: "Yes."] Then when you and I read what He says, just as He says it in the Bible, I want to know whether it is any use for you and me to go over to some other part of the Bible and hunt up some other text to see whether that does not contradict this? Is the Lord able to tell His own story in His own way without contradicting Himself? [Congregation: "Yes."] We have been at that long enough. So I do not propose to harmonize any texts of Scripture in all the work that I shall have to do here in this institute. I think the Lord has everything straight, exactly as it is. I do not think He needs any of my help. I think rather that I need His help to see that there is no contradiction at all. And I think that if there appears to me to be a contradiction, then I need more of His Spirit to see that there is none. And instead of trying to harmonize the supposed contradiction, I am going to say that the Lord knows all about that, and I am going to wait until He gives me breadth of mind enough to see it is no contradiction there at all.

So what I want here to decide now and forever is that when you read anything in the Bible, that that means exactly what it says, and you need not hunt up anything in the Bible to see whether that tells the other side of it. There is no other side; it is all one. "Well, then, how are you going to explain everything in the Bible when people ask you?" There is the difficulty; men go out preaching the gospel, and they think if they cannot explain everything that people ask them it is going to be a great discredit to their ministry. No, sir. It will be well for you to acknowledge that there are some things even in the Bible that you have not grasped fully yet.

What the Lord asks of you and me is stated in 2 Timothy 2:7, and it is the key of all Bible study; it is God's directions for Bible study: "Consider what I say, and the Lord give thee understanding in all things." The only things He asks of you and me to consider is *what He says,* and if we have to consider it for ten, fifteen, or twenty years to find out what it means, we will find that it was worth twenty years of waiting. We need not be disappointed at all. Bear in mind that the longer you have to consider a text to find out what is in it, the more it will be worth when you get it. So there is no place for discouragement ever. Therefore if I cannot measure the depths of it, I am going to be glad that it is so deep that when I do get it I shall rejoice as long as I live.

All we have to do in these lessons is to consider what He says, and depend upon Him to give us the understanding of it. That is all. That is all I can do, and everyone that will do that will get more out of it than the one who does not consider what He says.

Then "their righteousness is of me, saith the Lord." That is what He says. [Congregation: "Yes."] It is a gift of righteousness; it is a gift; is that so? [Congregation: "Yes."] Now how do we receive a gift? "The righteousness is of me," He gives it. A free gift. How do we get it? [Congregation: "By faith."] By faith. By faith. Let us bear in mind also the definition which we have studied, of what faith is. Not a satanic belief. That is not faith at all, but a submission of the will to God, a yielding of the heart to Him, the affections fixed upon Him – there is faith. That is God's idea of faith. And when we read of faith and get His word of belief which He has spoken in His word – that is what He means.

Mark this: It is received by faith. It is known by faith. But let us read the text and see that it is so. Romans 1:17. The 16th verse is talking about the gospel. "For therein is the righteousness . . . revealed from *faith* to *faith*." What alone can obtain it, then? [Congregation: "Faith."] Not from faith to works, but from faith to *faith*. But what is faith? Submission of the will to Him; yielding of the heart to Him, the affections fixed upon Him. That is surrender of self and takes what God says as the fact; in other words, faith is simply this: that when God says a thing and you and I read it, we say, "that is so." That is faith.

Faith comes by hearing, and hearing by the word of God. Romans 10:17. What is the source of faith, then? [Congregation: "The Word of God."] How does faith come to us? [Congregation: "By hearing the word of God."] Faith comes to us by the word of God. That is the source, the fountain of faith. Then when that word is read, you yield to that and say, "That is so." I take that as it says; with no attempt to explain it even to myself. I take it as God says it; I receive it just as He says it; I rest upon it just as He says it; He giving me understanding of it – then I want to know whether I do not receive in that word and from it just what He has in it to give to me. Assuredly. That also precludes our getting any thread of human invention into it.

Then it is of faith. It comes by faith. We receive it that way. Then don't you see that with the man who does not understand and begins to question righteousness by faith alone, the trouble is that his soul is not submitted to God, his heart is not yielded to God, the affections are not fixed upon Him? That is the difficulty. All the trouble that ever comes to anybody in this world over justification by faith is in the heart – in the refusal to submit to God – and that is the carnal mind; as we read the other night, the carnal mind cannot comprehend it – does not know it.

Now let us turn to the third chapter of Romans, and begin reading with the 20th verse.

"Therefore by the deeds of the law there shall no flesh be justified in his sight."

Justified is made righteous, so whenever we read it here, you can just put the words, "made righteous," there instead, and you have the same thing always. "For by the law is the knowledge of sin. But now the righteousness of God without the law is manifested, being witnessed by the law and the prophets, even the righteousness of God which is by faith of Jesus Christ unto all and upon all them that believe," and then do their best? [Congregation: "No, sir, 'for there is no difference.'"] Unto all and upon all them that *believe,* for there is no difference, for all have sinned and come short of the glory of God.

Now the verse I am after:

"Being justified" (made righteous) how? [Congregation: "Freely."] "Being made righteous freely." Is it so? [Congregation: "Yes."] Is it so? [Congregation: "Amen."] Let us thank the Lord that it is so. Let us take it right now. [Congregation: "Amen."] "Being made righteous freely by his grace." Now let us stop here with that word "grace" and turn over to Rom. 11:6, where we read as follows, "And if by grace, then it is no more of works: otherwise grace is no more grace." And when grace is no more grace what in the world then are the people in this world going to do? When the grace of God is gone what are we going to do? [Voice: "We would be gone too."] Yes. Brethren, let us submit. Let us submit. "But if it be of works, then it is no more grace; otherwise work is no more work." A man's works is all gone if there are no more works. Don't you see, then, what becomes of a man who takes that course?

Now Romans 3:24: "Being justified freely by his grace through the redemption that is in Christ Jesus: whom God hath set forth to be a propitiation through faith in his blood, to declare his righteousness." Whose righteousness? [Congregation: "God's."] God has set forth who to declare it? [Congregation: "Christ."] Yes. "For the remission of sins that are past, through the forbearance of God; to declare, I say, at this time." When is that? [Congregation: "Now."] Is that right now, just now, tonight? [Congregation: "Yes."] Just now, four minutes of nine o'clock? [Congregation: "Yes."] *His* righteousness? [Congregation: "Yes."] To you? [Congregation: "Yes."] Thank the Lord. "For the remission of sins that are past, through the forbearance of God, to declare I say at this time." Will you go out of this house realizing that? I want to ask, if any man goes out of this house without that what in the world is the matter? [Voice: "Unbelief."] Who is to blame? [Voice: "The man himself."] Then let us not do it. The Lord wants us to receive the latter rain. And shall we ask for it, and then when it comes not take it as He gives it because it does not come quite as we thought it would come. It is none of your business how it comes. It is for Him to give it, and for us to have discernment to see that it is He who gives it.

"To declare, I say, at this time his righteousness; that he might be just." That He might be righteous. Oh He is all right then; it is not going to tangle Him; it is not going to disgrace Him. "That he might be just and the justifier of him which believeth in Jesus." And when God justifies I want to know what business in the world anybody has to condemn. He does it; He is able to do it; He has fixed the thing so He can do it and *be just* all the time – be just in the doing of it. Well then let us let Him have His own way. The law of God is satisfied. Let us be delighted. [Congregation: "Amen."] I can tell you when I found out that in the doing of this the Lord was justified and that the law of God was satisfied, I was delighted.

Now we will read right on: "Where is boasting then? It is excluded. By what law? of works? Nay, but by the law of faith. Therefore we conclude that a man is justified [made righteous] by faith without the deeds of the law." Is that a right conclusion? [Congregation: "Yes."] Now is it? [Congregation: "Yes."] Who drew it? Whose conclusion is it? [Congregation: "Yes."] Whose conclusion is it? [Congregation: "God's."] Let us let Him have His own way. Is not He able to argue straight? "What shall we say then that Abraham our father, as pertaining to the flesh, hath found? For if Abraham were justified by works, he hath whereof to glory, but not before God." What good is a man's glorying then if he cannot glory before God? We want something to glory in, when the heavens split open and the face of God shines into the hearts of men. We want something that we can glory in just then. I tell you God gives us something that we can do it with, too, and that is His own righteousness.

"For what saith the Scripture? Abraham *believed* God and it was counted unto him for righteousness." What does that say? Abraham believed God and it, it i-t, what? [Congregation: "Faith."] It, what? [Congregation: "Believed God."] His believing God – what did that amount to? [Congregation: "Righteousness."] Who counted it to him for righteousness? [Congregation: "God."] Well, did God make a mistake? [Congregation: "No."] Whether we understand it or not, the Lord did it, and He did right in doing it. He was perfectly just. He said so. We were not in the doing of it; we did not have the plan to lay. We could not have done it if we had tried anyway. Let us let Him have His own way, I say again, brethren, and when we let Him have His own way and we are in His own way, it will be all right, and we need not be a bit afraid.

What was counted to Abraham for righteousness? He *believed* God, and God said, "You are righteous, Abraham." Now that is said three times in that little short space. What was it that was counted to him for righteousness? His believing God. It, i-t, it.

"Now to him that worketh is the reward not reckoned of grace but of debt. But to him that *worketh not*" – Is that what it says? [Congregation: "Yes."] Did the Lord say it that way? [Congregation: "Yes."] "But believeth on him that justifieth the ungodly." But that is the Laodicean message again – miserable and poor and blind and naked. That is the kind of people that the Lord justifies. "His faith is counted to him for righteousness." The ungodly, his faith is counted for righteousness. What is counted to him? [Congregation: "His *faith* for righteousness."] And that is believing that God is justifying ungodly men? Will that bring righteousness to a man? [Congregation: "Yes."] To confess that he is ungodly and then believe that God makes that kind of man righteous. Yes, indeed.

I cannot tell how; I cannot understand it. I know it is so, and I am so glad that it is so that I do not care whether I ever find out how or not. The Lord wants us to have what He gives. Let us take it. The time has expired, and we will begin right there again. But do not forget what was counted to Abraham for righteousness, and "if we be Christ's," then are we "Abraham's seed."

Sermon 16

February 24, 1893

I received a letter a little while ago from Brother Starr in Australia. I will read two or three sentences because they come in well just at this place in our lessons:

> Sister White says that we have been in the time of the latter rain since the Minneapolis meeting.

That is just what we have found in our own study of these lessons, is it not? Brethren, how much longer is the Lord going to wait before we will receive it? He has been trying these four years to have us receive the latter rain. How much longer is He going to wait before we receive it? Now this subject will join right on to Brother Prescott's and his talk is simply the beginning of mine, and what he called upon every one here to do is what every one should have done four years ago.

And the fact of the matter is, something is going to be done. Those who will seek the Lord that way, who will receive His message that way, will get what He wants to give. Those who will not do that will be left to themselves, and when that is done it will be forever. And that is the fearfulness of the situation at this meeting; that is what lends to this meeting its fearful character. The danger is that there will be some here who have resisted this for four years or perhaps who have not resisted it that long, who will now fail to receive it as the Lord gives it and will be passed by. A decision will be made by the Lord, by ourselves in fact, at this meeting. On which side are you going to be found?

Here is another word that teaches the same point that we had last night in our lesson, to receive the word of God just as it is, just as He says it, with no question of our own. Brother Starr says that he was talking with Sister White one day about the angels at Mt. Sinai at the giving of the law, and he says this:

> She saw that the angels, ten thousand times ten thousand, and thousands of thousands, surrounded the people of God as they assembled around the mountain, and all above them, thus making a great living tabernacle from which every evil angel was excluded that not one word that was to come from the voice of Jesus should be altered in any mind or one suggestion of doubt or evil to a soul be made.

Now that is what we want here. [Congregation: "Amen."] What we want right here is for each one to just put up his own prayer himself, for himself, to the Lord to cover us with such a canopy as that at this Institute that when the words of the Lord are read not one word shall be altered in any mind from just what God speaks and that not one suggestion of doubt or evil shall come to a single soul, but that we, each one, may receive just what the Lord says in His own way, *as He* says it and as *He* means it.

Then further from Brother Starr:

> In a late testimony to an individual here, Sister White was forbidden to send it to him in writing but to read it personally, for the reason that evil angels are at work *substituting words* for those that are written. Other words are pronounced in his ears and he gets a meaning just opposite from that designed of God.

Well if that man needs that, is he the only one in the world that needs it? If Satan is working that way, is he going to confine himself to Australia? Then don't you and I need to have our ears anointed as well as our eyes, that we may hear? And does not that word of Jesus, "Take heed how ye hear," come to us?

Then another instance there: A brother had been carried away by connection with secret societies and had gone through with them until he was about ready to take the highest degree.

A testimony came for him. God presented his case to her as a man just upon the brink of a precipice to whom it was dangerous to call out even. Sister White asked the Lord what she could do for him, and as she prayed, the angel said, "Give him the pass word. Give him the pass word into the heavenly society, '*Jesus Christ and Him crucified.*'"

What is the pass word into the heavenly society? [Congregation: "Jesus Christ and Him crucified."] That is the only thing that you and I have any business to know anything about. That is His message to the world, "Jesus Christ and Him crucified"; that is the passport.

Now turn again to Romans 4th chapter. We want to read of the righteousness of God and while we read of this righteousness of God, we want to receive it just as the Lord has spoken it. Don't forget now, we want that canopy of angels over us and around us, that no word may be perverted to our understanding. We want to receive it just as he gave it.

"What shall we say then that Abraham our father, as pertaining to the flesh, hath found? For if Abraham were justified by works, he hath whereof to glory; but not before God. For what saith the scripture? Abraham believed God, and it was counted unto him for righteousness." What was it that was counted unto Abraham for righteousness? [Congregation: "He believed God."] When God said a thing, Abraham believed it. He said "that is so." What was it that the Lord said to him?

Let us turn and read, because that is important to us. Genesis 15:4-6. "And, behold the word of the Lord came unto him, saying, This shall not be thine heir; but he that shall come forth out of thine own bowels shall be thine heir. And he brought him forth abroad and said, Look now toward heaven and tell the stars, if thou be able to number them: and he said unto him, so shall thy seed be. And he believed in the Lord and he counted it unto him for righteousness."

Now do you believe that Abraham became righteous in just that way? [Congregation: "Yes."] Honestly now, do you? [Congregation: "Yes, sir."] Do you know he did? [Congregation: "Yes."] The Lord called Abraham out and said, Look at the stars and tell the number of them, so shall thy seed be. Abraham said, "Amen." That is the Hebrew, Abraham said, "Amen." And the Lord said, "You are right."

"Now do you know that it was as simple a transaction as that? Was it just like calling you and me out of this tabernacle and the Lord saying to us, See the stars? Tell the stars if thou be able to number them. Yes, so shall such and such be. And we say, "Amen." And He should say, "You are righteous." Suppose the Lord called you and me out tonight. No, He can do it without calling us out. He called Abraham out doors to show him the *stars*, but He can show us *sins* without calling us out doors. Has He shown you a great many sins? Has He? [Congregation: "Yes."] Now He says, If thou be able to number them, "they shall be white as snow." What do you say? [Congregation: "Amen."] Then what does the Lord say? [Congregation: "You are righteous."] Are you? [Voice: "Yes."] Do people become righteous as easy as that? Is it as simple a transaction as that? [Congregation: "Yes."] Amen. Thank the Lord! Now let us turn again to the 4th of Romans and get the particular verse where this is told. Romans 4:23, 24: "Now it was not written for his sake alone, that it was imputed to him, but *for us also,* to whom *it shall be imputed,* if *we believe on him* that raised up Jesus our Lord from the dead."

Some of the brethren were saying this morning in the social meeting that last night they felt as though they would like to praise the Lord out loud, but they thought they had better not. "Quench not the Spirit." If you want to praise the Lord for anything, the Lord tells you to do it. We might as well start here as any other time to have Seventh-day Adventists praise the Lord or say, "Praise the Lord" in meeting. We might as well start that here as anywhere.

What the Lord said to Abraham, Abraham believed. And what He says to you and me, you and I believe, then we get the same results. It is not some particular thing that the Lord says, that we must believe in order to be righteous; *whatever* He says, *believe* it, and then He says, "you are right."

I would like to know whether it is not so, that when the Lord says a thing He is right? [Congregation: "Yes."] Then when I say that is so, am I not right? [Congregation: "Yes."] What in the world hinders me from being right? Can you tell? I will say it again: When the Lord says a thing, is He right? [Congregation: "Yes."] He *is right* in saying it; then when I say "that is so"; when I say "Amen"; when I say "be it so"; when I say "yes, that is so," then am I not right? Yes. Am I not right just as certainly as He is? Certainly. Can even He say I am wrong? [Congregation: "No."] He says a thing, and I say the same thing; can He say I am wrong? [Congregation: "No."] When you say the same thing, can He say that you are wrong? [Congregation: "No."] Well then, when we are in such a situation that the Lord Himself cannot say that you and I are wrong, I would like to know what in the world is the reason we are not right? And believing God puts us in just that situation, as He did Abraham. I would like to know what can keep us out of heaven then? What can keep us out of the kingdom of God *then*?

The only thing that can keep you and me out of the kingdom of God is to tell the Lord that He lies, and if you and I will stop that business we will get into heaven all right. That is just what people need to do, to stop telling the Lord that He lies. "He that believeth not God hath made him a liar." But whoever would make God a liar is a liar himself, and liars cannot get into the kingdom of God. "Without are liars" and all those other people referred to in Revelation 21:8, 27, and 22:15. Then the thing we want to do is to stop lying. Let us quit right now. Stop lying. No difference what the Lord says, you say, "That is so."

Don't you see this is the whole story and the very idea that Brother Haskell was trying hard to inculcate upon us here in our lessons, that there is salvation in every line of the Scriptures. For God says it, doesn't He? Well, when God says it, and we say it, then we are righteous, that is the end of it. God said that to Abraham; Abraham said, "Amen, that is so, I take that." So this shows that there is salvation in every line of the Scriptures, in everything God says.

Romans fourth chapter tells more about what Abraham said, or rather what he thought. Romans 4:20-22: "He staggered not at the promise of God through unbelief, but was strong in faith giving glory to God: and being fully persuaded that, what he had promised he was able to perform. And therefore it was imputed to him for righteousness." Now as I read last night without reference to the third chapter of Romans, that Christ was set forth to be a propitiation for sin that is past. "Whom God hath set forth to be a propitiation through faith in his blood, to declare his righteousness for the remission of sins that are past, through the forbearance of God: To declare, I say, at this time his righteousness; that he might be just and the justifier of him which believeth in Jesus." The thought is, that God is righteous in the doing of it; this is sufficient; He has met every demand. He is perfectly able, then, to justify the believer in Jesus, is He not? He is perfectly able to make the man righteous who believes in Jesus. He has promised to do that for every one who will believe in Jesus: Well, do you believe He is able to perform what He has promised? Has he not promised to do that? [Congregation: "Yes."] Do you believe He is able to perform what He has promised? [Congregation: "Amen."] Is He? [Congregation: "Yes."] Amen. *Therefore* it *is imputed to you* for *righteousness*. [Congregation: "Thank the Lord."] That is all the story. [Congregation: "Praise the Lord."]

The story is simple enough, the mischief of it is though that we allow so much of Satan's devices to get in to mystify it. That is the mischief of it. He does not want that; He wants it to be just as simple as He has told it, and He has told it so simply that a little child can understand it and |receive it. And you who do not receive it as a little child, cannot receive it. So I say again, that it is no difference what God says or when He says it; *whatever He says,* we, like Abraham, say, "Amen. Lord, I believe that; that is so." Then He says you are right. And you are right, too.

Let us read on now, in Romans 4:3-5: "For what saith the scripture? Abraham believed God and it was counted unto him for righteousness. Now to him that worketh is the reward not reckoned of grace but of debt. But to him that worketh not but believeth on him that justifieth the ungodly, his faith is counted for righteousness."

Believeth on him that justifieth who? [Congregation: "The ungodly."] Who is it, in this world, that the Lord justifies? [Congregation: "The ungodly."] The ungodly. I am glad of it, for that assures me everlasting salvation. If it were otherwise there would be no hope for me. If God justified people who were only half saints that would leave me out. If He justified people who had only *one* good thing, that would leave me out. If He justified people who had only a little good about them, that would leave me out. But thank the Lord, *He* is so *good, He* loves me *so much;* He has such wondrous *power,* the divine power of His righteousness is so *great,* that when He pronounces that word upon such a corrupt sinner as I am it makes me through and through righteous in the sight of God. [Congregation: "Amen."] That is the worth of God's word "righteousness."

And because He is so good; because there is such divine power in His righteousness and because He justifies the ungodly; therefore, I have the perfect security of His everlasting salvation.

Then what in the world is going to keep me from being glad? Can you imagine anything that is going to keep me from being glad? Can you imagine anything that is going to keep you from being glad? It is not enough for me to be glad; I want you to be glad; I can attend to my part of it. [Voice: "I am glad."] Amen.

"To him that worketh not." Yes, if it required works I could not do enough. If there was anything at all required it would leave me out. But Oh, as we read the other night, ye have "sold yourself for naught" and "ye are redeemed without money." But not without a price. But lo, *He* has paid the price. And the blessing of it is that He was rich enough to pay the price and the other blessing is He was good enough to spend all His riches in paying the price that He might have me. He can have me.

I have heard brethren say, "I thank the Lord I have confidence in Him." I thank the Lord He has confidence in me. I think it is little enough for *a man,* for whom the Lord does that much, to have confidence in the Lord, but to think that the Lord would make such a wondrous investment in me with the confidence of ever getting the worth of it; *His confidence* in me I cannot grasp. That is too wonderful for me. And I am thankful that the Lord had that much confidence in His risk upon me. For that reason I am so glad I don't know what else to do. Brethren, the Lord is good. [Congregation: "Amen."] Then let us trust Him.

"Even as David also describeth the blessedness of the man"? Well, I should say so. I should say so. The blessedness of the man "unto whom God imputeth righteousness *without works.*" Brethren, do *you* know the blessedness of that man? Or are there some in this house who know only the distressedness of that man, who tries to get it by works? There is no *blessedness* of that kind; the Bible does not describe any blessedness of that kind. That is all distressedness only and you know it. But God describes the blessedness of the man to whom God imputeth righteousness without works saying, "O the blessedness of the man." That is the way David said it in his own language, but in ours it is translated simply "Blessed is the man." O the blessedness of the man whose iniquities are forgiven, and whose sins are covered.

There is a blessedness to that man; I tell you there is. O the blessedness of the man to whom He will not impute sin. To whom the Lord will not impute sin, because that man has received the gift of Jesus Christ, and all that God has given in Him, and when He looks at that man, He sees Jesus Christ; He does not impute sin to that man at all. Oh the blessedness of the man to whom the Lord will not impute sin!

"Cometh this blessedness then upon the circumcision only, or upon the uncircumcision also? For we say that faith was reckoned to Abraham for righteousness." Three times, you see, there inside of nine verses, three times the Lord has said it over, Faith counts for righteousness. Look at it. "Abraham believed God and it was counted unto him for righteousness"; "To him that believeth on him that justifies the ungodly, his faith is counted for righteousness." "We say that faith was reckoned to Abraham for righteousness." Brethren, let us do like Abraham did; let us say "Amen." [Congregation: "Amen."] Counting that what God has promised He is able to perform. [Congregation: "Amen."] And then thank the Lord that He imputes to us righteousness and makes us free.

"How was it then reckoned? When he was in circumcision or in uncircumcision?" Did not he have to go and circumcise himself and all his house before he could be righteous? [Congregation: "No, sir."] "When he was in circumcision or in uncircumcision? Not in circumcision but in uncircumcision." When he was a Gentile. Is that so? [Congregation: "Yes, sir."] Before he was circumcised? "And he received the sign of circumcision, a seal of the *righteousness*" that he had? [Congregation:

"Righteousness *of the faith* which he had."] Doesn't it say, he received the sign of circumcision, a seal of the righteousness which he had? [Congregation: "No. 'A seal of the righteousness of the faith which he had.'"] Yes, sir. Yes, sir. "He received the sign of circumcision, a seal of the righteousness of the faith which he had." [Congregation: "Amen!"] A seal of the righteousness of the faith which he had, not the righteousness that he had, because the *righteousness* that he had came by the *faith* that he had.

"And he received the sign of circumcision, a seal of the righteousness of the faith which he had yet being uncircumcised, that he might be the father of all them that believe, though they be not circumcised." Is that you? Father of all them that *believe* God. [Congregation: "Amen."] All them that *believe*. Is that so? [Congregation: "Yes, sir."] That righteousness might be imputed unto them also. He is the father of all them that believe, what for? "That righteousness might be imputed unto them also." Come along, then. "Father of all them that believe." No wonder he could not count them. Only the mind of God could count the seed of Abraham. They are indeed numberless as the stars, but lo, of the stars it is said, "He calleth them all by their names," and he is able to number us, he knows us by name, and the blessing of it is, he is going to give us a new name. I tell you, brethren, the Lord loves us. Indeed He does.

"For the promise, that he should be the heir of the world, was not to Abraham, or to his seed, through the law, but *through the righteousness of faith*." Is that so? [Congregation: "Yes."] "For if they which are of the law be heirs, faith is made void, and the promise made of none effect: because the law worketh wrath." Does it? [Congregation: "Yes."] Does it now? [Congregation: "Yes."] Then how much righteousness is any man going to get out of the law? [Congregation: "None."] That is not what the law is for; "the law worketh wrath."

"For where no law is, there is no transgression. Therefore it is of faith, that it might be by grace; to the end the promise *might be sure*." Oh! The Lord wants His promise to be sure to us, does He? And in order that it might be sure to us, where did He put it? Therefore it is of *faith, that* it might be by *grace; to the end* the promise might be *sure*."

Look now; think of that carefully. I will say it slowly. "Therefore it is of *faith, that* it might be by grace. The word "that" is what I am after. What does it mean? In order that, just this way. "That it might be by grace." Then it is of grace, is it? [Congregation: "Yes."] It is of *faith,* that it might be by *grace,* what for? "That it might be *sure*." Then he who receives anything from God by faith, he is the man that is sure of that thing, isn't he? [Congregation: "Yes."] And he who thinks of getting anything from God in any other way than *by faith,* never can be sure that he has it, because in fact he does not have it at all. Do you see that? [Congregation: "Yes."] Let us act that way.

"Therefore it is of faith, that it might be by grace; to the end the promise might be sure *to all*." Good. [Congregation: "Amen."] To *all*. To all.

"To the end the promise might be *sure* to *all* the seed; not to that only which is of the law, but to that also which is of the faith of Abraham; who is the Father of us all (as it is written, I have made thee a father of many nations), before him whom he believed, even God, who quickeneth the dead, and calleth those things which be not as though they were." What does he do? [Congregation: "Quickeneth."] What does He do? [Congregation: "Makes alive."] Giveth life unto the dead. "Calling those things that be not as though they were." When He calls a thing that is not as though it were, then *is* it? [Congregation: "Yes."] Did not He do that when He made the worlds? There were no worlds; He called them; what then? [Congregation: "They were."] There was no light; He called the light; "there was light."

In me is no righteousness; here is all ungodliness; here is all uncleanness; God has set forth that same One who declared the word and the worlds came and who declared the word "light," and light came – He has set forth that same One to declare righteousness in place of this body of sin. [Congregation: "Praise the Lord."] In this place, this body, this character of sin, He calls that which is not as though it were, and, thank the Lord, it is. [Congregation: "Amen."] In this place which is all uncleanness he has set forth that blessed One to declare holiness and He calls this thing which is not as though it were, and, thanks be to His almighty power, it is. [Congregation: "Amen."] And I am glad of it. "Calleth those things which be not as though they were." A sinner is not righteous; the ungodly are ungodly; but God calls that which is not, as though it were and it is. [Congregation: "Amen."] It is.

"Who against hope believed in hope, that he might become the father of many nations, according to that which was spoken, so shall thy seed be. And being not weak in faith, he considered not his own body now dead, when he was about a hundred years old, neither yet the deadness of Sarah's womb: he staggered not at the promise of God through unbelief; but was strong in faith, giving glory to God and being fully persuaded that what he had promised, he was able also to perform. And therefore it was imputed to him for righteousness. Now it was not written for his sake alone that it was imputed to him but for us also, to whom it shall be imputed, if we believe on him that raised up Jesus our Lord from the dead; who was delivered for our offenses and was raised again for our justification." He was raised that we might be justified; raised for our justification. I am going to let Him accomplish what He was raised from the dead for. That is settled. He knows how to do it, and He can do it, and I am going to let Him.

Now the fifth chapter of Romans: "Therefore being *justified* by *faith*." What do you say? [Congregation: "Amen."] Therefore being made righteous, being justified by faith, "we have peace with God." And I know it, don't you? We *have* peace with God. He says so. Then it is so. Even though it were not so. Then it is so. Even though it were not so, it is so after He calls those things that be not as though they were. We cannot understand it, but we can know it. I know it, and that is all I care to do.

> Therefore being justified by faith, we have peace with God through our Lord Jesus Christ: by whom also we have access by faith into this grace.

How did we get into this grace? By faith. We have it, thank the Lord. "Wherein we stand." Do we stand there indeed? [Congregation: "Yes."] He says so; it is so, isn't it? He says so, and it is so. He says we stand there, and we do, thank the Lord. "Wherein we stand, *and rejoice* in hope of the glory of God." Don't we? He says we rejoice, and we do. Because when He says we do, He is right, and we say, "Amen," and then we are right. "And not only so, but we glory in tribulations also." Tribulations will come along as easy as can be, but they will not amount to anything against us. "For I reckon that the sufferings of this present time are not worthy to be compared to the glory that shall be revealed" – not *to* us only but "*in* us," which shall be a part of us. That is how we shall shine as the sun in the kingdom of our Father.

Well, that is the righteousness of God; that is how Abraham received it. What is the blessing of Abraham, then? What is it? [Congregation: "Righteousness by faith."] How did he get it? [Congregation: "By faith."] The blessing of Abraham is not received except by that man who has righteousness by faith; is that so? [Congregation: "Yes, sir."]

Now the text that Brother Prescott just read. I do not care if he did read it; it comes into my lesson as well as his, and it is all one lesson anyway.

Galatians 3:13,14:

"Christ hath redeemed us from the curse of the law." Has He? He says He has, then He has. "Christ hath redeemed us from the curse of the law, being made a curse for us, for it is written, Cursed is everyone that hangeth on a tree, that the blessing of Abraham might come on the Gentiles through Jesus Christ."

Why did Christ become a curse on the tree? That the blessing of Abraham might come on you and me. Why did He redeem us from the curse of the law? That the blessing of Abraham might come on you and me. What is the blessing of Abraham? [Congregation: "Righteousness by faith."] Christ died that you and I might be made righteous by faith. Brethren, isn't it awful when a man will rob Christ of the very thing for which He died and want righteousness in some other way? Isn't it awful? Brethren, let us believe in Jesus Christ.

"That the blessing of Abraham might come on the Gentiles through Jesus Christ."

Now then we are redeemed from the curse of the law; Christ is made a curse for us, that the blessing of Abraham might come upon us. And what does that come upon us for? "That we might *receive the promise of the Spirit* through *faith*."

Then when we as a people, we as a body, we as a church, have received the blessing of Abraham, what then? [Congregation: "The latter rain."] The outpouring of the Spirit. It is so with the individual.

When the individual believes in Jesus Christ and obtains the righteousness which is by faith, then the Holy Spirit, which is the circumcision of the heart is received by him. And when the whole people, as a church, receive the righteousness of faith, the blessing of Abraham, then what is to hinder the church from receiving the Spirit of God? [Congregation: "Nothing."] That is where we are. What is to hinder, then, the outpouring of the Holy Spirit? What holds back the outpouring of the Holy Ghost? [Voice: "Unbelief."] Our lack of the righteousness of God, which is by faith – that is what holds it back, for when that is received, it is given *in order* that we may receive the promise of the Spirit through faith. Then let us be sure we have the blessing of Abraham and then ask and we shall receive.

Sermon 17

February 26, 1893

The last verse that we had before us in the previous lesson was in the third chapter of Galatians, verses 13 and 14. Now whether that be the promise of the Spirit to the individual in his own individual experience, or the promise of the Spirit in its outpouring on the whole church, it is all the same. Nobody can have it without having the blessing of Abraham first. Whoever has not the blessing of Abraham cannot have the Holy Spirit. Because we read in Romans 4, "He received the sign of circumcision, a seal of the righteousness of the faith which he had yet being uncircumcised." What circumcision really is, you will find by turning to the 30th chapter of Deuteronomy and the 6th verse:

"And the Lord thy God will circumcise thine heart, and the heart of thy seed to love the Lord thy God with all thine heart and with all thy soul that thou mayest live." Now, put right with that Romans 5:5. After telling that we are justified by faith and that "we have peace with God through our Lord Jesus Christ: By whom also we have access by faith into this grace wherein we stand, and rejoice in the hope of the glory of God"; then he says, (verse 5): "And hope maketh not ashamed; because the *love of God* is shed abroad in our hearts *by the Holy Ghost* which is given unto us." Now, unto us, the Holy Ghost sheds abroad in the heart the love of God; but he said here, I "will circumcise thine heart . . . to love the Lord thy God with all thine heart, and with all the soul." The only way that we can love the Lord with all the heart and with all the soul, is by the love of God implanted in the heart and in the soul, converting the person to God. And "love is the fulfilling of the law."

To "love the Lord thy God with all thy heart, and with all thy soul, and with all thy mind," and "with all thy strength" is the first of all the commandments: "And the second is like unto it, Thou shalt love thy neighbor as thyself. On these two commandments hang all the law and the prophets." Circumcision of the heart is that condition of the heart by which we will "love the Lord" our God, "with all the heart and with all the soul." Then you see that that which this circumcision in the flesh was to Abraham, was simply a sign, a token, that they could see in the time when God was teaching them by object lessons – a token which they could see, signifying that which they could not see. And therefore, that circumcision in the flesh being the sign, "a seal of the righteousness of the faith which he had," before he was circumcised. It was simply the sign, outwardly, of the work of the Holy Spirit, which circumcised the heart. The Holy Spirit sheds abroad the love of God in the heart, but no man can receive the promise of the Spirit who has not the blessing of Abraham – the righteousness of God, which is by faith.

Then, the man who knows that he believes God can ask with perfect confidence for the Holy Spirit. Not the man who *thinks* that he believes God; a part of the time he does, a part of the time he does not; a part of the time he thinks he does; a part of the time he does not know whether he does or not. That is not believing God at all, but the Lord wants you and me to *know* that we believe God. He wants us to know that and to have that thing as firmly settled and fixed as that we live. Then, I say that the man who knows that he believes God can ask with perfect confidence for the Spirit of God, and receive it by faith, for "if ye ask, ye shall receive." He said so. But we must ask according to His will. But it is not according to His will to give the Holy Spirit to anybody who has not the blessing of Abraham, and just as with the individual, so with the church: When the people of God reach that place where they *know* that they believe God, they can ask with perfect confidence for the outpouring of the Holy Spirit and wait in perfect confidence and faith that they shall receive it and they will. That is a fact.

Now let us study a little further tonight, how we may *know* that the blessing of Abraham is our own and how we may *know* that with perfect confidence we may ask the Lord to give us His Holy Spirit and then just simply wait His own good time and we receive it according to His own wish – we have not anxiety about whether we are going to receive it or not. We want to learn how all that anxiety as to *whether* we can receive the Holy Spirit or not – learn how that can be taken away from us and then we can present our petitions to the Lord in faith, expecting to receive it, expecting just that and expecting nothing else and simply waiting for Him to give it in His own good time, while we still ask and still seek Him that it may be so.

I tell you, brethren, when we get into that place it will not be difficult for us all to be "with one accord in one place." Now, at this meeting, when we reach that condition – that place where we know that we believe God and know that we may ask with perfect confidence for the Holy Spirit, it will be an easy thing for every one of us – and it will be so, too – to be with one accord in one place, every time there is a meeting. The fact of the matter is, each one will be afraid to be away, because if he should be away from any one of these meetings and the promise of the Holy Spirit be fulfilled, he would miss it. Every one will be here waiting and watching for the Lord to do what He says, just when He gets ready. Don't you see how that will bring all with accord into one place? It will do it.

Of course, if the work of the Lord should call us away from some meeting in the order of our work and the order of the Lord, and the Holy Spirit should be poured out while we were away, we would get it anyhow, wherever we were. But it will not be so with those who are away from the meeting from their own inclinations. I am afraid to be away from any of our meetings here. I am afraid to be away from these morning meetings. For I can't tell at what meeting the Spirit may be poured upon us. I cannot risk being absent.

Now let us take up the Scriptures and read just how the Lord has led us and will lead every one right through to that place tonight, if you will go. If you will start where I begin to read, the Lord will lead you and me right straight through. Let us not question how that can be. When the Lord speaks, that is the end of the whole story, no difference what He says; that is the end of it, and we say "Lord, that's so." Now, let us go together tonight and we will arrive at that place where every one of us can *know* that we believe God and that we have the blessing of Abraham and then we can ask God for His Spirit in perfect confidence and wait to receive it, as He gives it in His own good time.

Let us see what the Lord has done and how He works and how He brings us up to that place. Let us begin where He began. We will read first from Ephesians 1:3-6. That takes us to the point where God began concerning us, and that will be as far back as we need to go. The third verse:

"Blessed be the God and Father of our Lord Jesus Christ, who hath blessed us with all spiritual blessings in heavenly places in Christ." What is it He "hath" done? [Congregation: "Blessed us."]. Is it so? [Congregation: "Yes."] Has done it? [Congregation: "Yes."] He has blessed us with how many blessings? [Congregation: "*All* spiritual blessings."] All the blessings He has? He has given us all? [Congregation: "Yes."] How? [Congregation: "In Christ."] In Christ. Then in giving Christ, what did God give? [Congregation: "All spiritual blessings."] All the spiritual blessings that He had.

Well, then, when you and I believe in Jesus Christ, are we not blessed? Have not we all the blessing that the Lord has? Then what is going to bother us? A person that is blessed like that, is he going to be anything else than happy? [Congregation: "No."] Can he have the blues? [Congregation: "No."] Can he get into the sulks because things don't go just right? [Congregation: "No."] They are going just right any way. However things go they can't take his blessings away. "All things work together for good to them that love God."

But the fourth verse is the one particularly that I want to read: "According as He hath chosen us." *Will* choose us? [Congregation: "Hath chosen us."] Has He? [Congregation: "Yes."] When did He do it? [Congregation: "'Before the foundation of the world.'"] Thank the Lord! "Before the foundation of the world" He chose you and me. [Congregation: "Praise the Lord!"] Now, will you say "amen" to that every time? [Congregation: "Amen!"] I do not mean just now. Will you say it *all* the time? [Congregation: "Yes."]

How long is that Scripture going to remain there? [Congregation: "Forever."] Then how long is it going to be true that "he hath chosen you before the foundation of the world?" [Congregation: "Always."] Then how long are you going to be bothered to know whether you are the Lord's or not? Hasn't He *chosen* you? Hasn't He chosen you?

[Congregation: "Yes."] What did He do it for? Because He wanted us? Did He? [Congregation: "Yes."] He chose me because He wanted me and He shall have me. I am not going to rob Him and disappoint His choice. He has chosen us, hasn't He? [Congregation: "Yes."] "Before the foundation of the world." Now the rest of that verse: "That we should be holy and without blame before Him in love." His blessed purpose is, He wants us to "be holy and without blame before him in love." Then we can let Him have His own way, because it is our everlasting salvation to let Him do it.

Next verse:

"Having predestinated" – appointed the destiny that He wants us to reach, long before hand. The destiny that God fixes for man is worth having. "Having predestinated us unto the adoption of children by Jesus Christ to Himself, according to the good pleasure of His will." Why did He do it then? Not because we were so good, but because He is so good; not because we were so well pleasing to Him, but because of the good pleasure of His own will. It was just Himself to do it. That's why He did it.

Verse 6: "To the praise of the glory of His grace wherein he hath made us accepted in the beloved." Now what do you say to that? [Congregation: "Amen."] When did He do that? [Congregation: "Before the foundation of the world."] Precisely. "Before the foundation of the world." That answers all this idea about whether we can do anything in order to be justified or not. He did it all before we had any chance to do anything – long before we were born – long before the world was made. Don't you see that the Lord is the one that does things, in order that we may be saved and that we may have Him?

Now see what He has done: (1). "He hath blessed us with all spiritual blessings" in Christ. (2). "He hath chosen us in him before the foundation of the world." (3). "He hath predestinated us unto the adoption of children by Jesus Christ." (4). And "He hath made us accepted in the beloved." Well, I am glad of it. I *know* that that is so. [Congregation: "Amen."] Don't you? [Congregation: "Yes."] For He says so. He *says* so. Here then are four things that we can be everlastingly sure of.

A word further about those blessings the Lord hath given us. We have all the blessings that God has, when we believe Jesus Christ. Then they are our own. We don't need to be so very particular about praying for blessings. Would we not do better, think ye, to spend our time in *thanking Him* for the blessings that we have, than in asking Him for blessings? How does that look? Which do you think looks the better, to thank the Lord for the blessings He has already given, or to ask Him to give us some, when He hasn't any more to give? Now which is the better? [Congregation: "To thank Him."]

He hath given us all the blessings He has in Christ. Christ says, "I am with you." Brethren, let us feed on the blessings. We have them, and they are our own.

Then we can be sure all the time that we have *all spiritual blessings.*

We can be sure all the time that He has chosen us. He says He has.

We can be sure all the time that He has predestinated us unto the adoption of children.

We can be sure all the time that He has made us accepted in the Beloved.

We can be sure of all these things, for God says so and it is so. Then isn't that a continual feast itself?

Now He has done all that and has done it freely. For how many people did He do this? [Congregation: "All."] Every soul? [Congregation: "Yes, sir."] Gave all the blessings He has to every soul in this world; He chose every soul in the world; He chose Him in Christ before the foundation of the world, predestinated him unto the adoption of children and made him accepted in the Beloved, did He not? [Congregation: "Yes."] Of course He did.

We will read other verses on that presently. The thought I am after just now is that no one can have these things and know they are his without his own consent. The Lord will not force any of these things upon a man, even though He has given them already, will He? [Congregation: "No."] This is a cooperation, you see. God pours out everything in one wondrous gift, but if a man will not have it, the Lord will not compel him to have a bit of it. Every man that will take it, it is all his own. There is where the cooperation comes in. The Lord has to have our cooperation in all things.

Now let us turn to Titus 2:14, speaking of the Lord it says, "who gave himself for *us*." That is the past tense too is it not? That is done. He did give Himself for how many people? [Congregation: "All."]

How many people on the earth can read that text and "say that means me"? Every soul on the earth. Wherever we go, then, on this earth and find a man, we can read to him that "Christ gave Himself for you," can we not? [Congregation: "Yes."] He gave Himself for you, then. That is the price that Peter refers to in 1 Peter 1:18-20: "Forasmuch as ye know that ye were not redeemed with corruptible things, as silver and gold, from your vain conversation received by tradition from your fathers: but with the precious blood of Christ, as of a lamb without blemish and without spot: Who verily was foreordained before the foundation of the world."

Now we want each individual to know where he stands.

"He gave Himself for me." That is stated in Galatians 2:20: "The life which I now live in the flesh I live by the faith of the Son of God, who loved *me,* and gave himself for *me.*" How many people in the world can read that and say that means me? [Congregation: "Every one."] "Loved me and gave himself for *me.* That was the price that was paid. Then He bought me, did He? [Congregation: "Yes."] He bought you? [Congregation: "Yes."]. Whether you or I let Him have us, that is not the question just now. What has *He* done? What did He do? [Congregation: "Paid the price."]

Before the foundation of the world He bought me, did He not? And you? Then whose are we? [Congregation: "The Lord's."]

Well, then, is there any prospect of your getting into doubt as to whether you are the Lord's? How is a man who wants to be the Lord's and has confessed his sins – how is it possible for him to get into doubt as to whether he is the Lord's or not? It is only by going back on the word of God altogether and not believing it at all and saying the Lord has lied. Is not that the only way he can do it? "He that believeth not God has made him a liar." Then the only way a man can doubt as to whether he is the Lord's or not is by going back on the word of God and saying that the Lord lies. That is the only way he can do it. Because for a man to doubt is to do that; he may not do that in so many words, but when he gets into doubt as to whether he is the Lord's that is what he has done. He has allowed unbelief to overthrow him and Satan to get the advantage and sweep everything away. That is so.

But still though the Lord has bought us, He will not take what He has bought without our permission. There is a line which God has set as fixing the freedom of every man and He Himself will never go over that line a hair's breadth without our permission. He respects the freedom and dignity which He has given to intelligent creatures, whether man or angel. He respects it and He Himself will not transgress the limit. He will not go over the limits without the permission of that person. But when the permission is given, then He will come for all that He is. Then that opens the flood gates and the Lord flows in. That is so.

Well, then, He has bought you, has He? [Congregation: "Yes."] Do you want to be the Lord's [Congregation: "Yes."] Now, friends, let us make this a real practical, tangible thing. He has bought us, has He not? He has paid the price for us. We are His by His will. Now then, when our will is there, whose are we then? [Congregation: "The Lord's."] He has shown His will on that subject by paying the price, has He not? And when we make known our will on the subject by saying, "Lord, that is my choice, too; that is the way my will goes, too, then I want to know how in the universe anything is going to keep us from being His. Then can you *know* that you are the Lord's? [Congregation: "Yes, sir."] Can you, now? [Congregation: "Yes, sir."]

Well, suppose you get up in the morning with a headache and your digestion has not worked very well during the night and you feel rather bad all over and don't feel just right. How do you know you are the Lord's? [Congregation: "Because He says so."] But suppose you get up in the morning and feel bright and hilarious and feel pretty good generally. How do you know you are the Lord's? [Congregation: "Because He says so."]

Sometimes people say when we ask them, "Have your sins been forgiven?" "Yes, I was convinced that they were for awhile." "What convinced you?" "I *felt* as though they were forgiven." They did not know anything about it. They did not, in that, have a particle of evidence that their sins were forgiven. Why, brethren, the only evidence that we can have that these things are so is that God says so. *That* is the evidence. Don't look to feelings. Feelings are as variable as the wind. You know that is so. Never pay a particle of attention to them. It is none of your business how you feel. When God says so, it is so, whether I feel so or not.

I will give that illustration again. I have given it before but it emphasizes this point, that feeling has nothing to do with facts. Twice two is four, is it not? You know that is so, but there are some people in the world who do not know that twice two is four. But suppose you should tell someone, and he should believe it, how do you think he would *feel*? Do you suppose he would feel as though he had been picked up and whirled in a sort of half somersault and set down in a new place? No. What in the world has feeling got to do with that? Then what does he care how he feels?

Now that is not saying that there will be no experience as the fruit of this, but it is saying that if you look for feelings as an evidence, you will never find the evidence, but if you look to the word of God for the evidence, then you will get the evidence which God gives in His word; that is, His own divine power in that word effectually working in the man who believes.

Well then, the Lord has bought us, has He not? Now as far as you and I are concerned, we need not have any more doubt as to whether we are the Lord's; that is so? [Congregation: "Yes."] But there are some people in the world who are not, really, in real experience and as a matter of fact so far as the consummation of the bargain is concerned; they have not submitted themselves to the Lord and are not practically His. He has made them His by purchase; now how can they know that they are His practically and indeed? By His word. By choosing for themselves to have it just that way. By choice. Page 44 in *Steps to Christ* gives the whole philosophy of it; it tells how to make the surrender of ourselves to God. It says that your promises and resolutions are like ropes of sand, and the knowledge of your broken promise and forfeited pledges, weakens your confidence in your own sincerity. And finally: "What you need to understand is the true force of the will. You cannot save yourself; you cannot change your heart, but you *can choose* to serve Him."

When the man chooses to put his will on the side where God's will is, then the thing is accomplished. Then it is at a man's *choice* that he practically, in his own experience, becomes the Lord's indeed. Then is it not by the man's own permission in choosing the Lord's way that the man becomes the Lord's in practical experience? Then having done that, don't you see that so long as your choice is there, so long as your wish is there to be the Lord's don't you see that you are the Lord's indeed? Do you see that? Whenever we deliver ourselves up to Him, that is so. But some of you delivered yourself up long ago, but then, since that, you have been discouraged and wondering whether you were the Lord's or not.

We want people tonight to get that doubt and question forever out of the way so that whatever comes up, you will not be bothering about whether you are the Lord's. Just as certainly as your choice is there to be His, you *are* His, for He bought you long ago. That is the thing I am after. Is that what you are after? You are to *take* it if you ever get it. [Congregation: "Amen."] Then we can *know* that we are the Lord's.

But now we sometimes hear people talk as though that was going to sanction sin. No. It will not do that. No. It will *save* you from sinning. When a man gets into that place and his choice is there to be the Lord's, then God works in him both to will and to do of his own good pleasure, and he is a Christian. God will make him a Christian. That is the divine power there is in this thing. There is no sanction of sin about it. In fact, it is the only way to keep from sanctioning sin. Any other profession *does* sanction sin. Any other profession does do just what the Lord complains of – that men have made Him to serve with their sins. What does the Lord say? "You have made me to serve with your sin." Isaiah 43:24. Let us stop it. Let our will and our choice be the Lord's every moment of our conscious days, and then it is a fact.

Let us turn and read that verse that says so. 1 Corinthians 6:19 and the last words of the verse: "Ye are not your own." That is so, is it not? I don't care who the man is, is he his own? [Congregation: "No, sir."] The Lord has bought him and if he does not let the Lord have him, he is robbing the Lord of that which is the Lord's own. That is the mischief of it. Though he be not consciously and practically the Lord's, yet the Lord has bought every one and any man who refuses to let the Lord have him, he is robbing the Lord of that which He bought and for which He paid the price and he is counting the price which bought him as worth less than *himself*. Is not that the same satanic spirit that sought to put itself above God in heaven? The Lord gave *Himself* for us; then when I will not let Him have me, in that very thing I count myself worth more than the price that was paid – that is, worth more than the Lord, and that is the same self that puts itself above God all the time. Oh let this mind be in us that was in Christ, who emptied Himself that God and man might again be united in one.

"Ye are not your own," are you? [Congregation: "No."] Are you not glad of it? Are you not glad you are not your own? He says so, and it is so, is it not? Why is it? "For ye are bought with a price." He bought us, therefore, we are not our own, and before all people in the world who are not their own, is the man who has yielded himself to the Lord who has bought him. "Therefore glorify God in your body and in your spirit which are God's." Whose are they? [Congregation: "God's."] But I need not dwell longer on these verses, brethren. You do that, will you? You dwell on them.

Well now we have read the verses, "He gave himself for us." He bought us. How much of us? [Congregation: "*All* of us."] When was it that He did it? [Congregation: "Before the foundation of the world."] What kind of folks were we before the foundation of the world? What kind of folks were we when God bought us?

We were just ourselves; just as we were in this world. And He bought us, sinners, just as we are? [Congregation: "Yes."] Now did He? Honestly now? We are coming to another thought here. Now did He pay that price and buy us just as we were? Sinners? [Congregation: "Yes."] Evil beings and willing to go into evil ways? Willing to do the evil thing? Making no profession of religion and not particularly wanting to? Did He buy us then? [Congregation: "Yes."] What did He buy just then? He bought us, and *all* there was of us. And as He bought *what* there was of us; He bought our sins. Isaiah describes it – wounds and bruises and putrefying sores; no soundness at all. Is that so?

Here is another text, Titus 3:3-7: "For we ourselves also were sometimes foolish, disobedient, serving divers lusts and pleasures, living in malice and envy, hateful and hating one another. But after that the kindness and love of God our Saviour toward man appeared, not by works of righteousness which we have done, but according to his mercy he saves us, by the washing to regeneration and renewing of the Holy Ghost; which he shed on us abundantly through Jesus Christ our Saviour: that being justified by his grace, we should be made heirs according to the hope of eternal life." He did it; He says so. Then do you know that that is so? [Congregation: "Yes."]

Well now let us carry that a little further. He gave Himself for our sins, but the same thought goes through all. He will not take our sins – although He bought them – without *our permission*. Look at it a little further, carrying the same thought forward. "He gave himself." for whose sins? [Congregation: "Ours."] Whose were they? [Congregation: "Ours."] He gave Himself for them. They being ours, *to whom* did He give Himself when He bought them? [Congregation: "To us."] He gave Himself *to* me, *for* my sins? [Congregation: "Yes."] Then the choice is forever with me as to whether I would rather have my sins than to have Him, isn't it? [Congregation: "Yes."] That is the living choice before me, is it? [Congregation: "Yes."] Is that the choice before you? [Congregation: "Yes."] Which would you rather have, your sins or Christ? [Congregation: "Christ."] Then from this time henceforth can there be any hesitation about letting anything go that God shows is sin? Will you let it go when it is pointed out? When sin is pointed out to you, say, "I would rather have Christ than that." And let it go [Congregation: "Amen."] Just tell the Lord, "Lord, I make the choice now. I make the trade. I make Thee my choice. It is gone, and I have something better." Thank the Lord! Then where in the world is the opportunity for any of us to get discouraged over our sins?

Now some of the brethren here have done that very thing. They came here free, but the Spirit of God brought up something they never saw before. The Spirit of God went deeper than it ever went before and revealed things they never saw before and then instead of thanking the Lord that that was so and letting the whole wicked business go and thanking the Lord they had ever so much more of Him than they ever had before, they began to get discouraged. They said, "Oh what am I going to do? My sins are so great." There they let Satan cast a cloud over them and throw them into discouragement and they get no good out of the meetings day after day.

Isn't that too bad? Isn't it too bad that a person whom the Lord has loved so much as to give Himself for Him at all, should act that way with the Lord when the Lord wants to reveal more of Himself? Brethren, if any of you have got into discouragement, let us quit. If the Lord has brought up sins to us that we never thought of before, that only shows that He is going down to the depths and He will reach the bottom at last and when He finds the last thing that is unclean or impure and that is out of harmony with His will and brings that up and shows that to us and we say, "I would rather have the Lord than that," then the work is complete and the seal of the living God can be fixed upon that character. [Congregation: "Amen."] Which would you rather have, a character – [Someone in the congregation began praising the Lord and others began to look around.] Never mind. If lots more of you would thank the Lord for what you have got, there would be more joy in this house tonight.

Which would you rather have, the completeness, the perfect fulness of Jesus Christ or have less than that with some of your sins covered up that you never know of? [Congregation: "His fulness."] But don't you see, the Testimonies have told us that if there be stains of sin there, we cannot have the seal of God. How in the world can that seal of God, which is the impress of His perfect character revealed in us, be put upon us when there are sins about us? He cannot put the seal, the impress of His perfect character, upon us until He sees it there. And so He has got to dig down to the deep places we never dreamed of, because we cannot understand our hearts. But the Lord knows the heart. He tries the conscience. He will cleanse the heart, and bring up the last vestige of wickedness. Let Him go on, brethren; let Him keep on His searching work. and when He does bring our sins before us, let the heart say, "Lord, thou gavest thyself for my sins. Oh, I take thee instead of them." They are gone, and I rejoice in the Lord. Brethren, let us be honest with the Lord, and treat Him as He wants us to.

Then He gave Himself to us for our sins. Then I say again and you see that it is simply with you and me a living choice, as to whether we will have the Lord or ourselves, the Lord's righteousness or our sins, the Lord's say or our say? Which will we have? [Congregation: "The Lord's way."] There is no difference in making the choice when we know what the Lord has done, and what He is to us. The choice is easy. Let the surrender be complete. And when these sins come up – why, they were surrendered long ago. That is all they are brought up for, that we can make the choice. This is the blessed work of sanctification. And we can know that that work of sanctification is going on in us. If the Lord should take away our sins without our knowing it, what good would it do us? That would simply be making machines of us. He does not propose to do that; consequently, He wants you and me to know when our sins go, that we may know when His righteousness comes. It is when we yield ourselves that we have Him.

It is true that the Scriptures say we are instruments of God, and don't you forget that we are always intelligent instruments – not like the instrument, a pick or a shovel, that a man would use. That is utterly senseless. That is not it, but we are *intelligent* instruments. We will be used by the Lord at our own living choice. Our own living choice upon His side, choosing that He will do that with us and then it is done, because His almighty power carries on the work.

Then He gave Himself for our sins, and now He comes and says, there is sin. What then? "Lord, it is sin." That is confession. The root idea of confession is to speak the same thing. The root idea of the Greek word translated confession is to speak the same thing. That is confession. The Lord said to David, "You have sinned and done this evil." David said, "I have sinned." That is confession. The Bible says, "If we confess our sins he is faithful and just to forgive us our sins." What does God show them for anyway? The only thing that He shows men their sins for, is that He may take them away. When He shows me sins, I say, "Lord, they are sins." And what then? They are forgiven. They are gone.

Now you folks have confessed your sins since you have been here, haven't you? All that the Lord has shown you, have you? [Congregation: "Yes, sir."] Everyone who has done that, his sins are forgiven. The Lord has said so. What do you say? [Congregation: "Amen."] But Satan says, "It is not so." He is a liar. But some folks here have been saying that Satan tells the truth upon that point. People in this house have been telling Satan that he told the truth upon that very point. Satan says, "They are not forgiven," and they say, "No, they are not." *Let us quit that.* We confess our sins that they may be forgiven, and the Lord says they are forgiven, and when they are forgiven why then in the Lord's name, let us say so.

"Abraham believed God, and it was counted to him for righteousness." "And he received the sign of circumcision, a seal of the righteousness of the faith which he had." The Lord says, "Come now, let us reason together, saith the Lord: though your sins be as scarlet, they shall be as white as snow; though they be red like crimson, they shall be as wool." What do you say? [Congregation: "It is so."] How do you know? [Congregation: "The Lord says so."] Very good. Then you know that is so, do you?

Micah 7:19: "He will turn again, he will have compassion upon us; he will subdue our iniquities; and thou wilt cast all their sins into the depths of the sea." Then where are they? [Congregation: "In the depths of the sea."] How do you know? [Congregation: "He says so."] Then you know *that,* don't you? Then how in the world is anybody going to bother you about getting your sins back to you?

Psalm 103:12: "As far as the east is from the west, so far hath he removed our transgressions from us." How far are they away from you now, you who have confessed them? How far are they away? [Voice: "As far as the east is from the west."] Why don't you say so then? Satan comes and says, "They are not forgiven; every sin is right there before your face; don't you see them?" Are they? [Congregation: "No."] Says one,

"I have seen them there." It is nothing of the kind. Satan is a magician and can make things appear so that are not so. But you look at them and say, "Yes, that is so." It is not so. The Lord says they are as far from us as the east is from the west. They are in the depths of the sea, and they are as white as snow. Thank the Lord.

Isaiah 38:17, and that verse is the last one we need tonight. "Behold, for peace I had great bitterness; but thou hast in love to my soul delivered it from the pit of corruption: for thou hast cast all my sins behind thy back." How many? [Congregation: "All."] Behind His back. Where are they, then? [Congregation: "Behind His back."] We are before His face and the sins are behind His back; who is between us and them? [Congregation: "God."] And He is upon His throne, isn't He? Then when I have confessed my sins to the Lord, He and His living eternal throne stand between me and those sins, and Satan and everybody else in this universe cannot bring them back; for he has got to get the Lord and His throne out of the way before they can get those sins back to me again. And I am going to be glad of it.

Can we know these things? Can we know that we know them? How can we know that we know them? The Lord says so. When He says so, and we believe it, that is faith. Satan says, "They are not." We say, "I know they are." Satan says, "No, there they are." We say, they are not there. They are in the depths of the sea. [Voice: "Praise the Lord."]

When the man stands there, there is something that God can put His seal on. When the Lord says, "Thy sins are forgiven," that He has "cast them behind His back" and the man will not believe it, is there anything there that God can put His seal on? No.

[Someone asked that Isaiah 43:25 be read, which Elder Jones did.] "I, even I, am he that blotteth out thy transgressions for mine own sake and will not remember thy sins."

There are many other texts like that which we might notice. One is found in Heb. 8:15: "Their sins will I remember no more," and another in Ezekiel 33:16: "None of his sins that he hath committed shall be mentioned unto him." Here the Lord says, He will not remember our sins. the Lord will never mention them. It is Satan's work to do that. Brethren, let us believe the Lord.

When we believe that, then God will give you and me the circumcision of the heart, the seal of the righteousness of the faith that we have and He can do it, because there is something there that He can put His seal upon. And when a man does that as an individual, he receives the seal of righteousness. And when we as a whole body, as a church, believe that, we can ask with perfect confidence for the outpouring of His Holy Spirit and wait patiently and confidently, knowing that it will surely come in His own good time.

Sermon 18

February 27, 1893

Our study last night was in order to know for ourselves and how we may know that we have the blessing of Abraham, and thus be prepared to be sure, that with confidence we may ask for the Spirit of God. There is more of that yet. The Lord has given us yet further evidence, yet further proof, upon which to base our perfect confidence in Him, in His righteousness; that that is our own – that we have the righteousness which is by faith, so that we can ask in perfect confidence for His Holy Spirit and thank the Lord that it is our own. For remember the verse reads: "Christ hath redeemed us from the curse of the law, being made a curse for us: for it is written, Cursed is everyone that hangeth on a tree: That the blessing of Abraham might come on the Gentiles through Jesus Christ; that we might receive the promise of the Spirit through faith."

The blessing of Abraham is the righteousness of faith; that we are to have in order to receive and that we may have, the promise of the Spirit – and *that also* through *faith.* Well then when we have the evidence, the proof, the perfect work of God demonstrating to our complete satisfaction, that we can ask in perfect confidence for the Holy Spirit, then is it not ours to receive that by faith? Is it not ours to thank God that that is our own? And that it simply remains for Him to manifest it at His own will, whenever occasion may require and as occasion may need?

Well, let us study, then, some other evidence that He has given us – study this tonight in connection with what we had last night, so that we may have before us fresh what the Lord Himself has opened for us, upon which to base our confidence before Him, upon which we may be sure where we stand and upon which we may ask with the full assurance of faith. And when we ask according to His will and ask that we may have that which He has promised, then He heareth us. "This is the confidence that we have in Him that, if we ask anything according to His will, He heareth us: and if we know that he hear us," then "we know that we have the petitions that we desired of him." 1 John 5:14, 15. And then we can thank Him that that is our own.

Let us begin with the fifth chapter of Romans, twentieth verse. The real point, or we might say, one of the main points of the study tonight is to see what place the law of God occupies in the subject of righteousness by faith; what place the law of God occupies in our obtaining righteousness alone by Jesus Christ, and this is simply another phase of the same thought we had last night, as to what proof the Lord has given us to give us confidence that we can claim by faith the promise of the Holy Spirit.

"Moreover the law entered, that the offense might abound." In other words, Romans 3:20, the last words – words with which you are all familiar – "by the law is the knowledge of sin." What was the law given for on tables of stone – the first purpose of its given? [Congregation: "To show us what sin is."] To make sin abound; to give the knowledge of sin. So, "the law entered that the offense might abound"; that sin might appear; that it might appear as it is. Paul, speaking in the 7th chapter of Romans, says how it appeared to him, 12th and 13th verses:

> Wherefore the law is holy and the commandment holy and just and good. Was then that which is good made death unto me? God forbid. But sin, that it might appear sin, working death in me by that which is good; that sin *by the commandment* might become *exceeding sinful.*

Then to make sin abound and make it appear as it is, exceeding sinful – that is the first object of the giving of the law, isn't it?

Now let us read right on in Romans 5: "Moreover the law entered, that the offense might abound. But where sin abounded, grace did much more abound." Then did the law come alone, making sin to appear alone, and that alone? [Congregation: "No."] It is simply the means to another end – the means to an end by which to attain another object beyond the knowledge of sin. Is that so? [Congregation: "Yes."] So then, where sin abounds – where is it that grace abounds? [Congregation: "In the same place."] Right there? [Congregation: "Yes."] But does it read that way, "Where sin abounded grace abounded"? [Congregation: "No. 'Much more.'"] That would be pretty good wouldn't it, if it was only where sin abounds there grace abounds? That would be pretty good, but that is not the way the Lord does things, you know. He does things absolutely well – entirely good, – just as good as God *could* do.

Well then, "where sin abounded, grace did *much more* abound." [Congregation: "Amen."] Then, brethren, when the Lord, by His law, has given us the knowledge of sin, just at that very moment, at that very point, *grace* is *much more abundant* than the knowledge of sin. Is that so? [Congregation: "Yes."]

Now another word:

"By the law is the knowledge of sin"; and we have found this much: that when the law gives the knowledge of sin, at that particular moment, in that very place and at that very point, in that very thing, the grace of God is much more abundant than the knowledge of sin. But when the law gives the knowledge of sin, what puts the *conviction* there? [Congregation: "The Spirit of God."]

Before we read the passage which says so, however, let us see what we are to get so far, from what we have read – what are you and I henceforth to get from the knowledge of sin? [Congregation: "Abundance of grace."]

Then there is no possible place for discouragement at the sight of sins any more, is there? [Congregation: "No."] No possibility of that. It is impossible, you see, for you or me to get discouraged or under a cloud any more at the knowledge of sin. Because, no difference how great the knowledge is, no difference how many sins are revealed to us and brought to our knowledge, why, right there, at that very moment, in those very things, and at that very time in our experience, the grace of God much more abounds than all the knowledge of sins. Well then, I say again, how is it possible for us ever to be discouraged? Brethren, isn't it so, that the Lord wants us to be of good cheer? [Congregation: "Amen!"] Be of good cheer.

Well, now, this verse that we have before us brings the same thing to view. John 16:7,8: "Nevertheless I tell you the truth." What is He telling us? [Congregation: "Truth."] Good! And He told us also that "Ye shall know the truth and the truth shall make you free." That is it then, isn't it? "Nevertheless I tell you the truth; it is expedient for you that I go away; for if I go not away, the Comforter will not come unto you." Who will not come? [Congregation: "The Comforter."] The Comforter? Is that His name? Is that what He is – the Comforter? [Congregation: "Yes."]

"But if I depart, I will send him unto you. And when *he* is come," Who has come? [Congregation: "the Comforter."] Who? [Congregation: "The Comforter."] "And when he is come, he will reprove [or convince] the world of sin." Who is it that does it? [Congregation: "The Comforter."] Is it the Comforter that convinces of sin? [Congregation: "Yes."] Is He the Comforter *when He does it?* [Congregation: "Yes."] Now, each one wants to get hold of that. Is not He the reprover when He does it and the Comforter some other time? [Congregation: "No."] It is the *Comforter* that *reproves,* thank the Lord! The Comforter reproves, thank the Lord! Then what are we to get out of the reproof of sin? [Congregation: "Comfort."] Whose comfort? [Congregation: The Lord's comfort."] The comfort we get, comforts just at the time when it is needed. Then where is the room for our getting discouraged any more at the knowledge of sin? Isn't that the very thought that we have read in the fifth chapter of Romans?

Don't you see, then, that when we bear in mind just at the moment and at the time and at the place that where sin abounds there grace much more abounds, and just at the time when the Holy Spirit is giving conviction of sin, He is the Comforter that does it. Don't you see that in all that – remembering all that – we have an everlasting victory over Satan? Does Satan get the advantage of that man who believes God right then? No. Satan comes and says, "See what a sinner you are." Thank the Lord, "Where sin abounds, grace does much more abound." [Congregation: "Amen!"] "Well," says another, "I have such a deep conviction of sin. It seems to me I was never convicted of sin so deeply before in all my life." Thank the Lord, we have got more comfort than ever before in our lives. Don't you see, brethren, that that is so? [Congregation: "It is so."] Well, then, let us thank the Lord for that. [Congregation: "Amen!"] I should like to know why we should not praise the Lord right along.

But there is some more in that Romans 5:20. What is this all for? First, we found that the law makes sin abound in order that grace may abound so that we may have the grace to lead us to Christ. Now what are the two things together for? The law making sin abound in order that more grace may abound. What are they both together for? "*That* as sin hath reigned unto death." We know that's so, don't we? Now that is so. The law makes sin abound, *that* we may be lead to more abundance of grace, *in order* "that as sin hath reigned unto death, even so might grace reign."

What does "even so" mean? Just as certainly. Just so. Then, isn't it so that God will make that abundance of grace to reign in our lives just as certainly as ever sin did in the world? [Congregation: "Yes, sir."] But, mark you, when the grace much more bountifully reigns, then what is the comparison between freedom from sin now and the slavery to it before? The freedom is much more abundant even than the slavery was. "That *as sin hath reigned* unto death, *even so* might *grace reign* through *righteousness* unto *eternal life* by *Jesus Christ*."

Now let us see the whole story. "The law entered that the offense might abound," in order that we might find the more abundant grace abounding right there in all those places, and the grace abounds "through righteousness unto eternal life by Jesus Christ our Lord." Then what did the law enter for? [Voice: "To bring us to the Lord."] What did the law enter for? [Voice: "To bring us to Christ."] Yes. Don't you see? Then whenever anybody in this world uses the ten commandments – when any sinner in this world uses the ten commandments for any other purpose than to reach Jesus Christ, what kind of a purpose is He putting them to? [Congregation: "A wrong purpose."] He is perverting the intent of God in giving the law, isn't He? [Congregation: "A wrong purpose."] He is perverting the intent of God in giving the law, isn't he? [Congregation: "Yes, sir."] To use the law of God with men for any other purpose, therefore, than that they may reach Christ Jesus, is to use the law in a way that God never intended it to be used.

Well, the law then brings us to Christ. That's certain. What for? [Congregation: "That we may be justified."] What does the law want of you and me? Does it make any demands of us before we reach Jesus Christ? When the law finds us, does it want anything from us? [Congregation: "It wants righteousness."] What kind? [Congregation: "Perfect righteousness."] Whose? [Congregation: "God's."] God's righteousness? [Congregation: "Yes."] Just such righteousness alone as God manifests in His own life, in His own way of doing things? [Congregation: "Yes."] Will that law be content with anything less than that from you and me? Will it accept anything less than that, a hair's breadth less? [Congregation: "No."] If we could come within a hair's breadth of it – that's too far short; we miss it.

Turn to Timothy, and Paul tells us what the law wants *out* of you and me and what it wants in us, too. 1 Tim. 1:5: "Now the end (the object, the aim, the intent, the purpose) of the commandment is charity." What is charity? [Congregation: "Love."] What kind of love? [Congregation: "The love of God."] "Out of a pure heart." What kind of a heart? [Congregation: "A pure heart."] "And of a good conscience." What kind of a conscience? [Congregation: "Good."] "And of faith unfeigned." That is what the law wants to find in you and me, isn't it? Will it accept you and me with anything less than that which it demands – perfect love, manifested "out of a pure heart, a good conscience, and of faith unfeigned"? No, never. Well, that is simply *perfection*, that it demands.

Well, now, have we – has any man in the world – any of that kind of love to offer to the law of God? [Congregation: "No."] Has any man naturally that kind of a conscience? [Congregation: "No."] No, sir. Well, then, the law makes that demand of every man on the earth tonight, no difference who he is. He makes it of you and me; he makes that demand of people in Africa and of all the people on the earth, and he will not accept anything less than that from anyone of them. But, we are talking about ourselves tonight. So, the law comes to you and me tonight and says: "I want charity; I want perfect love – the love of God. I want to see it in your life all the time. And I want to see it manifested out of a pure heart and through a good conscience and unfeigned faith." That is where we are.

"Well," says one, "I have not got it. I have done my best." But the law will say, "that is not what I want. I don't want your best. I want perfection. It is not *your* doing I want anyhow; it is God's I want. It is not your righteousness I am after; I want God's righteousness from you. It is not your doing I want. I want God's doing in your life." That is what the law says to every man. Then, when I am shut off thus at the very first question and even then when I said I did my best, then I have nothing more to say. Is that not what the scripture says: "That every mouth may be stopped." It does just that, does it not?

But there comes a still small voice saying, "Here is a perfect life; here is the life of God. Here is a pure heart; here is a good conscience. Here is unfeigned faith." Where does that voice come from? [Congregation: "Christ."] Ah, the Lord Jesus Christ, who came and stood where I stand in the flesh in which I live. He lived there. The perfect love of God was manifested there. The perfect purity of heart manifested there. A good conscience manifested there, and the unfeigned faith of the mind that was in Jesus Christ is there.

Well, then, He simply comes and tells me, "Here, take this." That will satisfy, then, will it? [Congregation: "Yes."] The life manifested in Jesus Christ, that will satisfy the law.

The purity of heart that Jesus Christ gives – that will satisfy the law. The good conscience that He can create, that will satisfy. The unfeigned faith which He gives – that will satisfy. Will it? [Congregation: "Yes."]

Well then is that not what the law wants all the time? It is Jesus Christ that the law wants, is it not? [Congregation: "Yes."] That is what the law wants: that is the same thing which it calls for in the fifth of Romans, is it not? But why does it call for it in connection with me? It calls for Christ in me, because the law wants to see that thing *in me*. Then is not the object of the law of God, the gospel of Christ alone? "Christ in you the hope of glory?" Ah, that is so.

Romans 5:1,5. "Justified by faith we have peace with God through our Lord Jesus Christ, and the love of God is shed abroad in our hearts by the Holy Ghost which is given unto us." And that is charity. Supreme love. Acts 15:8, 9, "And God which knoweth the hearts, bare them witness, giving them the Holy Ghost, even as he did unto us, and put no difference between us and them *purifying their hearts by faith*." There is the love of God out of a pure heart.

Hebrews 9:14: "How much more shall the blood of Christ, who through the eternal Spirit offered himself without spot to God, purge your conscience from dead works to serve the living God?" There is a clean conscience, brethren, and there is the love of God out of a good conscience.

Then that faith which He gives, which He enables us to keep – the faith of Jesus which enables us to keep the commandments of God – there is the love of God by a faith unfeigned.

Oh then the message of the righteousness of God which is by faith in Jesus Christ, brings us to, and brings to us, the perfect fulfillment of the law of God, does it not? [Congregation: "Yes."] Then that is the object and the aim and the one single point of the third angel's message, is it not? [Congregation: "Yes."] That is Christ. Christ in His righteousness. Christ in His purity. Christ in His love. Christ in His gentleness. Christ in His entire being. Christ and Him crucified. That is the word, brethren. Let us be glad of it; let us be glad of it. [Congregation: "Amen."]

So then when we have Jesus, when we have received Him by faith and the law stands before us or we stand before it and it makes its wondrous demand of charity, we can say, "Here it is. It is in Christ and He is mine!" Out of a pure heart – "Here it is in Christ, and He has given it to me – a good conscience." The blood of Christ has created it in me. Here it is. "Faith unfeigned," the faith in Jesus. He has given it to me. Here it is. Then, just as *Steps to Christ* tells us, we can come to Jesus now and be cleansed and stand before the law without one touch of shame or remorse. Good. Brethren, when I have that which makes me at perfect agreement with the law of God, then I am satisfied, and cannot help but be glad that I am satisfied.

Now let us turn and read the third chapter of Romans. That tells the whole story without any further study than simply to read the texts.

Romans 3:19-22. We can say amen to every word of it now, right straight along. "Now we know." And that is so. "That what things soever the law saith it saith to them who are under the law. That every mouth may be stopped and all the world may become guilty before God." And is it not that? That which tells me that I am a sinner cannot tell me that I am righteous. "But now" – good. When? [Congregation: "Now."] All right, let us say so, brethren. "But now the righteousness of God without the law is manifested." That is so, is it not? [Congregation: "Yes."] The law cannot manifest it in us, because we cannot see it there. It is there, but we are so blind that we cannot see it there. Sin has so blinded and corrupted us that we cannot see it in the law. And if we could see it there, we could not get it there, because there is not anything in us to start with that is fit for it. We are utterly helpless.

So now "the righteousness of God without the law is manifested . . . even the righteousness of God which is by faith of Jesus Christ, unto all and upon all them that believe." What does that word "believe" mean when God speaks it? [Congregation: "Faith."] And what is genuine faith? Submission of the will to Him, a yielding of the heart to Him, a fixing of the affections upon Him. That is what He means here to those who will receive Him, because *believing* is *receiving* when God speaks. He says so in the first chapter of John, 12th verse. "But as many as *received* him, to them gave he power to become the sons of God, even to them that *believe* on his name." "Even the righteousness of God which is by faith of Jesus Christ unto all and upon all them that believe: for there is no difference." Then we can every one here have it tonight? *Can* have it? *Have* it, because we believe it.

Well now that is the object of the law then, is it not? To bring us to Jesus Christ that we may be justified by faith, made righteous by faith, that His righteousness – the righteousness of God in Christ – may be ours? That is it. Well, when that is true, when we have got there, *then* what is the use of the law? Then what is the law for? [Congregation: "It witnesses."] Exactly. Let us read now that part of the twenty-first verse that I did not read: "But now the righteousness of God without the law is manifested, *being witnessed by the law.*" That is as far as we need to read just now. The other belongs there, though. Then, when the law gives a knowledge of sin, in order that we may have the knowledge of the abundance of grace to take away the sin, then grace reigns through righteousness unto eternal life by Jesus Christ – and this righteousness of God by faith in Christ is our own through the working of the law, and this knowledge of sin has brought us to Christ, and we have Him, and the law is satisfied in all its demands that it has made upon us.

Now when it is satisfied in all its demands it has made upon us, then will it stick to that and keep on saying that it is satisfied. That that is all right? When the law has made demands upon us that we cannot satisfy by any other possible means except by Jesus Christ being present in ourselves, then, will the law of God, as long as we stay there, stand right there and say, "That is right, and I am satisfied with it"? [Congregation: "Yes."] Then if anybody begins to question it and says, "It is not so," then we have witnesses to prove it, have we?

Now you see this: that it is necessary for several reasons that we should have witnesses. One in our own connection and in our own personal experience is this: When God speaks and we believe it, then we know, each one for himself that the righteousness of God is our own, that we are entitled to it, that it belongs to us and that we can rest in perfect peace upon it. But there are other people that need to know this, too. Can they know it by my saying so? [Congregation: "No."] Can they know it by my saying that I assent to this and that I say that is so and therefore it is so? Will that convince them? Is that proof enough to them? [Congregation: "No."] They need something better even than my word. Don't you see, the Lord has met that very demand and has given us witnesses to which they can appeal and they can go and ask these witnesses whenever they please whether this that we have is genuine or not. Is that so? [Congregation: "Yes."]

They need not come and inquire of us; if they inquire of us, of course we can tell them what the Lord has told us to say and if that is not enough, they can go and ask those witnesses. We can say, There are some friends of mine. They know me from my birth till now. They know me better than I do myself and if you want any more than this that I say, go and ask them. They will tell you. How many of them are there? [Congregation: "Ten."] is their word worth anything? Do they tell the truth? Ah, they are truth itself. They are *the truth.* Psalm 119:142. Well then it is impossible for them to testify otherwise in bearing witness than that. When they say that that demand is satisfied, "This life is well pleasing to me," that is enough for anybody in the universe, is it not? [Congregation: "Yes."]

So then the man who claims to believe in Jesus and claims the righteousness of God which comes to the believer in Jesus, is his claiming it enough for this world? [Congregation: "No."] Or is our word in regard to it enough? [Congregation: "No."] Well, they will say and there are lots of them that will say it, "Why yes, we believe in the Saviour. I have a right to claim, too, the righteousness that He has, the perfect holiness and perfect sanctification and that I have not sinned for ten years and am above all temptation, even, and I know it." Well, how do you know it? "Why, *I feel it in my heart. I feel it* in my heart and have for several years." Well, that is no evidence at all, for "the heart is deceitful above all things and desperately wicked." Deceitful above *how* many things? [Congregation: "All things."] All things? [Congregation: "Yes."] Above Satan even? [Congregation: "Yes."] Is the heart actually deceitful above all things? [Congregation: "Yes."] He says so, whether we can understand it or not. It is more deceitful than Satan himself, isn't it? [Congregation: "Yes."] The heart will deceive me quicker and more often than Satan will.

Well then when that person *feels in his heart* is that a good kind of evidence? When my heart says that I am good, then what is it doing? [Congregation: "It is deceiving."] Solomon said, "He that trusteth his own heart is a fool." And he is not only a fool, but he is *fooled* in this thing, is he not? [Congregation: "Yes."] It is bad enough for a wise man to be fooled, but when a fool is fooled, what in the world is the thing coming to?

Therefore, we cannot afford to trust such things as that on such an important question as this. No, sir. We need better evidence than a man's heart that he has got the righteousness of God and that he is all right and is fit for the judgment and that he has not sinned for ten years, holy and sanctified and above temptation, etc., etc. We need something better than that, and the fact of the matter is, Jesus was here in this world a good while, and He never was above temptations while He was here. Christians are not, either, while they live.

Well then that evidence is not enough. We want something more than that. And if that person who claims to have the righteousness of God by faith in Jesus Christ has only that for a witness, and his testimony can go only that far, then what is his claim worth! [Congregation: "Nothing at all."] Just nothing at all. It is a deceptive claim. He never can realize upon it. So the Lord has not left us there. Last night we found in our lesson that when we want to know that these things are so in our experience we are not to look within to find out whether it is so, but to look at *what God says* to see whether it is so. When we have found Jesus Christ and have Him then the Lord does not want us to look within to see whether He is there. He has furnished us witnesses, whose testimony will tell us all the time that He is there and these will tell everybody else that He is there. The righteousness of God is now manifested which is by faith of Jesus Christ and when it is, it is witnessed *by the law.*

Then the law is, first, to bring us unto Christ and after it has led us to Christ and we have found Him, then it witnesses that that is just the thing. First, to give the knowledge of sin and second to witness to the righteousness of God which is by faith. Well then anybody who uses the law of God for any other purpose than these two purposes at any time, what is He doing with the law of God? [Congregation: "Perverting it."] He is perverting the whole thing. He is using it for purposes that God never intended at all. So then, though a man or an angel use the law of God in any other way or for any other purpose than those two things – a man can use it for both, but angels can use it for one – He has perverted the law of God.

Where is our righteousness from? [Congregation: "God."] "Their righteousness if of me, saith the Lord." 2 Corinthians 4:6. "For God, who commanded the light to shine out of darkness, hath shined in our hearts to give the light of the knowledge of the glory of God in the face of Jesus Christ." Where do we find the knowledge of the glory of God? [Congregation: "In the face of Jesus Christ."] In the face of Jesus Christ.

Now 2 Corinthians 3:18:

"But we all, with open face beholding as in a glass the glory of the Lord, are changed into the same image from glory to glory, even as by the Spirit of the Lord." Then what is it that we see in the face of Jesus Christ? [Congregation: "The glory of the Lord."] What is the glory of the Lord? We have read here, we have been told here, by the Spirit of God, that the message of the righteousness of God which is by faith of Jesus Christ, that is the beginning of *the glory* that is to lighten the whole earth. Then what is the glory of God? His righteousness; His character. Where do we find it? In Jesus Christ. There is the glory of God revealed in the face of Jesus Christ. He said so, you see. That is where we look for it.

Do we look to the law for righteousness? [Congregation: "No."] Even after we have been brought to Christ, do we look there for righteousness? [Congregation: "No."] Where do we look for righteousness? In the face of Jesus Christ. There "we all, with open face beholding as in a glass the glory of the Lord, are changed into the same image from glory to glory," from righteousness to righteousness, from character to character, from goodness to goodness, even as by the Spirit of the Lord.

Then don't you see how the righteousness of God and the Holy Spirit go hand in hand? Don't you see that when we obtain the righteousness which is by faith of Jesus Christ, the blessing of Abraham indeed, that then the Holy Spirit cannot be kept away from us. You cannot separate the two. They belong together. Then when we have that and know that we have that by the faith in His word, then He says we have a right to ask for the Holy Spirit and to receive it too.

Why, look at it. Galatians 4:5: He came "to redeem them that were under the law, that we might receive the adoption of sons. And because ye are sons, *God hath sent* forth the Spirit of his Son into your hearts." He *sends* it. He does not want to hold it back. He *sends* it into the heart. It is a free gift.

Then I say, don't you see that it is impossible to keep the righteousness of God and the Holy Spirit separate? So then, "changed into the same image from glory to glory, even as by the Spirit of the Lord" and when the image of God in Jesus Christ is found in us, what then? There is the impress, the seal of God. You have heard that in the other lessons. When by looking into the face of Jesus Christ, and there alone, having received the righteousness of God which is by faith in Him and looking ever into His glorious face that reflects the glory of God, the effect of that is to change us into the same image, to perfect the image of God, and restore it in us, by the working of the Spirit of God upon the soul. And when that is done, then the same Spirit of God is there to affix the seal of the living God, the eternal impress of His own image.

So then after we have come to Christ, after we have found Him, then we do not look into the law for righteousness. Where do we look? [Congregation: "In the face of Jesus Christ."] Into the face of Jesus Christ, and while we look there what does the law say? [Congregation: "That is right."] The law testifies, "That is the place to look. That is what

I want you to have. That is satisfactory. We are perfectly agreed." Where in heaven do the angels look? Don't they look into the law to see whether they are right or not? [Voice: "Always beholding the face of our Father."] "Their angels do always behold the face of my Father which is in heaven." Then where does the righteousness of the angels come from? [Congregation: "God."] From God through Jesus Christ, is it not? And what does the law in the throne of God, the foundation of His throne, what does the original copy of His law do there? When the angels look into the face of Him who sits upon the throne, what does the law, that never was touched by man, and never could be, what does it do there? It witnesses to the righteousness of God which they obtain without the law.

This was always the true idea of the uses of the law of God. When the people had sinned and done anything against the commandments of the Lord concerning things which ought not to be done and were guilty, then they were to bring the sacrifice they were forgiven. Leviticus 4. And *then* as *now* the commandments witnessed to the righteousness which they obtained by faith in Jesus. And therefore the Tabernacle was called "The Tabernacle of *witness.*" Acts 7:44 and Numbers 17:7, 8; 18:2. The tabernacle of the testimony is the same thing, because testimony is the evidence given by a witness. So that the tabernacle was the tabernacle of witness or testimony, the ark was the ark of the testimony or witness, because it contained the tables of the testimony. The tables of stone, the tables of the law, were the tables of the *testimony,* because they were the evidence of the witness, which God appointed to witness to the righteousness of God, which comes without the law, by faith of Jesus Christ alone. Then it is everlastingly true throughout the universe that "If righteousness come by the law, then Christ is dead in vain." Galatians 2:21. Forever and everywhere it is true that "Their righteousness is of me, saith the Lord." And the law witnesses to the righteousness which all obtain from God without the law, but by Jesus Christ.

Then isn't it true, as I said, awhile ago, that whether man or angel, if he uses the law of God for any other than one, or both of these two purposes, he perverts the law of God entirely from what God ever intended. Well then the righteousness of God which is by faith of Jesus Christ, that satisfies everything, does it not? Everything *now,* and how long? [Congregation: "Forever."] Now and evermore it satisfies everything. Well then we may know for our own selves that it is ours by the evidences that God gave us last night and they are everlastingly sure, and everybody in this world may know that we are entitled to it, by the witnesses that God has given.

Well, this is to fit us for the seal of God, the righteousness of God, in order that through this we may be changed from glory to glory, into the same image, and when that is completed what then? What witnesses to that? [Congregation: "The Sabbath of the Lord."] It will witness to that finished completed work all the way through.

As Professor Prescott gave us in his sermon, it is the presence of Christ that makes holy and sanctifies the place where it is. And when the presence of Christ is there in its fulness, then what is that place? That is sanctified. What is the sign of sanctification? [Congregation: The Sabbath."] And sanctification complete is God's complete work in the soul. Then when the work of God is completed in the soul, the law of God will witness to it all the way. But what particular part of the law of God is a witness to that particular thing, the complete sanctification of His people? [Congregation: "The Sabbath of the Lord."] It stands there as the witness and as the chief witness and the two coming together testify and the seal is affixed. That work is completed.

Brethren, how can we get away from the seal of God? Then are we not right now in the time of the sealing? [Congregation: "Yes."] And it is through the righteousness of God which is by faith of Jesus Christ, is it not? Yes, sir. And then when that seal is received; when that is affixed there, then these can stand through the time of the plagues, through all the temptations and trials of Satan when he works with all power and signs and lying wonders. For the promise is "as thou hast kept the word of my patience, I also will keep thee from the hour of temptation, which shall come upon all the world, to try them that dwell upon the earth."

And when that is past – then entrance into the heavenly city. Entrance into the heavenly city. Thank the Lord. There are the tests that we are to pass through, but, brethren, when we have this righteousness of Jesus Christ, we have that which will pass through every test.

And in that day there are going to be two parties there. There are going to be some there when the door is shut, and they will want to go in, and they say, "Lord, open to us. We want to come in." And someone comes and asks, "What have you done that you should come in? What right have you to enter the inheritance here? What claim have you upon that?" "Oh, we are acquainted with you. We have eaten and drunk in thy presence, and thou hast taught in our streets. Yes, besides that we have prophesied in thy name. In thy name we have cast out devils and in thy name we have done many wonderful works. Why, we have done many wonderful things. Lord, is not that evidence enough? Open the door."

What is the answer? "Depart from me, ye that work iniquity." What did they say? "We have done many wonderful works. *We* have done them. *We* are all right. *We* are righteous. *We* are just. Exactly right. Therefore *we* have a right to be there. Open the door." But "*we*" does not count there, does it?

There is going to be another company there that day – a great multitude that no man can number – all nations and kindreds and tongues and people, and they will come up to enter in. And if anyone should ask them that question, "What have you done that you should enter here? What claim have you here?"

The answer would be:

"Oh, I have not done anything at all to deserve it. I am a sinner, dependent only on the grace of the Lord. Oh I was so wretched, so completely a captive and in such a bondage that nobody could deliver me but the Lord Himself; so miserable that all I could ever do was to have the Lord constantly to comfort me, so poor that I had constantly to beg from the Lord; so blind that no one but the Lord could cause me to see; so naked that no one could clothe me but the Lord Himself. All the claim that I have is what Jesus has done for me. But the Lord has loved me. When in my wretchedness I cried, He delivered me. When in my misery I wanted comfort, He comforted me all the way. When in my poverty I begged, He gave me riches. When in my blindness I asked Him to show me the way, that I might know the way, He led me all the way and made me to see. When I was so naked that no one could clothe me, why, He gave me this garment that I have on, and so all I can present, all that I have to present as that upon which I can enter, any claim that would cause me to enter, is just what He has done for me. If that will not pass me, then I am left out, and that will be just too. If I am left out, I have no complaint to make. But, oh, will not this entitle me to enter and possess the inheritance?"

But He says,

"Well, there are some very particular persons here. They want to be fully satisfied with everybody that goes by here. We have ten examiners here. When they look into a man's case and say that he is all right, why then he can pass. Are you willing that these shall be called to examine into your case?" And we shall answer, "Yes, yes, because I want to enter in, and I am willing to submit to any examination, because even if I am left out I have no complaint to make. I am lost anyway when I am left to myself."

"Well," says He, "we will call them then."

And so those ten are brought up and they say, "Why, yes, we are perfectly satisfied with him. Why, yes, the deliverance that he obtained from his wretchedness is that which our Lord wrought; the comfort that he had all the way and that he needed so much is that which our Lord gave. The wealth that he has, whatever he has, *poor as he was,* the Lord gave it, and blind, whatever he sees, it is the Lord that gave it to him. And he sees only what is the Lord's. And naked as he was, that garment that he has on, the Lord gave it to him. The Lord wove it, and it is all divine. It is only Christ. Why, *yes, he can come in.*"

[Here the congregation began singing:

> *"Jesus paid it all,*
> *All to him I owe;*
> *Sin had left a crimson stain:*
> *He washed it white as snow."*]

And then, brethren, there will come over the gates a voice of sweetest music, full of the gentleness and compassion of my Saviour – the voice will come from within, "Come in, thou blessed of the Lord." [Congregation: "Amen."] "Why standest thou without?" And the gate will be swung wide open, and we shall have "an abundant entrance into the everlasting kingdom of our Lord and Saviour Jesus Christ."

Oh, He is a complete Saviour. He is my Saviour. My soul doth magnify the Lord. My soul shall rejoice in the Lord, brethren, tonight. Oh, I say with David, come and magnify the Lord with me and let us exalt His name together. He has made complete satisfaction. There is not anything against us, brethren. The way is clear. The road is open. The righteousness of Christ satisfies. That is light and love and joy and eternal excellence.

Isn't it true, then, of Isaiah 60:1: "Arise, shine, for thy light *is* come and the glory of the Lord *is* risen upon thee. For, behold, the darkness shall cover the earth and gross darkness the people, but the Lord shall arise upon thee and his glory shall be seen upon thee." Brethren, He can do it. He wants to. Let us let Him. [Congregation: "Amen."] And let us praise Him while He is doing it.

Now, can't we praise the Lord? Then everybody in this house that wants to do it, you just go right ahead now. I will say amen to every word of it, for my soul magnifies Him, too, brethren. My soul praises Him, too brethren, because He is my Saviour. He has completed the work. He has done His gracious work. He has saved me. He saves all. Let us thank Him forevermore.

Professor Prescott: The times of refreshing are here, brethren. The Spirit of God is here. Open the heart, open the heart. Open the heart in praise and thanksgiving.

Sermon 19

March 1, 1893

WE will begin tonight with the first verse of Revelation 14:

"And I looked and lo a Lamb stood on the mount Sion and with him a hundred forty and four thousand, having his Father's name written in their foreheads." This same number is referred to in the 7th chapter and 4th verse, but I read from the first verse, however: "And after these things I saw four angels standing on the four corners of the earth, holding the four winds of the earth that the wind should not blow on the earth, nor on the sea, nor on any tree. And I saw another angel ascending from the east, having the seal of the living God: and he cried with a loud voice to the four angels, to whom it was given to hurt the earth and the sea, Saying, Hurt not the earth, neither the sea, nor the trees, till we have sealed the servants of our God in their foreheads. And I heard the number of them that were sealed: and there were sealed a hundred and forty and four thousand."

All we read these two scriptures for is to get the connection, which shows that the seal of God and the name of God are inseparably connected. The 144,000 had the name of their Father in their foreheads, and they were sealed with the seal of the living God in their foreheads. Then, when we find out what the name of God is, we shall know what the seal of God is, for that which will bring to us His name and put in our minds His name and put upon us and in us His name will be the seal of God.

Now turn to Exodus 3:13, 14. This refers to the time when the Lord appeared to Moses in the burning bush. He sent Him to deliver the people of God from Egypt: "And Moses said unto God, Behold, when I come unto the children of Israel, and shall say unto them, The God of your fathers hath sent me unto you, and they shall say to me, *What is his name*? what shall I say unto them? and God said unto Moses, I AM THAT I AM. And he said, Thus shalt thou say unto the children of Israel, I AM hath sent me unto you." The Lord had said to Him so far only this, as we read in the sixth verse, "I am the God of thy father, the God of Abraham, the God of Isaac, and the God of Jacob."

Now, Moses asks, "When I come unto the children of Israel, and shall say unto them, the God of your fathers hath sent me unto you; and they shall say to me, What is his name? what shall I say unto them? and God said unto Moses, I AM THAT I AM:

and he said, thus shalt thou say unto the children of Israel, I AM hath sent me unto you. and God said moreover unto Moses, Thus shalt thou say unto the children of Israel, The Lord God of your fathers, the God of Abraham, the God of Isaac, and the God of Jacob, hath sent me unto you: *this is my name forever,* and *this is my memorial* unto *all generations.*"

But what is His name? "I AM THAT I AM." He had said, and they knew, that He was the God of Abraham, the God of Isaac, and the God of Jacob, and the God of their fathers. They knew their fathers had a God whom they worshiped. These folks had heard of the God of their fathers. They remembered, though dimly now, the God of their fathers, but now he reveals to them that the God of their fathers is the God whose name is "I AM THAT I AM," and "this is my name forever, and this is my memorial unto all generations."

Then the name of God and His memorial go together. Do you see? But, what is His name? "I AM," only? No. His name is not simply "I AM", BUT "I AM" *what?* "I AM." That is the idea of "that"; "I AM" that which, or what, "I AM." Now it is not enough you see for the Lord to state to men that He is, but we need to now that He is *what* He is, for the knowledge of *Himself* to do us any good. Existence is to us not enough to know of God – it is not enough for us to know that He exists, but we need to know *what* He is and what He exists for in respect to us. Therefore He did not say simply, "'I AM,' that is my name." No, but "I AM" what "I AM." That is His name and if we will know God truly, we must know not only *that* He is, but that He is *what* He is and until we know what He is, we do not know *Him.*

The same thought is expressed in Hebrews 11:6: "Without faith it is impossible to please Him (God): for he that cometh to God must believe that He is, *and* that He is a rewarder of them that diligently seek Him." Well, what is the reward which God gives to those who seek Him? It is Himself; Himself, all He is, and all that He has. But, if we had all that He has without having Himself, what good would that do us? You see, if we had all that He has, and were still ourselves, we would be simply supreme – well the next thing to devils, would we not? To give a man all that God has and he still remaining the man that He is, it would be a fearful thing. Therefore it is nothing to us that God gives us all that He has, unless He gives us what He is, unless He gives us *Himself.* Therefore, when He gives us *what* He is, giving us Himself, His character, His nature and His disposition, then we can use what He is as well as what He has, in His fear and to His glory. Consequently the same thought is there, not only that He is, but He is what He is, and "He that cometh to God must believe that he is" and that He is what He is.

Well, then, to follow this thought, what is God first of all to all things and all persons in the universe? [Congregation: "Creator."] Assuredly! The first thing that He is to anything, animate or inanimate is Creator; for by Him all things exist. He is author of all things. Then the first thing for men, for angels, or intelligences is to know Him as Creator.

Now, He says, "I AM THAT I AM." Then the first that comes to any creature as to what He is; that is, understanding His name, is that He is Creator. So we have found that in connection with His name His memorial stands inseparable. And therefore "this is my *name* forever, and this is my *memorial* unto all generations."

Turn to Ezekiel 20:20. You are familiar with the scripture: "And hallow my Sabbaths, and they shall be a sign between me and you, that ye may know that I am the Lord your God." What is the Sabbath a sign of, then? A sign that He is the Lord God. But that He is the Lord God in point of *existence,* that is not His name. It is more than that, but the Sabbath being the sign that He is Lord God, is it not the sign that He is *what* He is, as well as *that* He is? [Congregation: "Yes."] Now, think of that. Is it? [Congregation: "Yes, sir."] The Sabbath being the sign that He is the true God – and He having told us that He is *what* He is, therefore the Sabbath is the sign of *what* God is as well as the sign *that* He is. See? [Congregation: "Yes."] Then that being His name, "I AM" what "I AM," and the Sabbath being the sign that He is what He is, don't you see how that is His *name* forever, and that is His *memorial* forever? Then, He has given the Sabbath. "Remember the Sabbath day to keep it holy." He has given that as the *memorial* that He is the Lord. Consequently, "that is my name forever." That is His *memorial.*

[*Voice*: "Please repeat that."] All right. Let us go back and take the thought at the beginning. The Sabbath, He says "ye shall hallow," and it shall be a sign. Saturday is not a sign of the true God. Saturday is not anything. A man who keeps Saturday can do so without knowing the Lord just as He can keep Sunday without knowing the Lord, but He can't keep *the Sabbath* without knowing the Lord. There are three classes of observers of a day in the world: There are Saturday-keepers, Sunday-keepers, and Sabbath-keepers. What God wants is Sabbath-keepers. But there has been too many Saturday-keepers pretending to be Sabbath-keepers. That is the mischief of these last days.

"Hallow my Sabbaths, and they shall be a sign." That is the thing to start with. Then the Sabbath is a sign which He has set for us, which He Himself has given, "that ye may know that I am the Lord your God."

The Sabbath being the sign that He is the Lord God, He is not only God in point of existence, but He is, and He is what He is, for that is His name. See? "I AM" what "I AM," The Lord God. The Sabbath is a sign that He is the Lord God. The Sabbath, therefore, is a sign that He is, and that He is *what* He is. But His name, He says, is "I AM THAT I AM." "This is my name forever, and this is my memorial unto all generations." The sign that He is what He is is what? [Congregation: "The Sabbath."] But He says, "The Sabbath is my memorial." "He hath made a memorial for His wonderful works," and so on. Then, don't you see that that which is the sign that He is *what* He is, that being His name forever, that is His *memorial* forever? Now, shall I say it over? [Voice: "No, I can see that."] Have you got that now? [Congregation: "Yes, sir."].

Well, now let us go on with it. The Sabbath being the sign that He is, and that He is what He is, and the first thing that He is is Creator, the first thing that the then must signify is Creator. But, is that the only thing that it will signify? No, because He is more than that not more than that in the sense of being different from that – because all things are in that, but what He is in that is more largely expressed in other places, so that we can know more fully what He is in that. Well then Exodus 31:17: "It is a sign between me and the children of Israel forever: for in six days the Lord made heaven and earth, and on the seventh day He rested and was refreshed." Now, it is a sign "that ye may know that I am the Lord your God." And wherein is it this sign? Is it not because "in six days the Lord made heaven and earth and on the seventh day he rested and was refreshed." It being a sign of that because He did that, it is a sign of Himself in the doing of that. Is that so? [*Voice*: "Yes."]

Now put the two together: It is a sign that He is the Lord, *because* "in six days" He "made heaven and earth." Then, as we have found, the first thing that God is is Creator. The first thing that the Sabbath signifies is Creator, *in* signifying what He is. But the Sabbath commandment is, "Remember the Sabbath day, to keep it holy. Six days shalt thou labor, and do all thy work: but the seventh day is the Sabbath of the Lord thy God: in it thou shalt not do any work. . . For in six days the Lord made heaven and earth, the sea, and all that in them is, and rested the seventh day: wherefore the Lord blessed the Sabbath day and hallowed it."

Now remember the Sabbath day. What is the Sabbath day? As we have already read in the twentieth chapter of Ezekiel: "A sign that ye may know that I am the Lord." Remember that thing which signifies that I am God. We are to remember that thing which signifies that He is God. Then is not that the memorial which brings Him to people's remembrance? For that is what a memorial is for, to bring to remembrance. He wants to be brought to the remembrance of His creatures and has given that which will do it. And now He tells us "remember that thing which will do it."

Now a thought right there:

We are to remember the thing that brings Him to remembrance, or, in another word, brings Him to *mind*. When He is brought to mind, He is not only brought there as He who exists, but as *what* He is. And when He for *what* He is, is brought to our minds, that is His name, is it not? Where is the name? [Congregation: "In the forehead."] "With the mind I serve the law of God." See? Then God wants to be in people's minds? And the Sabbath is that which brings Himself – not a theory of Him – but *Himself,* to bring *Him* to the remembrance, to bring *Him* to mind, because the Sabbath is the sign "that I am the Lord your God." And now remember the sign, remember that which signifies and brings to mind Myself, brings to mind the Lord thy God. And He is *what* He is. To bring *Him* and *what* He is to your mind. That is the thought. Then is not that His memorial?

The very purpose of a memorial, the very object of it is to bring the thing that is touched upon to mind. So you can see that that being the case, the name of God and His memorial, His Sabbath, cannot be separated at all. Consequently when He told Moses that "I am *that* I am," that *is* His name forever, and that *is* His memorial to all generations; because the memorial brings Him to mind, and bringing Him to mind, as *what* He is, that puts God into the mind in His real name, and so the Father's name in the minds of those people who are mentioned is the seal of the living God in their foreheads.

The first thing, then, that is signified thus in the Sabbath is Creator, creative power, but that is brought to mind through the things which are made. It is a sign that He is the Lord because He made all these things. Consequently the Sabbath is the sign, the memorial of the Lord our God as manifested in creation.

Now let us study a moment how He manifested Himself in creation. Hebrews 1:1,2: "God, who at sundry times and in divers manners spake unto the fathers by the prophets, hath in these last days spoken unto us by His Son, whom He hath appointed heir of all things, by whom also he made the worlds."

And the first verses of John: "In the beginning was the Word, and the Word was with God and the Word was God. The same was in the beginning with God. All things were made by him, and without him was not anything made that was made." Now the 14th verse: "And the Word was made flesh and dwelt among us."

There is another verse we will read right upon the same thing, which tells it in a different way. Ephesians 3:9, and the last words of the verse: "God, who created all things by Jesus Christ."

Then God in creation manifested Himself in and through Jesus Christ. Is that so? [Congregation: "Yes."] Then the man who does not know Jesus Christ, will he get right ideas of created things, of creation? [Congregation: "No."] He will not find God there; he will not find the ideas of God there, because God is manifested in Christ in creation.

Now further: How did He manifest Himself in Christ in creation? In creating, we had better say, perhaps, because we are at the origin of all things now. How, then, did He manifest Himself in Christ in creating? Psalm 33:6, 9: "By the word of the Lord were the heavens made, and all the host of them by the breath of his mouth." "For he spake, and *it was;* he commanded, and it stood fast." I was there.

Hebrews 11:3: "Through faith we understand that the worlds were framed by the word of God, so that things which are seen were not made of things which do appear." So far we have found that God manifested in creation is the first thing in which *what He is* can be known. But God is manifested in creating, in Jesus Christ; and God is manifest in creating in Jesus Christ, *by His word*. And that word by which He created all things has in it the power to make a thing appear which before could not be seen at all, because it was not. See? "The worlds were framed by the word of God, so that things which are seen were not made of things which do appear." Then after God spoke, things were seen which before He spoke did not appear at all. Nobody could see them. Then there is power in the word which God in Jesus Christ speaks, that is able to make a thing; in other words, able to produce the thing which He names in the word He speaks. That is, God can call those things which be not as though they were and not lie. A man can speak of those things which be not as though they were, but there is no power in His word to produce the thing which He speaks, and consequently He lies.

And there are many people who do that thing. They speak of those things that are not as though they were, but it is a lie. And the reason that it is a lie is that there is no power in them or their word to produce the thing. They would willingly have it that way, they would willingly have what they are speaking to be real; but it is not so, and they speak of it as though it were, yet it is a lie, however much they would like to have it be real. There is no power in their word to produce the thing desired in their minds when they speak the word.

But God is not such. The thought that is in His mind, expressed in a word, the word produces the thing that was in the thought. The creative energy, the divine power, is in the word which God speaks. Consequently, when there were no worlds that appeared at all, God in Jesus Christ spoke, and there the worlds were, and there they are yet, because He spoke then.

Now let us read two verses that have these thoughts in them. Not only does the word of God which He speaks, produce the thing that is in the thought, but it keeps that thing in existence after it is produced, and in the place where God wants it, after it is produced. I want you to see that the word which God shall speak has all that power in it.

Now turn to Colossians 1:14-17. He is speaking of Christ the Son of God, "in whom we have redemption through his blood, even the forgiveness of sins: who is the image of the invisible God, the firstborn of every creature: for by him were all things created, that are in heaven and that are in earth, visible and invisible whether they be thrones or dominions or principalities or powers: all things were created by him and for him and he is before all things and by him all things *consist*." Or by Him all things *hold together*. But what made them? What made this world as it is? The power of His word. [Voice: "He commanded and it stood fast."] The world is quite large. There are a good many ingredients in it, but when He spoke, it came, with all the ingredients in it. The word, then, that produced it holds it together in the shape that it is.

Well then, now the other thought in the third verse of Heb. first chapter: "God, who at sundry times and in diverse manners spake in time past unto the fathers by the prophets, hath in these last days spoken unto us by his Son, whom he hath appointed heir of all things, by whom also he made the worlds; who being the brightness of his glory and the express image of his person, and *upholding all things* by *the word of his power.*" What holds these up since they were made? [Congregation: "The word of His power."] Has he been compelled to keep on talking since He spake that time, in order to keep these things in place? [Congregation: "No."] Is it necessary that He should keep on talking to the world every day, to hold it together? [Congregation: "No."] Is it necessary that He should keep on talking all the time to the worlds and the planets to keep them in their courses and in their places? No. the word which produced them in the beginning has in it the creative power which holds them together and holds them up.

2 Peter 3:1-7: "This second epistle, beloved, I now write unto you; in both which I stir up your pure minds by way of remembrance; that ye may be mindful of *the words* which were spoken before by the holy prophets." Mindful of what? The *words* which were spoken before by the holy prophets. Why are we to remember them? Because He wants us to find out what those words are worth, and, remembering the words, to obtain in our minds, in our lives, the strength and the force of the words. Because the words which were spoken by the prophets were the *words of God,* which they spake by "the Spirit of Christ which was in them, when it testified beforehand the sufferings of Christ and the glory that should follow."

Mindful of *those* words, then; "and of the commandment of us the apostles of the Lord and Saviour: knowing this first, that there shall come in the last days scoffers, walking after their own lusts, and saying, Where is the promise of his coming? for since the fathers fell asleep, all things continue as they were from the beginning of the creation. For this they willingly are ignorant of" – that is, people that talk that way, that all things continue as they were from the beginning, are willingly ignorant – "that by *the word* of God the heavens were of old, and the earth standing out of the water and in the water: whereby the world that then was, being overflowed with water, perished."

By what did the world overflow with water? [Congregation: "The word of God."] God spoke. "But the heavens and the earth, which are now, *by the same word* are kept in store, reserved unto fire." What does he call our attention to there, in respect to the word which he wants us to remember. He wants us to be fully minded of the *words* of God, because *that word* at the first produced the worlds; that word holds them there; that word brought the flood; that word rescued the earth from the flood, and still keeps it.10 Then that word that can produce worlds and recover worlds; *that word* he would have us to keep fully in mind, that we may know the *power* of that word.

Well, then you see in all this there is the same thought still, that that word which produced all, holds all together, holds all up, and preserves all, until God speaks again. When He speaks again, then everything goes to pieces; for when that day comes in which there comes "a great voice out of the temple of heaven, from the throne, saying,

It is done," then there are thunderings and lightnings and voices and an earthquake, such as was not since men were upon the earth, so mighty an earthquake and so great, and "every island fled away, and the mountains were not found"; and the cities of the nations fall; the heaven itself splits open and rolls away. I tell you when that day comes the man who is fully minded of *the word* that does it all, he is perfectly safe. Because when that word which produces these things is my confidence, when that word is my foundation, when that word itself is my trust, why, no difference if the earth does go, His word remains; that is all right.

So then God was manifest in Christ by His word in creating and is still manifest thus, in the created things – in creating, in preserving, holding together, and holding up. So that gravitation is God in Jesus Christ. Science tells us that the law of gravitation holds things up, you know; but what is gravitation? "Why, that is what holds things up." There is a better answer than that. That answer is gravitation, the law of gravitation, holds all these things up and in their places. But what is gravitation? It is the power of God manifested in Jesus Christ in creation; that is gravitation.

Cohesion, in science, is to hold together. But what is cohesion? All the answer that science can give is, The word "cohesion" is from two Latin words, *co* and *haerere*, signifying to hold together; in other words, cohesion is cohesion; that is the answer. There is a better answer than that. There is God's answer, and He tells us that cohesion is the power of God manifested in Jesus Christ in creation; for by Him all things consist, cohere, hold together; that is cohesion.

The origin of all things is not spontaneous generation; it is not evolution. It is God manifest, the power of God manifested in Jesus Christ by His word producing all things that are seen, which before did not appear at all. Then God in Jesus Christ is the origin of all things; that is creation. God in Jesus Christ is the preserver of all things; that is cohesion. God in Jesus Christ is the upholder of all things, and that is gravitation.

Sermon 20

March 2, 1893

Beginning just where we stopped last night – the thought last night and what we wanted to dwell upon particularly last night, was to find God in Christ in His word in creation; in creating, preserving, holding together and holding up, all things.

Six days He employed in creating, and then the record is (Genesis 2:1-3): "Thus the heavens and the earth were finished and all the host of them. And on the seventh day God ended his work which he had made. And God blessed the seventh day, and sanctified it: because that in it he had rested from all his work which God created and made." And this made it the Sabbath day *for man;* but the thought still before us is that the Sabbath is the sign that He is *what* He is, in creating, and in all things else that He is; at the same time, however, that all things that He is, is in the fact that He is Creator.

Then, when He had finished creating, He rested and was refreshed, that is, took delight in the reflection in the created things, of the thought of His mind, the completion of the purpose, as it was manifested in the finished creation. That is the thought in the word "refreshed" in Exodus 31:17. Six days He employed in making the heavens and the earth, and "the seventh day he rested and was refreshed," took delight, rejoiced in His completed purpose, in the creation – the purpose that was in His mind before creation was spoken into existence. Then He blessed the day, made it holy and sanctified it.

Therefore the commandment tells us:

"Remember the Sabbath day," that is, the rest day, "to keep it holy; six days shalt thou labor, and do all thy work": But the seventh day is the "rest" – "the Sabbath" – the rest "of the Lord thy God." Whose rest is it? [Congregation: "God's."] Whose rest is it then that we should take and enjoy on the Sabbath day? [Congregation: "God's."] Then the man who takes his own rest and enjoys his own rest and not the Lord's rest, does he keep the Sabbath? [Congregation: "No."] He keeps Saturday, doesn't he? [Congregation: "Yes."] A man who takes his own rest on Saturday, even though he enjoys his rest on that day, is not keeping the Sabbath, the Lord's rest, and even though he enjoys it, he keeps Saturday only and not Sabbath.

The man who receives and enjoys *the Lord's rest* on the seventh day, he keeps the Sabbath, because it is God's rest that he keeps. That is what he does. It is God's rest day. "Six days shalt thou labor, and do all thy work: But the seventh day is the" rest of the LORD thy God, not yours. It is His; His rest, and when we remember the rest day, whose rest day is it we remember? Ours or His? [Congregation: "The Lord's."] Yes, the Lord's. It is altogether God's rest, and the idea of God's rest in the thought of the Sabbath commandment, and the reasons that are given in the commandment, are the same. We are to work six days. The reason is: because the Lord in making heaven and earth worked six days and rested the seventh. And we are to rest the seventh day, because the Lord rested, and blessed it, and sanctified it and hallowed it.

What kind of rest was that, or is that, which is in the seventh day? [Congregation: "Refreshing."] Whose refreshing? [Congregation: "God's."] What is God? [Congregation: "Spirit."] God is Spirit. The only kind of rest which He could possibly have is spiritual rest. Then the man who does not obtain and enjoy spiritual rest in the seventh day, he does not keep the Sabbath, because Sabbath rest is spiritual rest; it is God's rest, and that alone. It is spiritual rest, and the sabbath is a spiritual thing, and God's rest is in the day; spiritual rest is in the day. And by observing the day by faith – "spiritual things are spiritually discerned", by observing the day by faith, that spiritual rest comes to him who observes the Sabbath. That spiritual rest which God put into the day, which became a part of the day, that spiritual rest which is there, comes to a man and is enjoyed and known by him who keeps the Sabbath, the only way it can be kept, by faith in Jesus.

Then He blessed the day. Then the blessing of God is also in the day; the rest of God is in the day, and the joy that we have found, the refreshing, the delighting, the joy of the Lord is also in the day. The blessing of the Lord is in it, too; for He blessed the day. Now, is that blessing in the day yet? [Congregation: "Yes."] If a man does not observe it or pays no attention to it, is the blessing in it? [Congregation: "Yes."] But it does not reach the man, if he does not believe.

Now the thought we had last night – the force of the word of God – the word of God, which spoke the worlds into existence, what effect has it on the worlds and has it had since that day? [Congregation: "It upholds them."] That word that He spoke then keeps the worlds together and in their courses ever since. How long will it do so? [Congregation: "Forever."] "The word of our God abideth forever."

Now there is the word of God, that He blessed the seventh day. What is the effect of that blessing which, away back there, He put upon the day? It is there yet, and it will always be there, because to all eternity it will be a fact that God did bless the seventh day; that He Himself cannot contradict, you see. He Himself cannot say that He did not bless the seventh day, for He says He did. Even if He should blot out the whole of creation, it would still be a fact that He blessed the seventh day when it was there. Wouldn't it? [Congregation: "Yes."] Then that is settled. Then to all eternity it will remain a fact that God did bless the seventh day. And just as long as it remains a fact that He did it, so long will it remain a fact that the blessing of God is in it and so long it will remain a fact that the man who observes it as only the Sabbath can be observed – by faith in Jesus – he will get the blessing of God out of it and enjoy it as such.

Now, referring to the first chapter of Genesis, there we read in the twenty-seventh and twenty-eighth verses: "God created man in his own image, in the image of God created He him; male and female created He them. And God *blessed them*." What day was that? [Congregation: "The sixth day."] Then God blessed the *man* before He blessed the *seventh day*. That is settled, is it not? [Congregation: "Yes."] Now is it as much of a certainty that He blessed *the day* as it is that He blessed *the man*? [Congregation: "Yes."] Is the blessing with which He blessed *the day,* as real as the blessing with which He blessed *the man*? [Congregation: "Just the same."] It is as real. What was the blessing? Whose blessing was it that He put upon the man? [Congregation: "The blessing of God."] Whose blessing did He put upon the day? [Congregation: "God's blessing."] Well, then, when that *blessed man* came to that *blessed day,* did he receive additional *blessing* in the *day* beyond what he had, before he came to the day? [Congregation: "Yes."]

Then the Sabbath was intended to bring to the man, who was already blessed of God with spiritual blessings – the Sabbath was to bring to man additional spiritual blessings? Well, is that so still? [Congregation: "Yes."] "The word of God liveth and abideth forever." It is so now.

Well then He made the day holy. But *what* made the day holy? Now I need not go through the texts on this; you have had these in Brother Prescott's talk Sabbath before last. What was it that made the day holy? [Congregation: "The presence of God."] The presence of God makes things holy. It makes a place holy. It makes a man holy. The presence of God made the *day* holy. Then the holiness of God is attached to the day. The presence of God, the holy presence of God, is attached to the seventh or Sabbath day. Well then when the man comes to that day, as only man can come to it, spiritually-minded – with the mind of the Spirit of God – and receives the spiritual rest, the spiritual refreshing that is in it, the spiritual blessing that is in it, does he not also receive that *presence,* become a partaker of that *presence,* in which is the holiness of God to transform him? He does indeed. And that is Sabbath-keeping.

Well then He *sanctified* the day, but I need not rehearse those texts either. What is it that sanctifies? [Congregation: "The presence of God."] Then the presence of God, His sanctifying power is in the seventh day. Is that so? [Congregation: "Yes."] Then the man who comes to the Sabbath of the Lord according to the Lord's idea of the Sabbath of the Lord, and his intent, obtains spiritual rest. He finds that there. He finds spiritual refreshing, delight; he finds spiritual blessing. He finds the presence of God and the holiness which that presence brings to transform him. And he finds that sanctifying power in that presence which sanctified the day to sanctifying him. For what purpose was all this done? Why was the sabbath made? [Congregation: "For man."] It was made for man. Well then, God rested and put His spiritual rest upon the day for man, did He?

[Congregation: "Yes."] God's refreshing, His rejoicing in that day was for man. The blessing with which He blessed it was for man. The holiness which His presence brought to it and which His presence gave to it, was for man. His presence sanctifying it was for man. Well then was it not that man through the Sabbath might be a partaker of His presence and be made acquainted by living experience with the spiritual rest of God, the spiritual blessing, the holiness, the presence of God to make holy, the presence of God to sanctify him? Is not that what God intended the Sabbath to bring to man? Well, the man who gets all that in the Sabbath is the man who is a Sabbath-keeper. *And he knows it too.* He knows it and he is delighted to know it.

Now another thing: Who was the real present agent in creating? [Congregation: "Christ."] Who was it that rested? [Congregation: "Christ."] Who was refreshed? [Congregation: "Christ."] Who blessed? [Congregation: "Christ."] Whose presence made it holy? [Congregation: "Christ's"] Whose presence is in the day? [Congregation: "Christ's."] *Then the man whom the presence of Jesus Christ does not sanctify, and does not make holy and does not bless and to whom it dos not bring rest, why, he can't keep the Sabbath.* Don't you see, it is only with Christ in the man that the Sabbath can be kept; because the Sabbath brings and has in it the presence of Christ.

So you see when God set up the Sabbath, He had set creation all before man to start with and man could see God in creation. But the Lord wanted to get nearer to man than that. Man could study creation and find a knowledge *about* God. But God wanted him to have the knowledge *of* God. In creation he could know *about* Him. In the Sabbath he would know *Him,* because the Sabbath brings the living presence, the sanctifying presence, the hallowing presence, of Jesus Christ, to the man who observes it indeed. Therefore we see the creation was before man and he could study God in creation and thus know *about* Him. But God came nearer than that and set up that which signifies that God is *what* He is, and when the man would find what God is there, then he would not only know *about* Him *from the created things,* but would know Him *in Himself.*

So then the original purpose of God in creation and the Sabbath as the sign of it was that man might know God *as He is* and *what* He is to the world in and through Jesus Christ. Is not that so? [Congregation: "Yes."] Do you see that? [Congregation: "Yes."] *What is it for now, then?* [Congregation: "The same."]

Now, another thought here. The Sabbath was thus made at the end of creation and the real thing that made creation week. The Sabbath then was a sign of the power of God manifested in Jesus Christ and the sign of a finished creation – the sign of God as manifested in Jesus Christ in a completed and finished creation. He saw all that He had made in the five days and behold it was good, but when it comes to the sixth day, He saw all things, and behold it was *very good.* Genesis 1:31. And His purpose stood completed. "Thus the heavens and the earth were finished, and all the host of them," and there they were, the expression of the thought that was in His mind, that the word expressed when

He spoke them into existence. Then the Sabbath – the sign "that I am the Lord your God," because in six days He made heaven and earth and on the seventh day He rested and was refreshed – is the sign of the finished and completed work of God in creation.

Now, let us go on from that. Did man, at that time, in the garden of Eden, standing as God made him, know all of God that he ever could know? [Congregation: "No."] Then as each Sabbath day came, it would bring to him additional knowledge and presence of God. But who is this? [Congregation: "Christ."] Additional knowledge and presence of Christ in Himself. Then if he had remained faithful, he would still have grown in the knowledge of God, in Himself, in His own experience, growing more and more in all that the nature of God is. But he didn't stay there. He didn't remain faithful. The creation was completed as God finished it, and all the host of them, and they were according to His own mind. That is so. But Satan came in and swung man and all this world clear out of God's purpose entirely. Didn't he? [Congregation: "Yes."] Reversed God's order, so that, where God was reflected to man's mind in all things above and in man himself before, *now* Satan is reflected in man and that puts a blur upon the reflection of God in anything, so that the natural man does not see God, even in nature.

Well, then, when Satan had swung this out of God's purpose, and turned it about and reversed God's order, the Lord did not leave it then. He said, "I will put enmity between thee and the woman, and between thy seed and her seed." That broke the power of Satan over man to that extent that it released him from total depravity; set him free to find God. But in whom was that done? [Congregation: "Christ."] Christ again. God in Christ wants to bring man and the world back again into His original purpose. And was it not the same power in Christ and by the same means – His word – that He would bring back men and the world into His purpose, that produced them in the first place? [Congregation: "Yes."]

It was God in Christ, by His word, that produced the world and man, in the first place. Now Satan has taken it all away from God and turned it contrary to God's purpose. Now it is God in Christ, by His word, that brings men and the world back into His purpose. Then is not the work of *salvation* simply the power of God in another way than that which brought all things in the first place? In other words, is not salvation creation? Assuredly.

Now another thought on that to see it still more plainly, if need be. Is God's original purpose in creation completed now? [Congregation: "No."] It was completed, but is it now? [Congregation: "No."] No, sir. When the salvation of mankind is completed will His original purpose *then* be completed? [Congregation: "Yes."] Then what is the work of salvation but God's carrying out and completing His original purpose in creation? [Voices: It is the same thing."] "My Father worketh hitherto and I work." Then what can the work of salvation be but original work of creation? The same God, in the same Son, by the same means, to accomplish the same purpose. Well, then isn't the sign of *this* work in *salvation* the same as the sign of *that* work in *creation?* To be sure it is.

Then the Sabbath of the Lord is just as certainly the sign of the creative power of God manifested in Jesus Christ through His word, *in the salvation of my soul* as it was in the making of this world in the first place.

But God is revealed everywhere in Christ, in all places, you see. That is the thought before us continually. Then His name is I AM WHAT I AM. But what He is can be known only in Jesus Christ. Therefore to men, to all intents and purposes, to men in this world, Jesus Christ is God Himself and what He is, isn't He? [Congregation: "Yes."] I say to all intents and purposes – not that it is making them one, identical and the same individual, but as no man can know the Father save the Son, and *He to whom the Son will reveal Him,* no man can know God except as He is revealed in Jesus Christ; consequently, to man, Christ is God and all that He can know of God is in Christ. And therefore Christ becomes practically, to all intents and purposes, God to us; and God said when He was born, He is "God with us."

Well then the Sabbath is the sign that He is the Lord our God. But it is the sign that He is *what* He is. Then Christ being God to us, is not the Sabbath the sign of what Jesus Christ is to the man who believes in Him. [Congregation: "Yes."] At creation it was the sign of what Jesus Christ is in creation. And now as Christ has to carry on His own work in salvation in order through this means to finish His original purpose in creation, the Sabbath is the *same sign* of the *same creative power,* in the *same one, Jesus Christ.* So it is still the same thing right along. Only now the *power* is manifested in a different way from what it was before, because of the reversal of the order, but it is the same creative power from the *same Person* in the *same One* by the *same means,* and accomplishing the *same purpose.* And therefore the *same sign* is the only one that ever could be attached to it. You cannot have any other sign of it. It is impossible. So that it is literally true that the Sabbath of the Lord, the seventh day, the blessed seventh day, is God's own sign of what Jesus Christ is to the man who believes in Jesus Christ.

Now let us study that a little further.

"All have sinned, and come short of the glory of God." "The wages of sin is death; therefore death passed upon all men, for all have sinned." All are dead. Is that so? [Congregation: "Yes."] They are all gone out of the way. They are gone from God's original purpose entirely. What is the first thing that Jesus Christ is to the man who believes in Him? [Congregation: "Creator."] "Created anew in Christ Jesus." God in Christ unto the sinner is still Creator, the very first thing, because God speaks and he lives. By the word of God we live. And "we are his workmanship, created in Christ Jesus unto good works, which God hath before ordained that we should walk in them." Ephesians 2:10. *Then* God made man to walk in good works, but man walked the other way. *Now in Christ* God brings man up to the place where He started him. So salvation is only the accomplishing of the original purpose of God in Christ in creation.

Well, therefore, "if any man be in Christ he is a new creature." The first thing that Christ is to anybody and the first thing that God is to anybody – to the sinner – in this world is Creator, making him a new creature. "Create in me a clean heart, O God; renew a right spirit within me." Then the work of God in salvation is creation.

Well, when we have thus found Jesus Christ as our Creator and been made new in Him, then what is the first thing we find in Jesus? [Congregation: "Rest."] Yes, rest, of course. And there is the first thing that He did in the beginning. He rested. So first thing we find in the manifestation of His power in us is rest. What kind of rest? [Congregation: "Spiritual rest."] That is the invitation: "Come unto me all ye that labor and are heavy laden, and I will give you rest." Then He says, "I am with you." I am with you. "I will never leave thee nor forsake thee." And when He spoke to Moses in the wilderness, "My presence shall go with thee, and I will give thee rest." What does His presence give? [Congregation: "Rest."]

And when that man has become a new creature in Christ and finds that rest what then does He do? [Voice: "Works the works of God."] No. He rejoices first, and he goes to work rejoicing. What did God do? Rejoiced. What does the man do? He rejoices in the purpose of God accomplished in himself. But is that all the rejoicing there is? No. "I say unto you that likewise joy shall be in heaven over one sinner that repenteth, more than over ninety and nine just persons, which need no repentance." Then God rejoices again in the rest which He gives to us and which we obtain in Him. And again He is refreshed; again He delights in His people.

Well then the next thing that belongs to the Sabbath day and the next thing that belongs all through this is blessing. Last verse of Acts, third chapter: "Unto you first, God, having raised up his Son Jesus, sent him to bless you, in turning away from every one of you from his iniquities." Then Christ is a blessing to the sinner, isn't He? He is a blessing to the man who believes in Him. But further: That text that we have studied here so deliciously, Ephesians 1:3; "Blessed be the God and Father of our Lord Jesus Christ, who hath blessed us with all spiritual blessings in heavenly places in Christ Jesus." God has given to us all the spiritual blessings He has. They are given to us in Christ, though.

But the Sabbath brings to us spiritual blessing. Where did the Sabbath get the spiritual blessing? [Congregation: "From Christ."] Yes, from Jesus Christ. Then in the matter of spiritual blessing which the Sabbath brings to us, it brings it to us from Jesus Christ only and through Jesus Christ only, so that in that respect, the Sabbath is a channel through which spiritual blessing flows from Jesus Christ to the people of God. That is a fact; because all spiritual blessings are given to us in Christ, and the Sabbath has the spiritual blessing of God in it, and therefore it being spiritual blessing it could not get it in any other place or way that in, by, and from Jesus Christ. Consequently the Sabbath is one of those links that Brother Prescott referred to awhile ago that binds us to Christ, that we may have spiritual blessing.

Then further:

"My presence shall go with thee." His presence makes holy the person where he is. And further: Another thought, to come up to the same point another way. "I am not ashamed of the gospel of Christ, for it is the power of God unto salvation to every one that believeth." What is the gospel? [Congregation: "The power of God."] What is manifested in Christ? [Congregation: "The power of God."] What is manifested in the gospel? [Congregation: "The power of God."] To what purpose? [Voice: "Creation."] But the power of God unto *salvation* is the same power in the *creation*. It is the power of God in both places. Then whatever the sign of the power of God is in one place, it is the sign of the power of God in every place and in every way, because it is the power of God alone all the time, and you cannot set the power of God against the power of God. So you do not need any other sign of the manifestation of the power of God. You cannot have it; it is impossible.

Well then the gospel is the "power of God unto salvation," and the gospel is "Christ in you, the hope of glory." Then the man who believes in the gospel of Jesus Christ, Christ dwells in him. Christ's presence is there, and Christ's presence makes holy. That is what made the Sabbath holy. Then the Sabbath, in the point of the matter of holiness, is exactly the sign of what Christ is to the man who believes in Him.

Further, the presence of Christ sanctifies. Then in sanctification the Sabbath is the sign of what Christ is to the believer. Don't you see. So unto the believer in Jesus, God in Christ creates anew; to him God is rest, refreshing, delight, rejoicing, blessing, holiness, sanctification. That is what Christ is to the believer, but that is what He was to the Sabbath long ago, *for* the believer.

He made the Sabbath for man, as we found, at creation. He made it there, at creation, that the man, even though he had remained faithful to God and had never sinned at all, it would have been to man the sign of what God was to man in Jesus Christ and the presence of Christ in the man. And now in the new creation it is the same thing. In the work of salvation it is the same thing.

Then another thing: Christ is made unto us wisdom, righteousness, sanctification, and redemption. He is our sanctification.

He sent Paul to preach the gospel, you remember. To preach to the Gentiles, "to open their eyes and to turn them from darkness to light and from the power of Satan unto God that they may receive forgiveness of sins and inheritance among them which are sanctified *by faith that is in me.*" But sanctification and its ultimate purpose, accomplished purpose, is the complete work of Christ finished in the individual. The image of Christ completely formed in the believer, so that when Christ looks upon the believer He sees Himself. That is so. That is sanctification.

The Spirit of prophecy has defined sanctification for us in these words: "Sanctification is the keeping of all the commandments of God." – not *trying* to keep them, or *doing our best* to keep them. It is the *keeping* of all the commandments of God. No man will be the keeper – the keeper as God expects and calls a keeper – of all the commandments, in whom Jesus Christ is not completely formed, His own image impressed there, and when He looks upon that man, He sees Himself. That is so.

Now the righteousness of God in Jesus Christ is that which makes us righteous, which saves us, which sanctifies us, which is all in all to us. When we have obtained that righteousness, and that righteousness is there according to righteousness, God's idea of righteousness, what is it that witnesses to the righteousness of God in the believer in Jesus? [Congregation: "The law."] The law of God. But here is this work of Christ growing up in the individual, that progressive work; that is the work of sanctification – the work of sanctifying; for that is the thought, the work of sanctifying. It is the growth of Christ in the individual. When Christ has grown to the fulness there, then that is the completed work of sanctification.

What is the sign that God sanctifies? [Congregation: "The Sabbath."] What is the sign, then, that the presence of Christ is sanctifying the individual? [Congregation: "The Sabbath."] When the work is completed, what will witness to that? [Congregation: "The law."] What part of the law, particularly? [Congregation: "The fourth commandment."] Just as the whole law will witness to the complete work of the righteousness of God in a man, but the Sabbath stands there as God's sign of a completed work. It is the sign of a completed work at creation, isn't it? But when that was undone, and God's order reversed, now the Lord has to carry on His work through this means in order to finish that original purpose of creation.

Then the Sabbath stands there in this finished work of God in salvation – the Sabbath stands there at the pinnacle of the law itself, as the witness of the sanctification completed, so that the Sabbath is the sign of the completed work of God in the original creation, and in this secondary creation, which is the carrying out of the original purpose of creation.

Now another thought: The Sabbath being the sign of what Christ is to the believer, will the believer know fully what the Sabbath is until he knows fully what Christ is? [Congregation: "No."]

So then when the knowledge of God in Jesus Christ has absorbed all of the mind itself, then the Sabbath will be also known fully to the mind itself. But the Sabbath is the sign of what God is in Christ, and when that is brought fully to the mind itself, what is that but the image of God, the name of God, in the mind of the believer, and that the seal of the living God, through the Sabbath of the Lord?

Well, then, you see at every step of the way, every line of thought, brings us only face to face with that, that the Sabbath as it is in Jesus Christ, and as the believer in Jesus observes it, that alone is the seal of the living God. Saturday keeping is not the seal of God. Christ as He is reflected in the Sabbath of the Lord, through the Sabbath of the Lord, and in it, in the mind and heart of the believer, in the living image of God completed – that is the seal of the living God. Then there is written in the foreheads of that people the name of the Father.

Now see here. Turn to Numbers 6:23-27: "Speak unto Aaron and unto his sons, saying, On this wise ye shall bless the children of Israel, saying unto them, The Lord bless thee, and keep thee: the Lord make his face shine upon thee: the Lord lift up his countenance upon thee and give thee peace. And they shall put my name upon the children of Israel, and I will bless them." Now that is the blessing with which the high priest blessed when the Day of Atonement was over. When the work of atonement was finished and the priest come out of the temple to sanctify and bless the people, that is the blessing. And in that blessing what did he put upon them? He "shall put my name upon the children of Israel." The judgment was passed, and they were secure. That was in the figure.

Now turn to Revelation 3:9-12: "Behold, I will make them of the synagogue of Satan, which say they are Jews and are not but do lie; behold, I will make them to come and worship before thy feet, and to know that I have loved thee. Because thou hast kept the word of my patience, I also will keep thee from the hour of temptation, which shall come upon all the world, to try them that dwell upon the earth. Behold, I come quickly: hold that fast which thou hast, that no man take thy crown." That message was the message that was given when the Day of Atonement began, was it not, our Day of Atonement?

That was fulfilled when the Day of Atonement began.

Now: "Him that overcometh will I make a pillar in the temple of my God, and he shall go no more out: and I will write upon him the name of my God, and the name of the city of my God, which is New Jerusalem, which cometh down out of heaven from my God: and I will write upon him my new name." Then when His work of atonement is finished, the name of God is completed in the mind, and He pronounces the work finished; for what God is there, in the believer and in the Sabbath, is the sign of a finished work in sanctification.

Now Isaiah 58:13, 14: "If thou turn away thy foot from the Sabbath, from doing thy pleasure on my holy day, and call the Sabbath a delight, the holy of the Lord, honorable, and shalt honor him, not doing thine own ways, nor finding thine own pleasure, nor speaking thine own words: then shalt thou delight thyself in the" Sabbath. [Congregation: "No. 'Delight thyself in the Lord.'"] Why not in the Sabbath? Doesn't it say you are to call the Sabbath a delight? That you are to call it the holy of the Lord? honorable? Not doing thine own ways. They why not delight yourself in the Sabbath? Ah, there is that meaning there, you see. You do that to the Sabbath, and you delight yourself in the Lord, because the Sabbath is the sign of what the Lord is to the man.

Therefore He put that just right. You do that with respect to the Sabbath, and you will delight yourself in the Lord, because it is the sign of what the Lord will be to you and what you will be to the Lord. Well, then, I want to know how in the world anybody is going to compromise with any other rival institution, when the Sabbath is the sign of what Christ is to him. The man to whom the Sabbath is the sign of what Christ is to him, will he be asking whether he shall work or not on Sunday? [Congregation: "No, sir."] Why, no! He knows well enough that that does not come into it. He knows he cannot compromise and have half of Christ and half of something else, and besides, Christ is all in all, and the Sabbath is the sign of what Christ is to him, and Christ is all in all to him, and to suggest anything else is to insult him.

Then those people who are asking these questions do not know what Christ is, anyway. They might as well keep Sunday as not. They are not keeping Sabbath.

But there is the thing. The Sabbath has the living image of Jesus and the presence of Jesus Christ in it. He put it there. He put it there for the man, and the man who believes in Jesus Christ can get it there. In addition to the blessing he has of the Lord when he comes to the Sabbath day, he gets additional blessing from the Lord. It matters not how much the presence of Christ is with him, when he comes to the Sabbath day, additional presence of Christ comes to him. He knows it.

No difference how much of the rest of the Lord he is enjoying, when he comes to the Sabbath, which is the sign of what Christ is to the believer, and has the presence of Christ in it, it brings to him additional rest in the Lord. No difference how much holiness of Christ he has in him, when he comes to the Sabbath more of it is revealed in him from observing it in the fear of Christ and by faith in Him. No difference, though he be completely sanctified and all of self is gone and none but Christ there, even then, when he comes to the Sabbath day, in the depths of eternity it will reveal to him still more of the wonderful knowledge and the sanctifying, growing power there is in Jesus Christ to the man who believes in Him.

Sermon 21

March 3, 1893

We take up the thought tonight just where it was left last night, that the work of God in salvation is the same as the work of God in carrying out His original purpose in creation, because as stated then, at the time the creation of the heavens and the earth was finished, and all the host of them, God's completed purpose stood there in which He took delight in that day. Yet through the deception of Satan, this world was swung clear out of His creative purpose and turned to the opposite.

Therefore, in order to complete His purpose, He has to gather from this world a people who will fill the earth when made new as it would have been filled if it had never fallen in His original purpose. And when that is accomplished through this word of salvation, the power of God in salvation that will be the real finishing indeed, the real accomplishment of His original purpose in making this world with all things – a complete universe, when everything that is in heaven and on earth and under the earth and in the sea and all that in them are, are saying, "Blessing and honor and power be unto him that sitteth upon the throne and unto the Lamb forever and ever."

And therefore, the Saviour, when He was here, said, "My Father worketh hitherto and I work." God's work was finished when the seventh day began of old. He rested. But His work on this earth and forming man here was undone, so that He had to set to work again in the work of salvation to complete His original purpose, and therefore Jesus says, "My Father worketh hitherto, and I work."

Now I will read three passages in the Old Testament and three in the New and you can multiply on them just as far as you please, especially from the 40th chapter of Isaiah and onward, showing that in the work of salvation He puts His original work in creation and Himself as Creator and His power as manifested in creation as the basis of our confidence in His power to accomplish our salvation.

Turn first to Psalm 111:4: "He hath made his wonderful works to be remembered." The revised version, the Hebrew, Jewish, and others give it: "He hath made a memorial for his wondrous works." That is what we have been talking about. That is the first part of the verse, and now the latter part: "The Lord is gracious and full of compassion." His wonderful works, then, that are signified in the memorial which

He has established, are attached right there in that verse, to His graciousness, His fullness of compassion for man in this world, who needs it so much.

Now the 40th chapter of Isaiah, and you can follow on through, then, clear through the rest of the book of Isaiah, and you will see it all the way through. I will begin with the first verse, which is, you remember, "Comfort ye, comfort ye my people, saith your God. Speak ye comfortably to Jerusalem." The margin reads: "Speak ye to the heart of Jerusalem, and cry unto her, that her warfare is accomplished, that her iniquity is pardoned: for she hath received of the Lord's hand double for all her sins. The voice of him that crieth in the wilderness, Prepare ye the way for the Lord, make straight in the desert a highway for our God." That is the message of John the Baptist.

> Every valley shall be exalted, and every mountain and hill shall be made low: and the crooked shall be made straight, and the rough places plain: And the glory of the Lord shall be revealed and all flesh shall see it together: for the mouth of the Lord hath spoken it. The voice said, cry. And he said, What shall I cry? All flesh is grass, and the goodliness thereof is as the flower of the field: The grass withereth, the flower fadeth; because the Spirit of the Lord bloweth upon it; surely the people is grass. The grass withereth, the flower fadeth; but the word of our God shall stand forever.

And Peter quoting that text in the last two verses of the 1st chapter of 1st Peter says: "And this is the word which by the gospel is preached unto you." He is quoting this from Isaiah, that "the word of our God shall stand forever," and he says, "This is the word which by the gospel is preached unto you."

Then Isaiah goes right on and speaks in other words of the gospel: "O Zion, that bringest good tidings, get thee up into the high mountain; O Jerusalem, that bringest good tidings, lift up thy voice with strength; lift it up, be not afraid; say unto the cities of Judah, Behold your God! Behold, the Lord God will come with a strong hand and his arm shall rule for him: behold his reward is with him, and his work before him. He shall feed his flock like a shepherd: he shall gather the lambs with his arm, and carry them in his bosom, and gently lead those that are with young."

Now that is the gospel. Up to that point he is teaching the gospel by the word of God. Now read: "Who hath measured the waters in the hollow of his hand, and meted out heaven with a span, and comprehended the dust of the earth in a measure, and weighed the mountains in scales, and the hills in a balance?" Who did that? The same One who comes and says, "I will tenderly lead like a shepherd those who are mine" – the same Whose word now speaks to us in the gospel and liveth forever.

"Who hath directed the Spirit of the Lord, or being his counsellor hath taught him? With whom took he counsel and who instructed him and taught him the path of judgment and taught him knowledge and shewed to him the way of understanding? Behold the nations are as a drop of a bucket and are counted as the small dust of the balance:

behold, he taketh up the isles as a very little thing. And Lebanon is not sufficient to burn, or the beasts thereof sufficient for a burnt offering. All nations before him are as nothing; and they are counted to him less than nothing, and vanity. To whom then will ye liken God? or what likeness will ye compare unto him?"

Then skip to the 25th verse: "To whom then will ye liken me, or shall I be equal? saith the Holy One. Lift up your eyes on high, and behold who hath created these things, that bringeth out their host by number: he calleth them all by names by the greatness of his might, for that he is strong in power; not one faileth." Not one gets away. "Not one faileth" the text is. They are all kept: but what keeps them in place? [Congregation: "The power of His word."] He upholds "all things by the word of his power."

Now He tells us to look up and see who created all these things and "bringeth out their host by number." He "bringeth out their host" how? [Congregation: "'By number.'"]

Well, then, what is that for? Now, then, the 27th verse: "Why sayest thou, O Jacob, and speakest, O Israel, My way is hid from the Lord, and my judgment is passed over from my God? Look up to the heavens and see who made all these things, and he calls out their host by number and not one fails. Now, Jacob, why are you saying that God has forgotten you? What do you get discouraged for? What do you think He has forgotten you for? Why, He does not forget any of the planets in the universe; He knows them all by their names. Is He going to forget your name? What are these two things put there together for? [Voice: "For our comfort."] Because the same one who created all these things is the one who comforted Israel. The One who knows all these things is the One that gives you and me our new name.

Twenty-eighth verse: "Hast thou not known? hast thou not heard, that the everlasting God, the Lord, the Creator of the ends of the earth, fainteth not, neither is weary? There is no searching of his understanding. He giveth power to the faint, and to them that have no might he increaseth strength." Who does it? [Congregation: "The Lord."] Well, lift up your eyes and see who created all these things, and then that He has power to give to the faint. He has power for the faint, by His word; so He says, "Be of good cheer. Be of good courage." It is so. For, when He spoke to Daniel, "Be strong," Daniel said, I am strong, for Thou hast strengthened me.

Now the remainder of the chapter: "Even the youths shall faint and be weary, and the young men shall utterly fail: but they that wait upon the Lord shall renew their strength; they shall mount up with wings as eagles; they shall run and not be weary; and they shall walk and not be faint." Because the power that keeps the planets in their courses and in one place, that same power will be with the weak and the faint, and so they can "run, and not be weary," and they can "walk and not faint." Then don't you see that the Lord puts the creation and His power in creation there as the foundation of our hope in His salvation? Then isn't it all one?

Another blessed verse that touches so intimately everybody – I read it principally for that purpose – is found in the 147th Psalm, 3rd and 4th verses: "He healeth the broken in heart, and bindeth up their wounds. He telleth the number of the stars; he calleth them all by their names." Then the one who can tell the number of the stars, call them all by their names, is He who binds up and heals the broken hearts – binds up their wounds. Well then, have you been wounded in spirit, broken-hearted and almost in despair and thought everything and everybody had forgotten you? Why, just remember the very next verse. The thought connected with it is – He not only "healeth the broken in heart and bindeth up their wounds," but He tells the number of the stars and He calls them all by their names and He will not forget your name. That is the Lord. That is our Saviour, but the foundation of our confidence in Him as Saviour is that He created all these things and knows all their names and holds them up by the word of His power, which saves.

Now reading hurriedly in the New Testament, you remember that scripture in the 1st chapter of John, 1-3: "In the beginning was the Word, and the Word was with God, and the Word was God. All things were made by him, and without him was not anything made that was made. In him was life, and the life was the light of men." And the 14th verse: "And the Word was made flesh and dwelt among us . . . full of grace and truth." "And of His fullness have all we received, and grace for grace."

Then that one who created all things came here Himself, "full of grace and truth"; flesh like ourselves, and through Him we are partakers of His fullness. Don't you see then, that the only thought that God would have us have about salvation is that He who created us saves us; that the power by which He created is the power by which He saves; and the means by which He created – His word – that means is the very one by which He saves. And this was His word, "unto you is the word of this salvation sent."

Ephesians 3, speaks of the gospel, beginning with the 7th verse and ending with the 12th: "whereof I was made a minister, according to the gift of the grace of God given unto me by the effectual working of his power. Unto me, who am less than the least of all saints, is this grace given, that I should preach among the Gentiles the unsearchable riches of Christ, and to make all men see what is the fellowship of the mystery, which from the beginning of the world hath been hid in God, who created all things by Jesus Christ." Now, what was he to preach? "The unsearchable riches of Christ" and to make men see what is the mystery that is "in God, who created all things by Jesus Christ." Then the gospel is to bring men to understand God's purpose when He started out to create in the first place. Then if the gospel were engaged in any other work and teaching any other thing or any other power than that original creation, don't you see, the preaching of it would not bring them to that? But that being the design of it, that simply shows the force that is before us always, that God's purpose in the gospel is to make known to men who have lost the knowledge of it, the knowledge of His original purpose in creating all things by Jesus Christ.

So we read on: "To the intent that now unto the principalities and powers in heavenly places might be known by the church the manifold wisdom of God, according to the eternal purpose which He purposed in Christ Jesus our Lord." But we read in another place that He purposed that before the world began. He would have to, if it was an eternal purpose. Then, in Christ, in the salvation of this world and men, and the working of Christ in it, God is carrying out His eternal purpose that He began at the beginning. "In whom (in Christ) we have boldness with confidence by the faith of him."

Let us read that eternal purpose again: "According to the eternal purpose which He purposed in Christ Jesus our Lord." Then that original creating purpose that we spoke of last night, that was in Christ, this carrying out of it that was frustrated, is Christ. Then it was Christ back there, and it is Christ now. It is Christ all the time and the power of God in Christ all the way: the power of God manifested in the word all the way for the accomplishment of His purpose at the beginning and the accomplishment of that purpose at the close. Satan came in and swung the world off in a crooked way. The Lord says, "All right, we will carry it out that way." Satan didn't do anything. He swung the world off, and so it has gone on, as it were, in a little by-way, and God will carry the thing through in that by-way and accomplish His eternal purpose so that it will astonish the universe and destroy the devil. *It will do it.*

The same thing is in Colossians 1, beginning with the 9th verse. I will read hurriedly from the 9th to the 17th verse: "For this cause we also, since the day we heard it, do not cease to pray for you and to desire that ye might be filled with the knowledge of his will in all wisdom and spiritual understanding: That ye might walk worthy of the Lord unto all pleasing, being faithful in every good work, and increasing in the knowledge of God. Strengthened with all might, according to his glorious power, unto all patience and longsuffering with joyfulness: Giving thanks unto the Father, which hath made us meet to be partakers of the inheritance of the saints in light: Who hath delivered us from the power of darkness and hath translated us into the kingdom of his dear Son: In whom we have redemption through his blood, even the forgiveness of sins: Who is the image of the invisible God, the firstborn of every creature: For by him were all things created, that are in heaven, and that are in earth, visible and invisible, whether they be thrones, or dominions, or principalities, or powers: all things were created by him and for him: And he is before all things, and by him all things consist." Creation, salvation, the blessing of God, and His grace, and deliverance from the power of darkness, also, it is all one story – the creative power of God, and God in Jesus Christ.

First chapter of Hebrews has it all through. Well it is all through the Bible. Now then the thought. We do not need to dwell any further upon the thought that salvation is creation and is given as a sign signifying creative power manifested in Jesus Christ. And the only way that that power is manifested at all is in Jesus Christ; the only way we can know God is in Him. Now He has set up that sign to signify the creative power of God in Jesus Christ, and whether that creative power be in the original creation or in the work of salvation to carry out that original purpose in creation, it is all the same power, the same purpose, by the same one, in the same way, and by the same means and the same sign signifying all in all, in all its bearings and workings.

Now then if you have another sign set up, to signify the work of salvation, another sign than that which God has set up – will that other sign signify the power of God and the salvation that is expected? [Congregation: "No."] Now think carefully of this. God set up a sign to signify His power working everywhere and in every way, in Christ Jesus. If you or anybody else sets up another sign, it cannot signify the power of God, because it is some other one than God that sets it up. Then it is impossible to signify the power of God by another thing, another sign; that is impossible. Is that so? [Congregation: "Yes."]

Further, if anybody should find anywhere in history another thing set up to signify salvation, it would signify salvation by another power than the power of God in Jesus Christ. It would have to do it. Well, has there been any effort, any pretense ever made in history, by any other power, to save people, apart from Jesus Christ? [Congregation: "Yes."] Has there not arisen in the world a power called antichrist? [Congregation: "Yes."] "Anti" is against or opposed to Christ. That power does propose to save people, doesn't it? [Congregation: "Yes."] Let us read the description of what it does in the first place: "Who opposeth and exalteth himself above all that is called God or that is worshipped, so that he as God sitteth in the temple of God, shewing himself that he is God." 2 Thessalonians 2:4.

Daniel 8:25 also says: "He shall also stand up against the Prince of princes." He shall "stand up" to reign, to rule, and to show forth his power "against," opposed to, "the Prince of princes." Who is the Prince of princes? [Congregation: "Christ."] He stands up against Him; he will reign; he will exercise his power, manifest his work, in opposition to Christ. Take the eleventh verse. "Yea, he magnified himself even to the prince of the host." But the margin reads, "He magnified himself *against* the Prince of the host of heaven," because the previous verse shows it is the host of heaven. Then, as Paul says, he exalted himself, opposed and exalted himself above all that is called God and that is worshiped. Magnified himself, exalted himself against the Prince of the host.

What power is that? [Congregation: "Papacy."] That power is the papacy, the church, the Catholic church, the Church of Rome. Now is it not the doctrine of that church that there is no salvation anywhere else? [Congregation: "Yes."] Or by any other means than that church? Isn't that settled? [Congregation: "Yes."] Further, that church, that power opposed to Christ, that exalts and sets up itself as the way of salvation, is itself opposed to Christ. And yet that church says there is no other way of salvation. Then is it not plain that if it is going to have any sign to signify its power to save, it has got to have another one than the Sabbath. That is settled.

Now then another thought. As it must be a sign other than the Sabbath, which is the sign of the power of God in Jesus Christ in salvation, then any other power setting up a sign to show and signify its power unto salvation, would it not have to be in the nature of things a rival sabbath? It would have to be that; there is no room for anything else. If they would set up anything else as a sign, the sign that God has set up would stand alone and distinct in the world, and it would take precedence of it and there would be no rivalry at all. Therefore, to make the rivalry complete and to make his power manifest in opposition to Christ, the man of sin has to have a sign of *his* power unto salvation, and it must be, in the nature of things, a rival to the sign which is the sign of the salvation in Christ. It has to be that.

And the Church of Rome makes no pretense to anything else. It makes no pretension to anything else than that the Sunday which it has set up is the sign of the power of the church to command men under sin into the way of salvation. That is settled. That is the object of it. That is all it has started out to do, and that is all it did.

Now when the Sunday was set up and enforced upon the people by the power of earthly government, it made the practical living papacy, as it exists in the world. When it was done, Sunday was put in the place of the Sabbath of the Lord by a direct and definite purpose. That was done. Here is the record. This is said by one of the men who did it. On page 313 of *Two Republics*, we read as follows:

> All things whatsoever that it was duty to do on the Sabbath, these we have transferred to the Lord's day. *Eusebius.*

Then the law was there to enforce the observance of Sunday and what was the purpose of that? From *Two Republics*, p. 315, I read:

> Our emperor, ever beloved by Him, who *derives the source of imperial authority from above,* and is strong in the power of his sacred title, has controlled the empire of the world for a long period of years. Again, that Preserver of the universe orders these heavens and earth and celestial kingdom, consistently with his Father's will. *Even so our emperor* whom he loves, *by bringing those whom he rules on earth to the only begotten Word and Saviour, renders them fit subjects of his kingdom. Eusebius.*

Then that purpose was to save people by that means, and the Sunday was put there as the sign of the power that was doing it, instead of the Sabbath of the Lord, which signifies the Lord's power to do it.

I read further on page 316:

> He commanded, too, that one day should be regarded as a special occasion for religious worship (*Ibid.*).

And again,

> Who else has commanded the nations inhabiting the continents and islands of this mighty globe to assemble weekly on the Lord's day and to observe it as a festival, not indeed for the pampering of the body, but for the comfort and invigoration of the soul by instruction in divine truth? *Eusebius.*

That is all it was set up for, to take the place of God, to take the place of the Sabbath of the Lord. It is appropriate enough that it should do so, because we have found if there is going to be another power that is going to save men, it has got to have another sign than God's to signify its power. It belongs there.

That made the papacy; that set up the government of the church, and made the church the channel of salvation by absolute earthly power and compelling men into that way.

Now we have read the doctrine of the church here – the doctrines of the church of Rome in the way that men must be saved, and it was altogether man's self. It was altogether the power of self alone that could save. That is not the salvation of Christ. Her doctrines are that a man must fit himself, good enough, and the Lord would take him and make a regular bargain with him. "If you will do so and so, then I will be good to you." That is the record itself there in that book; I have not time to read it tonight. Her doctrine is that a man must do that, but there is not power in him to do it, but there is the argument. If he does it, then he gains all. That is not the salvation of Christ. That is not the salvation of God.

Further than this: the professed Protestant churches of the United States have taken that same course now, and have also exalted Sunday, the day that they place in this government, as the Catholic church did in the Roman empire, and for the same purpose.

Further than this, these professed Protestant churches know that there is no commandment given for that thing. They say that. They say that it began with the primitive church. I do not care how far back they claim to get it in the primitive church. If it be a church institution, a church ordinance, that the church commands men to perform, it is the same thing. It is the same *evil* thing. Because any church that would attempt to do it, becomes in the nature of the attempt, an apostate church. Trace it to the days of the apostles if you want to, yet the church that did it is, in the nature of things, an apostate church, attempting to save itself and others without the power of God. Therefore whatever church did it, it is in the nature of things a fallen church, because it is not the church's office in the world to command men. The church's office in the world is to obey God and not to command men.

Any church, therefore, that presumes to command men is, at the very motion of it, an apostate church. The church that obeys God is the church of God. God commands; His is the power. His is the authority. He used the church, that through it He may reflect His power and His glory unto men. But the church has no right to command anybody. It obeys God *alone,* too.

Now I will put that in another way or state it a little more plainly. It is not the church's place to command anybody, and it is not the church's place to obey anybody, but *God only.*

Now look at that a little further. The church as a whole – Catholic and apostate Protestant – has already put herself in the place of Jesus Christ. Because any church that exalts *herself* and makes *herself* the way of salvation is, in that thing, an apostate church and puts herself in the place of Jesus Christ, who is the Saviour, don't you see?

Then no church can exalt herself as a saviour of men. She may exalt Jesus Christ as the Saviour of men, and Jesus Christ in her as the Saviour of men, but not *herself,* because it is the same with the church as with individuals. I have the righteousness of Jesus Christ. I have the presence of Jesus Christ dwelling in me. That is the word of the individual Christian, but the individual Christian cannot say, *I* am the Saviour. The individual Christian cannot say *I* am righteousness, that *I* am good and have goodness to bestow upon others that they may be saved. No, the Christian can say, I have the righteousness of Christ. Christ dwells in me and sends in me and through me His blessed purpose in reaching others and saving them. But *He* is the Saviour. *He* is the righteousness. *He* is the power. *He* is all and in all.

As with the individual so with the collection of individuals. As Christ dwells in the individual, so He dwells in the collection of individuals, in an additional sense beyond that which He dwells in the individual, and the righteousness of Christ in the collection of individuals is only the idea of the righteousness of Christ in a greater measure, if anything could be, upon the collection of individuals which is the church. So as Christ in the individual works through the individual to save, so Christ *in the church* works through the whole church to save. But if the church grows proud and thinks *she* is above all and begins to give *herself* credit for her glory and her power to save, she, in that moment, puts herself in the place of Jesus Christ as the Saviour.

That is the same self-exaltation in the church that there is in the individual, and it was the self-exaltation in the individuals that made the self-exalted church and brought on the apostasy.

Now then, that is the church putting herself forth as the way of salvation, as the Saviour indeed, as the only channel of salvation and all must be saved by the way she lays down. And she thus exalted herself against God and against the Prince of the host, against Jesus Christ, and set up that sign of her power to save, against the sign which God set up. And, as we have found, she did it with the direct intent and purpose to put it in the place of the Sabbath of the Lord.

And in the second apostate church – that which has come in this land – she has done the same thing. She has by a direct act of the government of the United States, the congressional action, put the Sunday institution, the sign of the power of the Church of Rome to save men – the professed Protestant churches have put that by a direct congressional act, in this land, in the place of the Sabbath of the Lord. So that both mother and daughters have put the Sabbath of the Lord out of the way and have put the Catholic church's sign of salvation in its place.

Now let us see what that amounts to. What have we found the Sabbath is? The Sabbath we have found by every consideration is the sign of what Jesus Christ is to the believer. The sign of what God in Jesus Christ is to men, that it has in it the presence, the blessing, the spirit, the refreshing, the presence of Christ which makes holy and the presence of God which sanctifies. It has in it the presence of Jesus Christ, and the man who keeps it by faith in Jesus has the presence of Jesus. And as each Sabbath day comes he finds additional presence of Jesus.

Then when that apostate church put that out of the way and put her own sign in its place, did she put only the day out of the way? [Voice: "She put Christ out of the way."] Was not that putting Jesus Christ away from the minds and lives of men? When the apostate daughters have done the same thing in our land, before our eyes, have not they by that put away the presence and the power of Christ and thus taken Him away from the knowledge of men and from the lives of men? [Congregation: "Yes."]

Now it seems to me that there is a point there that is worth our consideration, as to why it is that progress has not been made in Christian profession in the ages that are past, in the way Christ intended always that progress in Christian life should be made. What did He put into the life of man when He made him, even though he had remained faithful and never sinned, to carry him on in everlasting progress in the knowledge of God, in Himself – what did He put there? Let me ask it over again now. When God made man at the beginning, put him here upon the earth to live, if he had remained faithful forever and had never sinned, was there anything that God had put there and attached to him that would carry him on in an everlasting progress in the knowledge of God in his own heart's experience? [Voice: "The Sabbath."]

Didn't we read it last night over and over? Didn't He put Himself, His name, His living presence, His sanctifying power, into the Sabbath day, and give that to man, although He was already blessed, although He was already glorified, so that when the blessed man came to that blessed day, He received additional blessing? Is not that so? [Congregation: "Yes."] Then has not God put into the world something that will, if observed, if kept as God chooses and intends – be something that will keep man, carry him onward, in a channel of growth and progress in the knowledge of Jesus Christ, in himself? What is that? [Congregation: "the Sabbath."]

It is there since man fell. Now then, when the Church of Rome took the Sabbath away from the minds of men – that by which they might be brought to the recognition of Christ and to the converting power of Christ – was there anything there to carry them forward in the sanctifying work of Christ? That is the secret, then, you see, why each church, starting out in the knowledge of God, salvation by faith and righteousness by faith came to a stand-still; then another church had to rise up and reach righteousness by faith, salvation by faith, and come to a stand-still. And another one had to rise up and do the same thing and come to a stand-still. But when we came to this, the everlasting gospel is to be preached again, and a church is to rise up again at the last which has that sign which brings the presence of Jesus Christ to men in His living presence, in a progressive work unto a completion. That is the church that has the Sabbath of the Lord, and the church which has the Sabbath of the Lord is brought to that completed work in the salvation of Christ.

Then who can measure, who but the mind of God could possibly measure the iniquity and the evil that has been done to the world by that fearful thing that the apostate church has done? None but the mind of God can comprehend the mischief and the loss that has been wrought in the world by that thing.

Well, then, the effect of that was to take away the presence of Christ – take Christ away from the knowledge, the heart's experience, of men and to put another, to put a human power, a satanic power, to put *self,* in the place of God and in the place of Christ, Who emptied Himself that God might appear.

Now here is a historical parallel so apt and so perfect that I read it. First, mankind altogether, as men, without any church at all, are subject to God. Can they exist without Him? [Congregation: "No."] If any man by his own act could indeed become independent of God, could he exist? [Congregation: "No."] What did Satan start out to do in the first place? Was it not to become independent of God, self-existent? If he could have accomplished his purpose, what would it have been? [Voice: "His destruction."] Bound to be, because he could not exist without Him who created him, but in his wild ambition, in his intense all-absorbing selfishness, he thought he could live without God Who created him.

Is not that the same thought in this self-exaltation that has put itself in the place of God? Well, whether it be man as man, or men professedly as Christians organized into a church, they are equally dependent upon God and God in Jesus Christ, and they are subject to the law of God. The law of God is the supreme law. The law of God is the government of His whole universe, and everybody on the earth is subject to that law.

Now see the parallel: About two hundred and sixty years ago Ireland had Home Rule, as she is after it now. She had a Parliament of her own, governing her own internal affairs, the affairs of Ireland, but she was subject to the supreme government in England. Now I read from the fifth volume of Macaulay's History of England, page 301 of this particular edition, chapter 23, however, and if you have other editions you can find it in that chapter. Now notice:

> The Irish Lords and Commons had presumed not only to re-enact an English Act passed expressly for the purpose of binding them, but to re-enact it with alterations. The alterations were indeed small, but the alterations even of a letter was tantamount to a declaration of independence.

Now is the law of God enacted to bind the church as well as every other man? [Congregation: "Yes."] Has that apostate church presumed to alter that law? [Congregation: "Yes."] The alteration of it in a single letter would be what? [Voice: "A declaration of independence."] She has altered it more than a single letter, in the actual thought, in the very idea, in the very thing that reveals and brings the presence of God above every other part of the law. She has taken Him out of it. Then what has she done? [Congregation: "Put herself there."] She has established her own independence of God and proclaimed it to the world.

The Protestant churches – professedly Protestant, not Protestant any longer – the professed Protestant churches have drawn the Congress of the United States into the same identical position; they have drawn the Congress of the United States into a re-enactment of the fourth commandment, haven't they? [Congregation: "Yes."]

It was quoted bodily and put upon the statute book of legislation. Gov. Pattison, the other day, in Pennsylvania, speaking in the capitol of that State, arguing in behalf of Sunday laws that are already on the statute books, said that this law is only a part of that system of the law of God which is "*re-enacted*" in the statutes of Pennsylvania. He says that the law of God is there "re-enacted."

But did they re-enact the law of God as it is? [Congregation: "No."] To do that, to undertake to enforce it, would put themselves on an equality with God, but they re-enacted it with alterations, and that puts them above God. And the churches of this nation have proclaimed themselves independent of God, in the act which they have taken of setting up His own law and then deliberately altering it in the course of the legislation which set it up.

Let me read another sentence from Macaulay's History of England, from the same page as before:

> The colony in Ireland was therefore emphatically a dependency; a dependency, not merely by the common law of the realm, but by the nature of things. It was absurd to claim independence for a community which could not cease to be dependent without ceasing to exist.

Was there ever a more complete parallel on earth to illustrate in the place of government and government law this principle, than that which occurred there and was recorded for our instruction?

Now a thought. Jesus Christ came into the world Himself, didn't He? [Congregation: "Yes."] He made the Sabbath Himself, didn't He? [Congregation: "Yes."] He was Lord of the Sabbath Himself, wasn't He? [Congregation: "Yes."] He knew, and He alone, the true idea of the Sabbath, didn't He? [Congregation: "Yes."] Yet He did things on the Sabbath, carrying out the true idea of the Sabbath, which did not suit the ideas of the priests and Pharisees and the politicians of that day, didn't He? [Congregation: "Yes."] And that stirred up their hatred against Him. The thing that did stir up their hatred against Him was that very thing – that more than anything else He disregarded their ideas of the Sabbath. Isn't that so? [Congregation: "Yes."] And their hatred put Him out of the world for that reason more than any other under the sun, that He disagreed with their ideas of the Sabbath. They did it.

In the fourth century there was another apostate church disagreeing with God's idea of the Sabbath, and they put the Sabbath and Him with it out of their minds and out of the world as far as their power could go. The other put Him out of the world, but He came back again, and they put Him out only so far as their power was concerned; that is all.

Here is another apostate church, a third one, following the example of the other apostate two which have gone before. It has put Him in His Sabbath out of the world because their ideas of the Sabbath disagree with His, and they will not submit to His. That is a fact. You know that is a fact.

In order that that original apostate church might accomplish her purpose of putting Him out of the world and thus maintain their ideas of what the Sabbath is, they joined themselves to an earthly power. They joined themselves to Caesar and turned their backs upon God. That was done. In the second apostasy of the church, that she might accomplish her purpose of putting Him in His Sabbath out of the world, she joined herself to Caesar, likewise to accomplish her purpose. In the third apostasy, in order that these also may carry their idea of the Sabbath against Christ's idea of the Sabbath, they must put Him in His Sabbath out of their way. But in order to accomplish it they must join themselves again to the powers of earth, again to Caesar, as the others did before them.

In the first apostasy, when they joined themselves to Caesar in order to get rid of Him and sustain their own ideas of what the Sabbath is, against Him, the result of that, although it was accomplished by a mere minority, a very small minority – in fact so small that they did not dare to let the people know what they were about for fear they would rescue Him out of their hands entirely – that minority, small as it was, was composed most largely and was led entirely by leaders of the church, and these leaders of the church, by threats, compelled the representative of Caesar's authority, by their threats, to yield to their ideas and execute their will. You know they did it.

That is the record, and that was the utter ruin of that nation, wasn't it? [Congregation: "Yes."]

It is possible, then, is it, for a minority, a *very small* minority, led by even a minority of the church managers – but the leading ones – to take a course that will ruin the nation of which they are a part? [Congregation: "Yes."]

When we come to the second apostasy, they did the same things again by trading off their influence to worldly power and by this means get governmental power in their hands to accomplish their purpose of putting Christ in His Sabbath out of their way and maintaining their own ideas of the Sabbath against His.

That was done by the minority; it was done by chief leaders of the church and but a few at that. What was the result of that intrigue to the empire of Rome? It was its utter ruin. Then it is possible that a minority, a very small minority, insignificant, as compared with the great mass – led, though, by a few of the church prelates – I say it is possible for such a few as that to establish such a system of things and take a course and put the government into such a course of work as will prove its utter ruin. That has been demonstrated twice in history.

Then in this land, last year, before your eyes and mine, a minority of the people of this country, led by a few – a minority only of the church leaders – did, by threats, bring the politicians to surrender the power of government into their hands to accomplish their purpose of sustaining their ideas of the Sabbath against Christ's idea of the Sabbath. It has been demonstrated twice in history that such an act as this ruined the nation in which it was done. Does that double demonstration mean anything in the third instance? [Congregation: "Yes."] The lesson that is taught in both instances will be felt in the third instance. It *means that*. Ruin and nothing but ruin can come out of it. They themselves cannot prevent it. It cannot be done. They have set a-going a train of circumstances that nothing in the universe can stop. *That is fixed.*

Now this Congress is about to expire. It is altogether likely from the whole situation that it will expire without touching the question further. If the next Congress should repeal it outright, it would not affect the situation and the results. That thing has started and it will go on in spite of everything they can ever do. You and I need not be surprised that if it be not repealed by the next Congress, that it will be repealed some day and when that day comes, then let every Sabbath-keeper on the earth rise up with all the vigor that the Spirit of God can give him, cut loose from everything on earth, and put it into the cause of God. For in but a little while the tide will swing back and take all with it to ruin. You and I need not be surprised that that may come. When it comes, that will be the meaning of it.

But those who have not had an experience in the cause of God will mistake the meaning of it, and they will say to you, "We told you all the time that you were making too much out of that. There was nothing in it." And so, they will settle back, but when the tide swings back, they are caught in ruin. Let not your minds and your hearts be deceived by anything of that kind, even though it should come twice. You *believe* it. Believe what is being said here. Study it for your lives, for your lives are in it. Bear in mind that that which has been done means, in itself, exactly what these two previous lessons teach – it means ruin, though there might be the repeals once or twice. The tide is set, and the result of that follows, in spite of anything that the universe can do. Then, it is no difference what a man tells you, you tell him you know better. No difference if Congress undoes it. You tell them that that is the surest reason that the thing is that much nearer than ever, and put your whole soul into it. If he laughs at you, God has promised that the day will come that you will laugh and he will mourn. It is dangerous business.

Well then, these are *some* of the things. We will call your attention to other things at another time.

Now then the question as to whether the Sabbath – the seventh day – the Sabbath of the Lord is the day or Sunday is the day has considerable meaning in it. It means more than anyone on the earth has yet dreamed, unless taken personally into the counsels of God. Further than that, let us look at it. We have found that the Sabbath is the sign of the power of God in Jesus Christ, working the salvation of men. We have found that the Sabbath brings by itself and in itself the presence of Jesus Christ into the living experience of a man as nothing else can and keeps it there. That is a fact; if you have not found it out in your own experience, you believe it, and you *will* find it in your own experience. Everyone may know who will believe.

Well, then, we have found that the attempt in that was to take the Lord away from the knowledge of man. That has been demonstrated.

Now, upon that question, then, as to whether the seventh day is the Sabbath of the Lord or not, hangs man's salvation. That is settled. Upon that question hangs their salvation or their destruction *now*. There are instances of that kind.

Let us turn and read it, and with that thought we will close for this time. Acts 25:19, 20: "But had certain questions against him of their own superstition, and of one Jesus, which was dead, whom Paul affirmed to be alive. And because I doubted of such manner of questions, I asked him whether he would go to Jerusalem, and there be judged of these matters."

That was a great question to make such an uproar about, as to whether a man was dead or alive. Here the whole Jewish nation was stirred up against one of their own people and all the question that was involved was as to whether one was dead or alive. That is all that Festus saw in it. But you and I know that upon whether that person was dead or alive, depend the salvation or the perdition of this whole world. You know that is so. And the same thing is asked today. "What is the use of all this stir about whether it is Saturday or Sunday, about the keeping of the day. Why, it is only a day anyhow.

What is the use of getting up a new sect – a new denomination – and making a great stir? What is the use of making all that stir about it, whether Sunday is the Sabbath, or another day; whether we rest on one day or another? Never mind as to whether that day is the Sabbath or not."

Upon the decision of that by men as individuals and as bodies depends the salvation or the destruction of this earth today. That's settled. Whether that day is the Sabbath of the Lord or not, upon that hangs the salvation of men today as it did back there that day. Those people, in their envy against Christ and determination to maintain their own idea against God's idea – they got Him out of the world, and then they got up a controversy as to whether He was dead or alive, so these same people will put the Sabbath out of the world and then raise up a question as to whether it is the Sabbath or not.

They know well enough it is the Sabbath, but like those back there, they will maintain their own ideas of the Sabbath against God's idea, and though He has told them that He is Lord of the Sabbath, just as certainly as that was so in that question depended the salvation of men, just so certainly today on this question depends the salvation of men, because we can say boldly that the salvation of men does depend and does hang upon their keeping the Sabbath of the Lord because the keeping of the Sabbath of the Lord has the presence of Jesus Christ, His life, and man cannot be saved without it.

So I say again, we may boldly say that the salvation of a man depends upon his own observance of the Sabbath of the Lord as it is in Jesus Christ, for that means Jesus Christ. Jesus Christ means the Sabbath, and the Sabbath means Jesus Christ. In this day, when men are enlightened upon it, when the message of the everlasting gospel is to be preached to the world, when the third angel's message is to go to them with Christ in it and Christ the all and all of it then they also that reject the Sabbath of the Lord, they turn their backs upon Christ, and they themselves know that there is no salvation in that way.

But haven't we in our previous study seen that there is nothing else to preach to men in this world but Jesus Christ and Him alone? That is the only thing, and haven't we seen that we are to preach Him in the face of every earthly consideration, every consideration of protection of earthly powers, every consideration of wealth or influence of any kind and life itself? That is in the message to the world. Christ is the message to the world. Christ as made known in the Sabbath of the Lord, which is "a sign between me and you, that ye may know that I am the Lord your God," and My name is "I AM" what "I AM!"

Sermon 22

March 7, 1893

> ARISE, shine; for thy light is come, and the glory of the Lord is risen upon thee. For, behold, the darkness shall cover the earth and gross darkness the people, but the Lord shall arise upon thee, and his glory shall be seen upon thee. Isaiah 60:1,2.

A week ago tonight the text with which the lesson closed was this same one. And you remember the question was asked at the end of the reading of those scriptures which we were then studying, Is not this the time? Is it not now time for the fulfillment of this text which we have been reading, "Arise, shine; for thy light is come, and the glory of the Lord is risen upon thee"?

On Sunday following there came this word, and it was read in the Conference:

> Arise, shine, for thy light is come, and the glory of the Lord is risen upon thee. For, behold, the darkness shall cover the earth, and gross darkness the people: but the Lord shall arise upon thee, and his glory shall be seen upon thee.

This was the point which we had reached by a number of different lines of study and that is the point where we now stand. He who will claim that light and that glory by faith can have it. [Congregation: "Amen."] He who does not, cannot have it. I read a passage to you from Brother Prescott's talk the other night, on page 444 of the *Bulletin*. It is a word of caution and instruction which he gave us that is worth repeating:

> It is so easy for us to get wrong ideas about these things and in that way we ourselves be deceived about it. I have thought that some would have a wrong idea about what is meant when we say that we must go forth in the power of the Spirit, and that we must have power when we go forth.

So have I, and that has been done. But we had the caution over and over several times at the beginning of the Conference, against anyone setting any theory or fixing any thought as to how this thing that God had given, was to come. Because as certainly as we should think how it was going to come, that is the way it would not come. That is the one way in which it would not come at all. It would not come that way and could not possibly come that way.

> I do not understand that to mean that we are to come here to be consciously loaded up so that when we go from this place we have a certain feeling of a conscious power in our own selves that has been given to us and that we have it and carry it with us and can handle it, as it were, and measure it and look at it and when we need it take it out and use it.

I would not want to guarantee to you that nobody in this congregation had got that idea about it. I was especially pleased one morning in the ministers' meeting – those who were there will remember what I refer to – when one of the brethren got up and gave his testimony in regard to the manifestation of God's blessing and presence during the meetings of this Conference. He has jotted them down on paper in a long list. If every one of you had been marking the tokens of God's special favor in these meetings instead of looking for something you will never see, you would see vastly more than what you see now. I mean that we are not to have our ideas fixed that the Lord must work in a certain way and in that way look for something that will never come.

> All power is given unto me in heaven and in earth. Go ye therefore... Lo, I am with you.

The power is in Christ, *not in us,* and the *having the power* is the *personal presence of Christ* in us.

And when we have that personal presence of Christ in us and with us, the power is from Christ then and not from us.

Here is a thought: The apostles were not always able to work miracles at will.

> The Lord granted His servants this special power, as the progress of His cause or the honor of His name required. (*Sketches from the Life of Paul*, p. 135.)

A good many people think that when the apostles went out endued with the power to work miracles and all this, all they had to do when they came to a man who was sick was to work a miracle and restore him. There was nothing of that kind at all. They could work no miracle at all, except as the Spirit of Christ with them signified the will of God in that case. So that – I care not how great apostles they were – they were dependent upon the direct guidance of the Spirit of God in each individual case and all the time, and that means us.

"The power is the personal presence of Christ in us," and the having the power is that, "and that does not necessarily mean in the sense of a thrill of power in us all the time, but it means an abiding faith that Christ is in us," and it means not only an abiding belief in that but an abiding consciousness that He is there, that His power is there working in us, with us, for us, through us, always and in all things, to the glory of God alone, not at our bidding, not at our guidance in any sense.

> And then when we go out, no matter what the difficulties are we are not appalled by them, because of the conscious faith that Christ is with us and He is all-powerful. Well, when

> He is with us in the fullness of His power, our faith grasps Him continually. It is not a question of *feeling the power*; it is a question of *knowing* the power.

Now we have found in our study also that Christ redeemed us from the curse of the law in order that the blessing of Abraham might come upon us.

What do we find the blessing of Abraham to be? [Congregation: "Righteousness."] How? [Congregation: "By faith."] And Christ redeems us from the curse of the law that the righteousness which is by faith might come on the Gentiles, *i.e.*, on us, *that* we might receive the promise of the Spirit through faith. How did we receive the righteousness? [Congregation: "By faith."] Did you have a certain kind of whirl of feeling before you could receive that righteousness? [Congregation: "No."] Did you have a kind of whirl of feeling, a thrill or great commotion before you could know whether that righteousness was yours or not? [Congregation: "No."] How did you obtain the righteousness of God which is by faith of Jesus Christ? [Congregation: "By faith, and believing His word."] You know that God said to you and me in His word that that is a free gift to every man who believes in Jesus, do you not? And then you accepted that free gift, and thank God that His righteousness is your own; that is how you obtain it, and that is faith. Now, that was received and can only be received ever by faith alone.

That is received by faith in order that something else may be received by faith. What is that? [Congregation: "The promise of the Spirit."] Then, as we found that the righteousness of God upon His people is the one thing, the only then, the all in all, the fitting up of the people for receiving the promise of the Holy Spirit, and the outpouring of it, at God's own will – as we have found that that is so and that is received by faith, then in order to receive the other at all, it must be received exactly as that was received, that is *by faith*. Then, when God tells you and me – having given us His righteousness and we having received it gladly have therefore accepted it in its fullness by faith as God intends us to receive it and it is made our own by Jesus Christ bringing it to us – then when God tells you and me: "Arise, shine, for thy light is come, and the glory of God is risen upon thee," and when you and I do as God says, and arise *by faith* in Him, *He* will see that we shine. [Congregation: "Amen."] When He tells you and me that His glory is risen upon you and me which is by faith of Jesus Christ, then you and I are to thank Him that His glory *is risen upon you and me*. Thank Him that that is so and take our stand deliberately, fairly, openly, and candidly and honestly before God, under the canopy of angels of God and His glory which He gives, and then if He does not see that we shine, that is His fault. We need not doubt but what He will see to that.

Now, that message: "Arise, shine, for thy light is come, and the glory of the Lord is risen upon thee," is as certainly and as distinctly the message of God to you and me and through you and me as ministers to the people from this day henceforth, as was that message four years ago of the righteousness of God which is by faith alone in Jesus Christ. [Congregation: "Amen."] [The speaker upon request, restated the last proposition.] And the people of today who reject this message, which is now the message of today, as they rejected and slighted that four years ago are taking the step which will leave them everlastingly behind and which involves their whole salvation.

God has given us a message and has borne with us these four years in order that we might receive this which is now the message. Those who cannot receive that message are not prepared to receive this message, because they rejected that. And now when God gives the other in special measure in order that this may be received and both together are slighted, then what can become of those blind eyes? What can become of them!

So as we have been called upon to state several times during the Institute and this work, It is a fearful time. Each meeting is a fearful thing. But, brethren, though that has been so in the time that is past and of the meetings that are past, this meeting tonight is the most fearful one that we have yet come into.

So I turn again to the text and I say again that the message there given to us is the message for you and me to carry from this meeting. And anyone who cannot carry that message with him from this meeting had better not go. Anyone who cannot go from this meeting with the living consciousness of the presence of Jesus Christ in its power, with His light and His glory upon him and in his life, that minister had better not leave this place as a minister or as a professed minister, because he goes to a work that he cannot do. He goes to meet a people whom he cannot meet. He goes to meet responsibilities that he cannot meet. He goes to meet solemn scenes that he will not understand. He goes to take steps that he knows not which of the next ones will be to him a fearful one. That is where we are now, brethren and sisters.

It is for us now to face it and face it *joyously,* too. It is for us to face it, I say, in all its solemn responsibilities; to face it with all its fearful consequences. But we are to be so prepared by faith in Jesus Christ and clothed with His own righteousness alone and depending upon that alone – so prepared by this to face it, that we can face it with joy, with the confidence that God goes with us and desires to manifest His power and go joyfully and gladly to meet the scenes that are to be met, to take up the work that is to be taken up, and to meet the solemn responsibilities and scenes and actions and occurrences that will come, always gladly in the Lord.

That is for us. We need not be a particle discouraged because this is so. We ought to be the gladdest that we ever were in this world that we are there tonight. [Congregation: "Amen."]

Let me read that text again to get another thought out of it: "Arise, shine, for thy light is come and the glory of the Lord is risen upon thee. For, behold the darkness shall cover the earth and gross darkness the people, but the Lord shall arise upon thee and his glory. . ." *Thou shalt see* upon *thyself?* His glory *ye shall see in yourself* and upon *yourself?* [Congregation: "No! No!"] "His glory *shall be seen* upon thee." Let it.

Do not go about superintending that thing. That is none of your business. You are not to regard that matter at all. If it is the glory of the Lord, He will take care that it is seen upon you. You would not know that it was the glory of God if you should see it upon yourself, because it is not self-glory. When I see glory upon myself there will be self-glorification. Don't you see? It is not self-glory that we are seeking. It is not self-glory that God is going to manifest to the world. It is the glory of God that He is going to manifest. It is that glory that is going to be seen.

Therefore it says what it means and means what it says. "*His glory shall be seen upon thee.*" Thank Him that it is so, for He says so. Thank Him that He says so. Then thank Him that it is so *because* He says so. Then let Him do it. You have nothing to do with superintending that at all, just keep yourself out of it. He who undertakes that will lose the whole thing. Don't you see it is the same heart work there?

We want righteousness but so many people want to see it in themselves and upon themselves before they will believe that they have it. But don't you see that they will never get it in that way? They never will get it until they put self out of the way, until they turn their backs upon themselves and look at His word. Then when we turn our backs upon ourselves and look upon Him whose this glory is and in whom it is – when we look to the place where this glory is, then each one will know from that time that it is his so long as he looks to the place where it is. "We all with open face beholding as in a mirror the glory of the Lord, are changed into the same image from glory" to what? [Congregation: "To glory."] Has His glory appeared to us? [Congregation: "Yes."] *Has* it? [Congregation: Yes."]

Let me read that blessed text in 2 Corinthians: "God who commands the light to shine out of darkness." He did it once, didn't He? [Congregation: "Yes."] He has done it again. Darkness covered the earth; gross darkness. God commanded the light to shine and it did shine. Again He says, "Darkness shall cover the earth and gross darkness the people, but the Lord shall arise upon thee and his glory shall be seen upon thee." His light shall be seen upon thee, and therefore He says: "Arise, shine, thy light is come." Again, He has commanded the light to shine out of darkness. [Congregation: "Amen."] Is that not so? [Congregation: Yes."] He *hath* shined in our hearts." Well, then, He has done it, has He not? Are you saying that? [Congregation: "Yes."] I do not mean that you shall say that merely because it is in the text, but I want you to say it because in your heart you know it is so. By that yielding of the will, that submission of the will, that laying all upon Him – that is faith.

Well then, He says so. Now we can go on with this text: "God, who commanded the light to shine out of darkness, has shined in our hearts." Has He? [Congregation: "Amen."] Now can you thank Him that He has? [Congregation: "Yes."] Anyone who can thank God that God has shined in His heart, thanks Him from the heart; *he* can thank God that he does stand there by faith. He can do this just as certainly as he can thank the Lord that His righteousness is his own.

Let us read some more of that verse: "God who commanded the light to shine out of darkness, hath shined in our hearts." Thank the Lord. What is it for? "To give the light of the knowledge of the glory of God." Has He given you the light of the knowledge of His glory? [Congregation: "Yes."] *Has* He? [Congregation: "Yes."] Has not His glory arisen for you and me? Has not His glory then arisen for and upon each one of us and is each of our hearts? Has the light not shined as God commanded it to shine?

We will continue the text: "God who commanded the light to shine out of darkness, hath shined in our hearts to give the light of the knowledge of the glory of God *in the face of Jesus Christ.*" Then the man who can look with open face into the face of Jesus Christ, who can thank God with His whole heart that the glory of God is risen upon him, then God will see to it that that glory shall be seen upon him. Brethren, that is so, and O, that every heart in the house tonight might lift his face, unveiled, to that glorious face that shines so gloriously and graciously upon the sons of men and hath saved us from our sins and transformed us from glory to glory into His image – from glory to glory even as by the Spirit of the Lord.

Then that Spirit *has come* to those who can look into the face of Jesus Christ. And that Holy Spirit which God gives to those who look into the face of Christ will transform us into His own image and we shall see His glory reflected and men will see His glory too. Brethren, it is so, and tonight we must receive the promise of the Spirit through faith.

Moses was with the Lord that time in the mount, and when he came down his face shone with the glory of God. How much did *he* know about it? Nothing at all. "Moses wist not that the skin of his face shone." He did not know anything about it; the people knew about it. Did these people who saw the glory on Moses' face have faith? [Congregation: "No."] Moses had faith in order that it might shine. The faith of Moses received it in order that it might shine, and when it did shine from his face, though he was unconscious of it, even the unbelieving people could see it.

Stephen stood before the Sanhedrin – men whose hearts were steeled against God and against His Christ – but his face shone with the glory of God as it had been the face of an angel, and all they that stood in the council looked upon him and saw it. Did Stephen know it? No. It was not Stephen's glory. He had nothing to do with it. God was there in that presence, because that Stephen had such faith in Jesus Christ and was looking with unveiled heart with unveiled face by faith into the face of Jesus Christ and when he did that the glory of the Lord was risen upon him and the heathen and the worse than heathen – the wicked Pharisees – could see the glory of God upon him.

We have found in our study that the work today stands exactly as it did where the apostles left it. Well then when that promise of the Spirit came upon the people in that day, God manifested His own power, in His own way, at His own will, upon those who were His. That is the way He will do it again.

Let us read that verse again now. "God who commanded the light to shine out of darkness, hath shined in our hearts." Don't forget it. Well, how *can* we forget it. It is so, is it not? "To give the light of the knowledge of the glory of God in the face of Jesus Christ." Then we found in the lesson last Friday night that we were to obtain the righteousness of God which is by faith of Jesus Christ, by looking into the face of Jesus, and while we look there, receiving that righteousness more and more, being molded more and more into His image, the law of God stands there in all its glory witnessing that that is the way to look. We found that that was the occupation of the angels also in heaven. "Their angels do always behold the face of my Father who is in heaven." Well, then, brethren, when we go into the company of angels, looking where they look, to receive what they are looking there to receive, and the law witnesses that it is our own, then why shall not that blessed canopy cover us? And that is the covering of God drawn over His people. So then the requisite to this is the faith that lifts up the face to the face of Jesus, and it is not because of our goodness but because of our *need*.

[By permission of the speaker, Prof. Prescott read the following:]

> The hand of the Infinite is stretched over the battlements of heaven to grasp your hand in its embrace. The mighty Helper is nigh to help the most erring, the most sinful and despairing. Look up by faith, and the light of the glory of God will shine upon you.

Elder Jones: I did not know that that was there, but brethren, we can be thankful that the Spirit of God guides us to it here. And do not forget this passage that we have been wanting to get to so long and now it comes in just exactly: "Now the righteousness of God without the law is manifested. . . Even the righteousness of God which is by faith of Jesus Christ unto all and upon all them that believe. For there is no difference. For all have sinned and come short of the glory of God."

We have studied this before – that the righteousness of God without the law is manifested by the law. There is another phrase: "Being witnessed by the law *and the prophets*." Do not forget for a moment or fail to remember always that where the righteousness of God is, which is obtained by faith of Jesus Christ, *the prophets of God* will stand in that place and witness to that man that he has it. [Congregation: "Amen!"] That means at this time, for he is coming to us now. So, I am glad that the Spirit of God has led us to it in His way and His prophet stands and witnesses that that is true and that we have the truth in that thing as it is in Jesus Christ and as shining from His holy face. [By request the quotation was read again.]

Then, brethren, look up. Then, when we see the signs in the sun, moon, and stars, and upon earth distress of nations, then *look up*; lift up your heads. Rejoice, for your redemption draweth nigh. *Look up*, because that comes alone by looking up in the face of Him that has said it. We *need* to look up, for that brings the righteousness, the glory of Jesus Christ, and it is that glory which makes us immortal. But it is the same glory that *consumes*. We are to look up. He wants us to look up in order to receive it. And He wants us to look up before that great day in order that we may look up in that day.

Now, the Lord wants us to look up and He tells us what it is for. Look up and reach up the hand by faith, and He will take it. Then let Him. Then when God takes that hand of faith, He will hold you and me more securely than we could possibly hold Him if *we* took *His* hand. You see, it is the same way as we many times lead our own little children along. *We* hold *their* hand, and when they stumble, they do not fall. At other times we have been walking along, and *they* have had *our* hand; then they have stumbled and fallen. Thank the Lord, He says, "*I* will take *your* hand." Then, though we stumble, we shall not be cast down. [Congregation: "Praise the Lord!"] Oh, God is good.

[By request the following text was read: "For the Lord thy God will hold thy right hand, saying unto thee, Fear not; I will help thee." Isaiah 41:13.] When He says, "I will hold your right hand," Oh, let Him have it. Then you have no uneasiness at all.

"God, who commanded the light to shine out of darkness, hath shined in our hearts, to give the light of the knowledge of the glory of God in the face of Jesus Christ." In connection with that I will read: "But we all, with open face beholding as in a glass the glory of the Lord, are changed into the same image from glory to glory, even as by the Spirit of the Lord." What is His glory? Let us be sure of that. Here is a message which we had some time ago, to which I will refer you, on page 16 of the Bulletin:

> The work will be cut short in righteousness. The message of Christ's righteousness is to sound from one end of the world to the other. This is the glory of God which closes the work of the third angel.

Then that glory is that righteousness, that goodness, that character, of His own. Where then do we see righteousness alone? [Congregation: "In the face of Jesus Christ."] As we look at that, what effect has it upon us? It changes us into the same image – transforms us into the same image from righteousness to righteousness, from glory to glory, from character to character, even as by the Spirit of the Lord.

Well, arise, and shine, because the light has come. That is the Lord's command. That is why I said before – that is the message from this day henceforth as certainly as it is received. It is that to us. It is in fact the same thing, as certainly as it was four years ago, only with increased splendor, with increased power. Now, with the accumulated force of four years' exercise, God puts it forth to His people. The proposition is again: Arise, shine, for thy light is come, and the glory of the Lord is risen upon thee. Who will? Who will? [Numerous voices: "I will."] Good! Do it. How long will you? [Voices: "Always."] How constantly will you? How often will you? [Voices: "Always."]

I tell you brethren and sisters, those who will do this will find in their lives a subduing power such as they never knew before. It will bring that poverty of spirit and that humiliation of soul which will give the Spirit a chance to work in His own wonderful way. That is where we are. Well then, Arise and shine, because the light *has* come, and the glory of the Lord *hath risen upon thee.*

I will read from page 137 of the Bulletin:

> To him who is content to receive without deserving, who feels that he can never recompense such love, lays all thoughts and unbelief aside and comes as a little child at the feet of Jesus, all the treasures of eternal love are the free and everlasting gift.

All these treasures are a free and everlasting gift to us who have nothing with which to obtain it. The Lord says they are mine. I know they are mine too, for He says so. And I am going to thank Him all the time. Now there is another splendid text which we must read, that speaks to us now. Isaiah 52:1: "Awake, awake." We have been asleep, have we not? You know that we have. "Awake, awake; put on thy strength, O Zion." Put on what? Strength. We have found by examining the situation in which we stand that we need a power, we need a strength that is greater than all the power that this world knows put together. We have found that we need strength, have we not? [Congregation: "Yes."] Then we need it for this message just now. Put on your strength; you have got it. "Put on thy strength, O Zion; put on thy beautiful garments, O Jerusalem." What are the beautiful garments? [Congregation: "Righteousness."] The fine linen is the righteousness of the saints. "To her was granted that she should be arrayed in fine linen, clean and white: for the fine linen is the righteousness of saints." This is the righteousness which comes by faith in Jesus Christ. And here likewise is a word which the Lord addressed to us in this Conference. In the Bulletin, page 408, I read:

> At this time the church is to put on her beautiful garments – "Christ our righteousness."

Well then, there it is: "Put on thy beautiful garments, O Jerusalem, the holy city." What is she putting on her garments for? Where is she going? O, she is going home; she is going to the wedding supper, thank the Lord, and the people who went to the wedding suppers in those times had to have garments that were prepared by the master of the feast, and the Lord does the same thing now. [Congregation: "Amen."] Brethren, let us all thank the Lord; let us be thankful all the time. But that is only a part of it. Here is the most blessed promise it seems to me, that ever came to the Seventh-day Adventist church. "For henceforth there shall no more come into thee, the uncircumcised and the unclean." Thank the Lord. He has delivered us henceforth from unconverted people, from people brought into the church to work out their own unrighteousness and to create division in the church. Church trials are all gone; thank the Lord. All mischievous talebearers and tattlers are gone. The church now has something better than that to talk about. They can now talk of saving fallen men and women. They will have a goodness and a joy, and a holiness and a glory that is in Jesus Christ, to talk about, which is real indeed, and we know it.

That is a splendid promise. And do you not see how alone it can be fulfilled? When we go forth from this place, knowing nothing at all but Jesus Christ and Him crucified, refusing to know anything but that, refusing to preach anything but that, depending upon His power, depending upon His glory, knowing that it is come and that He has commanded us to shine, then it can be fulfilled. Do you not see that nobody will be drawn to that except those who are drawn from the heart and in whom the heart is converted? Do you not see that you yourself will know that they are converted before they are taken into the church? "No more shall come into thee the uncircumcised and the unclean."

Brethren, there is another thing that belongs there now. When God has graced His church with His power and His glory and the power of His Spirit, the most dangerous place in this world for a hypocrite to be in is that church. Ananias and Sapphira tried it, and that lesson was recorded as a lesson to all people, from this day forward, at least. There is no place now in the Seventh-day Adventist church for hypocrites. If the heart is not sincere, it is the most dangerous place that that man ever was in in the world.

Then, those who are not going along with this work had better get out quick. It is dangerous to stay here if you are not going along, and we cannot go along without having the glory of God and His light shining in the heart and in the life. We are to be called to stand before kings and before authorities and to speak against the oppressions and the wickedness of persecutors carrying out their venom against those who would love the Lord. "Awake, awake. Put on thy strength, O Zion; put on thy beautiful garments, O Jerusalem, the holy city, for henceforth there shall no more come into thee the uncircumcised and the unclean. Shake thyself from the dust. Arise, and sit down, O Jerusalem: loose thyself from the bands of they neck, O captive daughter of Zion."

Liberty is now proclaimed to the captives. Praise the Lord. "The Spirit of the Lord is upon me, because the Lord hath anointed me to bind up the broken-hearted, to proclaim liberty to the captives, and the opening of the prison to them that are bound, to preach the acceptable year of the Lord, and the day of vengeance of our God: to comfort all that mourn; to appoint unto them that mourn in Zion, to give unto them beauty for ashes, the oil of joy for mourning, the garment of praise for the spirit of heaviness; that they might be called trees of righteousness, the planting of the Lord, that he might be glorified." "Shake thyself from the dust; arise and sit down O Jerusalem: loose thyself from the bands of thy neck, O captive daughter of Zion. For thus saith the Lord, Ye have sold yourselves for nought, and ye shall be redeemed without money." Good, that is accomplished.

"For thus saith the Lord God, My people went down aforetime into Egypt to sojourn there, and the Assyrian oppressed them without cause." Then what did He do? [Congregation: "Delivered them."] Exactly. Then when does this apply? At the time of deliverance. Then we have reached that time, have we not? We have reached the time of oppression, and when that time of oppression has come, then the time of God's wondrous deliverance has come too. So let the oppression become more severe; let the fire become hotter. It only shows that deliverance is that much nearer. Thank the Lord.

"Now therefore, what have I here, saith the Lord, that my people is taken away for nought? They that rule over them make them to howl, saith the Lord; and my name continually every day is blasphemed." That is so. They have done it already. "Therefore my people shall know my name." What is His name? I AM that I AM. They will not only know *about* Him. They will know that *He is what He is* too, and He is the Almighty. And His people, knowing His name – the All-powerful One – will know His power manifested in them, for them, to them and through them.

"Therefore my people shall know my name; therefore, they shall know in that day that I am he that doth thus speak. Behold it is I." I am the one that is talking now. Good. Then what? "How beautiful upon the mountains are the feet of him that bringeth good tidings, that publisheth peace; that bringeth good tidings of good, that publisheth salvation; that saith unto Zion, *Thy God reigneth!*" Let kings and powers and governors and States – let them exalt themselves as much as they please. God has given you and me a message to the people – "*Thy God reigneth.*" "Thy watchman shall lift up the voice, with the voice together shall they sing." Why, of course, He said long ago we should sing as we go on the way to Zion. "For they shall see eye to eye, when the Lord shall bring again Zion." Brethren, while we look into the face of Jesus Christ and that light shines into our minds and hearts, we need have no trouble at all in seeing eye to eye, even though you are on the other side of the earth and I on this side. There will be that companionship of ideas and truth that will bind our hearts through the center of the earth. God is in it, and that is why it is so. God can make it so. There is no other power in the universe that can make it so.

"Break forth into joy." Why not, I would like to know? We need not have a special meeting to break forth into joy; it is not necessary to jump up and down and kick over the benches and chairs. It is the joy of the Lord and not fanaticism. It is not a feeling that is wrought up by such demonstrations.

"Break forth into joy, sing together, ye waste places of Jerusalem: for the Lord hath comforted his people; he hath redeemed Jerusalem." The Lord hath comforted His people. He has done it, hasn't He? Well, then, let us praise the Lord for His comfort. "The Lord hath made bare his holy arm." *He* is going to do something now. When a man has something to do and begins to roll up his sleeves, you know he means business. The Lord has taken that familiar figure to show the earnest work He has undertaken and that applies right now. He has made bare His holy arm – hath rolled up His sleeves – He is entering into a work now that will create a sensation, as in the days of Samuel when he said to Eli, "He will do a thing in Israel at which both the ears of everyone that heareth it shall tingle." Let us see that our ears tingle with joy. "The Lord hath made bare his holy arm in the eyes of all the nations: and all the ends of the earth shall see the salvation of our God." Let them; let them.

"Depart ye, depart ye, go ye out from thence." That means cut loose from this world, does it not? Are you cutting loose? Have you departed? Have you bidden farewell to earth? [Congregation: "Yes."] Is the world under your feet? [Congregation: "Yes."] Not only is it under your feet but is it stamped under your feet? I know and you know that when we separate ourselves from all things of this world, God can and does give you and me the consciousness of something that is better than all this world put together.

"Touch no unclean thing." That is the same word as that used in 2 Corinthians: "Wherefore come out from among them and be ye separate, saith the Lord, and touch not the unclean thing, and I will receive you, and will be a Father unto you, and ye shall be my sons and daughters, saith the Lord Almighty." "Be ye clean that bear the vessels of the Lord. For ye shall not go out with haste nor go by flight." No, we are not going to be scared or afraid of anything. "He that believeth shall not make haste." He is in no hurry. The Lord never gets in a hurry, but He can take His own good time and lots of it too. He that believeth shall not make haste. Another translation has it, "shall not be ashamed," another, "shall not be confounded," or not easily be put off his balance. And by the way, you will find yourself called to places where there will come a perfect storm of voices and tongues from twenty different sides. Then you do not want to get in a hurry or get off your balance. Then is the time when you are not to be frightened and run away. Oh, no! He has put us in the world to stay here just as long as He wants us here. "Ye shall not go out with haste, nor go by flight: for the Lord will go before you; and the God of Israel will be your rereward." Good. He is the vanguard and the rearguard. He is the advance guard and the rear guard also. That is good company to be in.

Brethren, that is the message now. That is the message that you and I are to carry from this place, and he who cannot carry it should not go. Oh, *do not go*. As we have been exhorted by the Spirit of the Lord in this place, let no one go without the consciousness of that abiding presence power of the Spirit of God. No one *need* go without it. For it is *obtained* and *kept* by faith in Him, into whose face we look, in order that we may receive by faith the righteousness of Jesus, that we may be prepared to receive and do receive the Spirit of God by faith.

Sermon 23

March 26, 1893

I wish we had six weeks in which to study the third angel's message now. [Congregation: "Amen."] I mean six weeks together; of course, we all have more than that separately. What I meant was that we might have six weeks together. Then we could begin to get a pretty good outline of the message for this time. But, keeping what the Lord has given us and going from here with that, all that remains is to study the message and preach it and it will grow as we do. And we will all see alike, if we keep what we have received here and preach that.

The time is so near past, though, now, and there is so much to be said before we separate, that about all we can do tonight is to touch just a few points that lead out from where we are, in lines that we need to follow and which will be our guide henceforth.

Let us turn to the 13th chapter of Revelation to begin with this evening, and study that passage of Scripture that refers to the United States and see if we may know where in the prophecy the working of this power comes in to deceive "them that dwell on the earth, by the means of those miracles which he had power to do in the sight of the beast." I know that a good many are losing sight of what has been done by looking for something that they had decided must be done first, and while looking for that which they had decided must be done and neglecting to use that which has been done, they will still go on, getting further and further from the light, still less and less prepared to meet any of these things, whether they have come, or whether they are yet to come.

Now, in the 13th and 14th verses is the statement of prophecy about the working of that power: "And he doeth great wonders, so that he maketh fire come down from heaven on earth in the sight of men, and deceiveth them that dwell on the earth by the means of those miracles which he had power to do in the sight of the beast, saying to them that dwell on the earth that they should make an image to the beast, which had the wound by a sword, and did live."

From the connection in which this is placed, a good many have been writing to me and saying that all these things must come to pass before the image is made; that these workings and wonderful manifestations are the workings of spiritualism and are to persuade the people *to make* an image of the beast. It is important therefore for us to study the prophecy and see what it *says* and as much as possible, what it does *not* say.

Let us now begin with the eleventh verse of the thirteenth chapter: "And I beheld another beast coming up out of the earth; and he had two horns like a lamb, and he spake as a dragon." When did he speak as a dragon? When he was coming up? [Congregation: "No."] When is it that he speaks as a dragon? Read the fifteenth verse: "And he had power to give life unto the image of the beast, *that the image* of the beast *should both speak* and *cause* that as many as would not worship the image of the beast should be killed." That is when he speaks as a dragon, is it? [Congregation: "Yes."] Isn't it the image of the beast that speaks as a dragon? [Congregation: "Yes."] was the image of the beast made, when he was seen coming up? [Congregation: "No."] When this beast was seen coming up out of the earth, was the image of the beast made? [Congregation: "No."] Was he then speaking as a dragon? [Congregation: "No."] Then all of that verse does not apply in the place where it is printed. That you may see this a little more plainly, turn to Testimony 32, page 208. This was printed in 1885:

> The Sunday movement is now making its way in darkness. The leaders are concealing the true issue, and many who unite in the movement do not themselves see whither the current is tending. Its professions are mild, and apparently Christian.

Has that any reference to the two horns like a lamb? [Congregation: "Yes."]

> Its professions are mild and apparently Christian, but *when it shall speak,* it will reveal the spirit of the dragon.

"When it *shall* speak." That was written in 1885; he had not yet spoken. Is that correct? [Congregation: "Yes."] When was he seen coming up? [Congregation: "In 1798."] "He had two horns like a lamb," when he was seen coming up and has had them all the time. Is that so? [Congregation: "Yes."] "Its professions are mild and apparently Christian." But there is the prophecy – "He spake as a dragon." And we have found by the connection that it is *the image* that speaks and causeth that as many as will not worship the image of the beast shall be killed. That is the dragon voice. But, "when it shall speak, it will reveal the spirit of the dragon."

Then, I say again, that that eleventh verse is not all fulfilled in the place where it stands in the prophecy and in the order in which the things that it mentions are mentioned in the prophecy. The last expression of the eleventh verse is not fulfilled until we reach the fifteenth verse.

Let us read on. Twelfth verse: "And he exerciseth all the power of the first beast before him, and causeth the earth and them which dwell therein to worship the beast, whose deadly wound was healed." Now, has this beast that was seen coming up out of the earth been exercising as yet all the power that the first beast before him did? [Congregation: "No."] Has he compelled them that dwell on the earth to worship the first beast? [Congregation: "No."] Is that verse, then, that 12th verse, fulfilled until the time of the 15th verse? [Congregation: "No."] Until the time after the image is made? [Congregation: "Yes."]

Then those two verses of the prophecy are manifestly not fulfilled in the order in which the statements are set down. Is that so? [Congregation: "Yes."]

The thirteenth verse: "and he doeth great wonders, so that he maketh fire to come down from heaven on the earth in the sight of men." Is that fulfilled before the image of the beast is made? [Congregation: "No."] We all know, who have read "Vol. IV," that that is one of the last things that is ever done before Satan comes himself, personally. You who have read "Vol. IV" know that, and you who have not read it, just read it and you will see that the making of fire to come down from heaven is one of the last things that is done before Satan appears personally, if not the last in fact. Vol. IV does not say positively that this will be wrought before Satan appears personally or after, but taking the most extreme view possible of it, it is amongst those things that are carried on when the very powers of the satanic agencies are exerted to their full extent, to deceive, if possible, the very elect. This miracle is wrought to prove to the children of God that they are wrong in keeping the Sabbath. This miracle is wrought as a deciding test, and it will be one of the very last things before the decree goes forth to put people to death; if not the very last before that, it will be one of the last. The contest will be between the powers of the earth and the Lord, between those who yield and obey the powers of the earth and those who obey the Lord.

Now, are these miracles all wrought openly and above-board, distinctly *as against the Lord?* Is that what they pretend to do? [Congregation: "No."] Are they wrought by those who openly and professedly deny Jesus Christ? [Congregation: "No."] Who then? Those who profess themselves to be Christ. "False Christs will arise and shall show great signs and wonders." This will be done by those who themselves profess that they are representatives of Jesus Christ and that Christ is with them and that God is the God of that side of the question. But it will be denied and it will be known that it is not so by those who know the Lord. But this challenge will be made. There was a contest once as to whether the Lord was God or whether the sun was god – Baal. The test which decided that day amongst the people that Elijah was a man of God and that God was the true God and not the sun – not Baal – that test was, fire came down from heaven.

Now that test comes again, but this time it will be done to deceive, and it will be done by those who claim now to be Baal's or rather those who are really Baal's servants, but profess that Baal is god, which is Satan, of course. And they will present that challenge to you and me: "Now, you say that the Bible is the word of God. You stand on that?" "Yes, sir." "You say that God is your God?" "Yes, sir." "And that the Sabbath ought to be kept because that is the sign of what God is to man and what Christ is to man?" "Yes, sir, that is the position exactly." "Now, a test was put once before which decided this question. That was that fire came down from heaven. That decided there that the

Lord was the true God. Now we offer you, upon your own proposition today the same challenge. We say to you that we challenge you to this decision; we give you an open, fair challenge; we say to you now: "If we are the men of God, if God is our God and not yours, if we are men of God, let fire come down from heaven upon the earth."

And what then? Fire comes. "He doeth great wonders so that he maketh fire come down from heaven on the earth in the sight of men." Men will see it and it is done to decide this question – to decide that they are the people of God, that they are men of God. And when the true people of God say that that is not the test, that that does not prove anything, then you see, they will say, "Well, you go back on your own evidences. You say you believe the Bible; you say that is your foundation and you agree that that decided this question once." "Yes, sir." But now, when we do the same thing you deny that that is any decision at all. What is the use of reasoning any more with such men as that? They all go back on the plainest evidence that they themselves say that they stand upon. What more should be done but to kill such people as that? You can't reason with them any more and the fate of the world, the plagues and pestilences and all these things are coming upon the people on account of your craze, because you will not surrender or yield; you are stubborn; you will have it your own way anyway. Now in order to save people whose lives are precious, the only thing we can do is to put you out of the way." So, we say, and you will see by reading, that that is not done before the image of the beast is made; it is after that, that it comes.

Brethren, it is not only time for every one of us to read Vol. IV but to read it over and over and to know the situation of things as they are. It is time to read it and we cannot afford not to read it.

So then the three verses which we have read you yourselves see they are not fulfilled in the order in which the statements are set down.

Now let us read on: "And he deceiveth them that dwell on the earth by the means of those miracles which he had power to do in the sight of the beast." Let us read another passage now in the 19th chapter of Revelation, referring to the coming of the Lord, 19th and 20th verses. "And I saw the beast, and the kings of the earth, and their armies, gathered together to make war against him that sat on the horse, and against his army. And the beast was taken and with him *the false prophet* that *wrought miracles* before him, *with which he deceived them* that *had received* the mark of the beast and them *that worshipped* his image."

Someone told me the other day about another translation, speaking of that – I do not know whether it is the Revised Version or some other – that reads, "the false prophet that wrought miracles before him, with which he deceived them that *had received* the mark of the beast and them that *had worshipped* the image."

[*Elder D. T. Bourdeau*: "So reads the French."]

Elder Jones: The same thought is in this. That shows then that the miracles, the deceiving miracles that are wrought are done to deceive them that had the mark of the beast. But do men receive the mark of the beast before the image is made? Under the message and the responsibility which the message brings are men held responsible for receiving the mark of the beast and worshiping the beast before the image comes on and undertakes to compel them to do it? No, because we found in our lessons here that until the image was made there was a way of escape from the worship of the beast. The way was open for a man to refuse, but *after the image is made* there is no way open for a man to refuse to worship the beast, because there is no place on the earth where the power of the beast is not found; consequently, after that comes there is no escape any more, and then it is that men become responsible for worshiping either the beast or his image. There is no other way of escape. The only way is to turn to God then. Then the time comes that the decision is clear cut and must be made between God and the powers of the earth alone.

Again, read the 16th chapter of Revelation. There the plagues, you know, are threatened to come upon the people because of worshiping the beast and his image. Under the sixth plague, we read verses 13 and 14: "And I saw three unclean spirits like frogs come out of the mouth of the dragon and out of the mouth of the beast and out of the mouth of."

What? Doesn't it read this way: "I saw three unclean spirits like frogs come out of the mouth of the dragon, and out of the mouth of the beast, and deceived people *into making* the false prophet? [Congregation: "No."] What is the false prophet, in other words? [Congregation: "The two horned beast."] The image of the beast is the false prophet, because that verse in the 19th chapter tells it: "And I saw the beast and the kings of the earth, and their armies, gathered together to make war against him that sat on the horse, and against his army. And the beast was taken, and *with him the false prophet* that wrought miracles before him, with which he deceived them that received the mark of the beast, and them that worshiped his image." In the 13th chapter, we read, "He exerciseth all the power of the first beast before him [in his sight] and causeth the earth and them which dwell therein to worship the first beast, whose deadly wound was healed." Then what is the false prophet? The image of the beast.

Now then these spirits, they are the spirits of devils. The next verse (Revelation 16:14) says, "For they are the spirits of devils, working miracles, which go forth unto the kings of the earth and of the whole world, to gather them to the battle of that great day of God Almighty."

But these spirits of devils working miracles come from where? They come from certain places *to do* these miracles. That is the truth, isn't it? And they come from those places, to gather the people to the battle of the great day of God Almighty. These spirits of devils come at that time with this miracle-working power, in this miracle-working power, in this miracle working way, to do a certain thing. Where do they come from? the beast and the false prophet (or the image of the beast). Then, from those testimonies and from those two verses, isn't it plain that the deceiving miracles – the great miracles that are wrought to deceive men come *after the image is made* and not *to make* the image? [Congregation: "Yes."]

Well, let us see whether we are right. *Testimony* 32, page 207:

| To secure popularity and patronage, legislators will yield to the demand for Sunday law.

Will they? They have done it. Is that fulfilled? [Congregation: "Yes."] That has been fulfilled. They have done it and they have done it so certainly that they themselves have publicly said that they did do it for that purpose. The evidence, more than we have had at any other time, is in this little pamphlet, The Captivity of the Republic. It is a report of the hearing before the Committee on the World's Fair Sunday Closing Bill, an account of which I gave here in my second talk. This is now being printed and coming from the press. It is entitled The Captivity of the Republic. And the idea is that the churches have captured the republic and hold it in the captivity in which they have taken it and the quotations there from congressmen themselves, lately, not simply those of Hiscock and Hawley and those of last summer, but those of the very latest – members of that Committee which heard our arguments and refused to hear what they would not hear willingly, but which they had to hear – statements from these very men, saying that they must not go any further in that direction for fear of the damage to the Fair and country at large, that the church element would do. You have it over and over there in several different ways; so there is further evidence than that which we had last summer, but they keep on saying that they did it then for that reason and they still maintain it for the same reason. So that is fulfilled over and over, if anybody wants evidence on that point.

| Those who fear God cannot accept an institution that violates a precept of the decalogue.

Does this institution that has been set up by those men to secure popularity and patronage refer in any way to a precept of the decalogue? [Congregation: "Yes."] Did they mention any precept of the decalogue in the doing of it? [Congregation: "Yes."] "Those who fear God cannot accept" it. Do you hear that? [Congregation: "Amen!"]

"Those who fear God cannot accept an institution that violates a precept of the decalogue."

And an institution that so entirely violates a precept of the decalogue that it itself could not be set up by the government without taking the precept of the decalogue out of the way, altering it entirely. It is not set *alongside* of the other one. They did not enact any Sunday law on its own merits, but they deliberately set up the precept of God and took out of it what He put into it and put into it what the Catholic church set up in the place of it.

> On this battlefield comes the last great conflict of the controversy between truth and error.

And the battle is joined and we are to go from this Conference into the midst of it.

> And we are not left in doubt as to the issue. Now as in the days of Mordecai, the Lord will vindicate His truth and His people. By the decree enforcing the institution of the papacy in violation of the law of God, our nation will disconnect herself fully from righteousness.

Now another thing: I want to ask you whether it has been fulfilled.

> When Protestantism shall stretch her hand across the gulf to grasp the hand of the Roman power...

That is, "when she shall." In 1884 it said, "She will." This says, "When she shall." that little special testimony, when it came a year ago now, said, "She is reaching." She is doing it. *We* know now that she *has done* it. Don't we?

Let us read from Testimony No. 33, page 240:

> When our nation shall so abjure the principles of its government as to enact a Sunday law, Protestantism will in this act join hands with popery.

But they joined hands with popery in the doing of it, in order to do it, and is it not all true in that one thing? She has joined hands with the papacy. That is fulfilled then, is it? [Congregation: "Yes."] Then the Testimony is fulfilled down that far. Is that so? [Congregation: "Yes."]

Then further, this same paragraph here, on page 240 of *Testimony* No. 33:

> When our nation shall so abjure the principles of its government as to enact a Sunday law, Protestantism will in this act join hands with popery; it will be nothing else than *giving life* to the tyranny which has long been eagerly watching its opportunity to spring again into active despotism.

We have found by our other studies and by the latest Testimonies that have come that it is through the influence of the United States government that all the nations are brought back to the papacy, and when that is done it is through this country that *life is given* to that same tyrannical spirit which passes all over the world. So then we are up to that point now, are we? [Congregation: "Yes."] Now let us see what remains. There is something else to come in this connection.

On page 207 of Testimony No. 32 we read:

> When she shall reach over the abyss *to clasp hands* with spiritualism...

It is fulfilled up to that point – up to that last one now. Is it? [Congregation: "Yes."] The other remains.

> When she shall reach over the abyss to clasp hands with spiritualism. . . When under the influences of this threefold union our country shall repudiate every principle of its constitution as a Protestant and Republican government. . .

When they joined hands with popery, it was to set up the papal institution, as the testimony which has been printed in the Bulletin told us, that God's memorial has been set aside, the false sabbath has been put in its place. In the doing of that, she has joined hands with popery, has set up the institution of the papacy instead of the institution of God. That much is fulfilled, then. That was accomplished in joining hands with popery. Now the next thing is to join hands with spiritualism. And then "under the influence of this threefold union" every principle, not only as a Protestant but as a *Republican* government goes. Now a Republican government is a government of the people, not monarchical. What is the object of Satan in working all these miracles? Well, I shall read the rest of that sentence first:

> When under the influence of this threefold union, our country shall repudiate every principle of its constitution as a Protestant and Republican government and shall make provision for the propagation of papal falsehoods *and delusion,* then *we may know* that the *time has come* for *the marvelous working of Satan* and that the end is near.

Now, why is it and for what purpose is it that Satan does these miraculous things? Isn't it to prove that he is Christ? [Congregation: "Yes."] "False Christs shall arise and shall show great signs and wonders, if possible to deceive the very elect." But he puts himself in the place of Christ.

Christ is King, isn't He? [Congregation: "Yes."] When Satan in those miracles puts himself in the place of Christ, it is to be the same thing, is it? [Congregation: "Yes."] When this is done, then upon the very face of it, every principle of Republican government has been taken away, and they will have a monarchy established. And so the object of spiritualism is to open the way for the professed coming of Christ and the setting up of his kingdom the earth.

So you see, having done so much already, it is easy enough to take the next step and to recognize "Christ" as king. That is the thing that is being urged now by the National reformers, who have been working for that which they have obtained, by those who recognize the strength of what has been done in making this a "Christian Nation." This will be done in much the same way. The principle will be recognized in some way, and they will clasps hands with spiritualism. Then, when that is done, when the way is opened, "Christ" is recognized as king, that opens the way for *Satan* to come *as Christ* and set up his kingdom here and do all these miracles and sweep the world with him, and then the cry is raised (Vol. IV gives it) "Christ has come! Christ has come!" Then does not all this show to us that the working of Satan in spiritualism, in these wonders and miracles that deceive men, is *after the making of the image,* even as the prophecy says?

> Saying to them that dwell on the earth that they should make an image to the beast, which had the wound by a sword and did live. And he had power to give life unto the image of the beast, that the image of the beast should both speak and cause that as many as would not worship the image of the beast should be killed. And he causeth all, both small and great, rich and poor, free and bond, to receive a mark in their right hand or in their foreheads: and that no man might buy or sell, save he that had the mark or the number of his name.

Then you can see again that up to the fifteenth verse, not one of the verses is fulfilled in the order in which its statements are set down. "Well, then," says one, "what in the world is that that way for? How are we to know, then, when it *does* come?" Vol. IV tells you that too. It says this on page 443:

> To learn what the image is like and how it is to be formed, we must study the characteristics of the beast itself, the papacy.

We are to learn of the fulfillment of the prophecy and be able to detect that from our knowledge of the thing of which it is an image. In other words, we are not to get the knowledge of the fulfillment of this prophecy from the prophecy itself alone but we are to detect and to learn of the fulfillment of this prophecy from the record of the nature, the working, and the disposition of *the beast* of which this is only *an image.* So you see, in order to see when these passages are fulfilled, in order to see when they are met, we must be acquainted with the beast and *well acquainted with it* that when anyone of these points appear we can see where that belongs, because we know where it belonged in the original, and then, knowing where it belongs, we can avoid that thing.

There is a peculiarity about this prophecy that is not about many others: There are some prophecies like the prophecy of Daniel seventh chapter, the passing away of Babylon, Medo-Persia, Greece, and Rome, and so on – those prophecies, men could see the fulfillment of them in the event and they could be perfectly safe in it. In other words, was it safe for men acquainted with the Scriptures to look for another kingdom to succeed Babylon and to look for it as Medo-Persia and know when that thing was fulfilled from the event itself? Yes, and they could see it fulfilled and the event itself. But mark you, here is this prophecy that comes at the end of the world, and in the whirl of events that bring the end of the world and the man who waits to see this fulfilled in order to act, he will be too late.

Therefore this is a prophecy with which God wants us to be so well acquainted beforehand that we will look at it from the right side and not be behind when it does come. And in order to do that, you see the Lord gives us a picture that has already been wrought out in history. He gives the course of events that have already been carried out, fulfilled before the eyes of men, in a slow process so that in studying it as it occurred slowly in that, we can become thoroughly acquainted with the principles that were established and their outgrowth and the result of them. And he does that in order that we may be so well acquainted with those things in all their bearings that when the first hint of those things is touched *here* we may know the outcome of it long beforehand, and, therefore, have ample time to take warning and never get caught.

This is why the Lord does not want us to look for the fulfillment of this prophecy in the prophecy itself, because if we wait for that, the most important things in the fulfillment of the prophecy will be those things upon which depends our salvation at the very moment that that thing is fulfilled, and if we are on the wrong side, if we are late, we are simply left. Therefore he fixes it and has fixed it so as to show us the beast in its fullness, in all his working, in order that by studying that, we may be able to detect the image in every phase and on every side. The first hint of anything of the kind is enough, because we know what the thing is. Everything is in it, and therefore just as soon as that thing is touched, we can say, "That means the image of the beast, the image of the beast is in that thing, and I must avoid every connection of it or with it from now until the end of the world." Watching the growth of that thing which has been started, which I know was the spirit and principle of the papacy when it was started, when I see that and avoid all of it at every step, I am on safe ground, and unless I do that I am on dangerous ground.

Therefore the Spirit of Prophecy has told us that if we would know about the image, we must study the original – the beast. And those who are watching it in this way will be able to detect the evil thing in every one of its phases. No difference how it comes up or where it comes up, even if it be only the merest glimmer. And God wants us to be so well acquainted with the original that we can detect the image even though it be only a glimmer.

Brethren, these things are important for us to consider, and for us to know, so that we shall not be overcome, so that we shall not be taken unawares on anything or at any point, but always be ahead in the thought and in the light of the Spirit of God.

So I say it over again. From the nature of things and in the fast whirl of these last days and these things all coming so fast, in order to be safe we have got to be ahead of the actual occurrence of events. And in order to prepare us for that God has drawn it slowly out before our eyes in the historical evidence of the beast.

He has drawn that out so that we can study it at leisure, and in this study as it occurred slowly even up to the full development and ruin that was wrought by it before, we can, by the Spirit of God enlightening us, always be ahead of these things that are coming now, so that when they do come, however fast, we are only glad, because we know beforehand what it all means.

That is all that I can say upon that particular line of prophecy or this particular passage. But did think that it was necessary as so many questions had been asked upon that, to call attention to it before we separate.

Now let us just sketch what is in the book of Revelation after that. The third angel's message warns against the beast and his image and the danger of drinking the wine of the wrath of God. And then follows the coming of the Saviour to reap the harvest of the earth, and the people of God standing on Mount Zion. So there, that is a sketch through from where we are to the final victory.

Then the sixteenth chapter takes up the plagues; the seventeenth refers to Babylon the great, the mother. The eighteenth is the message of warning; the times of refreshing, the latter rain, the lighting of the earth with the glory of God, the calling out from Babylon, because she is fallen and is become the habitation of devils, as well as the hold of every foul spirit, and a cage of unclean and hateful birds, and that ye receive not *of her plagues,* and God hath remembered her iniquities. And then the word goes on and gives the actual occurrence of the judgment of God upon that great Babylon, to her utter ruin and perdition.

Then the nineteenth chapter you will remember, is that song, that voice of a great multitude of much people in heaven, saying, "Salvation, and glory, and honor, and power, unto the Lord our God, for true and righteous are his judgments, for he hath judged the great" harlot, "which did corrupt the earth with her fornication, and hath avenged the blood of his servants at her hand." "And the four and twenty elders and the four beasts fell down and worshipped God that sat on the throne, saying, Amen; Alleluia. And a voice came out of the throne, saying, Praise our God, all ye his servants, ad ye that fear him, both small and great. And I heard as it were the voice of a great multitude and as the voice of many waters and as the voice of mighty thunderings, saying, Alleluia, for the Lord God omnipotent reigneth. Let us be glad and rejoice, and give honor to him: for the marriage of the Lamb is come, and his wife hath made herself ready. And to her was granted that she should be arrayed in fine linen, clean and white: for the fine linen is the righteousness of saints. And he saith unto me, Write, Blessed are they which are called unto the marriage supper of the Lamb. And he saith unto me, These are the true sayings of God." And the next thing he sees is heaven opened and behold a white horse and the coming of Christ, the destruction of the nations of the earth, the beast and his image are cast together into the lake of fire and the remnant are slain.

Then the 20th chapter is the binding of Satan, the resurrection of the righteous. Then the thousand years expire, and then comes the resurrection of the wicked and the judgment and destruction of them. The 21st chapter announces the new earth and the heavenly city upon it. And the 22nd chapter:

"And there shall be no more curse: but the throne of God and of the Lamb shall be in it; and his servants shall serve him: and they shall see his face; and his name shall be in their foreheads. And there shall be no night there; and they need no candle, neither light of the sun; for the Lord God giveth them light: and they shall reign for ever and ever."

Now, brethren, don't you see that from the message of Revelation 14, from the record of the third angel's message, when the image of the beast is made, that the rest of the book of Revelation is a straightforward story, as straight as can be written? From the time the image of the beast is made and the third angel's message goes forth as it reads, as now it goes forth from this Conference, as we go forth with the message, the rest of the book of Revelation is a straightforward story to you and me right through to the end of the book? Don't you see that? [Congregation: "Yes."] One event right after another, all coming in directly in connection and those things are right before us the rest of the book is just that, and you know that well enough.

Now here is another word that we want to read from where we are. You will recognize it. *Testimony*, Vol. I, page 186. It speaks of the Laodicean message:

> It is designed to arouse the people of God, to discover to them their backslidings, and to lead to zealous repentance, that they may be favored with the presence of Jesus and be fitted for the loud cry of the third angel. As this message affected the heart, it led to deep humility before God. *Angels were sent in every direction to prepare unbelieving hearts for the truth.* The cause of God began to rise, and His people were acquainted with their position.

There is where we are. He has said, "Arise," hasn't He? [Congregation: "Yes, sir."] He has brought us to the message which says to us, "Arise, shine, for thy light is come." Well, now the time has come for us to rise. We have arisen, for He told us to, and He says so. We have arisen, because we are not to forget that when He speaks the word and we yield, then the word is fulfilled. He says, Arise. We say, Lord, Arise it is, and then we are up. His word raises us. He says shine. We say, Lord, shine it is. And it is so. Back there, when darkness was upon the earth, He said, Let light be; light was. Now He says, Arise. That word, when we rest upon it, raises us. He says, Shine. And that word when we yield to it, causes us to shine. His word today which says, Shine, has just as much light in it as that word that said, Let there be light, back there. That word has light in it, and when we yield to that word, He will see to it that we shine.

But what I wanted to call your attention to especially was this promise that angels were sent in every direction to prepare unbelieving hearts for the truth. Now the angels of God have gone forth, haven't they? They are sent. What are you going to do?

When we go from this meeting, depending upon the power of God, we go with His power, in His presence, with His glory upon us, waiting for Him to manifest Himself in His own way, in His own good time, just as He pleases, then you can see, He, sending His angels ahead, and then sending us on, why He just sends us to meet the hearts that the angels have prepared already.

Then, brethren, we have got nothing more to do any longer with "getting up an interest." Don't you see that? We have nothing to do with getting up an interest, and to make a great display getting up an interest. The interest *is up*.

God wants us to get up *to the* interest. Get up *to the* interest, and not get up an interest. We will do well if we get up to the interest; that is all the Lord asks of us.

Then when He sends us we are to go with that promise; it is before us, and go to meet the work that God has prepared for us on every hand, in every direction. That is where we are. Is not that the way it was in the apostles' days? One reason why I wished we might have six weeks more to study together here was that we might study the book of Acts. Then we could see how God works when He has His own way, but you can study the book of Acts yourselves. That is our lesson book now. That is the way He worked when He had poured out the early rain, and that is the lesson book to see how He will work now in the time of the latter rain. Here is an instance at that time. Acts 16:4 and onward:

> And as they went through the cities, they delivered them the decrees for to keep, that were ordained of the apostles and elders which were at Jerusalem. And so were the churches established in the faith and increased in number daily. Now when they had gone throughout Phrygia and the region of Galatia and were forbidden of the Holy Ghost to preach the word in Asia...

Were *forbidden* of the Holy Ghost to preach the word in Asia! And that too when the Lord had sent them to preach the gospel to every creature! "And after they were come to Mysia, they assayed to go into Bithynia: but the Spirit suffered them not."

There were men who knew what the leading of the Spirit of God is. And you and I are to know it too. [Congregation: "Amen."] And that is what the Testimonies mean, and that is what the lessons of this meeting mean. Unless you are prepared to know the leading of the Spirit of God and to recognize the guidance of the Spirit of God, then don't you go from this place until you do. That is what this means.

Well, they could not preach the gospel in Asia any more, and they could not go into Bithynia, and all they could do was to go as far as they could in the only direction that was open, and so they came down to Troas; that was the limit. They could not preach anywhere behind them; they could not go to the right hand, and there was no place to the left, and there they were at the edge of the sea. There they were. What then? Then the Lord told them what to do.

> And they passing by Mysia came down to Troas. And a vision appeared to Paul in the night. There stood a man of Macedonia and prayed him, saying, Come over into Macedonia, and help us. And after he had seen the vision, immediately we endeavored to go into Macedonia, assuredly gathering that the Lord has called us for to preach the gospel unto them. Therefore loosing from Troas, we came with a straight course to Samothracia and the next day to Neapolis, and from thence to Philippi, which is the chief city of that part of Macedonia, and a colony, and we were in that city abiding certain days. And on the Sabbath we went out of the city by a river side, where prayer was wont to be made, and we sat down and spake unto the women which resorted thither. And a certain woman

> named Lydia, a seller of purple, of the city of Thyatira, which worshipped God, heard us, whose heart the Lord opened, that she attended unto the things which were spoken of Paul.

Why did the Lord want them to go over into Macedonia? To meet the interest which the angels of the Lord had opened already.

Cornelius, too, was seeking the Lord. An angel appeared to him and told him to send for Peter who would tell him words, whereby he should be saved. Peter went, but it was only to meet the interest that had already been raised. Philip, too, was sent away across the country to find the eunuch and meet the interest that was already raised in his mind and heart.

That is enough on that point. You can see by this that the book of Acts, from this day forward, is your lesson-book and mine on the work of God, how He will carry on the work and what place he wants us to occupy in it. And, brethren, bear in mind that what He says is so all the way through.

Let us turn to Isaiah and read a passage as to what the Lord wants us to do and what He has for us. You remember that I referred to the 60th chapter of Isaiah. We will now read the last two verses. "Thy people shall be all righteous: they shall inherit the land forever, the branch of my planting, the work of my hands, that I may be glorified. A little one shall become a thousand, and a small one a strong nation; I the Lord will hasten it in his time."

Then the 61th chapter: "The Spirit of the Lord God is upon me, because the Lord hath anointed me to preach good tidings unto the meek. He hath sent me to bind up the brokenhearted, to proclaim liberty to the captives and the opening of the prison to them that are bound, to proclaim the acceptable year of the Lord and the day of vengeance of our God, to comfort all that mourn."

Now the last two verses of that same chapter, and then the 62nd chapter: "I will greatly rejoice in the Lord. My soul shall be joyful in my God, for he hath clothed me with the garments of salvation, he hath covered me with the robe of righteousness, as a bridegroom decketh himself with ornaments and as a bride adorneth herself with her jewels. For as the earth bringeth forth her bud and as the garden causeth the things that are sown in it to spring forth; so the Lord God will cause righteousness and praise to spring forth before all the nations."

That is what He is going to do now.

"For Zion's sake I will not hold my peace, and for Jerusalem's sake I will not rest." What do you say? Afraid of getting tired, are you? "O yes, I have been at work quite a while now, and I think I had better go home and rest." You had better stay where you are and rest. Stay there and *work* while you rest.

"For Zion's sake will I not hold my peace, and for Jerusalem's sake I will not rest, until the righteousness thereof go forth as brightness, and the salvation thereof as a lamp that burneth." Brethren, I want to tell you that if you will take up the health reform and live it out according to God's idea, you will not have to rest. You will work while you rest, and you will need no vacation at all. I know it from experience. You know as well as I do that for the last three years I have been working all the time and have had no vacation. I have not needed it, do not want any. I have gone through institutes and camp meetings, right out of one into another, without any rest and have gained in weight and strength all the time. And I shall go out of this General Conference, where I have been working every minute of the time from early morning until sometimes midnight, just as fresh as I was when I started into the Conference, and I expect to stay so. But you must learn to work on your victuals, instead of on your vitals. A man cannot keep this up and work on his vitals, but he can work on his victuals and do it year in and year out. You get the health reform as it is and can do this as He said, "and for Jerusalem's sake I will not rest." I am bold to talk on this subject of health reform, because I think I am a pretty good specimen.

Well, says one, you have a good strong digestion. No, sir. I have a weak stomach and have had for years, and I have to be careful with my stomach all the time that it does not get all undone, but that is what health reform is for, to give a man sense enough to take care of himself.

So then, let us stick to that:

> For Zion's sake will I not hold my peace, and for Jerusalem's sake I will not rest, until the righteousness thereof go forth as brightness and the salvation thereof as a lamp that burneth. And the Gentiles shall see thy righteousness, and all kings thy glory, and thou shalt be called by a new name which the mouth of the Lord shall name. Thou shalt also be a crown of glory in the hand of the Lord, and royal diadem in the hand of thy God. Thou shalt no more be termed Forsaken; neither shall thy land any more be termed Desolate, but thou shalt be called Hephzi-bah, and thy land Beulah, for the Lord delighteth in thee, and thy land shall be married. For as a young man marrieth a virgin, so shall thy sons marry thee: and as the bridegroom rejoiceth over the bride, so shall thy God rejoice over thee. I have set watchmen upon thy walls, O Jerusalem, which shall never hold their peace day nor night. Ye that make mention of the Lord, keep not silence, and give him no rest...

Well, when we work without rest and give Him no rest either, I tell you there is something going to be done.

> And give him no rest, till he establish and till he make Jerusalem a praise in the earth. The Lord hath sworn by the arm of his right hand and by the arm of his strength, Surely I will no more give thy corn to be meat for thine enemies, and the sons of the stranger shall not drink thy wine, for the which thou hast labored; but they that have gathered it shall eat it, and praise the Lord; and they that have brought it together shall drink it in the courts of my holiness.

> Go through, go through the gates; prepare ye the way of the people; cast up, cast up the highway; gather out the stones; lift up a standard for the people. Behold, the Lord hath proclaimed unto the end of the world, Say ye to the daughter of Zion [This is our message], Behold, thy salvation cometh; behold, his reward is with him, and his work before him. And they shall call them, The holy people, The redeemed of the Lord; and thou shalt be called, Sought out, A city not forsaken. *Who is this that cometh* from Edom, with dyed garments from Bozrah? This that is glorious in his apparel, traveling in the greatness of his strength? [Who is this?] I that speak in *righteousness,* mighty to *save.*

That is the coming of the Lord. The 63rd, 64th, and 65th chapters of Isaiah speak of the new heavens and the new earth, and the 66th declares that as these remain so shall we remain.

> And from one new moon to another, and from one Sabbath to another shall all flesh come to worship before me, saith the Lord.

Don't you see that Isaiah, from the 60th to the 66th chapters, is a parallel of Revelation 13 on to the end of the book? All these things the Lord uses to show us what He is going to do now.

Well, brethren, the Bible is full of it. The Bible is full of it. Let us believe it; let us believe Him, and the message that He has given us, and the power of the message which He has given to every one, and may none go from this Conference without it.

Sermon 24

March 26, 1893

We will begin with that passage that we had last night in Volume IV. It is on page 443 of the canvassing edition of *Great Controversy*:

> To learn what the image is like and how it is to be formed, we must study the characteristics of the beast itself – the papacy.

And we need to study this now, just as much as we ever have needed to study it, because not all the features of the image of the beast have as yet been developed. The image has not yet appeared before the world in all its features and in all its developments. Each step that is to be taken and all that is to be done from this time forward will be the appearance of successive features of the image, creating more and more the full likeness, the perfect likeness, in all its parts, of the original. Only the start has been taken now, but as we have found in our lessons here, the start which has been taken is such that no power on earth or anywhere else can stop it. It will go on and develop all that is in it, in spite of all that can be done to prevent it. It will go on, even against the wishes and many times contrary to the intentions of those who have started it.

Now just see how this thing has grown with us, how it has grown right before our eyes. Several years ago, when we first began real, direct, active work upon this particular phase, we established the *American Sentinel*. That is eight years ago now, I think. There was then only one organization in the country that was set to obtain this thing. In a little while that organization gathered to itself others and within a year or two it gathered four or five. Then the movement got beyond the management and really beyond the power of the original organization. Then the original organization itself dropped out of our minds entirely and this new mold was put upon it, this increased power that was given to it carried it beyond the original organization by those that were added to it. That was what our opposition was against then. It was this new form that we had to deal with.

Now the increased power that has been brought to it by these additional organizations, has carried itself and the whole movement to the place where the original organization intended it to go, so that now we have no more to deal with these organizations. We have nothing to do with them, particularly any more. Our contention is not against them or their work. We have now to deal with the government of the

United States, and these things are, I was going to say, merely incidents, but they are less than that, because the government will take steps and will be forced to take steps that will be directly against the intentions and many times against the power of those who have done what has been done. And whereas our first work was against that first organization and as our second work was against the increased organization and the work that it was doing, *now* all those organizations are out of the way and we have now to deal with that which has been done by them.

That is our position now.

That is where we stand, and whether the American Sabbath Union does this, that or the other, it is nothing to us now, because steps will be taken and things will be done that the American Sabbath Union never did intelligently or conscientiously intend. Things will be done against the wishes and beyond the intent, the conscious intent, of the whole combination. Because they, even in their most radical intent, never intended anything but that they themselves should manage the government when they got it: but, behold, the Catholics will manage the government after these have got it. And that is where they will find themselves left in the fog. That is where they will find themselves at a disadvantage. And things will be done in spite of them that they never thought of when they were blinded by their own zeal to get power that did not belong to them, but they have nobody to blame but themselves.

Now, Congress has adjourned; and the action which that Congress took is fastened upon the government without any remedy. Not only that, but an additional step was taken in that line in the very last days of the session. I have not found the full particulars of the outcome yet, but I know the facts and they are these: It was found that the inaugural ball that was to be held celebrating Cleveland's inauguration had to be held Saturday night. It was expected, of course, that they would dance over beyond twelve o'clock in the night. The Marine Band – the National Band of the United States – was employed. They were to furnish the music for the ball and were also to give concerts on Sunday following.

The ministers of Washington city sent up a petition to Congress, and Senator Quay, of course, presented it. And here are the particulars that are reported on that:

> Feb. 28, 1893. Mr. Quay presented in the Senate today a petition signed by the pastors of many of the Washington churches and others, on the subject of the proposed concert by the Marine Band in the Pension Office building next Sunday as a part of the inaugural ceremonies.

I don't know how that was. This is the petition:

> SUNDAY CONCERTS IN PENSION OFFICE BUILDING
>
> *Mr. Quay*: I present a petition of sixty clergymen of the city of Washington, which I ask to have read.

The Vice-president: The petition will be read if there is no objection.

The Chief Clerk: The petition is as follows:

To the President of the United States, The Secretary of the Interior, and the Senate and House of Representatives in Congress assembled:

A PETITION

Whereas, It having been announced by the inaugural committee through the daily papers that, as a part of the program for the inaugural ceremonies, three concerts by the Marine Band are to be held in the Pension Office building on Sunday, March 5, proximo; and

Whereas, The Congress of the United States *in deference to the Christian sentiment of the nation* clearly and unmistakably expressed by the religious press, the pulpit, and by petition, has by legal enactment closed the doors of the Columbian Exposition on Sunday:

Therefore, believing to permit the holding of such concerts on Sunday by a band of musicians connected with one of the great departments of the government, in a government building which is occupied by another great department, and as a part of the ceremonies connected with the inauguration of *the President of this great Christian nation,* by and with the sanction of her chosen rulers, would be *a national sin;* believing also that such desecration as proposed is unprecedented, would result in incalculable harm and would be used as an authority and example for the complete secularization of Sunday:

We earnestly petition that orders be issued forbidding the use of any government building for such purpose on that day.

Signed by W. R. Graham, pastor of Congress Street Methodist Protestant Church; W. Sherman Phillips, pastor Mt. Tabor Methodist Protestant Church, and many others.

So you see, the Senate passed a resolution in answer to that petition, complying with its request so far as to ask the Secretary of the Interior for information. I have seen by a later paper, in giving the report of the outcome, the statement that the Secretary of the Interior had ordered that the Marine Band should not play on Sunday and that President Cleveland had signified his wish to the same effect. Therefore, when twelve o'clock struck, Saturday night, the band just stopped short, the great, brilliant electric lights were turned off, and everybody on the floor stopped dancing.

What I call attention to that for, is for you to see that the government, the United States Senate, at least, has taken an additional step in support of Sunday by passing that resolution, and there it stands.

Now another thought: That case that was in Judge Tuley's court in Chicago in which the Steamboat Companies thought to enjoin the World's Fair Commissioners from shutting Jackson Park to steamboat excursionists on Sunday – that failed, and Judge

Tuley decided that the United States government had sole authority in the park for exposition purposes and it had stated that Sunday should be observed there that shut out the State of Illinois and the City of Chicago from any word in the matter.

So then, you see, everything that touches this question, everything that comes up, all is turned to the support of what has been done. Now, if no extra session of Congress is called – and none has been yet, and doubtless will not be now, as the President has not signified his intention to do it – then that legislation goes on without any question or interference until the World's Fair is ended and the thing for which the act was passed has been accomplished. Then we shall have the United States government committed to and having lived through more than a year's history under the present statutory Sunday law. And thus the precedent will have been established which will be a part of the experience of the government, a part of its history, and as men who are not statesmen – and very few are nowadays, especially in Congress – are governed more by *what has been done* than by what *ought to be* done, that will be the strongest argument and the great bulwark forever after, in favor of Sunday as the sacred day of the government of the United States.

But as we have said formerly, if an extra session should be called and another Congress repeal that Sunday law, that would not affect the principle involved in the Sunday legislation in the least, because any succeeding legislation can repeal any law passed by any previous legislature and such action does not call in question the right of the previous legislature to *enact* that which has been repealed. When a legislature repeals an act of a previous legislature, it does not call in question the right of the previous legislature to enact it but simply the policy of it. The right to do the thing is just the same as though it were not repealed. Consequently, if an extra session should be called and should repeal that Sunday-closing act, the government would be just as clearly committed and pledged to the principle that Sunday legislation is right on the government, as it is now.

[*Voice*: "Suppose they repeal it on constitutional grounds."]

Elder Jones: If Congress should repeal it expressly upon the statement and for the reason that it was unconstitutional entirely, that would effect it but a very little more, because it would be simply the opinion of one Congress against the opinion of another, as is often done between the great parties. Even now this is precisely the position of the two great parties on the tariff question. The Democratic party insists that the Republican tariff bill is unconstitutional. Therefore if this Sunday legislation should not be repealed bodily because it is unconstitutional, any succeeding Congress could take it up again because Congress did that once before, so it would throw the thing into an even-going controversy, and that is all there would be to it.

But nothing that can be done can obliterate the legislation entirely in the principle of the thing and the right of the government to carry it forward. The fact is that the government is so thrown into the hands of this hierarchy that it never can be delivered. Controversies will arise and as soon as the Catholics begin to launch ahead a little and show their strength, the professed Protestants will resent it. We may expect that at any time. We may look for it to come from any direction and from almost any source. It will certainly come, and as a matter of fact, it has already started. When the World's Fair buildings were dedicated – the Catholics, Cardinal Gibbons and the representative of the pope, there, received great honors, and because of that, quite a number of professed Protestants, the preachers, got into a great "huff" about it. They said they would not have anything to do with the Fair anymore. They declared, "If the Catholics are to have precedence and they are to receive the honors and all this, why we'll just simply not have anything more to do with the Fair." Well, the Catholics don't care for that. They have got the honor, and they will have the power, and if "Protestants" don't like it, all they need to do is to stay away. And by their staying away, they will give the Catholics that much more to do what they wanted to do in the first place. So the sum of the matter is, that if they stay away, that gives the Catholics that much more power. If they *go*, it is a recognition of the Catholic supremacy. And thus they are taken captive and all they can do is to be moved about by that power at its will. That's all they can do.

There *is* just one thing that they can do. They can escape the whole thing and be delivered from it if they will, but the only way they can do it is to accept the third angel's message. There is no other way out.

These men, many of them, have been led into this by not seeing what was in it. They have been led into this by the influence of ministers who have a higher standing than they in the denominations round about, never dreaming what was in it. When they see that they are caught in a perfect labyrinth and the further they go in it and whichever way they turn, they get lost; when they see that and how completely they have allowed themselves to be sold, they will deliver themselves by fleeing unto God. And that is why the Lord lifts His people up above the world and causes His church to shine so that we cannot be hid and when they begin to look for deliverance, they will see where deliverance is, because in the third angel's message God has set deliverance before the world, and "a city set upon a hill cannot be hid."

Now, when God lifts us up, sets us up on a high mountain, as it were, and causes His light to radiate in every direction, then people in every direction will see it, and when they find that they are so badly lost where they are, they will be glad to get deliverance from any source. They will be glad to see that it is God that will deliver in this direction, and they would rather have God than the papacy, even if they have to come to the Seventh-day Adventists to find Him. They will do it.

Then another thing: This church Congress, this World's Fair Auxiliary that was dedicated or rather inaugurated at the dedication ceremonies – Archbishop Ireland was the grand magnate and the one orator – and it was opened up with the sanction and blessing and good will of the Catholic church. And in this to begin with, as well as in the ceremonies of the Fair grounds, the Catholics by the prominence that was given them, simply compelled these same Protestant ministers to say, "Well, if the Catholics are going to run the whole thing, we will not be there."

Now, when that World's Congress of Religions comes and all these things are brought out, then we may expect –we do not know how it will come, but we may expect– controversies to arise out of that governmental recognition of religion. And from this day forward, in everything that comes up, we may expect only the further development of the image that is already made. All that we can look for now is just simply that in each step and in everything that is done, other features will be developed which more perfectly fill out the living, standing, full image of the beast.

In all these things it will come, and when the turmoils, the riotings, and all the evils that this thing engenders, begin to be wrought and begin to come upon this nation, there will be an effort made to clear the government from it. There will be an effort made to rescue the government and free it from the evil that is being carried on through it. Persecutions will come. Oppressions will come from this more and more, and there will be a reaction, and if that reaction should lead to a governmental act, that would in its intent swing the government clear back to the original principles of the Declaration and the Constitution, as I stated the other night; when that thing is done, it will be time for everyone to get ready to go at a moment's notice. That will be the time for every one to increase his energies, deepen his consecration, put himself and everything, with all his might and main into the work, because when that reaction itself reacts, and the evil tide sways back again, as it surely will, into the religious persecuting, oppressing way, then it stays there.

In Europe this *may* be done *twice*. I will read a passage upon this from matter that never was published. It was given in a vision in 1850 and another in 1852. Brother Cornell had this and allowed us to copy it. He says that Brother O. Hewitt was present when the visions were given and secured these copies. Upon that point, this was said:

> I saw in Europe just as things were moving to accomplish their desires, there would seemingly be slacking up once or twice, thus the hearts of the wicked would be relieved and hardened, but the work would not settle down (only seem to) for the minds of kings and rulers were intent upon overthrowing each other and the minds of the people to get the ascendancy.

So you can see, though it slacks up once or twice, it does not *really*. It only *seems* to. And it says that thus the hearts of the wicked will be relieved. Relieved of what? What had affected the hearts of the wicked? Why, the message telling them what these distresses mean, as the Lord has said, "Distress of nations with perplexity, the sea and the waves roaring, men's hearts failing them for fear and for looking after those things which are coming on the earth." They will be convinced by the Spirit of God that that thing is so, and they will be afraid that it is – not glad that it is so, but afraid it is. Then, when it slacks up, that will relieve them, you see. Then they will say, "We thought that was all a false alarm." And then when it swings back and the message goes on saying, "That is what we told you and now be sure to get ready," then they will say, "That's what you said before, and it has slackened up and swung back." That is where the hardness of heart comes in, just as Pharaoh's heart was hardened, and consequently the hearts of the wicked will be relieved and hardened, and when it does swing back, the end comes and they are caught.

Now about our own country:

In 1888, when I went to the Senate, I had the hearing before the Senate Committee. When I came back, Sister White asked me what the situation was there and what was the prospect. I told her what the Senators told me, that that being a short session, Congress would expire on the 4th of March, that the session was so far gone that they could not possibly get the legislation through, even if it were introduced. From the calendar they had, they saw no possibility of its getting into the Senate even, and if it did, still there was no possibility that it could be passed and go through both houses, as it would have to. I told her the situation as it was. The answer she made was: "Then it is nearer than we expect." The natural thought would be, if it should *not* pass then, these things that we are looking for –troubles, persecutions, and so on– would be farther off, but if it *should* go through, then these things would be nearer. Well, as that would be the natural way to look at it, of course God's way being the right way and ours the wrong way, His is bound to be the opposite of ours, and what we would naturally think the sign that it was farther off would indeed be the sign that it is nearer.

Well then, she went on to say that when this passed, when they did get the government into their hands and begin their oppression and carry out the spirit that is in them, the oppressions and persecutions that will be set up will cause a reaction by men of fair minds, who abhor persecutions and there will be a lull and a little time of relief and apparent peace. And *then* when the tide should swing back after the reaction, all things would wind up shortly. So you can see the situation here is similar to what she saw it would be in Europe, as expressed in this testimony of 1852.

So that is why I said the other night that none of us want to get caught or deceived by anything that will be done hereafter, professing or expecting to undo what has been done. Whatever comes, bear in mind, when it does come, it is only a little relief that God gives us in which to do more work than we ever did before in the world. And that it only opens up the way for us to do *in an easier way* what we have to do. And so, every one that will take that view of it and who acts upon it – then when the work of God is finished, he simply goes onto the triumphant assembly on Mount Zion.

But every one that is saying, "O, no. You were going too fast. You were making too much of this," as a good many will say, we want to be warned against these things also.

Here is the record of what some will say (*Testimony* 33, page 243):

> When the watchman, seeing the sword coming, gives the trumpet a certain sound, the people along the line will echo the warning and all will have opportunity to make ready for the conflict. But too often the leader has stood hesitating, seeming to say, "Let us not make too great haste. There may be a mistake. We must be careful not to raise a false alarm." The very hesitancy and uncertainty on his part is crying, "Peace and safety."

Then don't you see in this that anyone who hesitates, anyone who wavers, his very conduct says, "Peace and safety"? He may not say it out loud, but he says it. That is why in the other place we read, in previous lessons, "Calebs are wanted who will say 'Now is the time for action.'"

I read on:

> The very hesitancy and uncertainty on his part is crying, "Peace and safety. Do not get excited. Be not alarmed. There is a great deal more made of this Religious Amendment question than is demanded. This agitation will all die down."

See? That shows that some will say that. Well then, don't you see, those who say that and take that hesitating, lingering, questioning, wondering position when they see something that appears like the undoing of all that has been done, they will say, "Yes, that's what we told you. We told you that long ago. But you have gone ahead and got the people all stirred up and alarmed and now it is all undone and what's your work worth? It is a false alarm that you have sent. You have deluded the people."

It is no such thing! Because when that lull comes, that is the very thing that those who stand in the fear of God and in the council of God will see is their very grandest opportunity. [Voice: "Isn't it in answer to our prayers to hold the winds in check?"] Yes, sir. And when that lull comes instead of saying, "peace and safety," everyone who stands in the council of God, will exclaim, Now get ready, quick. Get ready, for soon the tide will swing back, and then, everyone that is caught is caught forever. That is the danger, you see.

Let us read a little further from *Great Controversy*, p. 443:

> When the early church became corrupted by departing from the simplicity of the gospel and accepting heathen rites and customs, she lost the Spirit and power of God, and in order to control the consciences of the people, she sought the support of the secular power.

That was the papacy, bear in mind.

> The result was the papacy, a church that controlled the power of the state and employed it to further her own ends, especially for the punishment of "heresy." In order for the United States to form an image of the beast, the religious power must so control the

civil government that the authority of the State will also be employed by the church to accomplish her own ends.

Has anybody here seen anything of that kind done in the United States? [Congregation: "Yes."] Now, honestly, do you believe there is a person in this house besides yourself that has seen such a thing as that in the United States? [Congregation: "Yes."] Is there anyone that has *not*? [Congregation: "No."] No difference what he says about it; no difference what he thinks about it or how he views it himself, is there anyone in this house or in the United States that has *not* seen that thing? The question is not what he believes about it. That is not the question at all, but is there anyone that has not seen just that thing done? [Congregation: "No."] There is not one that has not seen that thing done: they know it is done, whether they allow it is the image of the beast or not. That is not the question, but *it is done*. They have seen it done. If anybody should say it is not the image of the beat, we can answer that it is something just like it anyhow. We could go that far together perhaps.

Then another thing that comes in right here. Some have wished that they might have a statement by the Supreme Court of the United States as to what the Court meant in that decision or as to what the Court intended by it.

But, brethren, that would not do a bit of good. If the Supreme Court of the United States should write out an express statement that the Court did not mean at all to make this a Christian nation, that it did not intend at all to establish a national religion here, it would not affect the thing the snap of your finger.

The question is not what the Court *intended;* it is what the Court has *done*. It is that that counts. And what the Court has done will be seen and the fruits of it will be reaped and the effects of this will be carried on in spite of anything that the Court even may have intended. That has nothing to do with it. I do not suppose that anyone in the Court intended what is in what the Court said, because the Court does not know what is in what it has said, and therefore it could not have intended what is in it. The Court does not know what is in it. They do not dream what is in it.

Did Congress know what was in the Sunday act, closing the World's Fair on Sunday? Did they know what was in that? [Congregation: "No."] Suppose Congress should rise up and pass a resolution for the nation, the American people, saying, "we did not intend at all by this act to put the government of the United States and the power of the government into the hands of the churches." And they could say so honestly, don't you suppose they could?

Question: Did the bishops of Constantine's time know what was in it back there?

Answer: No, they did not see what was in it. They did not know what was in it; that is the point.

So now if Congress should plainly say that we did not intend to give the government into the hands of the churches and therefore the government *is not* in the hands of the churches, does the conclusion follow? No. It is there, whatever they intend.

The point is, they do not know what is in it, and they themselves *now* know that there is in it what then they did not know was in it. A senator from the State of Washington told Brother Decker that if he had known before what he knew afterward, he would not have voted as he did. Exactly. And members of the house have said the same thing. But there is the mischief of it. Satan does not care and the papacy does not care whether they know what is in it or not or whether they intended it or not. It is done, and the fruits of it will appear and the wrong that is in it will come, in spite of what the court intended, in spite of what Congress intended, in spite of what the court knew and in spite of what Congress knew.

That is not where we are to look anyhow for interpretations of these things that have been done. In the word of God is where we are to look for the interpretation of these things that have been done. In the history of the papacy is where we are to look for the interpretation of these things that are done. And only those who do look there will be able to see what there is in these things which have been done. He who is not acquainted with the history of the papacy; he who has not studied that and seen the origin of these things and the encroachments and the building up and the logic of each step as it went on in its way until the final outcome – he who has not followed this, will not be prepared to see what is in these things and what is to come out of them.

And therefore the Lord has pointed us to that thing as the source of our knowledge. Let me read that again. "to learn what the image is like and how it is to be formed." Just as I stated last night, God has given us things by which to know long beforehand what is going to be, in order that when it appears, we shall be able to recognize on the instant that that means the papacy.

Therefore what the Court intended in this has nothing at all to do with the question. And if a document could be secured from the Supreme Court of the United States signed by every Judge on the bench, saying that they did not intend anything of that kind, I would simply say, That has not anything to do with the question. There is just what they said. They said, "This is a Christian nation," and "proved" it. And all this will come out of it in spite of anything they ever intended or ever knew about it. That has nothing to do with it.

And there are those testimonies we read here. All have them in the little Special Testimonies. There it is said that we are not to get our information from those without; we are not to take counsel with the world. Our orders are to come from above; our counsel is to be received from there. In the Review and Herald of February 21, first page, is a statement to the effect that those who stand in the counsel of God will have wisdom to detect Satan's movements and avoid them. Brethren, the Lord has left us armed at every point against everything that Satan may do. Why, three distinct sources you see He has opened for our absolute knowledge of this thing – the Bible, the Testimonies, and the history of the papacy. There are three sources of knowledge upon this: there is the history, there is the Scripture, and there is the Spirit of Prophecy to explain both. Has not He left us fully armed, then?

Well, then let us make use of the documents and means that He has given us by which to be fully armed against these deceptions. That is what is wanted. It will require study, but what in the world is a preacher for if he is not to study? That is what I want to know. He has nothing else to do than to study, and nothing else to do than to work. Study and work, work and study *all the time.* Of course it will be harder work than a good many have done, to study up all these things and put your mind to it with all your might. But you need not be afraid of getting the brain fever; do not be afraid of that. I just wish – I would not confine it to ministers, because all must be ministers one time or another – but I wish that every Seventh-day Adventist would get down to it and study until his brain fiber snaps. It would do him good. Study until his brain fairly cracks because of the exertion. What does the Lord say? "Thou shalt love the Lord thy God with all thy heart, all thy soul," and how much of your mind? [Congregation: "All of it."] Then go at it. Come along. Let us get at it. "All of your mind" is what He wants. *All* of your mind. *All* of it. Let Him have it.

I will read that statement a little further concerning those who say it will all die down: *Testimony*, No. 33, pages 243, 244:

> Too often the leader has stood hesitating, seeming to say, "Let us not be in too great haste. There may be a mistake. We must be careful not to raise a false alarm." The very hesitancy and uncertainty on his part is crying, "Peace and safety. Do not get excited. Be not alarmed. *There is a great deal more made of this Religious Amendment question than is demanded. This agitation will die down.*" Thus he virtually denies the message sent from God, and the warning which was designed to stir the churches, fails to do its work. The trumpet of the watchman gives no certain sound, and the people do not prepare for the battle. Let the watchman beware lest through his hesitancy and delay souls shall be left to perish, and their blood shall be required at his hand.

Then another thing. Some of the ministering brethren and a good many of the people have said, "I do not think this religious liberty work, this church and State work is quite the thing. It is too much like politics. I do not think it is exactly the thing to work in the church and on the Sabbath and so on." Well, that depends altogether on what the condition of your heart is. It depends altogether on what it is to you. If it is simply a political thing to you, then all it is to you is politics. If it is religious liberty work indeed with you and in you, then it is the gospel. If it is with you only a theory, only an outward formalism, then all it is with you is politics. Policy is all you know. But if it is with you and in you the real soul liberty, the real liberty that Christ gives the converted soul, then it is religious liberty indeed, the gospel of Christ, and no politics about it. That is the difference between politics and the gospel of Christ.

I would like to know who is the greatest, the sharpest, and the most tricky politician on the earth. [Congregation: "The pope of Rome."] Of course, the pope. He always has been the greatest politician. Every one of them has been a politician, you know. But he professes the gospel. Where is there a broader *professor of religion* than the pope? But the principles of the papacy and the gospel as professed by the papacy are all on the outside. It never can be anything but politics. But let the principles of the gospel that these men put on the outside only and which they simply hold as a theory, as a creed, let those principles of the gospel reach the heart and bring Jesus Christ into the heart, and then you have got religious liberty indeed. But there would then be no popes.

And so those brethren that have supposed that the religious liberty work was too much like politics for them, what they need is to find out what religious liberty is and to get religious liberty for themselves and in their hearts and then they will know it is not politics. They will know that it is religion. Those folks have not found out what real religion is. No, sir. The man who finds the religious liberty that there is in Jesus Christ and which the gospel brings to him and which separates every religious thing from the State, separates Church and State – the man who does that, he knows that it is not politics, because he knows the straight way, and he will take the straight way and he will go that way in the face of every consideration that the earth can furnish or mention, and there is no politics in that. That is principle.

Well then this is where we stand. These are some of the things we are to consider. And the secret of all, the beginning and the ending of all, *the all in all* of it, is simply Jesus Christ in a man, the hope of glory. That explains everything. That gives understanding of everything. It supplies everything. Christ, Christ and Him crucified. That is all that any man wants. That is all that any man needs. It is all we can have, for "In him dwelleth all the fullness of the Godhead bodily and ye are complete in him."

Then as we separate, going forth to carry the message which God has given us, in the power which He has given with it, to carry the everlasting gospel to every nation and kindred and tongue and people and – do not forget – saying with *a loud voice,* "Fear God, and give glory to him; for the hour of his judgment is come, and worship him that made heaven, and earth, and the sea, and the fountains of waters," with the other angel following saying, "Babylon is fallen, is fallen, that great city, because she made *all nations* drink of the wine of her fornication." Has she? All nations now? [Congregation: "Yes."] Then let the *still louder* voice go, "If any man worship the beast and his image and receive his mark in his forehead or in his hand, the same shall drink of the wine of the wrath of God, which is poured out without mixture into the cup of his indignation. . . Here is the patience of the saints: here are they that keep the commandments of God, and the faith of Jesus. . . Blessed are the dead which die in the Lord from henceforth."

Well, then when one of your friends dies why do you mourn? God has promised a blessing upon him. Do not rob *yourself* of a blessing too by unbelief. "Blessed are the dead which die in the Lord from henceforth." And then it is confirmed: "Yea, saith the Spirit, that they may rest from their labors; and their works do follow them. And I looked, and behold a white cloud and upon the cloud one sat like unto the Son of man, having on his head a golden crown and in his hand a sharp sickle. And another angel came out of the temple crying with a loud voice to him that sat on the cloud, Thrust in thy sickle and reap, for the time is come for thee to reap, for the harvest of the earth is ripe. And he that sat on the cloud thrust in his sickle on the earth, and the earth was reaped."

"And I saw as it were a sea of glass mingled with fire: and them that had gotten the victory over the beast and over his image and over his mark and over the number of his name stand on the sea of glass having the harps of God." That is where we are going. It is a straight journey right through. That is where it is.

Well, then don't you see that everything we do, every subject we take, every word we utter, is in view of the coming of the Lord. He *is* coming. He is *coming*. Are you not glad of it? Yes, the Lord is coming, Himself. And we shall see Him as He is. Not as He *was*, but as He *is*. His face shining as the sun, His raiment white as the light, His voice like the voice of a multitude, speaking peace and everlasting joy to those who wait for Him. Yes, brethren, He is coming, all over glorious. He is coming. We shall see Him. We shall see Him. Yes, like that blessed hymn, which says:

> He comes, not an infant in Bethlehem born,
> He comes, not to lie in a manger;
> He comes, not again to be treated with scorn;
> He comes, not a shelterless stranger.
> He comes, not to Gethsemane,
> To weep, and sweat blood in the garden;
> He comes, not to die on the tree,
> To purchase for rebels a pardon;
> Oh no; glory, bright glory environs him now.

Exactly. Wrapped in a blaze of boundless glory it is. How many of the holy angels with Him? [Congregation: "All of them."] All of them? [Congregation: "Every one."] But shall we know Him then amongst such a company of them, each one shining above the brightness of the sun? Ah, brethren, He who has gone with us all the way, He who has been with us in suffering, He who has been with us in sorrow, He who has delivered us from trouble, He who has walked with us all the way, He who has walked with us all the way, He who has saved us from our sins, He who has made us acquainted with Him – can anything obscure Him in that day and hide Him from us? [Congregation: "No."] No. That blessed presence that has bound us to Him when He was so far away, can anything keep us from Him when He comes so near? No, and the ten thousand times ten thousand and thousands of thousands of angels are not there *to keep us from Him.* They are not there to surround Him like a bodyguard of soldiers to keep people away. Oh, no. They come to *take us to Him.* [Congregation: "Amen."] That is the only thing they are there for, to bring us to Him. And He will take us to Himself, for He says so. He says so. And we shall see Him for ourselves and our eyes shall behold Him and not a stranger. No, not a stranger. The last words of Paul were: "O Lord, when shall I embrace thee? when shall I behold thee for myself without a dimming veil between?" *Sketches from the Life of Paul, 331.* Can't we all say it too? [Congregation: "Amen."]

Brethren, it will not be long. [*Voices*: "No, indeed,"] It will not be long. Why, think. More than that, we shall see all the rest there. And did you ever notice that turn that is taken in Paul's words there when he is comforting us about the loss of our friends who have died, that they will all come from the dead again.

1 Thessalonians 4. Now let us read that:

"But I would not have you ignorant, brethren, concerning them which are asleep, that ye sorrow not, even as others which have no hope. . . For the Lord himself shall descend from heaven with a shout, with the voice of the archangel, and with the trump of God; and the dead in Christ shall rise first; then we which are alive and remain shall be caught up together with them in the clouds, to meet the Lord in the air: and so shall we ever be with" *one another?* [Congregation: "With the Lord."] Why, he started out to tell them that they would meet with their dead friends after a while, but when he came to the time he did not see them at all. What is the reason? Because *the Lord* is *all in all* that day. Why, of course, we will be glad our friends are all there, but, brethren, we will be gladder than all that *that Friend Himself* is there. He takes precedence of all our other friends in that day. We are so glad that that Friend is there that we have not time to look for these, and so He says. "The Lord himself shall descend from heaven with a shout, with the voice of the archangel, and with the trump of God, and the dead in Christ shall rise first: then we which are alive and remain shall be caught up together with them in the clouds, to meet the Lord in the air: and so shall we ever be with the Lord."

Brethren, then there will be no dimming veil between. We shall be like Him, for we shall see Him as He is. Then let us be glad. Let us be glad all the way. Tell the people that the Lord is coming. Tell them, Get ready, for He is coming. Tell them these things. Say, His coming is near. Get ready, for He is coming. Get ready to meet Him, for He is coming. Get ready to be like Him, for that glory of which He has given us a part now will make us like Him altogether in that day.

Where is that hymn book? Let us sing that piece –1175– *In the Resurrection Morning*. I think we can sing that together now.

In the resurrection morning we shall see the Saviour coming,
And the sons of God a shouting, in the kingdom of the Lord.

Chorus:

We shall rise; we shall rise,
When the mighty trumpet rends the azure skies;
Yes, the dead in Christ shall rise,
all the dead in Christ shall rise,
In the resurrection morning we shall rise.

We feel the advent glory; while the vision seems to tarry.
We will comfort one another with the words of Holy Writ.

By faith we can discover that our warfare'll soon be over,
And we'll shortly hail each other, on fair Canaan's happy shore.

We will tell the pleasing story, when we meet our friends in glory,
And we'll keep ourselves all ready for to hail the heavenly King.

www.ingramcontent.com/pod-product-compliance
Lightning Source LLC
Chambersburg PA
CBHW060457010526
44118CB00018B/2451